A Spirit
of Dissension

A SPIRIT OF DISSENSION

Economics, Politics, and the Revolution in Maryland

by Ronald Hoffman

The Johns Hopkins University Press · Baltimore and London

Note: In the interest of clarity, the spelling and punctuation
of quotations have occasionally been modernized.

Publication of this volume was assisted
by the Maryland Bicentennial Commission.

The Johns Hopkins University Press, Baltimore, Maryland 21218
The Johns Hopkins University Press Ltd., London

Library of Congress Catalog Card Number 73-8127
ISBN 0-8018-1521-5

Library of Congress Cataloging in Publication data
will be found on the last printed page of this book.

To Sandra

Contents

List of Tables

List of Maps

Preface

Men sought power for a variety of reasons during the revolutionary era. Some were committed reformers actuated by idealistic convictions, while others were clever opportunists. Whatever their personal motives, all were influenced by an array of economic, social, and regional factors. This study examines these influences and assesses their impact on the pattern of political behavior in a single colony, Maryland. The justification is not that Maryland was "typical" but that a closer understanding of developments in a particular colony should offer insight into the sources and meaning of the American War of Independence.

There are two major parts to this investigation. One concentrates on how the revolutionary movement developed in Maryland, the social, economic, and political milieu from which the decision for independence grew. The second concerns the dilemmas of those who provided leadership for the Revolution but who experienced intense anxiety over many of the social, political, and economic tendencies unleashed by the conflict. An intelligent and conservative elite led Maryland during the Revolution. Amid the threatening social cross currents of the period, they managed, often with great difficulty, to retain their popularity and their government's stability. Their ideals, their fears, and their compromises suggest much about the meaning of the American Revolution.

This study seeks to answer certain basic questions about the revolutionary experience in Maryland. Did the colony enjoy an economically stable position within the British Empire or had serious economic problems developed by the 1760s? If there were difficulties within the Tidewater economy, were they integrally tied to the pattern of political protest? Concerning the character of political behavior, were men motivated more by Whig ideology or by the desire to acquire power? And whatever their reasons, how did the specter of growing chaos affect the political elite's conduct? Were these fears responsible for their unanimous rejection of independence on May 21, 1776? And after they reluctantly agreed to separation, did these same persistent fears significantly influence the formation of a constitution and the subsequent policies of the state government?

If I have answered these questions satisfactorily, it is because of the generous assistance of a great many people. As every research historian knows, the degree of pleasure or pain accompanying an investigation is heavily dependent on the staffs of historical depositories. In this regard I have been extremely fortunate. At the Maryland Hall of Records, the director, Dr. Morris L. Radoff, his assistant, Mr. Gust Skordas, and all that institution's staff were of great assistance. I particularly want to thank Mrs. Phebe Jacobsen for possessing the characteristics that every historian hopes to find in a manuscript librarian: patience, intelligence, and enthusiasm. At the Maryland Historical Society the director, Mr. P. William Filby, and the manuscript librarians, Miss Bayly Ellen Marks, Mrs. Avril Pedley, and Mrs. Nancy Boles, were always considerate. While in graduate school I began this work under Professor Merrill Jensen, who read and reread the many drafts of an eventual dissertation. It has been my distinct privilege to study under his direction. At the University of Maryland I received further valuable assistance, both financially and intellectually. A summer grant from the General Research Board of the university enabled me to expand greatly my original investigation. All of my students and associates at Maryland have, at various times, served as sounding boards. One colleague especially must be cited, David Grimstead. His perceptive though kindly tempered criticisms and his steady endurance provided me with indispensable assistance in the book's final stages. My sister, Joanne Giza, also helped extensively in the editing and proofreading, as did Peter Albert and Dermott Hickey, both good friends and graduate students at Maryland. My parents provided further encouragement. My late father, Dr. Emanuel Hoffman, frequently hacked at an awkward sentence until it became clear; my mother, Mrs. Ethel Hoffman, logged many a weary hour at her typewriter as she turned out draft after draft. Lastly I must thank my wife, Sandra, for performing so much of the sheer drudgery demanded by historical research and editing—counting, key punching, typing, editing, correcting, checking, proofreading, indexing—my book is dedicated to her.

A Spirit
of Dissension

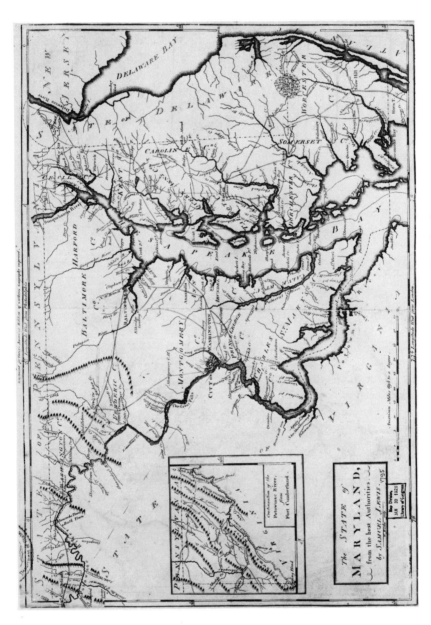

MAP 1. *Samuel Lewis's Map of Maryland, 1795*

1 : From Worcester to Frederick

By the autumn of 1776, Maryland's revolutionary leadership faced a crisis of alarming dimensions. Most of these men had not wanted independence. They had foreseen that uncontrollable chaos might result, but with other colonies agreeing to separation, they could not remain behind. Now their worst apprehensions were being realized. Since the previous fall, disorder within the colony had steadily mounted. The deterioration had been especially rapid since July. From the last months of 1776 through most of 1778, the revolutionary aristocracy knew intimately the agony of fear and uncertainty. At times its leaders gave in to despair as waves of discontent and social violence seemed about to engulf them. Reports from all parts of the province continually told of insurrectionist activities among blacks and whites, servants and slaves. Accompanying these accounts were numerous communiqués from frightened militia commanders emphasizing the extent of desertion and disobedience which had rendered their commands ineffective. Some dared not even issue arms, believing they would be murdered. The breadth of the insurrections, the chaos within the military, the brazen defiance of men who openly repudiated the Revolution, the presence of British ships sailing in the Chesapeake Bay at will—all of these elements gave rise to apprehensions of anarchy among the political elite. Most believed it imminent; a few felt it had already arrived.

The Maryland leadership had learned an important lesson by the time of independence: that revolution without some anarchy was impossible. In earlier more naive days, they had been gloriously euphoric about the future, but they soon grew somber and considerably wiser. Unlike many historians who have written of that era, they recognized the potential for convulsive social violence. The conflict with England had eliminated the presence of a strong visible authority and, in the process, created a political vacuum. That conflict had also unleashed previously suppressed social forces. Together, the absence of authority and the expressions of discontent were producing a condition of terrifying disorder.

The political elite believed its very survival threatened. They hoped that by securing both authority and popularity they could bring a return to order and stability. With these objectives clearly in mind, the revolutionary leadership followed a policy of institutional conservatism and economic radicalism. The constitution it designed in the fall of 1776 insured the wealthy a controlling voice in government. Because of the high property qualifications established for public office, none but the affluent could qualify to serve. But the revolutionary leaders correctly recognized that to write a constitution was one matter and to implement it another. Thus, to popularize their authority and to prevent what they foresaw as civil, if not class, warfare, they consciously drafted a program of radical economic legislation. Naturally, they disliked these acts which jeopardized their own financial interests. But they were thoroughly convinced that the desperate conditions demanded such action, if their class were to survive as a leadership force. By these concessions to "popular heresies," they hoped that the estranged, the aggrieved, and the disgruntled could be detached from the hard core of the resistance and the Revolution saved.

But why had conditions deteriorated to a point that the Revolution was in serious danger? Were there particular factors inherent in the colony's regional, economic, and social structure that had produced this crisis? Or more specifically, why had a movement initiated for imperial reform led to internal chaos? The history of Revolutionary Maryland was deeply embedded in the colony's geography and economy. Imperial conflict in the Chesapeake during the 1760s reflected very clearly the resentment of merchants and planters dominated by a market over which they had no control. By concentrating on tobacco, they had developed a vigorous economy. But this growth process was precarious. They prospered or declined in accordance with prices in Europe; profits could be extremely high one year and fatally low the next. Because of their dependence on external markets, life was particularly unstable. Each year the people waited apprehensively for news from England, where forces wholly beyond their control dictated their economic fate.

In certain areas problems of poor soil or transportation encouraged some diversification of crops. This resulted primarily in the production of wheat and corn for the West Indian and European markets. Indeed, the profits realized on grain sales were at times substantial, but as with tobacco, the market fluctuated greatly and Maryland planters had little control over their economic fortunes. Good harvests in Spain, France, and Italy could have disastrous consequences in the colony. Lumber products were also turned out in areas containing marginal soil. England's growing industrial output created a demand for these materials, and profits were possible. Still, most planters considered lumber production the least desirable. The work was hard, the hours long, and the returns small. The more prosperous planters considered it good winter work for their idle slaves. Farmers holding poor land turned to it out of necessity. By a "mean" combination of inferior tobacco, wheat, corn, and lumber, they managed a hard existence.

Maryland's planters and merchants knew both soaring profits and agonizing losses in the years immediately before the Revolution. The market was depressed in the first half of the 1760s but prosperous in the second. At the beginning of the next decade, depressions returned. Political protest followed these economic trends. Anger and frustration developed over the Stamp Act of 1765, which coincided with depression, while indifference characterized the reaction to the Townshend program initiated in 1767 during prosperous years. And when the economy worsened in the early 1770s, turmoil, confusion, and desperation again resulted. Once again the political protest and ideology which had developed in response to the Stamp Act depression took on social force. While other factors contributed to the rhythm of political protest, the very definite correlation between the strength of the economy and the forms of political behavior demonstrates that economic conditions exerted a particularly critical influence.

After 1774, however, economic conditions, while continuing to affect politics, played a gradually reduced role. Specifically, the disequilibrating social forces released by the revolutionary movement became the critical element influencing the character of political behavior. The revolutionary leaders reacted in a determined effort to save themselves by achieving popularity and order. Their struggle was a difficult one. Ultimately, they succeeded, but once having triumphed, the revolutionary elite lost its unity of purpose. Its more idealistic members became disturbed once again, this time by the aggressively self-seeking qualities of the society they had helped to create.

Maryland's peculiar geography heavily influenced the political and economic character of the revolutionary struggle. The colony actively participated in the eighteenth-century Atlantic trading community. Her most important connection with that sphere of commerce was the Chesapeake Bay. Transportation facilities afforded by the bay were put to much use, and an extensive commercialized agricultural system emerged and flourished during the colonial era. The Chesapeake is one hundred ninety-five miles in length, and its width varies from twenty-two miles at its widest point to between three and ten at the upper part of the bay. Its depth reaches a maximum of one hundred sixty feet, and there are many shallow areas of less than fifteen feet. Both the Eastern and Western shores of Maryland are deeply indented along the Chesapeake coast, and the bay contains numerous islands, especially in its eastern region. The shoreline takes on straight features only from the Calvert Cliffs, located on the shores of Herring Bay in Anne Arundel County, to Drum Point at Calvert County's southern end. Where the shoreline is broken, it is generally low and marshy, while along the relatively straight portions, the coast tends to be high and rugged.

Because of the marshes and swamps, parts of the Tidewater area were not suitable for settlement. The largest swamps were located along the Choptank and Nanticoke rivers on the Eastern Shore, and the most extensive inland swamp, Cypress Swamp, lay at the head of the Pocomoke River straddling the Maryland-Delaware border for some fifty thousand acres. Maryland's Atlantic coast, a mere thirty-one-mile stretch, now has a barrier of narrow, sandy beaches which encloses Chincoteague Bay or Lagoon. During the eighteenth century a navigable inlet existed between these sandy barriers, and this entrance, Sinepuxent Inlet, was used during the Revolutionary War to bring supplies into Maryland without necessitating entrance into the Chesapeake.[1]

Forty-eight principal creeks and rivers discharge into the bay. In the eighteenth century some of these tributaries were navigable for upward of one hundred miles, and these in turn, had one hundred and two branches which were navigable for up to fifty miles.[2] For the entire region, there were over one hundred and fifty channels in which vessels could sail. The waters of the bay are salty at the capes and lower bay, brackish further up, and fresh at the head and in the upper courses of the rivers. Vessels often sailed up into the fresher waters during the eighteenth century to rid their wooden hulls of the destructive ship worm, *Teredo navalis*, which could not survive the reduced salinity.[3]

[1] William B. Marye, "The Seacoast of Maryland," *Maryland Historical Magazine* 40 (1945), 108.
[2] Arthur Pierce Middleton, *Tobacco Coast*, edited by George Carrington Mason (Newport News, Va.: Mariners' Museum, 1953), p. 31.
[3] *Ibid.*

Throughout the bay were numerous local shoals. These were a special problem because bathygraphic charts of the bay were not available until after 1735, when Captain Walter Hoxton published his useful if limited map of the Chesapeake. Not until 1776, with the publication of Anthony Smith's map, was a reliable chart produced. Smith's work reflected the confidence of a Chesapeake Bay pilot who knew his waters well. Any pilot who sailed the Chesapeake had to have a detailed knowledge of the hazardous "shallows" and of the navigable rivers that fed into the bay. On the Eastern Shore the Wicomico was open to traffic for seventeen miles, the Choptank for thirteen, the Chester, a windy and treacherous thirty-five, and the Sassafras for ten.[4] On the Western Shore the Magothy, South, and West rivers were navigable for five miles, the Severn for ten, the Patapsco for fifteen, while the Northeast and Susquehanna could be negotiated for a very dangerous three. The big rivers, however, were the Patuxent and Potomac. Skilled mariners brought three-hundred-ton craft up the Patuxent for fifty-five miles, and vessels going up the Potomac to Georgetown had to cover one hundred ten miles.[5]

The soil of the colony was in many places rich. A number of eighteenth-century travelers to Maryland, as well as subsequent historians, have offered derogatory descriptions of the countryside. Soil erosion and its aftermath—a depleted, dust-ridden land—were reported everywhere. Such descriptions were misconceptions that arose primarily because most of the central lines of land transportation purposely crossed the more barren sections and did not pass through the more fertile areas. The best cultivated lands were near waterways, but the roads skirted these regions for the more solid, drier soils. The perceptive writer and traveler, the duc de La Rochefoucauld-Liancourt, noted this design. He pointed out that while he could see nothing but desolation from his carriage window, within four miles of either side of the road excellent farm lands existed.[6]

Good land abounded, and from it came rich yields. Besides the commercial crops of tobacco, wheat, and corn, other produce such as turnips, cabbages, and potatoes was raised. These vegetables, and the abundant fruits that grew everywhere, were not marketed extensively. They were raised in small patches and backyard orchards, and provided subsistence

[4] *Ibid.*, p. 78; Joseph Scott, *A Geographical Description of the States of Maryland and Delaware* (Philadelphia, 1807), pp. 45, 104; duc de La Rochefoucauld-Liancourt, *Travels through the United States of North America in the Years 1795, 1796, 1797* (4 vols., London, 1799), 3:561.

[5] Scott, *Geographical Description*, pp. 7, 15, 95; Middleton, *Tobacco Coast*, p. 32; Andrew Burnaby, *Travels through the Middle States of North America, 1759–1760* (London, 1789), p. 86; William Eddis, *Letters from America* (London, 1792), p. 33.

[6] La Rochefoucauld-Liancourt, *Travels through the United States*, 2:30.

crops and some income.[7] Generally, the commercial efforts of the Chesapeake farmer went into the growing of tobacco, wheat, and corn, and
since all of these crops were produced throughout the colony, distinctive
and simple regions of production are not easily identified. The staple
crops were grown in Worcester and Somerset counties at the southern
end of the Eastern Shore, but here marginal soil conditions led to an
emphasis on the production of lumber products. Caroline and Dorchester
counties contained stretches of better land, where tobacco, wheat, and
corn could be grown profitably. Yet, like their southern neighbors, these
people thought lumber to have equal importance because there were not
many areas of truly good soil.[8]

Talbot, Queen Anne's, Kent, and the southern part of Cecil County,
with large expanses of fertile soil, were the centers of prosperity on the
Eastern Shore. In the 1760s high tobacco yields strained storage facilities
there, a problem repeated whenever a good crop was raised. In addition
to tobacco, these counties were noted for their excellent wheat.[9] Cereal
products became an important money crop for the Eastern Shore before
the Revolutionary War, and after the Anglo-American conflict the change
to wheat was so widespread that by 1800 grain production definitely
overshadowed that of tobacco. The Eastern Shore also produced large
yields of corn to supply the slaves both in Maryland and in the West
Indies. Wheat, on the other hand, was generally considered too precious
to serve as fare for blacks.[10]

On the Western Shore, in Harford and Frederick counties, tobacco
and wheat were grown with equal emphasis by the time of the Revolution. The English, German, and Scotch-Irish who resided there, particularly in back-country Frederick County, wanted to raise tobacco in their
fertile valley regions, but faced difficult transportation problems. As the
anonymous author of *American Husbandry* commented, the "back country was quite fertile and generally capable of producing fine tobacco to

[7] For a typical example of this form of commerce, see Isaac Weld, Jr., *Travels
through the States of North America, and Provinces of Upper and Lower Canada,
during the Years 1795, 1796, 1797* (London, 1807), p. 141.

[8] La Rochefoucauld-Liancourt, *Travels through the United States*, 3:597; Scott,
Geographical Description, pp. 103, 113, 132–34; J. D. Schoepf, *Travels in the Confederation* [*1783–1784*], translated and edited by Alfred J. Morrison (2 vols., Philadelphia, W. J. Campbell, 1911), 2:354; Eddis, *Letters from America*, p. 132; Richard
Parkinson, *A Tour in America in 1798, 1799, 1800* (2 vols., London, 1805), 1:216–19.

[9] Parkinson, *Tour in America*, 1:99, 100, 130, 138, 140; Frederick Emory, *Queen
Anne's County, Maryland* (Baltimore, Md.: Maryland Historical Society, 1950), p. 21.

[10] Charles Carroll of Annapolis to Charles Carroll of Carrollton, May 22, 1770,
Charles Carroll of Annapolis Papers, Maryland Historical Society, Baltimore, Md.
(cited hereafter as MHS).

which it is in most parts applied where navigation is at a convenient place."[11] The Maryland tobacco country proper began, however, in the southern and western parts of Baltimore County. Rich tobacco was raised in all of the Western Shore's southern counties, but the finest grades were produced in the central part of Prince George's County and on the western side of Anne Arundel. As one writer noted after entering the area south of the Patuxent, the "houses for curing tobacco in (called here tobacco houses) begin to be more plenty than in the parts of Maryland I have travelled hitherto."[12] Wheat and corn, especially white corn, were also cultivated, but tobacco was king.[13] Here the soil was well suited to the demands of intensive tobacco farming and the intricate natural waterways made transportation easy and inexpensive.

Next to agricultural produce, the export of forest products constituted Maryland's largest commercial activity. By the end of the seventeenth century, Worcester, Somerset, Dorchester and Talbot counties were actively producing staves, shingles, planks, and timber. During the next century, this activity spread throughout the colony, with Harford County emerging as the most energetic producer on the Western Shore. The British colonial authorities were especially anxious to promote this enterprise and attractive bounties were offered to stimulate the trade. Tobacco planters found this industry beneficial to them. After a planter's slaves had completed their fall harvest, they were often hired out to work in camps where forest products were processed for exportation. The planters generally found the rental of their slaves to be quite lucrative.[14]

Shipbuilders provided one immediate market for the lumber pro-

---

[11] *American Husbandry* (London, 1775), p. 22; La Rochefoucauld-Liancourt, *Travels through the United States*, 3:247.

[12] Fred Shelley, ed., "Ebenezer Hazard's Travels through Maryland in 1777," *Maryland Historical Magazine* 46 (1951), 51.

[13] Scott, *Geographical Description*, pp. 8, 43, 45, 74, 96, 122, 125; Parkinson, *Tour in America*, 1:98; La Rochefoucauld-Liancourt, *Travels through the United States*, 3:534, 611, 708; J. F. D. Smyth, *Tour of the United States of America* (London, 1785), p. 184; Middleton, *Tobacco Coast*, p. 95. For a historian's view of the cyclical movements in Maryland's colonial tobacco trade, see John Hemphill II, "Freight Rates in the Maryland Tobacco Trade," *Maryland Historical Magazine* 54 (1959), 36–58, 153–187.

[14] Thomas Hall and Edward Hall Account Papers, 1784, Harford County Historical Society Papers, MHS. These papers illustrate the importance of slave hire. See also *American Husbandry*, p. 266; Parkinson, *Tour in America*, 1:65; La Rochefoucauld-Liancourt, *Travels through the United States*, 3:575, Schoepf, *Travels in the Confederation*, p. 372. For a perceptive discussion of Maryland's colonial settlement system, see the forthcoming study by Carville V. Earle, "The Evolution of a Tidewater Settlement System: All Hallow's Parish, 1650–1783" (Ph.D. diss., University of Chicago, 1973).

duced. By the end of the seventeenth century, shipbuilding had begun on a small scale in Talbot and Kent counties, where an abundance of oak, pine, and mulberry grew. Oxford and St. Michaels were the first centers of construction, with Chestertown and Georgetown entering later.[15] But with the increased settlement and population expansion of the Western Shore during the eighteenth century, the center of this craft shifted to the area around Annapolis, especially in the West River where Samuel Galloway and Stephen Stewart enjoyed excellent reputations for the ships they built for the London and West Indies trade.[16]

Another growing commercial activity in the colonial period was the production of iron. By 1762, eight furnaces and ten forges were located in Maryland. The largest firm was the Principio Company of Cecil County, followed by the Baltimore Iron Works, the Hampton Furnace on the Monocacy, Stephen Onion's Iron Works on the Gunpowder, Richard Snowden's on the Patuxent, Charles Ridgely's Nottingham Iron Works on the Patapsco, and the Harley Forge, whose location is unknown.[17] During the 1750s these companies produced 2,500 tons of pig iron and 600 of bar iron annually, enabling Maryland to lead all other colonies in the export of iron. After the Revolution the production of iron, along with the milling of wheat, remained an important manufacturing process.[18]

Thus by the 1760s Maryland's economy was partially regionalized. Production patterns varied but tobacco and grain were the central commodities raised. The colony's geographical character determined this pattern. In the areas of rich soil and adequate transportation the staple crops flourished. The poorer sections were more diversified and were forced to rely on the less profitable industry of forest goods. Each of the areas suffered from different liabilities. Marginal soil made life hard for some; richer soil made life frustrating for others. The more prosperous farmers, because of their heavy emphasis on staple crop production, were ex-

[15] Oswald Tilghman, *History of Talbot County, Maryland, 1661–1861* (2 vols., Baltimore, Md.: Williams & Wilkins Co., 1915), 2:354, 379.

[16] Middleton, *Tobacco Coast*, p. 224; Burnaby, *Travels through the Middle States of North America*, pp. 62, 177; Samuel Galloway to Captain William Tippell, February 22, 1770, Samuel Galloway Letterbook, Galloway Papers, Library of Congress, Washington, D.C.

[17] Jedediah Morse, *The American Geography* (Elizabethtown, N.J., 1789), p. 354; Paul H. Giddens, "Trade and Industry in Colonial Maryland, 1753–1769," *Journal of Economic and Business History* 4 (1932), 523; Middleton, *Tobacco Coast*, p. 168; La Rochefoucauld-Liancourt, *Travels through the United States*, 3:246, 584, 678; Schoepf, *Travels in the Confederation*, pp. 348–49; Weld, *Travels through the States of North America*, pp. 24, 141.

[18] Giddens, "Trade and Industry in Colonial Maryland," p. 523.

tremely dependent on external markets. They invested considerable capital and felt the most anxiety when world markets were depressed. Part of the Revolution's impetus resulted from this condition, for these planters, needing a scapegoat to blame for conditions beyond their control, frequently pointed to the British mercantile system. At the same time the people residing in the poorer regions had little reason to reproach the British for their difficulties. What they resented most was the wealth held by others, and since the Revolution was dominated by a colonial elite, the "lesser sort" were frequently indifferent. Many of them, in fact, supported the British in the hope that they might be rewarded.

By 1776 Maryland contained some 233,000 persons, 95 percent of whom lived on farms. Of this number approximately 65 percent were white freemen, 25 percent slaves, 5 percent white indentured servants, and 5 percent free Negroes.[19] They were a heterogeneous mixture of English, Scotch-Irish, Irish, Germans, and Negroes imported from the West Indies and Africa. One of the best means of determining where these groups resided is to plot the locations of the various eighteenth-century religious establishments. These data, along with the remarks made by contemporary travelers, suggest the locational patterns of population.

Starting in 1680, the Scotch-Irish began migrating to northeastern Maryland and "raising" their Presbyterian churches. From New Castle, Delaware, they moved first into Pennsylvania's counties of Chester and Lancaster and then south into Maryland's Cecil County and down the Eastern Shore.[20] Governor Francis Nicholson reported in 1697 that six or seven hundred Scotch-Irish had been living in Somerset for over a decade. This early group was a precursor of the extensive migration of the eighteenth century, and Presbyterian churches were widespread throughout the Eastern Shore by the time of the Revolution. Still, they were greatly overshadowed in number by the Anglican churches that served a large English population.[21] Other English religious groups included a growing number of Methodists, a minority of Quakers, and a small number of Irish Catholics. Before 1770 a few Acadians had also settled in Talbot and Queen Anne's counties.[22]

---

[19] A. E. Karien, "Numerical and Distributional Aspects of Maryland Population 1631–1840" (Ph.D. diss., University of Maryland, 1958), p. 74.

[20] Stella Helen Sutherland, *Population Distribution in Colonial America* (New York: Columbia University Press, 1936), p. 187; Middleton, *Tobacco Coast*, p. 160; Scott, *Geographical Description*, pp. 105, 132.

[21] Scott, *Geographical Description*, pp. 70, 72, 101, 105, 132.

[22] Tilghman, *History of Talbot County*, pp. 521–30; Emory, *Queen Anne's County*, p. 228.

On the Western Shore, Irish and English Catholics settled heavily in the southern counties, with some in the west; Germans resided predominantly in the central and western counties; and the Scotch-Irish in the north and far western areas. And again throughout all of these areas, the Anglican church existed, attesting to the presence of the English, as did the Methodist Church.[23] J. F. D. Smyth estimated that in St. Mary's, Charles, Calvert, and Prince George's, Catholics constituted six-sevenths of the population.[24] The Catholic church in these counties held major properties and it seems likely that Catholics resided here in large numbers, though Smyth's estimate of their pervasiveness is probably exaggerated. To the west another ethnic group was also concentrated. Ever since 1732 the General Assembly had actively encouraged the settlement of Germans on the frontier.[25] Whether as a result of legislative encouragement or simply because of the prospect of good land, an estimated 36,000 Germans were living in Frederick and Washington counties by 1781.[26]

The religious denominations of Baltimore's population serve as an excellent illustration of the heterogeneity of Maryland's inhabitants. Religious opinions divided the city into Anglicans, German-Calvinists, Lutherans, Presbyterians, Roman Catholics, Methodists, Quakers, Nicolaitans, Anabaptists, New Jerusalemites, Universalists, and a few Jews.[27] Yet, despite the many churches, one wag commented that the object of the majority "appears to be to make their fortunes for this world—while preparation for another is either unthought of or deferred to a *more convenient* season."[28] Baltimore, by 1776, contained approximately 5,700 persons. This figure illustrates the city's remarkable growth, since its population in 1750 consisted, at best, of only several hundred families. Two other relatively large towns, Annapolis and Frederick, of 1,500 and 1,700 people respectively, were also thriving. The former was the capital and

[23] Thomas Anburey, *Travels through the Interior Parts of America, in a Series of Letters, 1776–81* (2 vols., London, 1789), 2:181; La Rochefoucauld-Liancourt, *Travels through the United States*, 3:708; Scott, *Geographical Description*, pp. 90, 96, 122, 135, 140, 145, 149, 154; Smyth, *Tour of the United States*, pp. 180, 183, 187, 258; Schoepf, *Travels in the Confederation*, pp. 61, 64, 315; Eddis, *Letters from America*, p. 99; Weld, *Travels through the States of North America*, p. 75; Giddens, "Trade and Industry in Colonial Maryland," p. 514; Sutherland, *Population Distribution in Colonial America*, p. 195.

[24] Smyth, *Tour of the United States*, p. 180.

[25] Sutherland, *Population Distribution in Colonial America*, p. 195.

[26] *Ibid.*

[27] Ferdinand M. Bayard, *Travels of a Frenchman in Maryland and Virginia*, translated and edited by Ben C. McCary (Ann Arbor, Mich.: Edwards Brothers for Ben C. McCary, Williamsburg, Va., 1950), p. 160.

[28] Morse, *American Geography*, p. 353.

center of political activity, and the latter was the focal point for the back country trade.[29]

Negro slaves made up some 25 percent of the population, and were most heavily concentrated on the southern part of the Western Shore in the prime tobacco region. In Calvert, Prince George's, Charles, Anne Arundel, and St. Mary's counties, they made up close to 50 percent of the population. On the Eastern Shore in Queen Anne's, Kent, and Somerset, slaves made up 40 percent to 45 percent of the population. These areas were also engaged in the growing of tobacco, with the exception of Somerset, where blacks were used extensively in forest industries. In Worcester County slaves comprised 30 percent of the population and were also employed in the production of lumber materials. These heavily concentrated centers of black population were severe sources of worry and strain during the Anglo-American conflict. Maryland's revolutionary leaders agreed to independence reluctantly because they were unsure of their ability to control a restive white and black population. And in the early war years the rhetoric of the Revolution and the efforts by the British to exploit the dissatisfaction present in these communities contributed to conditions approaching civil war. Throughout the rest of Maryland the proportion of slaves ranged from 20 percent to 25 percent in the north and north-central counties to around 10 percent in Frederick and Washington counties.[30]

By the 1760s a number of important towns had been built to serve as shipping and distribution centers. The multitude of rivers and streams originally discouraged the development of large commercial centers. Indeed, for much of the seventeenth century English captains made their ships fast alongside the planters' wharves.[31] But three eighteenth-century developments led to the growth of towns: the settlement of the Piedmont, the adoption of a tobacco inspection system, and the supplementing of the traditional consignment trade with resident factors and the British outport system.

Prior to the establishment of entry ports on the Eastern Shore in the latter part of the seventeenth century, planters carried tobacco across the bay to the Patuxent for export to England. This became unnecessary in the 1690s, when the port of Oxford in Talbot County was created. The town afforded a fine harbor and grew into an active port by the time of the Revolution. Throughout most of the eighteenth century a large number

---

[29] Karien, "Numerical and Distributional Aspects of Maryland Population," pp. 159–63.

[30] "Census of Maryland 1782," *The American Museum* 7 (1789), 159.

[31] Giddens, "Trade and Industry in Colonial Maryland," p. 514.

of English factors, as well as some independent traders, conducted their business from Oxford.

Ships unloading cargoes on the Eastern Shore normally reported first to Oxford, though some checked in at Annapolis. After a survey had been conducted, and customs fees paid, they landed their cargoes either at Oxford or at other places nearby. Captain Jeremiah Banning described the commerce of Oxford before midcentury:

The store keepers and other retailers both on the Western and Eastern side of the Chesapeake, repaired there to lay in their supplies. Seven or eight large ships, at the same time were frequently seen at Oxford, delivering goods and completing their landing; nor was it uncommon to dispatch a ship with 500 hogsheads of tobacco in twelve days after its arrival. At that time tobacco was not examined or inspected by sworn officers as now. Men skilled in the article were employed by the merchants or store keepers and called Receivers, to view, weigh, mark and give receipts to planters after which vessels were sent to collect it, when it underwent a pressing and packing preparatory for shipping.[32]

Small collection boats were especially vital in facilitating the process of exportation. Merchants who owned more than one store would have ships anchor at their major agency, and from there smaller vessels, normally sloops, carried goods to their outlying stores. These sloops also played a key role in gathering cargoes. Large ships would anchor in open roadsteads, and the various small craft would bring hogsheads of tobacco and bushels of wheat from the landings in their area.[33] To encourage this practice most ship captains offered a reduced freight rate to those who would bring their goods alongside.[34]

Other Eastern Shore ports included Pocomoke, Chestertown and Georgetown. Pocomoke and Oxford were naval offices by the middle of the eighteenth century, but despite this status only limited trade passed through Pocomoke's harbor. Essentially, Pocomoke catered to the lumber trade, and normally the small vessels that traded there hauled their cargoes to Oxford or Annapolis for reloading onto larger vessels.[35] Chestertown was not a naval office, but by the 1760s the port performed an important commercial function as the center for the Eastern Shore's wheat trade. Wheat transported from the Eastern Shore went either directly down the bay to foreign ports, or up the Chesapeake to Phila-

[32] Tilghman, *History of Talbot County*, 2:357.
[33] Clarence P. Gould, *Money and Transportation in Maryland, 1720–1765* (Baltimore, Md.: Johns Hopkins Press, 1915), p. 154.
[34] Hemphill, "Freight Rates," pp. 36–58.
[35] Port of Entry Books, 1751–1757, MHS.

delphia or Baltimore. To reach Philadelphia, Chestertown traders sent ships up the bay to Elkton, where the grain cargoes were shifted to wagons for the land passage to Christiana Bridge. At Christiana, shallops picked up the wheat for the run to Philadelphia.[36] Whenever the weather was bad and bay conditions precluded safe passage, wagons carried grain from Chestertown to Philadelphia. Land transportation costs ran about three times as high as water, but the prices offered in Philadelphia were an inducement to using this route.[37] Georgetown, located north of Chestertown on the Sassafras, performed a similar function, though on a lesser scale.

At the head of the bay lay the strategically located port of Elkton. Situated almost midway between Philadelphia and Baltimore, this settlement handled a heavy volume of traffic. Corn and wheat, sent to Philadelphia from the Eastern and Western shores, went first to Elkton. During the Revolution, Maryland established its chief commissary there, and for one year, 1780, it handled close to 20,000 barrels of flour alone.[38] After the war, Elkton reportedly sold over 250,000 bushels of wheat annually.[39] In addition it continued as the primary market for the sale of livestock and other products between Maryland and Pennsylvania.[40]

A little further to the west two other shipping towns, Charlestown and Havre de Grace, conducted a trade different from that of Elkton. Charlestown on the North East River and Havre de Grace on the Susquehanna endeavored to attract wheat from the central counties of Pennsylvania for export down the bay. The two rivers, particularly the Susquehanna, were used to bring wheat from Pennsylvania. Neither was entirely navigable, but a supplemental network of rough roads along the rivers allowed Pennsylvanians to ship their produce more cheaply to the bay's head than to Philadelphia. By the outbreak of the Revolution, Baltimore had become the directing influence in this trade, with Charlestown and Havre de Grace providing secondary transshipment functions.[41]

On the Western Shore the town of Annapolis, located on the Severn

---

[36] Zebulon Hollingsworth to Hollingsworth and Rudulph, June 5, 1769, and February 24, 1771, Hollingsworth Correspondence, Historical Society of Pennsylvania, Philadelphia, Pa.

[37] "Aggregate of Wheat, Flour and Indian Corn Annually Exported from the Eastern Shore of Maryland, on an Average, from the Years 1770–1775," manuscript located in Chalmers Papers, New York Public Library, New York, N.Y.

[38] Harold T. Pinkett, "Maryland as a Source of Food Supplies during the Revolution," *Maryland Historical Magazine* 46 (1951), 160, 163.

[39] Scott, *Geographical Description*, p. 117.

[40] *Ibid.*

[41] Schoepf, *Travels in the Confederation*, p. 373; Scott, *Geographical Description*, pp. 141–42.

River, possessed a protected harbor. In spite of this facility, its exports were limited.[42] The Severn offered a good anchorage, but large vessels found it difficult to sail into Annapolis because of the local shoals. More important, the town served a small hinterland. The roads that led there crossed many streams, and for most merchants it was quicker and more profitable to ship their goods on the interior waterways. When traders sent commodities to the coast, the goods invariably went to Baltimore, which was favored by an uninterrupted land route.[43] The injurious *Teredo navalis* also filled Annapolis' harbor, and ships putting in there often sustained damage because there were no fresh water streams to limit the destruction to their hulls.[44] This same condition held true for the two other rivers surrounding Annapolis, the West and the South rivers.

Nevertheless, Annapolis performed an important commercial function because it served as the colony's largest naval office.[45] All ships leaving the upper bay region were required to register at Annapolis and pay their export fees.[46] By 1770, Baltimore exported far more than Annapolis, but every vessel that sailed from Baltimore paid export duties at Annapolis. Such payments did not necessarily require the ships to put into Annapolis proper, since collection agents from there maintained a facility on the Patapsco. Nonetheless, this regulation was an irritant to the increasingly powerful Baltimore merchant community. After the Revolution began, they exerted greater influence and gained a central customs house in 1780.

The Western Shore naval offices at Port Patuxent and North Potomac expanded greatly in the eighteenth century as a result of trade from the interior Piedmont region. Directly south of Annapolis, Patuxent became a central base for many of the English and Scottish factors. Along the Patuxent, several trading communities thrived, the most important of which were Queen Anne's, Upper Marlboro, and Benedict.[47] A similar development occurred on the Potomac and its tributaries, where Bladens-

[42] Burnaby, *Travels through the Middle States*, p. 82; Eddis, *Letters from America*, p. 95.

[43] Schoepf, *Travels in the Confederation*, p. 366; Eddis, *Letters from America*, p. 19.

[44] Scott, *Geographical Description*, p. 76; Hemphill, "Freight Rates," p. 57.

[45] Annapolis Port Record Books, "Exports, 1758–1774," MHS.

[46] Port of Entry Books, 1751–1757, MHS; Donnell M. Owings, *His Lordship's Patronage* (Baltimore, Md.: Maryland Historical Society, 1953), p. 66.

[47] Smyth, *Tour of the United States*, p. 210; Burnaby, *Travels through the Middle States*, p. 80; Scott, *Geographical Description*, p. 128.

burg, Piscataway, Port Tobacco, and Georgetown emerged.[48] Of these two naval offices, the North Potomac consistently exported more tobacco and earned greater revenues during the period.

The principal Western Shore towns that specialized in shipping were generally located on the rivers that fed into the bay. The rivers on the Western Shore, rising in the Piedmont plateau and emptying into the tidal bay, flowed across two geological divisions, the plateau and the coastal plain. The first was composed of a hard rock; the latter, of sandy marine deposits. The fall line where these two regions met represented the limits of navigation into the interior, and below the fall line the rivers were accessible to ocean tides. For most of the seventeenth century, the planters did not settle west of this zone. This meant that they could ship their goods directly on the navigable rivers located nearby and did not require towns. The consignment trade and the lack of a tobacco inspection system also diminished the need for central commercial centers.[49] During the eighteenth century a tobacco inspection system was established and resident factors settled on the Patuxent, Piscataway, and the Potomac. The Piedmont was also populated by farmers who began to produce tobacco, wheat, and corn, and to carry their goods in small boats or overland to places on the navigable rivers which led to the bay. Here, at these river trade junctions, they also picked up the imports they needed. To accomplish these transactions, enterprisers, traders, and innkeepers constructed warehouses, stores, and ordinaries to handle the flow, and around these structures small towns grew.[50]

Retail centers were required as much in the back country as they were along the various rivers. These centers were set up to allow the people to purchase and sell what they needed near their homes. Frederick was the West's principal exchange center and its location was conveniently situated near the Monocacy River, a branch of the Potomac. By 1775, it was Maryland's second largest city.[51] Hagerstown, about forty miles to the west, was the only other community to rival Frederick for the back-country trade by 1775.[52]

Transportation among these various communities and between the two shores was often difficult, but never impossible. Because of the many

[48] La Rochefoucauld-Liancourt, *Travels through the United States*, 3:652; Scott, *Geographical Description*, p. 127; Smyth, *Tour of the United States*, p. 179.

[49] Scott, *Geographical Description*, p. 40; Middleton, *Tobacco Coast*, p. 39.

[50] Middleton, *Tobacco Coast*, p. 40.

[51] Eddis, *Letters from America*, p. 101.

[52] Scott, *Geographical Description*, p. 134; La Rochefoucauld-Liancourt, *Travels through the United States*, 3:245; Eddis, *Letters from America*, p. 102; Schoepf, *Travels in the Confederation*, p. 313.

rivers and the bay itself, transportation depended on a series of ferries and the tidewater roads that connected the various ferry lanes. For example, from Williamsburg to Annapolis, a distance of 120 miles, it was necessary to take a dozen ferries. Two types of ferries were used. In protected creeks, flat-bottomed scows with sides two and one-half feet high were adequate. These boats varied in size, the largest running thirty feet long and eight feet wide. On the lower courses of the larger rivers, in estuaries, and on the bay, sloops or schooners capable of carrying upward of fifteen people were used.[53] The most important of the larger ferries hauled passengers and freight across the bay from Rockhall to Annapolis. What accounted for its popularity was the desire of most travelers, moving up or down the coast, to use Eastern Shore roads and then cross the bay, instead of taking a route around the head of the Chesapeake. The combination of land and water routes also encouraged a number of shippers on the Eastern Shore to use the portages. Wherever the heads of two rivers came close to meeting, one flowing into the Chesapeake and the other into the Delaware, traffic developed between them. Portages were located at the head of the Elk, the Sassafras, Chester, Choptank, and Nanticoke.[54]

Adequate roads ran through most of Maryland's settled regions, although the average eighteenth-century traveler would not admit it. Despite the acidity of their remarks, an occasional writer revealed the situation as it actually existed. The duc de La Rochefoucauld-Liancourt, for example, commented that the road between Baltimore and Philadelphia was "tolerably good for a horse, but almost impossible for a carriage. Notwithstanding which there are four stages that pass it every day."[55] Some commentators even remarked favorably on road conditions, and it is possible that those reporting adversely had experiences such as that of Ebenezer Hazard. While on his way to Philadelphia, Hazard came to the town of Charlestown where he found the people "so much offended at the Post Office having been removed to Susquehanna Ferry that they have stopped up a road which led thither, [with] near 100 trees across the road; some of them are very large."[56] Stage coaches using the colonial roads also appeared to make good time. The itinerary advertised by John Bolton in the *Maryland Gazette*, April 14, 1774, was, by necessity, based upon a quite usable network of roads:

[53] Middleton, *Tobacco Coast*, pp. 60–62; Gould, *Money and Transportation*, p. 136.
[54] Gould, *Money and Transportation*, p. 128.
[55] La Rochefoucauld-Liancourt, *Travels through the United States*, 3:679.
[56] Ebenezer Hazard quoted in Shelley, "Ebenezer Hazard's Travels," p. 50.

John Bolton's stagewagon continues to ply from Chestertown to New Castle and Rockhall as usual; she sets out from Chestertown every Monday morning and gets to New Castle on Tuesday where there is a commodious stageboat; takes in the passengers and proceeds directly for Philadelphia, and arrives there on Wednesday at Crooked Billet Wharf; the boat leaves Philadelphia on Sunday and returns to New Castle on Tuesday afternoon or Wednesday and returns to Chestertown on Thursday.[57]

The roads in Maryland were not developed according to a systematic plan; rather, each county designed its own system.[58] The best roads composed the main line between Philadelphia and Virginia. This route divided in Delaware and came into Maryland by two separate branches. One branch led down the Eastern Shore, crossing the Elk at Bohemia Manor, then continued on to Frederick and Georgetown on the Sassafras, Chestertown on the Chester, and from there to Rockhall or East Neck Island on the bay side of Kent County. From either Rockhall or East Neck Island, ferries could be boarded for Annapolis. The other branch went around the head of the bay, passed the head of the Elk River and the Susquehanna Ferry near Port Deposit, then ran through Joppa and Baltimore to Annapolis. Below Annapolis the main road branched again, one fork leading to Queen Anne's and Upper Marlboro on the Patuxent, the other to Nottingham and Piscataway to the main Potomac ferry near the mouth of Pope's Creek. The law required that all the major roads leading to ferries, courthouses, churches, and the towns of Annapolis and Oxford be marked by two notches cut into trees at each side of the road.[59]

Several major commerce-carrying roads extended into the west by 1775. In 1720 Prince George's County extended a road as far west as Rock Creek. By 1728 a road went from this county to the Monocacy, bringing the western area into land contact with the Tidewater. The people of western Maryland did not consider this road suitable, however, and from 1739 on they petitioned for a road running directly from the Monocacy to the Chesapeake.[60] Although no clear records exist, a road was constructed around 1745 from the head of the Patapsco, the present site of Baltimore, to Fredericktown, and eventually north into Pennsylvania and south into Winchester, Virginia.[61] These transportation developments helped knit the colony together despite serious stress between

---

[57] *Maryland Gazette*, 14 April 1774.
[58] Gould, *Money and Transportation*, p. 124.
[59] *Ibid.*, p. 132.
[60] *Ibid.*, p. 129.
[61] *Ibid.*, p. 127.

different economic and population groupings. They also welded the colony economically to other colonies, especially Pennsylvania and Delaware, and made the break with England less traumatic than it might otherwise have been.

By the middle of the eighteenth century the face of colonial Maryland had been considerably changed. Roads crisscrossed the terrain, the beginnings of a diversified economy were clearly in evidence, and a heterogeneous lot of people had settled permanently on the land. The people's labor and the fertile soil created a profitable economy, emphasizing principally tobacco, but also including wheat, corn, and lumber. During the next twenty-five years several new developments of major economic significance took place. Specifically, there developed rapidly both a massive wheat trade with southern Europe, and an excessive imbalance of payments with England. Before the Seven Years' War, wheat had been exported to Europe, but never in the quantities to be registered in the 1760s.[62] Adverse balances of trade and the resulting imbalance of payments were, however, a new and vexing phenomenon. During two critical cycles, from 1759 to 1762 and from 1768 to 1773, Marylanders imported goods far in excess of the value of their exports. Massive debts were piled up in each of these periods, and panics to secure remittances followed. The structure of colonial trade was built upon the confidence English merchants had in their colonial correspondents. Whenever England's traders lost that faith, a crisis ensued.

The alterations that took place during these twenty-five years revealed important structural weaknesses in the colony's economy, and Maryland merchants suffered greatly. The independent merchants of Baltimore were particularly hard hit, and this encouraged their role in the political controversies leading to the Revolution.

During the 1760s and 1770s, both the merchants and planters made their basic profits from the exportation of tobacco, wheat, and lumber. Colonial statistics admittedly are unreliable, and the figures on the value of exports and imports from Maryland are further clouded because they are listed in combination with Virginia. (See table 1.) Certain differences existed between the two colonies but the same debt cycles occurred in both. At the time of the Revolution the debt Maryland owed to Britain was exceeded only by the debts of South Carolina and Virginia.[63] Mary-

[62] For an original study of this early trade see Gaspare J. Saladino, "The Maryland and Virginia Wheat Trade from Its Beginning to the American Revolution" (Master's thesis, University of Wisconsin, 1960).

[63] Benjamin R. Baldwin, "The Debts Owed by Americans to British Creditors, 1763–1802" (Ph.D. diss., Indiana University, 1932), pp. 72–109; Richard Sheridan, "The

land and Virginia enjoyed a favorable balance of trade from 1735 to 1756, but in 1757 the value of their imports exceeded their exports. After regaining a favorable balance the following year, both colonies registered negative balances from 1759 to 1763.

In 1763 the Seven Years' War ended. Soon the unfavorable balances that the colony had accumulated returned to haunt the merchants. England's mercantile firms faced a grave financial crisis. European merchants had extended extensive credit to British traders during the war, but after the conflict subsided a currency crisis developed in Europe and panic-stricken investors began to flood English counting houses with demands for payment.[64] Naturally, the English merchants turned to their colonial correspondents, but many of the tidewater merchants had imported far too much and were hopelessly in debt. The realization of this fact among English commercial circles produced widespread alarm, and England's merchants demanded in shrill tones that they be paid.[65]

All of these demands and restrictions occurred in a period of rising political passions. Faced with a sagging economy and a mountainous debt, Maryland's merchants and planters also confronted a new stamp tax. To many traders, even before the levying of this additional tax, nonimportation appeared to be the only real solution to the balance of payments problem. Parliament's apparent disregard for the welfare of her colonies made the nonconsumption program seem both necessary and justifiable.[66] By a combination of credit restriction and nonimportation, the colony painfully reduced its balance of payments. Importation into Maryland and Virginia was cut drastically. From a high of £605,882 in 1760, the value of goods brought into the tidewater colonies plummeted to a low of £383,224 in 1765 and an even lower £372,548 the next year.

Maryland merchants were greatly aided in the difficult process of regaining equilibrium by an expanding wheat trade to southern Europe, where a series of poor harvests had raised the possibility of famine. Wheat had been traded to Europe before, but the expansion that began in 1765 and lasted through 1770 was unprecedented. Many merchants

---

British Credit Crisis of 1772 and the American Colonies," *Journal of Economic History* 20 (1960), 167. Virginia owed £1,383,245; South Carolina, £412,772; Maryland, £310,473.

[64] David Macpherson, *Annals of Commerce* (4 vols., London, 1805), 3:373.

[65] *Ibid.* The economic cycles outlined here will be intensively analyzed in subsequent chapters.

[66] William Lux to James Russell, Baltimore to London, September 17, 1765, William Lux Letterbook (cited hereafter as WLLB), New York Historical Society, New York, N.Y.

TABLE I *Value of Sterling Imports and Exports of*
Great Britain with Virginia and Maryland

Year	Imported into England	Exported from England	Year	Imported into England	Exported from England
1735	£ 394,995	£ 220,381	1756	£ 337,759	£ 334,897
1736	380,163	204,794	1757	418,881	426,687
1737	492,246	211,301	1758	454,362	438,471
1738	391,814	258,860	1759	357,228	459,007
1739	444,654	217,200	1760	504,451	605,882
1740	341,997	281,428	1761	455,083	545,350
1741	577,109	248,582	1762	415,709	417,599
1742	427,769	264,186	1763	642,294	555,391
1743	557,821	328,195	1764	559,408	515,192
1744	402,709	234,855	1765	505,671	383,224
1745	399,423	197,799	1766	461,693	372,548
1746	419,371	282,545	1767	437,926	437,628
1747	492,619	200,088	1768	406,048	475,954
1748	494,852	252,624	1769	361,892	488,362
1749	434,618	323,600	1770	435,094	717,782
1750	508,939	349,419	1771	577,848	920,326
1751	460,085	347,027	1772	528,404	793,910
1752	569,453	325,151	1773	589,803	328,904
1753	632,574	356,776	1774	612,030	528,738
1754	573,435	323,513	1775	758,356	1,921
1755	489,668	285,157			

SOURCE: *Historical Statistics of the United States, Colonial Times to 1957* (Washington, D.C.: U.S. Government Printing Office, 1957), p. 757.

were saved by this market. The traders also received much needed additional assistance when the legislature, after considerable dispute, agreed to an emission of currency in 1766.[67]

But these years of return to favorable balances did not see reinstitution of the pre-1757 trade relationship. Contemporary traders believed that the Anglo-American system of trade was financially secure, but they were wrong. By 1769 the structural weaknesses of the colony's trade pattern began to reappear. Starting in that year and continuing through 1772, the value of commodities imported exceeded substantially that of those exported. These imbalances occurred despite the fact that Maryland adopted a nonimportation policy from June 1769 to November

---

[67] William Lux to William Molleson, April 4, 1776; William Lux to William Alexander and Sons, June 29, 1767, both in WLLB. See Annapolis Port Record Book, export figures for the statistical expansion of the wheat trade.

1770. Virginia also agreed in principle to nonimportation, but the program was never enforced. The extent of the imbalances acquired during these years was staggering. A high was reached in 1771 when the colonies shipped £577,848 worth of goods to England and received merchandise valued at £920,326. Virginia, no doubt, received more of these goods since importation into that colony was never restricted, but the anguished cries of Maryland's merchants and planters, which began in late 1772 and extended through 1773, clearly indicated that the traders were dangerously overextended.[68]

Given the lesson of the early 1760s, why had such imbalances so quickly reemerged? Several factors must be analyzed and considered in exploring the reappearance of this pattern. After 1766 Maryland's principal exports went to markets that were stable or rapidly expanding. During these years the Atlantic commercial community appeared deceptively sound. The tobacco trade enjoyed a steady pattern of prosperity. Wheat, corn, lumber, and iron exports rose impressively. Lumber and iron went mainly to England, while wheat and corn traders found excellent markets in the West Indies and Europe.[69] Wheat shipments to southern Europe were especially important because British merchants dominated much of that area. Indeed, English traders became so powerful in Portugal that the government there attempted official measures to lessen the hold exerted by Britain. Such efforts proved to be futile.[70] As for Maryland's traders, Britain's economic presence was especially convenient since the shipping of wheat to southern Europe provided an excellent channel for making up adverse balances.

The combination of a stable tobacco trade with advances into other prosperous markets created a pervasive sense of well-being within the commercial community. Reacting to the improved conditions, the colony's traders imported heavily on the basis of the ample credit eagerly extended by Britain's merchants. Most British firms thought the colonies to be a safe risk. The tobacco trade was good, and more important, British traders were receiving regular remittances from the Iberian Peninsula. If they needed more security British firms found it in the Currency Act of 1764, which appeared to insure financial stability in the colonies.

It was not until late 1770 that the new structure of prosperity began to show signs of unsteadiness. With the return of good harvests to

---

[68] James Anderson to James Hollyday, June 25, 1773, Corner Collection, MHS.
[69] Annapolis Port Record Book, MHS. Chapters 3 and 4 discuss these trade years in greater detail.
[70] Macpherson, *Annals of Commerce*, p. 503.

southern Europe, the demand for wheat and corn dropped suddenly. This decline was temporarily overshadowed by an upsurge in the tobacco and lumber markets. But in 1771, all the markets went slack. As a result, no extensive remittances came to England from any trade sector. Once again the enormity of the debt produced by the imbalanced pattern of trade became apparent. When a credit crisis developed in England and on the continent, a panic for remittances began.[71] Of course the orders for payment could not be fulfilled: the debt was too extensive. The Atlantic merchant community recognized the bankruptcy that it faced, but it was powerless to avoid the consequences produced by a pattern of imbalanced trade based on an overextension of credit. In sum, the growth of a viable wheat, corn, and lumber trade, in concurrence with a steady tobacco market, had encouraged competing merchants to extend credit unrealistically. After the early stages of the crisis, a redress of the balance was partially achieved, but the grief and anxiety of the experience caused many American traders to think their best interests might lie outside the British economic empire.

The importance of these commercial cycles was great because they vitally influenced the attitudes of the merchant community in the years before the Revolution. This community was composed of three general categories: consignment traders, factors, and independent merchants. Consignment was the earliest and most traditional method of trade. To consign tobacco, a planter shipped his crop to an English merchant who sold it for the market price. Accompanying the tobacco, the planter generally sent a list of needed goods to be purchased from the profits of the sale. He assumed the profits would be sufficient, although often they were not. This trade was expensive and risky because the planter had to pay all shipping costs, and the tobacco never became the responsibility of the British trader until it arrived at his English storehouses. As a result, the consignment method was usually, but by no means always, the province of the larger planter who, for a price, normally handled the trade for his smaller neighbors. For the lesser planter, consignment was always hazardous. Selling at home for a good price appeared to be obviously preferable, since none of the anxieties and dangers associated with the consignment were present. A more secure method, involving far less risk, entailed selling tobacco to a resident factor. In this transaction the planter did not run the risk of cargo damage or overextension, and if he spent too much, he at least knew exactly where his credit stood.

Factors began settling in Maryland early in the eighteenth century,

---

[71] See chapter 5 for a discussion of the 1772–1773 credit crisis.

and acquired a greater share of the tobacco market after mid-century. Tobacco firms, both English and Scottish, found it profitable to have a permanent representative settle in the colonies. Before resident factors were used to buy tobacco, a ship's captain might spend months gathering a cargo. Since shipping costs were the trade's highest expense, this delay was costly. With factors in the colonies actively securing tobacco for incoming ships, the turnaround time and length of the voyage were greatly reduced, significantly increasing profits.[72]

Normally the factors got on well with the planters, except in periods of poor prices, when friendships obviously became frayed. Henry Callister observed somberly in 1746 that "it's a sad thing to hear the planters cursing us continually for fixing the price of their tobacco."[73] Echoing this theme, Charles Carroll of Carrollton reported, almost twenty years later, to an English friend, "our factors are closely combined; tho hating and hated by each other they confederate to oppress us."[74] And when the repercussions of Europe's 1772 depression reached America, the factor-planter relationship took on forms of organized opposition. Planters in the major tobacco counties, believing that the factors were combined against them, formed counterassociations which agreed not to sell tobacco below a certain level. Small growers as well as larger planters joined, and besides concurring on price levels, agreed to consign their produce or ship through the independent merchants whenever possible.[75]

With the coming of more factors, the introduction of more vigorous price competition, and the improvement of tobacco quality because of the inspection system started in 1747, the home market attracted more sellers. Nevertheless, consignment remained for many the basic marketing procedure, and in the late 1760s this method showed signs of a definite revival. Consignment merchants, taking some cues from their factor competitors, began offering cash advances to attract the smaller planters, and by this practice they began to cut sharply into the factors' traffic. Samuel Galloway, a prominent Annapolis trader, took note of this in a letter to an English correspondent. "Merchants trading to this province have loaded their ships this year (as I am told) without purchase. The trade is getting into a very different channel from what it was some years

[72] Jacob M. Price, "The Rise of Glasgow in the Chesapeake Tobacco Trade, 1707–1775," *William and Mary Quarterly*, 3 ser., 11 (1954), 189–94.

[73] Henry Callister (Oxford) to Foster Cunliffe (Liverpool), Fall 1745, Callister Papers, MHS.

[74] Charles Carroll of Carrollton (Maryland) to William Graves (London), September 15, 1765, Charles Carroll of Carrollton Letterbook 1765–1768, MHS.

[75] Charles Carroll of Annapolis to Charles Carroll of Carrollton, September 4, 1770, Charles Carroll of Annapolis Papers, MHS.

past."[76] In 1771 the Annapolis firm of Wallace, Davidson, and Johnson became interested in the consignment method and sent their own representative, Joshua Johnson, to England to investigate its possibilities. Similarly, a Scottish factor, Alexander Hamilton, spoke worriedly of the resurgence of consignment in 1774. From his residence on the Potomac he observed that "there is more shipped on consignment from Port Tobacco Warehouse this inspection than there has been since the inspection law first took place."[77]

The lure of the consignment method lay in a kind of market gambling; risks were great but the potential profits were also greater. Producers played the market and hoped to get more than by selling at home. Charles Carroll of Annapolis emphasized this prospect in 1770 when the Carrolls were haggling over prices with resident factors. Because prices were high in the colonies, the elder Carroll reasoned that the market in Europe was strong. Tobacco at the time was selling at 22/6 to 25/ sterling per hundred weight higher than it had been for five years. The elder Carroll wanted at least 25/ and if he did not receive it, he instructed his son to "direct measures for shipping it."[78] Because of his wealth, the old man believed his situation was unique. "Our case is quite different," he wrote; "we are known to have a large quantity for sale and have always been apply'd to. . . . I would not by any means offer our tobacco to anyone; that is not the way to sell."[79]

Though the Carrolls were indeed wealthy, lesser planters could also indulge in such gambling tactics. They were never solely at the factors' mercy. Admittedly their crops were not prizes sought after, but in good times they, too, bargained effectively. The firm of Wallace, Davidson, and Johnson, which consigned goods for many of the smaller planters in the early 1770s, often handled orders of a hogshead or less.[80]

The third type of trader, the independent merchant, can be considered in two essentially distinct categories. By the early 1720s, planter-merchants had developed. Dr. Charles Carroll handled goods for his smaller neighbors, sometimes purchasing and at other times consigning

---

[76] Samuel Galloway to Sylvanus Grove, August 20, 1769, Samuel Galloway Letterbook, Library of Congress, Washington, D.C.

[77] Alexander Hamilton to James Brown and Company, Port Tobacco to Glasgow, August 6, 1774, Richard K. MacMaster and David C. Skaggs, ed., "The Letterbooks of Alexander Hamilton, Piscataway Factor," *Maryland Historical Magazine* 62 (1966), 309.

[78] Charles Carroll of Annapolis to Charles Carroll of Carrollton, August 31, 1770, Charles Carroll of Annapolis Papers, MHS.

[79] *Ibid.*, September 4, 1770.

[80] Joshua Johnson to Wallace, Johnson, and Muir, London to Annapolis, August 30, 1775, Wallace, Johnson, and Muir Letterbook, Maryland Hall of Records, Annapolis, Md.

and importing products for them to buy.[81] The scope of his trade was large—in 1724 he dealt with six merchants in London alone.[82] After the French and Indian War, a different type of independent merchant became prominent. These men resided in the port areas and made their living solely from commerce. Generally they concentrated on the European and West Indian wheat and corn trade, or dealt with other colonies.[83] Some were former factors who had accumulated enough capital to enter business for themselves.[84] Others came from Pennsylvania and even England to settle and to export wheat.[85] As the volume of trade increased through the 1760s and 1770s, most of the new traders settled near Baltimore or at other strategic locations.[86] A few earned enough capital to enter the tobacco business. William Lux, a man of major political importance in Baltimore during the years 1765 to 1775, bought tobacco on his own and also worked as a purchaser for English tobacco merchants.[87] Charles Ridgely, another prominent political figure, worked for William Molleson in a factor-like capacity as an independent purchaser during the 1760s and 1770s.[88]

Because of the various methods of marketing, a Maryland planter had several options for selling his crop. He could dispose of it at home to either a factor or an independent merchant, or consign it to England. If he was a small producer, he might also sell it to one of his more prosperous neighbors. The question for the planter was whether to gamble on the open English market for more, or settle for a lesser but assured price at home.

Consignment traders, factors and independent merchants provided the essential human services in the conduct of the trade between planter and market. For the Tidewater colonies the Atlantic trade consisted es-

[81] Dr. Charles Carroll to Phillip Smith, October 27, 1729. "Extracts from Accounts and Letter Books of Dr. Charles Carroll of Annapolis," *Maryland Historical Magazine* 18 (1923), 336: "I am conveniently seated for business and have a desire to fall into a little trade and being satisfied that I could take advantage of terms of the above kind and also serve you here (which I have a very good inclination to do) make my application to you on this occasion not in the least doubting your sincerity and generosity from what I have had to do with you."

[82] Dr. Charles Carroll to Edward Hankin, Annapolis to London, June 10, 1724, *Maryland Historical Magazine* 18 (1923), 213. Other letters that year were sent to Phillip Smith, John Hyde, John Hanbury, Richard Burbydge, William Hunter—all London merchants.

[83] Oxford Port Record Book, 1760–1773; Annapolis Port Record Book, 1758–1774, both in MHS.

[84] Henry Callister to his brother, December 29, 1763, Callister Papers, MHS.

[85] Thomas W. Griffith, *Annals of Baltimore* (Baltimore, 1824), pp. 30–60.

[86] "The Autobiography of Robert Gilmor," Gilmor Papers, MHS.

[87] William Lux (Baltimore) to James Russell (London), June 5, 1766, WLLB.

[88] William Molleson to Charles Ridgely, March 10, 1765, Ridgely Papers, MHS.

sentially of importing dry goods and remitting in hard coin, tobacco, or bills of exchange. Bullion shipments were relatively infrequent because the colonies normally lacked enough money to make this possible. The principal forms of payment were tobacco or bills of exchange.

The bill of exchange was "an unconditional written order from one person to another to pay a third party a certain sum in money at a specified time."[89] Many planters and traders in Maryland did not have English correspondents to draw upon in order to make payments and yet they had sterling debts to pay. As a result, people who had English correspondents sold bills to those who did not. Such bills could be purchased with sterling, but since it had limited circulation they were generally purchased with the currency issued by the colony. The difference between the amount of Maryland currency necessary to purchase an equivalent sum in sterling was called the exchange rate. The official exchange rate in Maryland after 1753 stipulated that £166 2/3 of Maryland currency was required to purchase £100 sterling.

The level of exchange also afforded a barometer of the economy's strength. Alterations in the rates were determined by the relative legal value of the two currencies, the amount of paper money and specie in use, the supply and demand for bills, the balance of trade, and the credit of the colonial drawer and his English correspondent. High rates resulted from excessive demands for payment which usually accompanied credit restrictions. Currency went out of circulation at such times and its scarcity seemed to aggravate payment problems and raise the rates. Conversely, when the rate was low or falling, it indicated that credit was easy and currency adequate to meet the needs of trade. These rates bore a direct relationship to the actual balance of trade and the connected balance of payments. When the balance of trade was in Maryland's favor, or at least believed to be under control, English merchants did not press for payments and the exchange rate rested at lower levels. But when a crisis set in and the creditors realized their overextension, payments were demanded and the rate began to rise. As a rule, a rising rate of exchange reflected the declining credit standing of the colony, while a low rate indicated faith in the state of trade.[90]

[89] Sir James Murray, comp., *A New English Dictionary on Historical Principles* (Oxford, 1887).

[90] For two valuable discussions of the internal workings of the eighteenth-century commercial system as pertaining to the tidewater region, see John Mickle Hemphill II, "Virginia and the English Commercial System, 1689–1733; Studies in the Development and Fluctuation of a Colonial Economy under Imperial Control" (Ph.D. diss., Princeton University, 1964); and Robert Polk Thomson, "The Merchant in Virginia, 1700–1775" (Ph.D. diss., University of Wisconsin, 1955).

Exchange rate levels also correlated with the degree and form of merchant political opposition. When the rates were high, the merchants invariably formed the vanguard in condemning British policies. Conversely, as the rates declined, so did the fires of agitation in the merchant community sink and expire.

2: The Economics
of Nonimportation

Throughout most of the Seven Years' War economic conditions in Maryland remained generally favorable. Substantial crops and good prices prevailed. England's merchants willingly extended credit to the colony and imports surged upward. This situation began to change in 1761 as the tobacco markets became glutted. By September Glasgow's merchants were refusing to sell to the continent for the low prices being offered. In the summer of 1762 bankruptcies followed in Britain. English merchants reacted in the traditional manner, calling for payments from the colonies and establishing tight credit restrictions there. Tobacco prices eventually dropped below shipping cost. The European market faltered badly and only exchange rates rose. Bills of exchange soared to £170 in 1763, a £20 increase over the exchange price of 1759.[1] The hard money that had been spent in the colonies during the Seven Years' War was soon drained out.

The big bust came in 1763. A credit crisis gripped the continent's financial circles. Two events, both central to the Seven Years' War, produced the collapse. After the war ended, European financiers, particularly Dutch bankers, realized that Britain and France would never be able to pay off the massive debts they had incurred. Second, Germany's currency system failed. The money issued by the German princes during

[1] The author owes a debt of gratitude to Joseph A. Ernst for the use of exchange figures he compiled. For the depression of 1761–1765 see also Paul H. Giddens, "Trade and Industry in Colonial Maryland, 1753–1769," *Journal of Economic and Business History* 4 (1932), 518; Richard Sheridan, "The British Credit Crisis of 1772 and the American Colonies," *Journal of Economic History* 20 (1960), 161–82; Calvin B. Coulter, "The Virginia Merchant" (Ph.D. diss., Princeton University, 1944), pp. 208, 222, 229.

the war had maintained its value because of the heavy war trade going through neutral German ports. With peace, this traffic ended.[2] Soon the continental crisis extended to England and the colonies.

The effects of this crisis are reflected in the case of one Maryland factor, Henry Callister, whose business prospects rose and fell during this period. His experience bears witness to the problems that confronted the mercantile community in the early 1760s. During the Seven Years' War the Cunliffes, the family owners of a Liverpool firm for whom Callister worked, withdrew from the tobacco trade. Callister, the firm's chief factor, saw an opportunity to strike out on his own. He bought the company's facilities and went into business. When he made his purchase in late 1759, prices looked good, but by the mid-1760s the declining trade had ruined him. Callister explained to his brother, "My situation was fine, my credit flourishing, every view favorable. But the evil genius of the colonies had set off. Every honest fair trader fail'd more or less on my right hand and on my left; I floated with the stream and before I gained a penny, I sunk about two thousand guineas. I paid off all my debts in Maryland, but never shall receive those due me. As soon as I perceived for certain that it was impossible to stand it, I invited my English creditors and yet two years wasted before I could obtain a composition. . . . At length powers came in, and I resigned myself and my whole estate, real and personal."[3] Given the impossible times, he told another English correspondent, nothing could be done: "It is madness now to sue for debts. If people are not able to pay you must let them walk off or stay to defy you."[4]

Others portrayed conditions with similar force and desperation. Benedict Calvert offered his candid opinion of the commercial situation in June 1765 to Cecil Calvert, the secretary of Maryland: "Our trade is ruined, we are immensely in debt, and not the least probability of our getting clear." Debtors, he reported, were on every road and the gaols "not half large enough" to accommodate those incarcerated. The American people, he maintained, were "never in such a distressed situation."[5] Governor Horatio Sharpe gave the same picture of economic conditions in Maryland, but did more than simply describe conditions. Writing

[2] David Macpherson, *Annals of Commerce* (4 vols., London, 1805), 3:373.
[3] Henry Callister to his brother (n.d.), Callister Papers, Maryland Historical Society, Baltimore, Md. (cited hereafter as MHS).
[4] Henry Callister to Sir Ellis Cunliffe and Robert Cunliffe, September 8, 1765, Callister Papers, MHS.
[5] Benedict Calvert to Cecil Calvert, June 24, 1765, "The Calvert Papers, Number Two," *Maryland Historical Society Fund Publication* (37 nos., 1844–1899), no. 34; pp. 261–62.

Calvert to urge an emission of paper money, he diagnosed the basic illness of the colony to be the imbalance of trade and the resulting drain of specie. "The plenty or scarcity of specie here depends upon this, whether the whole balance of trade is or is not against us," he explained, "for if we import more than our exports will pay for, whether we have paper money or not, we must be drained of our specie to pay the balance till none remains."[6]

In the fall of 1765, the lower house reiterated the problem in the instructions it drew up for Charles Garth, a member of Parliament who was being commissioned as an agent to represent the colony's views at the time of the Stamp Act crisis. Low tobacco prices had resulted in a severe imbalance of payments. To continue importation, the merchants had increased their grain, lumber and iron exports. But England's restrictions on lumber and iron made it impossible for the colony to redress the balance. "We want British manufacturers but cannot pay for them."[7] Daniel Dulany succinctly explained the fundamental problem to Calvert. "Every shilling gained by American commerce hath entered in Britain and fallen into the pockets of the British merchants, traders, manufacturers and land holders, and it may therefore be justly called the British commerce."[8]

Dulany elaborated on this and other economic grievances in the appendix of his famous pamphlet, Considerations on the Propriety of Imposing Taxes, published during the height of the Stamp Act crisis: "From Virginia and Maryland are exported communibus annis, 90,000 hogsheads of tobacco to Great Britain of which it is supposed 60,000 are then re-exported. But these colonies not being permitted to send their tobacco immediately to foreign markets distributively, in proportion to their demands, the re-exported tobacco pays double freight, double insurance, commission and other shipping charges. The whole quantity is moreover, of course, much depreciated, for going all to Great Britain, the home market is overdone by which circumstances the quantity required for home consumption is without doubt purchased cheaper than it would be if no more than that were imported into Great Britain, and of this glut foreigners and purchasers on speculation also avail themselves." He further complained of the colonies' being exploited by the regulations placed on their imports: "If the colonies were not restrained from di-

[6] Horatio Sharpe to Secretary Calvert, December 21, 1765, Archives of Maryland, ed. William H. Browne et al. (68 vols., Baltimore, 1883——), 14:252.

[7] Ibid., 28:205–7.

[8] Daniel Dulany to Secretary Calvert, September 10, 1764, "Calvert Papers, Two," no. 34, p. 244.

rectly importing foreign commodities they would, it is presumed, pay less for them, even by 50 percent," he estimated, "than they do at present."[9]

The colony's merchants agreed with Dulany's assessment and that of the other proprietary officials. For the past several years, they had been dunned incessantly by their English creditors to make more ample payments. Resident factors such as Alexander Hamilton, the most prominent trader in Port Tobacco, were especially harrassed. Hamilton regularly received letters from his employers in Glasgow who used both pleas and threats in urging him to collect the firm's debts. James Lawson, head of the house, wrote with overtones of desperation, "For God sake do your utmost in settling, securing and remitting me so as I may be relieved of this dismal situation."[10] A large number of Glasgow firms, some said several hundred, fell during 1764 and 1765. Yet try as the factors might, they could not secure enough funds, and tobacco did not sell at any price.[11] A typical condition was that of Provost Christie in Glasgow. As of September 1764, Christie owed £24,000. His factors during the same year could collect only £10,000.[12]

To combat the depression, English merchants, besides demanding payments, cut off credit to traders in the colony. William Lux, a merchant and the future leader of the Baltimore Sons of Liberty, received word in July 1765 from James Russell that his credit was no longer honored. Lux responded quickly, requesting that his friend reconsider: "It's true remittances have been short but I appeal to yourselves whether any of your correspondents this way who have imported as many goods as I have, have made better. If not, as I am sure is the case, I must think your protesting bills amount to £90 was a step in itself cruel and unworthy the confidence of a long correspondence in which I think I never give you cause to suspect my credit."[13] Later in the month, Lux argued spiritedly that poor prices and short crops had prevented the people from paying the merchants who could not in turn pay their British creditors. "If I had been the only one you might justly have called my prudence

[9] Bernard Bailyn, ed., *Pamphlets of the American Revolution, 1750–1776* (Cambridge, Mass.: Harvard University Press, Belknap Press, 1965), pp. 653–54.

[10] James Lawson to Alexander Hamilton, January 31, 1764, Alexander Hamilton Papers, MHS. See also letters of October 18, 1764 and December 26, 1764.

[11] James Lawson to Alexander Hamilton, April 18, 1764, Alexander Hamilton Papers, MHS.

[12] William Allason to RA, September 25, 1764, William Allason Letterbook, Virginia State Library, Charlottesville, Va. (microfilm, Colonial Williamsburg, Williamsburg, Va.).

[13] William Lux to James Russell, July 3, 1765, William Lux Letterbook, New York Historical Society, New York, N.Y. (hereafter referred to as WLLB).

into question," he declared, "but as it is you have no right to do it."[14] Thomas Hyde, a merchant in Annapolis, received similar, but less severe, treatment. His creditors, Perkins, Buchanan, and Brown, did not cut him off entirely, but pared his orders considerably: "We have taken the liberty to assign the quantity of some of the articles which we hope you will excuse, as the present time is very precarious."[15] Other houses continued to give credit but only at excessively high interest rates. Charles Carroll, Barrister, a man who in the near future was to become a strong critic of British policy, received a note from Anthony Baron and Company that he owed £52 interest on a debt of £217. Carroll replied that a rate over 25 percent was grossly unfair.[16] High interest rates were a legacy of the depression in the early 1760s and, even when better times returned, merchants complained of the unreasonable levels charged. Charles Ridgely became involved in a heated dispute with several London firms over this issue. Confronting his creditors, Ridgely paid the principal but not the interest, and after a series of bitter exchanges, he severed ties with certain firms and achieved a limited compromise with others.[17]

Merchants and planters in 1764 and 1765 found themselves obstructed in meeting principal and interest payments, no matter what avenue they attempted to pursue. For several years the tobacco trade had been dismal. Prices plummeted from a high of £12 per hogshead in January 1760 to a low of £5 per hogshead in 1765.[18] Reports of bad conditions circulated on both sides of the Atlantic. From Baltimore, Lux complained that the sales of tobacco "are so exceedingly low that I can not support such continual losses."[19] From Glasgow, James Lawson told his Maryland factor, Alexander Hamilton, that one hogshead of tobacco could at best sell for £5 17s. 9½d. in Glasgow while the cost of shipping it would run £6 4s. 10½d. Tobacco, he related, did not "net above ¼ per lb. in Holland," a chief market for Maryland Oronoko and as a result in Glasgow "it will not sell at any price. God pity those who are concerned in such a

14 William Lux to James Russell, July 20, 1765, WLLB.
15 Perkins, Buchanan, and Brown to Thomas Hyde, January 13, 1766, Thomas Hyde Papers, MHS.
16 Charles Carroll, Barrister, to Anthony Baron and Co., October 21, 1764, Charles Carroll, Barrister, Letterbook, MHS.
17 James Russell to Charles Ridgely, September 4, 1766; James Russell to Charles Ridgely, September 20, 1766; Thomas Wagstoffe to Charles Ridgely, September 11, 1766; Charles Ridgely to Mildred and Roberts, September 23, 1766; Charles Ridgely to James Russell, November 13, 1766; James Russell to Charles Ridgely, November 26, 1766; James Russell to Charles Ridgely, March 10, 1767; Charles Ridgely to James Russell, March 19, 1767; all in Ridgely Papers, MHS.
18 Maryland Gazette, October 24, 1765.
19 William Lux to Samuel and Emanuel Elvane, December 13, 1763, WLLB.

trade."[20] Clement Hill, a large tobacco producer, was given a similar description of conditions by his British correspondent. Tobacco continued low because the Europeans "did not buy half their usual quantity." Great merchants failed everywhere and only a short crop could save the trade.[21]

These conditions continued in 1765.[22] Charles Ridgely, a merchant as well as an emerging politician, got similar reports from his English correspondents, Mildred and Roberts. Tobacco, they reported sadly, "has been low of late."[23] By July the outlook had become gloomier. From Glasgow word came that "there is no prospect of tobacco rising in price here, but a scarcity of it in America."[24] Unfortunately no real shortages occurred. Worse, the depression affected other areas of trade as well.[25] Shipments of foodstuffs to the West Indies and Europe sometimes earned a little but more often resulted in a loss, since both areas suffered from overstocks in 1764 and 1765.[26] "The markets in Europe are uncertain as well as the West Indies," observed Lux in September 1765, and "we got a very poor price for our wheat."[27] Earlier that year he had shipped flour and wheat with the hope of securing a small profit. Now, as autumn began, he received the wretched news of his sales suffering a 17½ percent loss. Such information, he commented, "is very discouraging business, but I have been so accustomed to bad markets that I very patiently acquiesce in my bad fortune without expectations of amendment." Since his last shipment to Cadiz had fared even worse, the 17½ percent was not as crushing as might have been expected.[28] The markets in southern Europe were down because large supplies of wheat had come from England and France.[29] Importers in Iberia, the Madeira Islands and the West Indies told their American correspondents not to send any grain.[30]

[20] James Lawson to Alexander Hamilton, January 31, 1764, Hamilton Papers, MHS.

[21] Perkins, Buchanan, and Brown (London) to Clement Hill (Upper Marlboro), January 17, 1764, Hill Papers, MHS.

[22] Thomas Philpot to Clement Hill, February 10, 1765, Hill Papers, MHS.

[23] Mildred and Roberts to Charles Ridgely, March 10, 1765, Ridgely Papers, MHS.

[24] James Lawson to Alexander Hamilton, July 8, 1765, Hamilton Papers, MHS.

[25] William Lux to Messrs. Lux and Potts, June 24, 1764, WLLB.

[26] Ibid.

[27] William Lux to James Russell, September 17, 1765, WLLB.

[28] William Lux to Robert Tucker, October 3, 1765, WLLB.

[29] Mayne and Co. (Lisbon) to Samuel Galloway (Annapolis), March 9, 1765, and October 23, 1765, Galloway Papers, Library of Congress, Washington, D.C. (cited hereafter as LC).

[30] John Searle (Madeira) to Samuel Galloway (Annapolis), June 20, 1764, Galloway Papers, LC; William Lux to James Russell, September 15, 1765, WLLB; James Lawson to Alexander Hamilton, October 18, 1764, Hamilton Papers, MHS.

Newspaper reports corroborated the descriptions in the private correspondence. A typical report printed in July 1765 read, "Yesterday arrived here, in 16 days from Barbados, the Brig Achsah, Captain Noel of Baltimore, who brings word that markets were low and provisions very plenty."[31]

Parallel conditions existed in the iron trade. As Lux informed James Russell in April 1765, British men of war lay in all the rivers and would "not suffer our vessels with iron to pass without a regular clearance the expense of which being so heavy the iron will not bear it so that every source of remittance is cut off."[32] These same British ships also made smuggling more difficult.[33] In 1763 Parliament had passed a Navy Act which authorized the use of naval vessels to help enforce the Acts of Trade and Navigation. The mercantile community unhappily found the ships stationed in the Chesapeake and Hampton Roads area extremely efficient in enforcing this policy. As a consequence the British by aggravating some of the colony's economic difficulties were frequently blamed for even more.

Two additional problems confronted the mercantile community in the years immediately before the Stamp Act. The task of making payments was made difficult by a rising exchange rate and a shortage of adequate currency. During the better years of the late 1750s, the exchange rate steadied around 150, but by December 1763 it had escalated to 170 and there it remained through 1765.[34] Occasionally it fluctuated downward, but never below 165. At this level the exchange absorbed what small profits the merchants and planters eked out from their sales.

Essentially the high exchange rate was the outgrowth of the colony's extensive debt created by the imbalance of trade and its declining credit standing. The lack of an adequate currency aggravated these problems. Paper money, if scarce, would normally bring the exchange rate down, but the law of supply and demand did not operate in a vacuum. The great demand for payments, coupled with a lack of confidence in the colony's ability to make good on its obligation, caused the exchange rate to rise. Currency in the colony went out of circulation to buy bills of exchange, but this did not lessen the basic fear that the debtors would be unable to pay. Consequently, the exchange rate and the level of currency worked adversely with the high rate perpetuating and compounding the difficulties of remittance.

[31] *Maryland Gazette*, July 4, 1765.
[32] William Lux to Russell and Molleson, April 11, 1765, WLLB.
[33] William Lux to Jesson Welsh and Co., April 14, 1765, WLLB.
[34] See n. 1.

Currency had been emitted in three issues prior to 1765. In 1733 £90,000 was struck; £28,000 of this issue had been retired in 1748 and the rest exchanged for new bills. During the 1750s two issues totaling £46,000 came off the presses, but both were retired in 1763.[35] As a result, less than half of the currency that had been circulating in the prosperous years, 1759–1761, remained in use, and much of what continued outstanding was being hoarded. Because of the assembly's action in 1753, doubling the rate at which currency would be redeemed from 33⅓ to 66⅔, speculators and the public in general were now holding on to their issues, with the retirement date approaching in 1765. As one Englishman explained it: "The consequence is that all this money is locked up in the chests of the wealthy and the trade is supported by notes issued by private persons."[36]

The Currency Act of 1764 further worsened the situation. Governor Sharpe, who complained frequently to the colony's secretary about the currency shortage and its ill effects, wrote in response to the parliamentary measure, "I am inclined to think that the trade of these colonies must flag much from the want of a paper currency. I could wish the legislature of Great Britain had not thought it necessary to prohibit absolutely anymore emissions."[37] Daniel Dulany expressed similar sentiments in a letter to Calvert. Currency was vital to American trade, and though the Currency Act prohibited the emission of paper money, he predicted the regulation would be circumvented: "We can no more do without circulation of paper in America than you can in England and therefore tho acts of Parliament may prevent our emitting bills of credit under one denomination, we shall have a paper circulation under another, if not under a public law; it may be upon the bottom of private security. The old course may be stopped but a new channel will be made." Indeed, he expressed bewilderment as to what Parliament actually intended to accomplish since "the importation of English money is prohibited by statute and much more effectually by the balance of trade being against us." Surely Parliament realized that the colonies required "some medium of internal intercourse" and "understood that the sheer necessity of it must ever prove an overmatch for volumes of statutes."[38]

The merchants agreed completely with Sharpe and Dulany. Samuel

[35] Joseph A. Ernst, "Currency in the Era of the American Revolution—A History of Colonial Paper Money Practices and British Monetary Policies, 1764–1781" (Ph.D. diss., University of Wisconsin, 1962), p. 276.

[36] Jerome Baker to Duncan Rose, February 15, 1764, William and Mary Quarterly, 1st ser., 12 (1903–1904), 240.

[37] Horatio Sharpe to Cecil Calvert, Archives of Maryland 14:174.

[38] Daniel Dulany to Cecil Calvert, September 10, 1764, "Calvert Papers, Two," no. 34, p. 246.

Galloway described their plight simply and yet accurately when he wrote, "I find difficulty in carrying on business at this time as money is not to be got here."[39] William Lux complained to his Barbados correspondent, Robert Tucker, of troublesome conditions "as cash is extremely scarce."[40] As the autumn passed, he saw no signs of improvement: "The great decline in the prices of our commodities and the scarcity of money makes times very difficult and I believe will cause a total stagnation of business."[41] Parliament, he maintained to James Russell, must be fully blamed for all of these difficulties: "The restraint on our trade by the late act of Parliament has made trade so dull and cash so exceedingly scarce that there is no doing any business."[42]

By November of 1765, all of these pressures—the adverse balance of trade, incessant demands for payments, reductions or discontinuations of credit, low prices, restricted trade channels, rising exchange rates, and the currency shortage—had placed the mercantile community in an ill temper. The Stamp Act with its extra taxes, small though they were, provided a symbol upon which discontent could be focused. Benedict Calvert characterized the bewilderment of the colony to Secretary Calvert: "I can't imagine where the different provinces will find the money to pay the duty; I am certain we have not enough in Maryland to pay one year's tax."[43] William Lux explained the same to his associates. "The Stamp Act is likely to oppress us so much," he suggested, "that it behooves us to think in time of getting a warm coat for winter, manufactured here, as I am sure we shall not be able to purchase one from our mother country, where all the produce of our labor has centered from our first settlement here."[44] Already trade and business were "stagnated" and the country distressed and confused. If the Stamp Act were executed, Lux and most others believed that all would be chaos. "At present our whole country is in great confusion," he related to James Russell, and should the measure "be put in execution it must inevitably ruin us."[45]

Lux's sentiments were identical to those held by New York's merchant community, and four days before the act was to take effect, a

[39] Samuel Galloway to ———, October 28, 1764, Galloway Papers, LC.

[40] William Lux to Colonel Robert Tucker, September 27, 1764, WLLB.

[41] William Lux to Charles Cornan, October 26, 1764, WLLB.

[42] William Lux to James Russell, November 17, 1764, WLLB.

[43] Benedict Calvert to Cecil Calvert, June 24, 1765, "Calvert Papers, Two," no. 34, p. 261.

[44] William Lux to Samuel Browne, July 29, 1765, WLLB.

[45] William Lux to James Russell, October 14, 1765, WLLB.

number of that city's traders announced their intention to resist by boy-cotting British goods. They pledged to import nothing more until the Sugar Act was amended, trade conditions revived, and the Stamp Act repealed. Three days later the merchants held a larger meeting and de-cided to make all orders for British goods, both past and future, contin-gent upon repeal of the Stamp Act. Two hundred merchants joined the agreement.[46]

On November 7, about a week after the New York action, the Phila-delphia merchants adopted a similar nonimportation plan. The Philadel-phians faced economic pressures comparable to those affecting Maryland. They too had imported enormous quantities of goods, and realized that a nonimportation ban was needed to reduce their inventories. John Chew, a Philadelphia merchant, explained the situation explicitly in a letter writ-ten to Samuel Galloway on the morning of the seventh:

This afternoon the body of merchants in this place are to have a public meeting to consult on a plan of the same nature [New York Non-Importation Association] which I presume from the prevailing spirit that seems to reign will produce an agreement of the same kind—Indeed we are well convinced something of this sort is absolutely necessary at this time from the great much too large importations that have for some time past been made—There will be no want of goods for twelve months and in that time 'tis hoped the riotous spirits of the manufacturers of Great Britain will take care.[47]

More than 400 merchants signed the boycott agreement and a committee was appointed to observe its execution.[48] Boston's merchants were more reluctant to follow, but after being subjected to a series of public attacks, they drew up a nonimportation agreement on December 9.[49] The other Massachusetts port towns of Salem, Marblehead, Newbury Port, and Plymouth took the same action. These Massachusetts agreements were the last formal nonimportation boycotts established.[50]

In Maryland the merchant community agreed to an informal program modeled on the ones adopted in New York and Philadelphia. While discussing the northern colonies' nonimportation arrangements on No-

[46] Merrill Jensen, *The Founding of a Nation* (New York: Oxford University Press, 1968), p. 129; Arthur Schlesinger, *The Colonial Merchants and the American Revolution, 1763–1776* (New York: Columbia University, Faculty of Political Science, 1918), pp. 78–80.

[47] John Chew (Philadelphia) to Samuel Galloway (Baltimore), November 7, 1765, Galloway Papers, LC.

[48] Schlesinger, *Colonial Merchants*, pp. 78–80.

[49] Jensen, *Founding of a Nation*, p. 129.

[50] *Ibid.*

vember 11, Lux noted that "we are on the eve of doing it here."[51] When this program was undertaken, and how effectively it was enforced cannot be measured, but a considerable number of merchants canceled their orders. No longer forced to compete with their colleagues for customers, many of them were more than willing to stop importation and sell off their surplus. For some time the merchants had realized the importance of curtailing their imports. In April 1765, William Lux wrote of this to James Russell: "I determined to quit the dry goods trade at least for some time for our country having suffered three years together by the frost has reduced the people greatly in their circumstances and consequently our remittances are very short."[52] Lux reiterated this same sentiment in September: "I do not intend importing any more goods till I have squared the old score or at least half of it."[53] Thus, the merchant protest against the new taxes conveniently justified the implementation of policies necessitated by economic troubles. And Lux indicated that even after the tax would be repealed, reordering might be expected to resume slowly. "When you consider it will be impossible to pay the debts already contracted," he told the English trader, William Molleson, "it is at least a principle of honesty not to desire to be trusted any farther when we know we cannot pay the old score and we must only endeavor to be content to live as our forefathers did on hominy and cover ourselves with Bearskins till we can learn to make clothing for ourselves."[54]

Besides canceling his orders for English goods, Lux fought the Stamp Act in still another manner. The Sons of Liberty, an organization dedicated to forcing a repeal of the tax, was being formed throughout the colonies in the latter months of 1765. New York was the center for this association, and some New Yorkers wrote to Lux proposing such an association in Baltimore.[55] By the beginning of 1766 Lux was actively working to create such an organization. What he actually did was to transform a local Baltimore "mechanical company" founded in 1763 into the Sons of Liberty. From 1763 to 1766 the company was responsible for policing, fire protection, drilling and mustering in Baltimore.[56] The or-

---

[51] William Lux to Joseph Watkins, November 11, 1765, WLLB.

[52] William Lux (Baltimore) to James Russell (London), April 12, 1765, WLLB.

[53] William Lux (Baltimore) to James Russell (London), September 17, 1765, WLLB.

[54] William Lux (Baltimore) to William Molleson (London), January 13, 1766, WLLB.

[55] Charles Carroll of Carrollton to Daniel Barrington, March 17, 1766, Charles Carroll of Carrollton Letterbook, MHS; Isaac Q. Leake, *Memoir of the Life and Times of John Lamb* (Albany, 1850), pp. 3-4.

[56] George W. McCreary, *The Ancient and Honorable Mechanical Company of Baltimore* (Baltimore, Md.: Kohn & Pollock, 1901), pp. 13-15.

ganization was composed of both merchants and tradesmen. Mark Alexander, a Baltimore merchant, proposed the name "mechanical company" specifically in deference to the large number of tradesmen enrolled. (See table 2.)[57] On February 24, 1766, two of the company's leading merchants, William Lux and Robert Adair, called a meeting of the membership to organize the Sons of Liberty. Lux was placed in charge at that session.[58] From its inception, the Baltimore Sons of Liberty, later known as the Whig Club, took a decidedly radical political stance. Maryland's last colonial governor, Robert Eden, labeled the group the most "pronounced rebellious and mischievious organization in the province of Maryland."[59]

When he first witnessed their proceedings, Charles Carroll of Carrollton referred to the Sons as "men of little note."[60] But in 1773, after he had become involved in a bitter conflict with the proprietary government, Carroll turned to the organization for support. Like others in the 1770s, Carroll considered the leaders of this association to be the voice of the Baltimore community. And for all practical purposes they were, since Baltimore, despite its size, was not accorded a seat in the legislature at Annapolis.[61]

All of Baltimore's major political leaders at this time were merchants. William Lux, the most active political organizer, was one of the first shipowners in Baltimore. His father, Darby Lux, had been a ship's captain in the London trade who had decided to settle in Baltimore around 1743. Quickly establishing himself, he became a town commissioner in 1745 and a few years later appointed his son, William, as commission secretary. Darby Lux died in 1750 and William inherited his dry goods business. Not content to remain a storekeeper, he made investments, and by 1754 he owned at least one ship. Continuing to expand, he bought more vessels, invested in others, established branch stores, and opened a rope walk with William Smith.[62] During the late 1760s he began selling and distributing goods for the Philadelphia firm of Willing and Morris through his Maryland stores. Once the war started, he was appointed a

[57] *Ibid.*

[58] *Ibid.*, pp. 18–19; John Thomas Scharf, *The Chronicles of Baltimore* (Baltimore, 1874), p. 58; Janet Bassett Johnson, *Robert Alexander, Maryland Loyalist* (New York: G. P. Putnam's Sons, 1942), p. 20.

[59] McCreary, *Ancient and Honorable Mechanical Company*, p. 25.

[60] Charles Carroll of Carrollton to Daniel Barrington, March 17, 1766, Charles Carroll of Carrollton Letterbook, MHS.

[61] Thomas W. Griffith, *Annals of Baltimore* (Baltimore, 1824), p. 29.

[62] *Ibid.*, pp. 33, 49; *Maryland Gazette*, April 2, 1761, August 16, 1764; William Lux to John Bradford, July 15, 1768, WLLB.

TABLE 2   *Names and Occupations of Members of the Mechanical Company*
of Baltimore Who Formed the Baltimore Sons of Liberty

Robert Adair	Merchant
William Aisquith	Merchant
Michael Allen	Innkeeper
William Baker	Storekeeper
Daniel Bowly	Merchant
Archibald Buchanan	Merchant
James Calhoun	Merchant
William Clemm	Cooper
Hercules Courtney	Merchant
James Cox	Storekeeper
John Dever	Storekeeper
George Duvall	Merchant
Benjamin Griffith	Merchant
Issac Grist	Merchant
Caleb Hall	Storekeeper
Samuel Hollingsworth	Merchant
Gerald Hopkins	Merchant
Melchner Keener	Merchant
George Leverly	Clock maker
Aaron Levington	No information
George Lindenburger	Merchant
William Lux	Merchant
William Lyon	Tailor
John Melane	Artisan
Richard Moale	Merchant
George Patton	Merchant
David Rusk	Innkeeper
David Shields	Hatter
William Spear	Merchant
John Sterrett	Merchant
Erasmus Uhler	Tanner
George Wells	Storekeeper
William Wilson	Merchant

NOTE: Those people who are defined as merchants are known to have invested in shipping. Individuals who imported goods, but did not invest in ships, are labeled storekeepers.

continental purchasing agent.[63] Closest to Lux was his cousin, Daniel Bowly, who established himself in Baltimore around 1752. Bowly's political and commercial career paralleled his cousin's, and he was executor of Lux's estate after the latter's death.[64]

[63] Robert East, *Business Enterprise in the American Revolutionary Era* (New York: Columbia University Press, 1938), pp. 140, 147.

[64] Griffith, *Annals of Baltimore*, p. 32; East, *Business Enterprise*, p. 140; *Maryland Gazette and Baltimore Advertiser*, January 23, 1784; Ward L. Miner, *William Goddard, Newspaperman* (Durham, N.C.: Duke University Press, 1962), p. 158.

James Calhoun, who settled in Baltimore during the early 1760s, was a member of the Sons of Liberty and later the chairman of the Baltimore Committee of Observation. Calhoun was appointed a magistrate after the Revolution and comptroller of Baltimore in 1784. In addition to his political activities, he served as first deputy in Maryland to William Buchanan, the commissary general of the Continental Army. Calhoun reached the pinnacle of his career in 1797, when he was elected Baltimore's first mayor. He was at that time president of the state's largest insurance company.[65]

Hercules Courtney, like Calhoun, was very active in prominent political organizations before the war. By 1780 he had shifted the emphasis of his business from that of a merchant to that of an insurance dealer, and in the 1790s he founded his own firm.[66] George Lindenburger came from Europe early in 1760. Through industrious service with the Sons of Liberty and various committees, he gained a magistrate's chair in 1771. Other newcomers who quickly rose to economic and political prominence included William Spear and James Sterrett from Lancaster, George Leverly from England, George Patton from Ireland, and Melchner Keener and Samuel Hollingsworth from Philadelphia. All of these men invested extensively in Baltimore properties during the 1760s and 1770s.[67] And as merchants they also imported sizable quantities of dry goods. In the years preceding the Revolution, this combination of local investments and heavy imports placed them in a precarious financial state.[68]

When the merchants instituted their nonimportation policy in November 1765, many of them were hoping for news of better wheat markets in Europe. Since early spring they had been requesting their contacts to forward all possible information on wheat and flour prices. These two commodities held out the best possibility of making favorable

[65] Griffith, *Annals of Baltimore*, pp. 49, 79; Miner, *William Goddard*, pp. 159, 169; *Maryland Journal*, January 8, 1777; *Maryland Gazette and Baltimore Advertiser*, April 30, 1784.

[66] Griffith, *Annals of Baltimore*, pp. 48, 114; Stuart Weems Bruchey, *Robert Oliver, Merchant of Baltimore, 1783–1819* (Baltimore, Md.: Johns Hopkins Press, 1956), p. 65.

[67] Griffith, *Annals of Baltimore*, pp. 37–39, 42, 43; Miner, *William Goddard*, p. 169; *Maryland Journal*, January 7, 1783, February 25, 1783; *Maryland Gazette and Baltimore Advertiser*, April 2, 1784, and April 30, 1784.

[68] Two of the most prominent political figures in the Baltimore trading community did not serve in the Sons of Liberty. Samuel Purviance, a man who came to rival Lux for leadership at the time of the Townshend Act controversy, lived in Pennsylvania during the period surrounding the Stamp Act. Charles Ridgely, a merchant politically active in the 1770s, did not join the organization, or if he did, no record of it has yet been found.

remittances.[69] "Pray," Lux requested, "don't omit letting me know the prices of wheat in England and Cadiz, Lisbon and Ireland."[70] Others asked for the same news and slowly some good reports began to circulate. Scattered at first in the summer, but increasingly frequent as the fall and winter months arrived, the reports from southern Europe told of excellent wheat markets. Mayne and Company, a Lisbon-based firm, informed Samuel Galloway that the European wheat harvest had turned out "very short so that there will be a necessity for great supplies from abroad till nearly next year's harvest."[71] On into winter and early spring, messages about poor harvests continued, not only from Portugal but from Ireland, France, and Italy.[72]

A rush to ship wheat to the continent began. William Lux busily engaged in sending wheat to Lisbon and Cadiz. In the letters he sent with his cargoes, he instructed his correspondents to remit the profits to London for the payments of debts.[73] By January 1766, trade conditions looked better. As Lux wrote to one of his British creditors, "Our last harvest proved very good and the great demand from Spain has been of real service to us in this general distress."[74] In February he rejoiced, "I have had very large orders for both wheat and flour this fall."[75] Through the spring and summer of 1766, prices continued high and indicators such as the exchange rate dropped. In April, Lux exclaimed, "We have had many vessels loaded here for Cadiz, Lisbon and Ireland, which has made the grain market very brisk and exchange low indeed. Nothing kept us from sinking but the demands for grain."[76] By June he could, with a shade of humor, report that "the large orders we have had has entirely drained us both of wheat and corn so that we ourselves are almost starving."[77] And with the shipping season's closing that fall, some

[69] William Lux to James Russell, April 12, 1765, WLLB.

[70] William Lux to James Russell and William Molleson, May 5, 1765, WLLB.

[71] Mayne and Co. (Lisbon) to Samuel Galloway (Annapolis), December 4, 1765, Galloway Papers, LC.

[72] Benson and Vaughan (Cork) to Samuel Galloway (Annapolis), December 4, 1765, Galloway Papers, LC; Edward Barn and Sons (Lisbon) to Samuel Galloway (Annapolis), February 26, 1766, Galloway Papers, LC.

[73] William Lux (Baltimore) to Reese Meredith (Philadelphia), November 16, 1765; to Clark and Huntley (Lisbon), October 28, 1765; to Parr and Buckley (London), June 13, 1766, all in WLLB.

[74] William Lux (Baltimore) to William Molleson (London), January 13, 1766, WLLB.

[75] William Lux to William Saunders, February 10, 1766, WLLB.

[76] William Lux to William Molleson, April 4, 1766, WLLB.

[77] William Lux to William Molleson, June 15, 1766, WLLB.

of the wonder of the year still remained as he reflected and marveled on the "extraordinary exportation to Europe."[78]

The other primary export, tobacco, also began to rise in price in late 1765 and early 1766. Thomas Philpot, a London tobacco importer, told Clement Hill that he hoped Hill was sending his tobacco since "our market at present is very good."[79] Prices offered by factors reflected this upward trend.[80] In February 1766, Perkins, Buchanan, and Brown of London predicted to their tobacco suppliers that there would be an excellent market the following summer.[81] With rising markets, the bitter feelings of the colony's merchants toward the British mercantile system changed and were no longer so pronounced, though most continued to long for a freer trading community. "The disadvantages we labor under of not being allowed to bring any of your commodities without touching in Great Britain," Lux told the European firm of Jesson, Welch and Company, "makes it very discouraging."[82] But this was only carping. By November, with the exchange rate resting at 155, the desperate times had passed. A combination of reduced imports and revived exports had eliminated Lux's vision of a disastrous commercial failure and pulled Maryland out of a depression.

Thus from 1763 to 1766 Maryland's mercantile community faced a serious crisis. Confronted with the task of paying off an enormous debt at a time when trade lagged badly, the merchants recognized clearly the value of nonimportation. The coming of the Stamp Act provided a focus for their frustration and gave them even more reason to discontinue the purchase of British goods. Because of their tactics the merchants quickly emerged as a political force within the colony. In achieving this prominence they had not only Lux to thank, but also Samuel Chase, who had much to do with merchant politics and the Stamp Act.

[78] William Lux to Jesson, Welch and Company, October 27, 1766, WLLB.
[79] Thomas Philpot (London) to Clement Hill (Upper Marlboro), October 12, 1765, Hill Papers, MHS.
[80] James Lawson (Glasgow) to Alexander Hamilton (Port Tobacco), March 11, 1766, Alexander Hamilton Papers, MHS; William Lux to William Molleson, February 24, 1766, WLLB.
[81] Perkins, Buchanan, and Brown (London) to Clement Hill (Upper Marlboro), February 4, 1766, and February 17, 1766, Hill Papers, MHS.
[82] William Lux to Jesson, Welch and Company, October 27, 1766, WLLB.

3 : The Emergence
of an Incendiary

The Maryland merchants were not alone in their opposition to the Stamp Act. The political ambitions of certain men and the economic plight of the merchants brought about a coalition of forces. Charles Carroll of Carrollton accurately named the components of this union to an English correspondent: "You may probably have heard of the Association of the Sons of Liberty at New York. Letters said to be written by some of those sons were sent to Mr. Lux of Baltimoretown proposing such an association there. The gentlemen readily came into it; the letters were communicated to Paca and Chase, who were to solicit a coalition of the inhabitants of Annapolis with the Sons of Liberty of Baltimore."[1] The impetus driving Lux and the Baltimore merchant community came basically from discontent with the mercantile credit structure. What provoked Chase and Paca is another story, which had its roots in the political background and structure of Maryland.

One principle dominated the government hierarchy in the colony— material gain. The entire ordering of official posts at all levels was geared to create a materialistic loyalty to the proprietor. Numerous positions of reward existed. As William Eddis, a government appointee, said, "In England there are few, even in the great departments of state who possess so extensive a patronage as the governor of Maryland."[2] Approximately

---

[1] Charles Carroll of Carrollton to Daniel Barrington, March 17, 1766, Charles Carroll of Carrollton Letterbook, 1766–1769, Maryland Historical Society, Baltimore, Md. (cited hereafter as MHS).

[2] William Eddis, *Letters from America* (London, 1792), p. 24.

£12,000 to £14,000 per year was available for distribution. This sum supported ten major officials, counting naval officers, and seventy lesser ones down to the county clerks. Most of these positions paid relatively well and new appointees were expected, as a matter of practice, to pay "kickbacks" to the higher proprietary officials.[3]

Such political patronage provided an indispensable vehicle for uniting the proprietary party. But patronage also presented a vulnerable target for the government's critics. Eddis wrote during a controversy over the extent of patronage in 1772 that its "influence is considered by many as inimical to the essential interests of the people; a spirit of party is consequently excited; and every idea of encroachment is resisted by the popular faction, with all the warmth of patriotic enthusiasm."[4] The opposition of the "popular faction" was not directed against an imagined specter of proprietary influence, for assemblymen voted regularly on the side of the proprietor in the hope of reaping lucrative posts.[5]

The practice of using material incentives within an institutional framework for the purpose of achieving efficiency in government apparently worked well. Proprietary incomes were always high. In 1748 the proprietor's gross revenue, including all funds from quit-rents, land offices, and trade duties, totaled £11,650 sterling. By 1754 it had risen to £16,440. During the French and Indian War the income fluctuated between a low of £10,655 and a high of £18,994. After the conflict the revenue averaged £13,171. Normally, £2,000 of this procurement constituted debits and the remaining 5/6th was net private revenue to the lord proprietor.[6]

The largest proprietary expense was the governor's salary. This official possessed extensive appointive and administrative power including the right to initiate and to veto legislation. Next to the governor in authority was the council, which consisted of twelve men named by the proprietor or approved by him after appointment by the governor. The council performed several functions. When meeting with the governor in executive session, it acted essentially as an advisory body. Together with the governor it also constituted the Provincial Court of Appeals. As a legislative body the council convened independently as the upper

---

[3] Charles Albro Barker, *The Background of the Revolution in Maryland* (New Haven, Conn.: Yale University Press, 1940), p. 148; William Fitzhugh to James Russell, July 1, 1774, Letters of James Russell, Coutts Bank Papers (microfilm copy in University of Virginia Library, Charlottesville, Va.).

[4] Eddis, *Letters from America*, p. 125.

[5] Lawrence C. Wroth, "A Maryland Merchant and His Friends in 1750," *Maryland Historical Magazine 6* (1911), 240.

[6] Barker, *Background of the Revolution*, pp. 143–44.

house. In this capacity it could introduce any form of legislation and its approval was necessary before a bill went to the governor for approval. The last major branch of the government was the lower house. Four delegates attended from each county when the legislature met. Throughout most of the eighteenth century the lower house, or House of Delegates, attempted to extend its powers. These attempts made some headway, and in the 1770s this confrontation provided the basic issue around which a party formed and eventually led the colony to independence.[7]

Those persons who held important positions at the various governmental levels, whether elective or appointive, invariably enjoyed membership in the upper class. Their widespread holdings afforded them both the means and opportunity to participate actively in politics. None of the poor or middling sort entered this exclusive circle, for office holding was reserved, as William Eddis once remarked, to "persons of the greatest consequence in their counties."[8] The elite's dominance of the colony's politics reflected the class structure of the society, but despite its monopolization of political power, parties—or more correctly, political factions—existed.[9] The leading and most powerful Anglican churchman in Maryland before the war, Jonathan Boucher, described politics as party-oriented and motivated by greed: "There, as well as here, the country and the people were divided into two parties. Placemen and their dependents took the part of government, but were always opposed by a faction whose leaders were instigated merely with the view of turning others out that they themselves might come in."[10] Boucher's opinion may have been biased by his having fled the colony prior to the Revolution, leaving wealth and valuables behind. But Charles Carroll of

[7] Adequate descriptions of Maryland's colonial government can be found in Barker, *Background of the Revolution*; Newton D. Mereness, *Maryland as a Proprietary Province* (New York: The Macmillan Co., 1901); and Donnell M. Owings, *His Lordship's Patronage* (Baltimore: Maryland Historical Society, 1953).

[8] Eddis, *Letters from America*, p. 178.

[9] The figures presented below for the distribution of wealth in one of Maryland's oldest counties, Anne Arundel, are perhaps suggestive though not necessarily representative of the general pattern of wealth distribution throughout the colony. These statistics have been compiled from taxation records located in the Maryland Historical Society for the year 1783. Unfortunately, copious tax records are not available prior to that date. Assessment figures for the colony's capital, Annapolis, have not been included in the analysis since they would distort the distribution pattern. According to these sources 75 percent of the county's total wealth was controlled by the upper 20 percent, with the wealthiest tenth of the population holding 54 percent. By contrast more than three-fourths of the entire community shared only 25 percent. The entire decile distribution follows: decile 1 (0%), 2 (1%), 3 (1%), 4 (1%), 5 (2%), 6 (3%), 7 (7%), 8 (12%), 9 (21%), and 10 (54%).

[10] Jonathan Boucher, *Reminiscences of an American Loyalist* (Boston and New York: Houghton Mifflin, 1925), p. 68.

Carrollton, upon his return from studies abroad in 1765, characterized politics in an identical fashion. "The basis for factions" he credited to a "want of a sufficient number of lucrative offices to gratify the avarice or ambitions of the outs." Such motives, he critically observed, mirrored only too well the more general currents of the society. Shortly after his arrival he began to take particular notice of the colonials' shoddy moral values. "As to the people," he told an English friend, "you know they do not want understanding nor the use of it; the common sort and indeed the better sort (be it spoken between friends) have not that opinion of strict justice and integrity and do not pay that regard to it in their dealings, which I could wish for their honor and for their advantage." He particularly lamented the people's considerable lack of deference for their betters: "There is a mean, low, dirty envy which creeps thro all ranks and cannot suffer a man a superiority of fortune, of merit, or of understanding in fellow citizens—either of these are sure to entail a general ill will and dislike upon the owner."[11]

The proprietary and antiproprietary factions, or the "court" and "country" parties, as they were called, divided on several key issues during the early 1760s. Legislation concerning defense appropriations, the disposition of collected revenue, the payment of the public debt, and the appointment of a provincial agent in London occupied the debates of the legislature. On all these matters the court party disputed the country party's position because the proprietor's champions interpreted the legislation advanced as tending to detract from the proprietary power.[12]

But in 1765 these internal debates took a secondary position to external political considerations. As Charles Carroll informed a friend in England, "Our political quarrels are now forgot or lay dormant while the dread of the Stamp Act continues and the common danger outweighs private concern."[13] While Carroll probably exaggerated the harmony within the colony, the focus of politics was indeed on imperial issues. This shift of attention, however, did not prevent local men with "private concerns" from using the imperial controversy for the same reasons that men had concentrated on provincial issues before, namely, to turn others out that they might come in.

[11] Charles Carroll of Carrollton to Edmund Jennings, November 23, 1765, Charles Carroll of Carrollton Letterbook, 1766–1769, MHS.
[12] Barker, *Background of the Revolution*, chapter 8. Barker's excellent study is one of the finest histories written of an eighteenth-century colony. Were there more works of this caliber, historians would know a good deal more about the foundations of the American Revolution.
[13] Charles Carroll of Carrollton to Edmund Jennings, November 23, 1765, Charles Carroll of Carrollton Letterbook, 1766–1769, MHS.

Samuel Chase was chief of those coveting entry. He was one of those Jonathan Boucher referred to when he wrote that "in Maryland the popular leaders have almost always been lawyers."[14] Besides Chase, other significant popular leaders included Thomas Johnson, William Paca, and John Hall—all lawyers. Chase rode the county court circuit with Johnson and studied under Hall. In 1763, Chase gained admittance to the bar. With an abundance of good lawyers handling the gentry's cases, Chase concentrated his talents in the role of a defense lawyer, with debtors constituting his primary clientele. The economic conditions of 1764 and 1765 contributed substantially to his practice, but since fees were not very high in the case of debtors, Chase worked on the principle of volume.[15] His income was good but not as high as he desired. To increase his earnings, he began speculating in land as early as 1762, while still a law student. By 1764 he was overextended and unable to pay the money due on his land. Looking for relief, Chase formed an association with Thomas Johnson. The latter agreed to make Chase's payments for half his shares. Chase, having little choice, accepted Johnson's offer.[16]

Politics constituted Chase's other passion. Beginning in 1764 he launched what was to become a three-pronged attack on the government at the local, provincial and imperial levels. A year before, Chase had been denied membership in the Forensic Club, a gathering of the Annapolis elite, and the implied social snub may have aroused his ire.[17] His first campaign was for local reform in Annapolis. His opponents were the top officials in the proprietary administration, because the leading men of the provincial government also held the higher town positions. Daniel Dulany served as recorder of Annapolis and deputy secretary of the province. The Annapolis aldermen included: George Steuart, judge of the land office; Upton Scott, clerk of the council and upper house plus examiner general and comptroller of North Potomac; John Ross, a naval officer; Michael MacNemara, clerk of the lower house; John Brice, chief justice of the provincial court; and Benjamin Tasker, president of the governor's council.[18] Chase criticized these men for refusing to maintain properly the public facilities of the town. Chase organized small trades-

---

[14] Boucher, *Reminiscences of an American Loyalist*, p. 68.

[15] Neil Strawser, "The Early Life of Samuel Chase" (Master's thesis, George Washington University, 1958), pp. 59, 67–68. Strawser's ably researched thesis contains a wealth of material on Chase and Annapolis politics in the 1760s. I am in his debt for portions of this chapter.

[16] *Ibid.*, p. 91.

[17] Neil Strawser, "Samuel Chase and the Annapolis Paper War," *Maryland Historical Magazine* 57 (1962), 181.

[18] *Ibid.*, pp. 178–82.

men, shopkeepers, and mechanics to demand the correction of these local abuses.[19] Victory came in the 1764 election when a ship's carpenter, Samuel Middleton, and a cordwainer, Allan Quynn, were elected to the Annapolis Common Council.[20] Chase, seeing his movement gaining popularity, immediately challenged George Steuart in October 1764 for his seat in the lower house.

Chase again emerged the victor, but in this election he owed a great deal to the Dulanys for their assistance. As deputy secretary, Daniel Dulany held the second most important post in Maryland. Despite the importance of his position, or possibly because of it, he suspected that a conspiracy was under way to remove him or, at least, to lessen his powers. Several recent developments prompted his concern. He had been getting on very poorly with the colony's governor, Horatio Sharpe, but felt he had done nothing personally to cause the estrangement. More important, he had recently received word that his brother's request for a proprietary position would be denied. Weighing these developments, Dulany became worried that "a very artful management" had been formed to reduce him.

Dulany believed George Steuart to be one of the plot's architects. He reasoned that Steuart and others were attempting to acquire the governor's support by telling Sharpe that the Dulany family was leading an attempt to reduce the authority of his office. At the time, Dulany conducted an extensive correspondence with the colony's secretary, Cecil Calvert, and visited England frequently. Dulany thought his enemies were using these facts as evidence against him. Because of these beliefs, Dulany backed Chase's candidacy.[21]

Charles Carroll, Barrister, also supported Chase in his first foray into politics. Carroll was then one of the leaders of the country party, while Steuart was the chief representative of the court party in the lower house. For Carroll, Steuart's party loyalties provided reason enough to support Chase. The son of Dr. Charles Carroll, the barrister had inherited a lucrative business upon his father's death. He was married to Margaret Tilghman, daughter of Matthew, who led the country party on the Eastern Shore. The barrister was also a cousin and intimate friend of Charles Carroll of Carrollton. In future years these two relationships

---

[19] Horace Wells Seller, "Charles Willson Peale, Artist and Soldier," *Pennsylvania Magazine of History* 38 (1914), 262.

[20] Strawser, "Samuel Chase and the Annapolis Paper War," pp. 182–83.

[21] Daniel Dulany to Cecil Calvert, September 10, 1764, "The Calvert Papers, Number Two," *Maryland Historical Society Funds Publications* (37 nos., 1844–1899), no. 10:230.

would become crucial, when the barrister helped forge an alliance between Carroll of Carrollton, Chase, and the country party.[22]

The Chase-Dulany alliance was short-lived. No sooner had it formed than internal tensions began to weaken it. Imperial and provincial conflicts produced its demise within two years. A difference of opinion over the Stamp Act precipitated the final break.

Governor Horatio Sharpe wrote Calvert in September 1765 that the Stamp Act was encountering strong opposition because "popular men and lawyers almost without exception have been exclaiming against it."[23] A month later he informed his brother more specifically that the "act being particularly hard on lawyers and those concerned with the courts of justice—they you may be assured took great offense at it and their influence in these colonies is really very great. The merchant people," he also observed, "have been very loud in their exclamations against the act."[24] Since 1764, with the enactment of the Sugar Act, taxation had been a principal concern. Most lawyers predicted that the proposed Stamp Act would never apply to Maryland since the express words of the colony's charter stated clearly that neither the king "nor his successors would ever lay impositions or taxes on the inhabitants of the province."[25]

In Maryland, there were two types of response to the Stamp Act. One was characterized by demagoguery and mob violence. Samuel Chase commanded this movement. The chief characteristics of the other approach were reason and restrained action. Daniel Dulany was the leading proponent of this form of political behavior. Governor Sharpe also disliked the Stamp Act, and other proprietary officials concurred. There was no split between these officials and the popular leaders over the substance of the issue, but the method of opposition became a sore point of disagreement. At the same time, both Chase and Dulany saw in the crisis the opportunity for personal political gain. For Chase, the Stamp Act provided an opening to acquire political recognition as the people's leader. Turbulence and agitation, not rational debate, were the methods he used in his bid for popularity.

Zachariah Hood provided the first target. Hood, an Annapolis mer-

[22] W. Stull Holt, "Charles Carroll, Barrister, the Man," *Maryland Historical Magazine* 21 (1936), 112.

[23] Governor Horatio Sharpe to Lord Baltimore, September 10, 1765, *Archives of Maryland*, ed. William H. Browne *et al.* (68 vols., Baltimore, 1883——), 14:223.

[24] Horatio Sharpe to his brother, October 1765, in Aubrey Land, ed., "Sharpe's Confidential Report on Maryland," *Maryland Historical Magazine* 44 (1949), 127.

[25] Governor Horatio Sharpe to Secretary Calvert, August 10, 1764, *Archives of Maryland* 14:175.

chant, had been in England at the time of the Stamp Act's passage and was appointed as the Maryland stamp distributor. When he returned to Annapolis, several of Chase's local followers prevented his landing.[26] Effigies of Hood were burned and an elaborate burial ceremony, directed by Chase, was conducted for the distributor.[27] Hood's warehouse next fell beneath the hands of a mob, and Hood judiciously fled to New York.[28] But his problems were not yet over. Hearing of Hood's presence, the New York Sons of Liberty resolved that fleeing stamp officers from other provinces could not seek refuge in their town. Hood left the city for Long Island, but a group of volunteers sought him out and forced him to resign his post as stamp distributor. As soon as the Baltimore Sons of Liberty received word of Hood's capture, their officers sent the following note to New York: "Our society orders us, in a particular manner to return thanks to your Sons of Liberty for obliging our fugitive slave master to resign his odious office, he having fled from the just resentment of his injured countrymen."[29]

After his capture Hood returned to Annapolis, but found the climate extremely unpleasant for the conduct of his business. Because of the community's open hostility, he left for the West Indies to try his luck there. He also began an unsuccessful campaign of petitioning Parliament for relief because of the loss he had suffered. In this matter the Maryland assembly showed more sympathy for Hood than Parliament had. At the insistence of Governor Sharpe, the assembly in December 1766 voted him £100, a full equivalent of the damage done by the "mob" to his storage facilities.[30]

On the heels of the Hood incident came another outbreak of violence. A Royal Navy vessel, the *Hornet*, put into Annapolis. Its commander, John Mewbray, and several of his passengers came ashore that evening, and while dining in a public house, got into an argument which almost cost them their lives. Mewbray's party had just begun their meal when a man walked in with a sign attached to his hat saying "No Stamp Act." The captain had four of his crew put the man out and prevented his return. This incident led to an argument between one of Mewbray's

[26] David Ridgely, *Annals of Annapolis* (Baltimore, 1841), p. 137.
[27] Elihu Samuel Riley, *The Ancient City, A History of Annapolis in Maryland, 1649–1887* (Annapolis, 1887), p. 149.
[28] Ridgely, *Annals of Annapolis*, p. 138.
[29] Isaac Q. Leake, *Memoir of the Life and Times of John Lamb* (Albany, 1850), p. 27.
[30] Governor Horatio Sharpe to Secretary Hamersley, December 8, 1766, *Archives of Maryland* 14:358; Paul H. Giddens, "Maryland and the Stamp Act Controversy," *Maryland Historical Magazine* 27 (1932), 98.

passengers "who was in liquor" and John Hammond, a prominent member of the country party in the lower house. To settle the argument the two agreed to a boxing match in which Hammond was worsted. Seeing Hammond fall, some of the spectators went screaming about the town that he had been killed. A mob quickly gathered and Mewbray's party was forced to run for the dock. All escaped safely except Mewbray, who received a knife wound and had to swim to his ship to save his life. Hood, writing from New York, summarized these events for a friend in September: "Our province is extremely heated. They have cut an officer of the tender in a shocking manner, pull'd down my house and obliged me to flee (with a single suit) or accept the same fate as the officer."[31]

Immediate action on the part of the colony's leaders was necessary to stave off further violence. Two strategies were employed. A letter to Sharpe from a majority of the practicing lawyers of the provincial court requested the governor to advance the starting date of the assembly's session from October to September. An earlier meeting was necessary, the lawyers pointed out, for the legislature to pick representatives to attend the Stamp Act Congress in New York. Sharpe promptly complied with the request, and the legislature convened on September 23, 1765. Three of the more eminent antiproprietary leaders, Edward Tilghman, William Murdock, and Thomas Ringgold, were selected by both houses to attend the New York congress.[32] The necessity of taking direct action in the face of a common danger had produced remarkable harmony between the two houses. Following the election of delegates, the lower house passed eight resolutions condemning the Stamp Act and asserting the colony's charter rights. With these measures offered for popular consumption, the assembly adjourned.

But the rhetoric of the resolutions was overshadowed by a pamphlet published by Daniel Dulany on October 14, *Considerations on the Propriety of Imposing Taxes*. Dulany had been petrified by the riots, especially the assault on Mewbray. He also realized the delicate situation into which Sharpe and the proprietary establishment had been thrust. Speaking for the proprietor, Benedict Calvert had openly castigated the act, but not to the point of sanctioning violence. Dulany's pamphlet accurately mirrored the proprietary position. He stressed the inequality of the Stamp Act and showed that its legality could best be refuted by reason. The pamphlet and its author received wide acclaim and carried

---

[31] Zachariah Hood (New York) to ——— (England), September 23, 1765, Fisher Transcripts, MHS.

[32] Sharpe to Calvert, October 2, 1765, *Archives of Maryland* 14:230; *Maryland Gazette*, September 26, 1765.

the force of reasoned opposition into other colonies and England.[33]

In publishing this pamphlet, Dulany's motives were, however, somewhat more subtle. Several of his recent proprietary requests had been rebuffed and Dulany felt threatened, particularly by Governor Sharpe. Late in 1764 he wrote at length of this to Cecil Calvert in an obvious effort to consolidate his connection with the proprietor. Referring to his reported differences with the governor, Dulany swore he had "not had the least visible difference with him. When business or amusement hath brought us together, I never perceived any symptoms of disgust, or coolness in his behavior—on the contrary we have ever since his residence here lived in a constant interchange of civilities. Upon my going last to England," he admitted, "there were a thousand conjectures formed and reports spread concerning the motive of my voyage and the letters I received, whilst I was there, informed me the governor suspected I entertained views to injure him and exalt myself at his expense." Soon after returning, Dulany told Calvert, he had confronted Sharpe with the rumor. On that occasion the governor assured him that he personally paid it no mind. Still, Dulany was "persuaded" differently. Despite the formally correct conduct of the governor "I must take the liberty to say," he continued, that Sharpe "has acted with a degree of disingenuousness which I never suspected him capable of." He felt certain that the governor not only believed the malicious rumors, but in his innocence had been repeating the charges. The explanation for all this was simple—both he and the governor were being injured by a coalition intending to reduce the Dulany family. "A very artful management hath given some persons an ascendant over him," Dulany maintained, and their motives "can be ascribed to no other course than the workings of malice and the intrigues of envy." The conspiracy appeared to him to be working only too well, and his single hope lay in justice from Calvert and the proprietor: "I utterly deny that I have in any instance offer'd the least personal neglect, or disrespect to him and flatter myself you will do me the justice to believe that, I would not deny, what I could not with the strictest veracity."[34]

By the time Dulany published his pamphlet in October 1765, his status within the proprietary structure seemed improved. The securing

[33] Aubrey C. Land, *The Dulanys of Maryland, A Biographical Study of Daniel Dulany, the Elder, 1685–1753 and Daniel Dulany the Younger, 1722–1797* (Baltimore, Md.: Maryland Historical Society, 1955), p. 262; Benedict Calvert to Cecil Calvert, June 24, 1765, "Calvert Papers, Two," no. 34, pp. 261–62; Barker, *Background of the Revolution*, p. 305.

[34] Daniel Dulany to Secretary Cecil Calvert, September 10, 1764, "Calvert Papers, Two," no. 34, pp. 228–39.

of a naval appointment for his brother, Walter, after a series of earlier rebuffs, seemed an especially good sign, but his relations with Sharpe continued to be characterized by mutual suspicion and distrust. Dulany, still insecure, realized that the Stamp Act crisis afforded him a perfect opportunity to display his worth and better his standing. By writing his pamphlet, he showed himself at one stroke to be both a popular political figure and yet an advocate of law and the status quo. His well-reasoned argument contained a clever attack on the tax's legality, and at the same time indicated that reason, not violence such as was then occurring, offered the best means for effecting change. Through this argument Dulany stood to gain the gratitude of the proprietary officials, and the accolades soon sent were undoubtedly pleasant to his ears. The only cost involved was the final rupture of his already severely strained alliance with Chase, a small price considering the fact that all possible benefit from that arrangement had by then evaporated.

The period of cooperation between Chase and Dulany had, in reality, been very brief. When they ran together in 1764, Chase and Walter Dulany attacked George Steuart on the grounds that as a proprietary appointee he had no business sitting in the popularly elected assembly. "No Placemen" was the motto of the Chase-Dulany ticket. After the election, Walter Dulany's appointment as a naval officer came through, and he accepted the well-paid position. Chase, with the backing of the lower house, then turned the "No Placemen" slogan against Dulany, and the assembly ordered a new election. Chase campaigned actively against Dulany. However, Dulany sat as an election judge, and after the balloting, declared himself reelected. A protest was lodged with the assembly and another election ordered. This time Dulany withdrew and John Hall won the vacant seat.[35]

Chase could easily afford the break since his popular opposition to the Stamp Act had increased his following. Because of his prominent role as the leading Annapolis "incendiary," he logically formed an alliance with William Lux and the Baltimore Sons of Liberty. The two men were similar in temperament, and in February 1766 they formalized their political connection.[36] Lux highly approved of the violence of the Chase organization in the expulsion of Hood.[37] Militant action did not frighten him, as he indicated in an offer to Samuel Browne of the New York Sons

[35] Strawser, "Samuel Chase and the Annapolis Paper War," p. 187.

[36] Charles Carroll of Carrollton to Daniel Barrington, March 17, 1766, Charles Carroll of Carrollton Letterbook, 1766–1769, MHS.

[37] William Lux (Baltimore) to Samuel Browne (New York), January 4, 1766, William Lux Letterbook (cited hereafter as WLLB), New York Historical Society, New York, N.Y.

of Liberty "to concur in any measures to prevent the vile act going into execution."[38]

The first action taken by the new Baltimore-Annapolis axis was to communicate its very intense feelings to Daniel Dulany. Signed ironically "your obedient servants," the coalition called upon all public officials to open their offices and conduct all regular business without stamped paper. Upon receiving the message, Dulany went before the council on February 26 to inform them of the demands. He predicted that "there is the greatest reason to apprehend from the present popular intemperance that if any officer should refuse to act as required, he will be exposed in his person and property to the rage of the populace."[39] Not wanting to be cowed, however, Dulany and the council, after weighing the matter, refused to open their offices. Chase and Lux's next step was to confront the government officials directly. On the last day of February their organization tendered another set of written demands to the chief justice of the provincial court, the secretary, the commissary general, and the judges of the land office. These men were ordered to open their offices no later than March 31. If these injunctions were not acted upon, the Sons promised that an association from all parts of the colony would meet in Annapolis on the 31st to take more decisive measures.[40] None of the officials agreed, but neither did they flatly reject the order. The 31st came and still the offices remained closed. On that day and the next a large group of the Sons of Liberty from all parts of the colony converged on the capital. This time they won their case. The court officials yielded and instructed the courts to be opened and business conducted without stamped paper.[41] Four days later news of the Stamp Act's repeal reached Maryland.

During the March interlude between the two Annapolis meetings, Chase did not rest. He realized only too well the powers he confronted and turned to attack them on the local level. Adopting the tactics he had used successfully in 1764, Chase published a list of complaints that detailed needed city repairs and oppressive local regulations—specifically restrictions on liquor sales—and alluded to chicanery in the use of public funds. Threats of a libel suit prevented Chase from publishing further attacks until June 19, 1766, when he once more restated his case.[42] The city officials, having received an advance text of Chase's remarks, replied

[38] *Ibid.*
[39] *Archives of Maryland* 32:122.
[40] *Maryland Gazette*, March 6, 1766; Riley, *Ancient City*, p. 140.
[41] *Maryland Gazette*, April 3, 1766.
[42] Strawser, "Samuel Chase and the Annapolis Paper War," p. 189.

in the same issue of the *Gazette*. His accusations were labeled fraudulent, but the emphasis of the reply was an attempt to discredit Chase personally. Here the officials miscalculated because their description amounted to flattery in the eyes of much of the populace: "A busy restless incendiary—a ringleader of mobs—a foul mouth'd and inflaming son of discord and passion—a common disturber of the public tranquillity."[43]

Not to be outdone in intemperate language, Chase penned so vitriolic a rebuttal that the owner of the paper, Frederick Greene, refused to print it, although he did agree to run it off separately. The pamphlet began with the author's assertion that he was proud to have served as a leader of the Sons of Liberty and to have participated in the disturbances they caused: "I heartily concurred in the measures then adopted to open public offices." Besides transforming criticism into compliment, Chase depicted in the most scurrilous language imaginable each of the Annapolis authorities. George Steuart he portrayed as a "man in universal odium —crept into the province from a foreign dunghill—raised by the hand of charity—and by cringing and fawning and pimping and lying sneak'd into proprietary notice."[44] The other officials were characterized in similar fashion. During the course of the dispute, several of them, including Steuart, resigned. At an election in October 1766, Chase, along with others of his party, won election to the Annapolis Common Council. As a result, Chase's party dominated the council by the end of 1766. His organization enjoyed a solid base of local power as well as an alliance with the Baltimore merchants.[45]

Meanwhile, during 1766 a program of more concern to Chase's allies, the merchants, was being discussed in the assembly. Even with the repeal of the Stamp Act and the return of good markets, the colony's economy and politics were not tranquil. The lack of sufficient colonial currency continued to hamper commercial dealings. Governor Sharpe had always recognized the necessity of an adequate currency supply and contended that an emission would contribute significantly to the relief of the colony's economic and political ills.

When the governor summoned the legislature in September 1765, he opened the session by suggesting that the lower house consider using the colony's funds held by trustees in England as a basis for a circulating currency in the colony. At the September session, however, the house resolved to consider no other business except the proposed Stamp Act

---

[43] *Maryland Gazette*, June 19, 1766.
[44] This pamphlet can be found in the microfilm copy of the *Maryland Gazette* for 1766. An original copy of this pamphlet is located at the Maryland Historical Society.
[45] Strawser, "Samuel Chase and the Annapolis Paper War," p. 193.

Congress. But at the next meeting, in November 1765, the delegates responded to the governor's proposal by appointing a committee to investigate the holdings of the colony's trustees as a basis for "emitting bills of credit."[46] The committee was specifically directed to look into the amount of bank stock owned by the colony. The colony's holdings of bank stock in the Bank of England were products of the paper currency act of 1733. With that act's passage, specific taxes and duties were established to earn revenue which would be used to purchase stock in the Bank of England. This stock was to be employed as a sinking fund for redeeming the 1733 emission. The committee appointed in 1765 reported a balance of £25,000 sterling remaining in bank stocks after the 1733 currency had been retired. After considerable debate, a bill backed by both parties emerged. It proposed issuing £140,000 on the basis of the remaining funds. The new currency would be used to pay off the public debt and the money was not to be legal tender. Public creditors could either accept or refuse it.[47]

After the members of the lower house reached an agreement on the fundamental plan, the emission became stalled for a year because of a minor, but long-standing, provincial dispute between the two houses. Since 1756 the upper chamber had steadfastly refused to appropriate money for the government because the House of Delegates insisted that the council's clerk should not be paid from public funds. The delegates argued that the council's clerk, being a creature of the proprietor, should be paid out of his and not the people's revenue. Consequently, after devising the currency scheme, the delegates passed a bill to pay the public creditors but again excluded the council's clerk. Under instructions from the proprietor, and at Dulany's insistence, the upper house returned the measures with the clerk's salary added. The delegates rejected this addition and neither bill passed.[48]

Angry demonstrations accompanied these proceedings and mobs periodically threatened to pull down the house of the council's clerk, John Ross. The frightened Ross requested a waiver for his claim, but the council refused. Other attempts to intimidate public officials were openly made and on several occasions rumors circulated telling of marches on the capital by discontented western elements.[49] Sharpe commented astutely to Calvert on the new strategy of violence: "The truth is that

[46] Archives of Maryland 59:17, 139.
[47] Ibid., p. 193.
[48] The details of this controversy can be found in: Archives of Maryland 14: 84–89, 221, 223, 225, 234, 251; 32:110–11, 124–25; 59:77–78, 82, 97–110, 235, 249; 61:106–109, 175, 182, 215–17.
[49] Charles Carroll of Carrollton to Daniel Barrington, December 22, 1765, Charles Carroll of Carrollton Letterbook, MHS; Archives of Maryland 32:124–25.

from all the people's succeeding so far by their riotous meetings and proceedings in their several colonies as to force the persons who had been appointed distributors of the stamps to resign their offices, they begin to think they can by the same way of proceeding accomplish anything their leaders may tell them they ought to do, and really I know not whether the civil power in any of the colonies will be sufficient of itself to re-establish order."[50]

The merchants echoed the bitter complaints voiced elsewhere in the colony. With the expansion of wheat and flour markets, they found themselves unable to take full advantage of the improved conditions because of the lack of cash. Somewhat sarcastically William Lux told John Norton, "Our scarcity of cash is a general complaint and the Parliament seems inclined not to let us have an opportunity of making more. I must always submit to higher powers and will suppose they act right, yet surely denying us a medium of commerce amongst ourselves must damp our trade and ultimately affect our mother country."[51] Lux was particularly hard pressed since bills of exchange, while acceptable for tobacco transactions, were of no value in the grain trade. This dilemma he accurately explained to another English correspondent. "The greatest difficulty I suffer will be want of cash which can't be got on bills here, and is exceedingly scarce at Philadelphia," and yet, he continued, "you surely must know that we cannot buy either wheat or flour for bills, for the millers want cash to pay the farmers and the farmers having no connections with London will not be concerned with bills."[52]

Despite the obvious need for currency, the delegates remained dead-locked during the spring session of 1766. At the fall meeting the wrangling finally ended. Both houses agreed to a face-saving compromise plan, which postponed paying the clerk pending an appeal to the king. With this matter out of the way, the currency emission passed immediately. Considering the critical economic situation, the legislature had been heavily pressured to reach a settlement—or so Charles Carroll of Carrollton believed. "A medium of trade," he informed an English friend, "is absolutely necessary to a trading people—such has been found the want of it in this province, that even the spirit of party itself has given way to so

[50] Governor Horatio Sharpe to Cecil Calvert, December 21, 1765, *Archives of Maryland* 14:253.

[51] William Lux to John Norton, August 20, 1766, WLLB; Thomas Ringgold to Samuel Galloway, December 6, 1766, Galloway Papers, Library of Congress, Washington, D.C.

[52] William Lux to William Molleson, November 9, 1766; for further references to the currency shortage, see William Lux to Christopher Choplin, April 15, 1766; to Captain Paul Loyal, April 23, 1766; to James Russell, June 16, 1766; to William Molleson, July 21, 1766; and to Reese Meredith, November 10, 1766, all in WLLB.

useful a measure." More specifically "the public necessity" had, in his opinion, "at last forced the houses into a compromise."[53]

The actual legislation provided for the emission of 173,733 dollars of nonlegal tender at the rate of 4s. 6d. sterling to the dollar. Backing for the currency came from £25,000 invested in Bank of England stock. The act specified that these bills should not be construed as legal tender. Governor Sharpe in 1765 explained to Calvert exactly what the assembly was then proposing in terms of a nonlegal tender. Since the Currency Act of 1764 prohibited the issuance of legal tender, the delegates had decided not to insert a clause making the new bills tender in all cases. But, he pointed out, because the bill had as a basis the Bank Stock fund in England which was more than equal to the nominal value of the bills, it could hardly be doubted that anyone would refuse to accept them.[54] The proprietor and his recently appointed secretary, Hamersley, who had replaced Calvert upon the latter's death, approved of the measure wholeheartedly.[55]

All parties appeared satisfied with the novel scheme. Sharpe thought the mercantile community would benefit, especially since it would now have money for trade while its counterparts in other colonies would not. As a result the Maryland merchants could take on a banking function, by lending currency and charging interest for its use.[56] William Lux shared the governor's good cheer. His personal fortune as well as that of Baltimore he now viewed with exuberant optimism: "As our town increases in its trade daily and the importation of European goods is much enlarged, and as we have lately had a currency emitted we are of opinion that in the future near as good an exchange can be got for bills here as at Philadelphia."[57] Prosperity's return had done wonders for Lux's disposition; all former bitterness was drowned in hope.

By the end of 1766 the anger and despair that marked the hard years surrounding the Stamp Act had disappeared. But the Sons of Liberty were more than a memory. They had confronted and successfully faced down the colony's power structure. And their leaders, Samuel Chase and William Lux, emerged from these years as men to be reckoned with. At a time of tension they had taken command. Both would do so again at a time of even greater drama in the future.

[53] Charles Carroll of Carrollton to Edmund Jennings, March 7, 1767, Charles Carroll of Carrollton Letterbook, MHS.
[54] Horatio Sharpe to Cecil Calvert, December 21, 1765, *Archives of Maryland* 14: 252.
[55] Hugh Hamersley to Horatio Sharpe, March 22, 1766, *ibid.*, p. 282.
[56] Horatio Sharpe to Hugh Hamersley, June 9, 1767, *ibid.*, p. 390.
[57] William Lux to William Alexander and Sons, June 29, 1767, WLLB.

4 : Economic Dependency and Political Disunity

In 1767 England again attempted to devise a formula for raising revenue in America. Under the Townshend program, new duties were laid on a variety of articles and an American Board of Customs Commissioners was established in Boston to reform the collection of customs. But this time word of the new taxes brought no reaction within Maryland. Unlike two years earlier, when the Stamp Act had been levied, the Townshend taxes came during years when prosperity rather than poverty characterized the economy. The flourishing mercantile community was in no mood to protest.

From 1767 until 1772 the colonies enjoyed steady commercial success. And yet, during the years 1769 and 1770, nonimportation agreements were adopted in all the important mercantile provinces. The pattern was the same everywhere: the popular leaders vigorously proposed the boycotts, and the traders, with equal vigor, opposed such schemes. As a result ambitious politicians drove a wedge between themselves and the merchants who had been their allies at the time of the Stamp Act.

In Maryland one additional factor had an important impact on the situation in 1769. At a meeting on March 30, Baltimore's merchants unilaterally agreed to nonimportation. Not one politician was present when this decision was made. The merchants took this action because Philadelphia's commercial community had been coerced into doing the same several weeks before. Immediately after their acceptance of nonimportation, the Philadelphians urged Baltimore to adopt a similar measure. To understand why Philadelphia's merchants could exert so great an influence, it is necessary to examine in some detail Maryland's and Baltimore's commercial ties with Pennsylvania in general and Philadelphia in particular.

Economically the relationship was crucial because much of the Chesapeake colony's produce entered the Atlantic community through the port of Philadelphia. Almost all merchants, with the possible exception of those factors who specialized in tobacco alone, were continually concerned about what transpired at Philadelphia. Wheat traders, active in the Eastern and upper parts of the Western Shore, were especially attentive, since these areas functioned as major grain suppliers for the Philadelphia trading region. The keen interest that Maryland's residents took in the newspapers published in Philadelphia illustrated the importance of this connection. Several of the Philadelphia papers circulated throughout the colony. The readership figures for one, William Bradford's *Pennsylvania Journal*, clearly point out how extensive was the interest. On the Eastern Shore, close to 350 persons received the newspaper while on the Western Shore, Bradford had 110 subscribers. Practically all his Western Shore patrons lived in Baltimore.[1] Through the *Journal*, merchants were kept well informed of the trends and commercial transactions taking place. Advertisements suggesting the intercolonial nature of the *Journal* covered a variety of services and topics, including transportation, investments, and ship schedules.[2] Enterprisers attempted to attract investments in land and mercantile activities, while retailers placed long descriptions in the paper detailing their wares for sale. Maryland buyers read all of this with keen interest and frequently placed orders. Richard T. Earle, a wealthy planter in Queen Anne's County, wrote Stephen Collins, a Philadelphia merchant, in specific reference to his advertisement. "I observe by your advertisement in Bradford's paper that you have many articles of merchandise which I am in want of, linens, stockings, dowlass's tickings, oznabrige and many other articles too tedious to enumerate. Pray write me by the next post," Earle requested, "if I can have between four and five hundred pounds' worth of these things and at what advance on the prime cost, to be paid for in six months from the date of purchase."[3]

Most important, Bradford's paper told its Maryland readers the prices current on the Philadelphia market. To one of the newspaper's patrons, Charles Carroll of Annapolis, the price lists constituted an essential reason

---

[1] Colonel William Bradford, "List of Subscribers on the 25th of August 1775 et postea to the Pennsylvania Journal." Bradford's circulation book is located in the vault of the Historical Society of Pennsylvania, Philadelphia, Pa. (cited hereafter as HSP).

[2] *Maryland Gazette*, October 22, 1767, August 14, 1768, September 22, 1768, February 23, 1769, October 26, 1769; *Pennsylvania Journal*, July 16, 1768, October 17, 1773.

[3] Richard T. Earle to Stephen Collins, May 22, 1775, Collins Papers, Library of Congress, Washington, D.C. (cited hereafter as LC).

for his subscription. When his son occasionally neglected to forward the paper fast enough, the elder Carroll became testy because he considered it particularly useful to have the Philadelphia prices whenever determining trade strategy.[4]

The price of wheat was of particular interest to Bradford's Maryland readers, for that was the most important commodity exported from Maryland through Philadelphia. Precisely when wheat began flowing to Philadelphia is unknown, but the trade certainly existed by the 1740s.[5] Grain was shipped from both shores. The preferred route was by sloop to Elkton at the Chesapeake's head. From there wagons hauled it to Christiana Bridge in Delaware, where it was loaded on shallops for Philadelphia.[6] (See map 2.) Wheat traders also employed two other channels. Shallops transported wheat to the upper courses of the Eastern Shore rivers, where it was portaged to the head of a similar river flowing into the Delaware.[7] And when ice obstructed water passages, wheat went to Philadelphia by land.[8] As the trade expanded, not all residents approved. A letter to the *Maryland Gazette* in 1762 complained that the colony was losing substantial profits to Philadelphia traders who were "buying up our grain, carting it overland to the branches of the Delaware, making up large quantities into flour and bread and sending it away in their own vessels to the West Indian Islands."[9]

---

[4] Charles Carroll of Annapolis to Charles Carroll of Carrollton, July 31, 1770, Charles Carroll of Annapolis Papers, Maryland Historical Society, Baltimore, Md. For the influence of Philadelphia prices see also William Lux to Colonel Robert Tucker, May 7, 1764, William Lux Letterbook, New York Historical Society, New York, N.Y. (cited hereafter as WLLB); Charles Carroll of Carrollton to George Meade & Company, May 10, 1774, Charles Carroll of Carrollton Letterbook, Arents Collection, New York Public Library, New York, N.Y.

[5] Dr. Charles Carroll to Mr. Brown, September 18, 1742, "Extracts from Accounts and Letterbooks of Dr. Charles Carroll of Annapolis," *Maryland Historical Magazine* 20 (1925), 165. For a discussion of early commercial conflicts between Maryland and Pennsylvania, see Gary B. Nash, "Maryland's Economic War with Pennsylvania," *Maryland Historical Magazine* 60 (1965), 231–44.

[6] Z. Hollingsworth (Head of Elk) to Hollingsworth and Rudulph (Philadelphia), June 5, 1769, and February 24, 1771; R. Gresham (Kent County) to Hollingsworth and Rudulph (Philadelphia), May 22, 1769, all in Hollingsworth Correspondence, HSP.

[7] Fred Perkins to Hollingsworth and Rudulph, June 13, 1771, Hollingsworth Correspondence, HSP. A remarkably accurate analysis of Maryland's colonial transportation can be found in C. P. Gould, *Money and Transportation in Maryland, 1720–1765* (Baltimore, Md.: Johns Hopkins Press, 1915).

[8] Abel James and Henry Drinker to Samuel Ember, March 2, 1768, James and Drinker Letterbook, HSP. Also see Samuel Patterson to Hollingsworth and Rudulph, June 12, 1769, and William Lux and Daniel Bowly to Hollingsworth and Rudulph, November 1770, Hollingsworth Correspondence, HSP.

[9] *Maryland Gazette*, April 8, 1762.

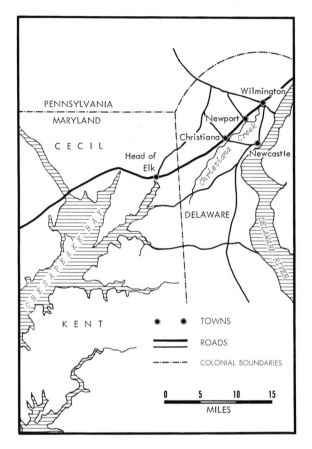

MAP 2. *Major Roads Connecting Chesapeake Bay and Delaware River*

There was more to the trade than this, for wheat flowed in both directions between Maryland and Pennsylvania. Heavy grain shipments from the northern portion of the Western Shore and much of the Eastern Shore went to Philadelphia for export, but at the same time, wheat from central and western Pennsylvania came into the Chesapeake, and merchants such as William Smith, William Spear, James Sterrett, and Melchner Keener moved from Pennsylvania to Baltimore to take advantage of this expanding trade. The combination of topography, shipping costs, and the absence of good roads explains this pattern. The wheat that went from Maryland to Pennsylvania encountered no major obstacles, whereas central and western Pennsylvania wheat shippers had to cross

TABLE 3   *Aggregate of Wheat, Flour, and Indian Corn Annually Exported
from the Eastern Shore of Maryland, on an Average, 1770–1775*

Towns from Whence Exported	Places to Which Exported	Bushels of Wheat	Barrels of Flour	Bushels of Indian Corn
Chestertown	Foreign markets only	100,000		
Chestertown	Baltimore and the head of the Bay	30,000		
Chestertown	Baltimore and foreign markets		5,000	
Chestertown	The head of the Bay, Baltimore, and foreign markets			50,000
Georgetown	Foreign markets	20,000		
Georgetown	Apoquinimink and Duck Creek	30,000	3,000	10,000
Turner's Creek	Foreign markets	10,000		
Head of Chester River	Apoquinimink and Duck Creek		3,000	
Still-Pond Creek	Apoquinimink, Duck Creek, and head of the Bay	40,000		
Still-Pond Creek	Baltimore and head of the Bay		2,000	
Still-Pond Creek	Baltimore, the head of the Bay, Duck Creek, and Apoquinimink			12,000
Worton Creek	Baltimore and the head of the Bay	3,000		4,000
Farlo Creek	Baltimore and the head of the Bay	3,000		2,000
Gray's Inn Creek	Baltimore and the head of the Bay	10,000		6,000
Gray's Inn Creek	Baltimore and the head of the Bay		1,000	
Langford's Bay and Eastern Neck Island	Baltimore and the head of the Bay	7,000		3,000
Queen's Town, Wye, and Choptank Rivers	Foreign markets	30,000		
Queen's Town and Kent Island	Duck Creek, Baltimore and the head of the Bay	20,000		

TABLE 3 *Continued*

Towns from Whence Exported	Places to Which Exported	Bushels of Wheat	Barrels of Flour	Bushels of Indian Corn
Other parts of Queen Anne's County	Duck Creek and other landings on the Delaware			9,000
Caroline County	Duck Creek and other landings on the Delaware	12,000	500	7,000
Talbot County	Baltimore and the head of the Bay	20,000		
Talbot County	Baltimore and foreign markets		1,000	
Talbot County	Baltimore, foreign markets, and the head of the Bay			30,000
Dorchester County	Baltimore, the head of the Bay, and landings on the Delaware	10,000		
Dorchester County	Baltimore, the head of the Bay, and foreign markets			20,000
Dorchester County	Baltimore, the head of the Bay and foreign markets	5,000		7,000
Somerset County	Baltimore, the head of the Bay, and foreign markets	3,000		5,000
Cecil County	The different landings on the Delaware	170,000	10,000	50,000
Church Hill	Duck Creek, head of the Bay, and Baltimore	30,000		10,000
Church Hill	Duck Creek, head of the Bay, and Baltimore		2,000	
Head of Corsica Creek	Duck Creek, head of the Bay, and Baltimore	30,000		8,000
Head of Corsica Creek	Duck Creek, head of the Bay, and Baltimore		1,500	

SOURCE: Chalmers Papers, New York Public Library, New York, N.Y.

long stretches of rugged terrain to reach Philadelphia. The lack of adequate roads through the region made the problem of shipping difficult. Prices were generally higher for wheat in Philadelphia. For Maryland's Eastern shoremen the extra shipping cost, which was low, still allowed a fine profit. But for wheat growers in the Pennsylvania back country, the expenses and dangers of traveling to Philadelphia made the journey not worth the undertaking, particularly when there were good roads following the Susquehanna and other water courses leading toward Maryland and especially Baltimore. Of course, had the Philadelphia prices been considerably higher than those in Maryland, these people would no doubt have managed to trade with Philadelphia, but for them the lower prices in Charlestown and Baltimore apparently sufficed.[10] At the same time it seems reasonable to suggest that these farmers and merchants traded with the Maryland towns at the head of the bay and Baltimore because they could buy imported goods cheaper there than from Philadelphia, since once again additional costs would have been involved in moving these wares westward.

An analysis of the Eastern Shore's annual exports for a five-year period, 1770–1775, indicates the extent to which that section of Maryland was a part of the Philadelphia trading area. (See table 3.) What these figures show is that wheat, flour, and Indian corn left the Eastern Shore in three principal directions. Two hundred eighty-two thousand bushels of wheat went to the Delaware River and from there to Philadelphia.[11] One hundred sixty thousand bushels were shipped directly to foreign markets, while one hundred seventy-one thousand bushels went to either Baltimore or Philadelphia for reexportation. The exportation of flour was similar. Sixteen thousand five hundred barrels were sent to Philadelphia, while twelve thousand five hundred barrels were divided between Baltimore and Philadelphia. Figures for Indian corn disclose a slightly different pattern. Eighty-six thousand bushels were shipped through Philadelphia while one hundred twelve thousand bushels were divided between Baltimore and Philadelphia. These data do not permit a precise conclusion concerning exact amounts of grain shipped to Philadelphia, but

[10] B. Rumsey to Hollingsworth and Rudulph, October 7, 1770, and Thomas Hollingsworth to Hollingsworth and Rudulph, August 3, 1771, Hollingsworth Correspondence, HSP. An interesting analysis of the shipping costs involved in sending produce to Philadelphia can be found in John Flexner Walzner, "Transportation in the Philadelphia Trading Area" (Ph.D. diss., University of Wisconsin, 1968).
[11] Both legal and illegal traders adopted the convenient practice of shipping goods from Maryland to Delaware by way of the Delaware River. For a vivid description of this route, see "The Perils of a Surveyor of Customs in Maryland," Fisher Transcripts, MHS.

obviously that port received a vast quantity of the Eastern Shore's produce. Further estimates made by customs officials indicate that in 1774 over one-fifth of all wheat and flour and one-half of the corn exported from Philadelphia came from the Eastern Shore.[12] During the war a loyalist from Dorchester County, while reading a copy of Andrew Burnaby's *Travels through the Middle States of North America*, commented in the margin that in the year 1774 the Philadelphia firm of Willing and Morris "exported three hundred thousand bushels of wheat, one hundred thousand of which they purchased in Maryland. This fact," he continued, "I had from a gentleman of character in Maryland who bought and paid ready money for every bushel purchased in that province; and he assured me I might depend on the authenticity of it."[13]

Philadelphia's merchants considered this trade to be of enormous importance. Naturally, they wanted it to increase. At the same time they hoped to attract more of their own colony's back-country produce, then being lost to Maryland's Chesapeake ports. With both these aims in mind the merchants subscribed £200 to the American Philosophical Society in 1769 asking that organization to undertake a commercial study. Specifically the society agreed to examine "in what manner a water communication might be opened between the provinces of Maryland and Pennsylvania; and particularly by what means the large and increasing number of settlers, especially those on the Susquehanna and its branches, might be enabled to bring their produce to market at the cheapest rate, whether by land or water."[14] Two years later the investigating committee published its findings in the first volume of the society's transactions.[15]

The published report offered four possible canal routes designed to be built upon existing land bridges between the Chesapeake and Delaware Bays. These land bridges, or more correctly portage routes, were already in use for the transfer of merchandise and agricultural products. Whenever the heads of two rivers came together, one flowing into the Chesapeake and the other into the Delaware, traffic developed between them, with the land transfer being made by portage. On the Delmarva Peninsula the most important portages were located at the head of the Elk, the

[12] Estimates made by custom officials can be found in the Chalmers Papers, New York Public Library.

[13] Andrew Burnaby, *Travels through the Middle States of North America, 1759–1760* (London, 1789), copy in Dorchester County Loyalist Notes, MHS.

[14] *Transactions of the American Philosophical Society* (2nd ed., corrected, Philadelphia, 1789), 1:537.

[15] "An Abstract of Sundry Papers and Proposals for Improving the Inland Navigation of Pennsylvania and Maryland by Opening a Communication between the Tidewaters of Delaware and Chesapeake Bay," *ibid.*, pp. 357–64.

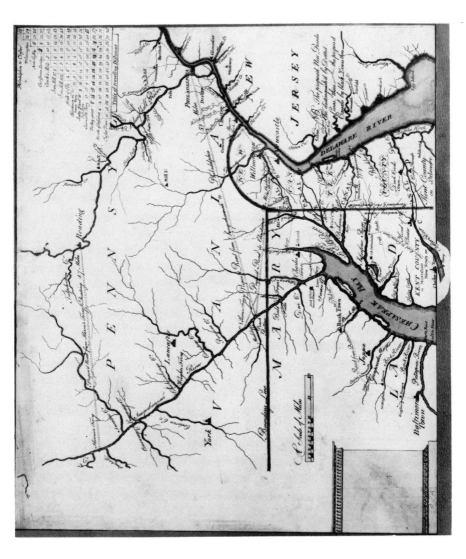

MAP 3. *Proposed Canals between Chesapeake Bay and Delaware River*

Bohemia, and the Chester Rivers. The committee proposed these locations as possible zones for construction. As part of its report the investigators included a relatively concise map illustrating the suggestions offered (see map 3). This chart, along with a rough sketch made by one of the men commissioned for the study, provides unique documentation emphasizing the commercial orientation of trade in the upper Chesapeake and what the Philadelphia merchants hoped to do with it (see map 4).

The commission proposed four possible routes, but found two of them unsatisfactory for different reasons. Between the Apoquinimink and Bohemia the site was good, but the estimated construction costs too expensive. Conversely, the connection of the Chester River and Duck Creek could be made at a reasonable cost, but the location did not serve Philadelphia's best interest. In the committee's own words this canal "would carry all the navigation of the river Susquehanna (which is the great object in view) too far down into the Chesapeake Bay, for an advantageous communication with Philadelphia."[16] Only the northernmost two routes, concluded the report, should be considered. Both contained the requisite geographical and commercial characteristics for either barge or lock navigation.[17] Since the building costs involved in lock construction were high, the committee urged the establishment of a barge canal complemented by extensive storage facilities at each end. "In the meantime," the investigators advised that the immediate opening "of the proposed new road from Peach Bottom on the Susquehanna to the Tidewater of the Christiana Creek is recommended as a matter of the utmost importance not only to the City of Philadelphia, but to a great part of the settlers on the waters of the Susquehanna."[18]

Philadelphia's merchants had high hopes for increasing their trade with the upper Chesapeake and Delmarva Peninsula region. Three different forms of fiscal and commercial arrangements were already in use to conduct the considerable commerce then underway: independent purchasing agents, partnerships, and factors. Joseph William of Bohemia Manor in Cecil County worked as an independent purchasing agent for Hollingsworth and Rudulph.[19] Thomas Ringgold, a Kent County planter, shipped as a partner with Willing and Morris.[20] As to the prominence of the factor method, the same contributor to the *Maryland Gazette* who criticized the loss of potential profits to Philadelphia merchants

[16] *Ibid.*, p. 359.
[17] *Ibid.*, pp. 359–60.
[18] *Ibid.*, p. 364.
[19] Joseph Williams to Hollingsworth and Rudulph, April 29, 1769, Hollingsworth Correspondence, HSP.
[20] Thomas Ringgold to John Galloway, March 2, 1769, Galloway Papers, LC.

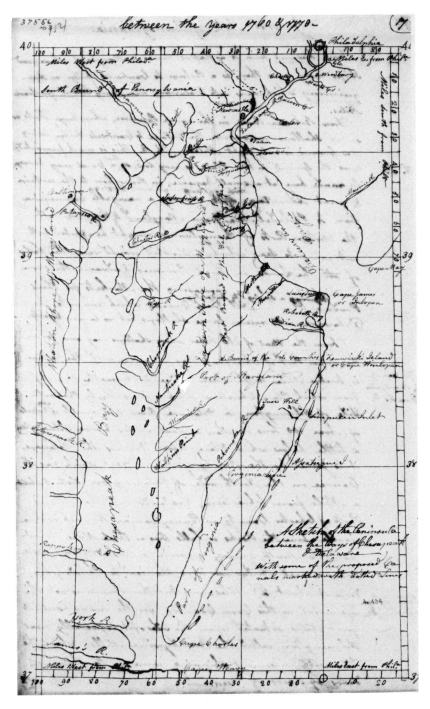

MAP 4. *"A Sketch of the Peninsula between the Bays of Chesapeake and Delaware . . ."*

wrote: "Our neighbors to the Northward can carry on a gainful trade upon our native produce or we should never see so many Philadelphia factors in the country."[21] On occasion the higher prices offered in that city even worked to the disadvantage of certain Eastern Shore planters. Generally, the larger growers bought up their smaller neighbors' harvests, but when the price was high in Philadelphia the smaller yeomen sometimes bore the shipping costs in hopes of making a more generous profit.[22]

Wheat, of course, was the most important commodity traded, but other products were also exchanged. Hogsheads of tobacco were forwarded as means of payment, normally on a small scale, although some larger shipments were made.[23] Samuel Galloway sent tobacco shipments of over 50 hogsheads to Hollingsworth and Rudulph when they offered a better price than the going rate in Maryland.[24] Iron constituted another item of exchange. Israel Pemberton of Philadelphia, and others, invested funds in Maryland iron works and in return received the finished product for shipments abroad.[25] Forest products, especially staves, also enjoyed a good market at Philadelphia. In fact, the prices paid there often determined the going rate in Maryland.[26] A sufficient demand for staves induced John B. Ennals of Dorchester County to propose to Hollingsworth and Rudulph a formal arrangement for handling them. Ennals suggested that he dispatch a sloop each week carrying staves, suitable for making packaging materials, to Philadelphia for "good back freights," particularly West Indian rum.[27] Rum, sugar, and other manufactured goods frequently came to the two shores from Philadelphia. Merchandise obtained by this route sometimes proved cheaper than when directly imported. This was especially true in the case of rum and sugar, because Philadelphia imported great volumes of both articles from the West Indies. In addition, coffee, tea, candles, ribbons, and chocolates, to men-

[21] *Maryland Gazette*, April 8, 1762.
[22] Thomas Ringgold to ———, August 26, 1765, Galloway Papers, New York Public Library.
[23] James Sullivan to Hollingsworth and Rudulph, July 14, 1769, and J. Barnaby to Hollingsworth and Rudulph, July 7, 1770, both in Hollingsworth Correspondence, HSP.
[24] Samuel Galloway and Stephen Stewart to Hollingsworth and Rudulph, July 18, 1770, Hollingsworth Correspondence, HSP.
[25] Joseph Pemberton to Israel Pemberton, July 24, 1767, Pemberton Papers, HSP; Thomas Clifford to Thomas and William Lightfoot, January 11, 1768, and Thomas Clifford to Lancelot Cowper, July 4, 1770, both in Thomas Clifford Letterbook, HSP.
[26] *Maryland Gazette*, March 9, 1769; John Chew to Samuel Galloway, July 3, 1766, Galloway Papers, LC.
[27] John Ennals to Hollingsworth and Rudulph, April 23, 1769, Hollingsworth Correspondence, HSP.

tion but a few items, were imported by storekeepers on both shores, though Eastern shoremen predominated in this business.[28]

A variety of financial connections supported and complemented the interlocking commercial structure of the two provinces. Credit entered Maryland from Philadelphia through several channels. Independent traders, Philadelphia factors, and even millers conducted purchasing activities on the basis of credit extended them by Philadelphia trading houses.[29] Similarly, Pennsylvania's currency standards were being employed in Maryland by the 1740s for wheat transactions. Dr. Charles Carroll instructed his purchasing agent to pay "eight shillings and six pence Pennsylvania currency per gross hundred" to have his wheat ground into flour.[30] Carroll also found it convenient to make wheat purchases in Pennsylvania currency. For that purpose he sold sterling bills in Philadelphia for the current money of that province.[31] The process of purchasing Philadelphia currency with sterling or current bills became easier in 1753, when Maryland's legislature altered the colony's exchange rate from 33⅓ to Pennsylvania's 66⅔. What this meant was that Maryland's and Pennsylvania's local currencies were now officially equal in value. In each colony, £166⅔ of local currency was required to purchase £100 sterling. This modification nicely accommodated the growing business relationships and also enabled Maryland's merchants to employ the more recognized Philadelphia exchange when dealing with other areas.[32]

Philadelphia's exchange market provided another important service for Maryland traders by offering a mechanism for the payment of international balances. William Bradford's *Pennsylvania Journal* published the

[28] Bishop and Walter to Hollingsworth and Rudulph, January 10, 1769; Tobin Rudulph to Hollingsworth and Rudulph, March 6, 1769; R. Gresham to Hollingsworth and Rudulph, April 21, 1769; Thomas Smyth to Hollingsworth and Rudulph, December 10, 1770; Henry Hollingsworth to Hollingsworth and Rudulph, October 17, 1770; Stephen Stewart to Hollingsworth and Rudulph, March 28, 1770; William Rooke to Hollingsworth and Rudulph, October 10, 1770; William Rooke to Levi Hollingsworth, April 17, 1772, all in Hollingsworth Correspondence, HSP.
[29] Israel Pemberton to William Cox, August 14, 1765, Pemberton Papers, HSP; Edward Sprigg to Hollingsworth and Rudulph, May 18, 1770, Hollingsworth Correspondence, HSP; James Hollyday to Stephen Collins, May 5, 1770, and Morris Birkhead to Hudson and Lawson, October 31, 1774, both in Stephen Collins Papers, LC.
[30] Dr. Charles Carroll to Jethro Brown, March 10, 1742, *Maryland Historical Magazine* 20 (1925), 263–64.
[31] Dr. Charles Carroll to Clement Plumshed, April 16, 1743, *Maryland Historical Magazine* 20 (1925), 267.
[32] *Archives of Maryland*, ed. William H. Browne et al. (68 vols., Baltimore, 1883——), 6:85, 23:362. For a later instance of the usefulness to merchants of such a fiscal alteration, see William Lux to Samuel Browne, April 29, 1765, and William Lux to Robert Tucker, November 12, 1765, WLLB.

exchange rates given by various firms for Maryland and Delaware bills, and traders both large and small bought bills in Philadelphia.[33] William Lux, in a letter he wrote to a potential investor, explained the two principal options by which credit and cash could be raised: "If you have thoughts of making a trial here the earlier your orders come the better, and you may either give us an order to be supplied with cash from Philadelphia or to draw on London."[34] Samuel Galloway suggested the same to a correspondent who requested £250 sterling, when he replied that "I am now at Annapolis to purchase it but must send to Philadelphia."[35]

The degree of Maryland commerce going to Philadelphia did not, of course, compare with the direct trade to Britain. Almost all the larger vessels, such as the ships, snows, and brigs, that left the colony went to England.[36] And though the Philadelphians were energetically attempting to attract the colony's most valuable crop, tobacco, this trade remained under the firm control of British mercantile houses. Nonetheless the Philadelphia trade was expanding before the Revolution, and many traders expected to make good profits. Indeed, as early as 1762 Governor Horatio Sharpe emphasized the size of this traffic to the proprietary secretary, Cecil Calvert, and offered his observations on why Philadelphia was able to attract Maryland produce. "A great part of our wheat, flour and other produce is now carried to Philadelphia, the price there being always higher than in Maryland, owing to the vast trade carried on from thence to the West Indies and other ports. As the merchants there can always load their vessels at once, they can afford," he observed, "to give more for cargoes than merchants in this province can give because ours must be a long time collecting a cargo for even a small vessel, there being no town or port of any size in Maryland where any considerable quantity of country produce can be purchased at once or together."[37]

Several reasons explain why so much of Maryland's commerce went to Philadelphia for exportation. The most basic was that Philadelphia

[33] *Pennsylvania Journal*, August 31, 1774; Charles Carroll of Annapolis to John Scerce, March 10, 1766, Henry O. Thompson Papers, MHS; Henry Hill to Samuel Galloway, March 10, 1771, Galloway Papers, LC; Tobias Rudulph to Hollingsworth and Rudulph, March 6, 1769, and William Thomas to Hollingsworth and Rudulph, June 16, 1769, Hollingsworth Correspondence, HSP.

[34] William Lux to Isaac Simon, January 15, 1767, WLLB.

[35] Samuel Galloway to Sylvanus Grove, August 20, 1767, Samuel Galloway Letterbook, Galloway Papers, LC.

[36] Ronald Hoffman, "Economics, Politics and the Revolution in Maryland" (Ph.D. diss., University of Wisconsin, 1969), pp. 418–33.

[37] Governor Horatio Sharpe to Secretary C. Calvert, September 25, 1762, *Archives of Maryland* 14:71–72.

offered the incentive of a competitive market. To ship goods there entailed some additional costs, but when crops arrived they were stored, and if the price was not right a trader could delay his sale until a better day. In other words, the market could be played in hopes of higher profits. The combination of competitive merchants and good storage facilities enabled a small wheat trader in Cecil County, Robert Thompson, to write his Philadelphia representative, Levi Hollingsworth, "I received your favor of the 8th inst. and am sorry to hear that the price of flour is so low and dull, therefore if you should think that the price of flour will rise in a few weeks I would be willing to wait a month longer rather than it should be sold at 21/; however I would take it a favor if you will act about the disposing of it as if it was your own."[38]

A year-round market was another advantage of Philadelphia, and merchants there emphasized this in their attempt to lure the tobacco trade. Normally ships weighed anchor and put to sea in the fall, which required a producer to ship his tobacco within a certain period or receive nothing for his labor. Hollingsworth and Rudulph of Philadelphia, recognizing the unattractiveness of the time restrictions, told Samuel Galloway to ship them his tobacco because they could give him a better return, "since we can dispose of it from 25/ to 35/ per 100 wt. at almost any season of the year."[39]

Lastly, shipping through Philadelphia was sometimes cheaper. All goods exported from Maryland directly overseas bore a 14d per ton proprietary levy, in addition to all the normal customs charges. The lower house protested this tax in 1769, specifically because it made Philadelphia a more attractive port of embarkation: "We must beg leave particularly to observe to your Lordship that the 14d per ton is burthensome to trade as to be accounted one principal cause why a great part of the produce of this province is exported through the channel of Philadelphia."[40]

No port in Maryland, prior to the Revolution, offered the attractions of a year-round competitive market. But one—Baltimore—was fast emerging, and once it developed a competitive market, much of the grain going through Philadelphia would be reoriented across instead of up the bay. The city of Baltimore is located at the northwest head of the Pa-

[38] Robert Thompson to Levi Hollingsworth, April 11, 1774. For further examples see Joseph Williams to Hollingsworth and Rudulph, March 14, 1769; Joseph Beaver to Levi Hollingsworth, February 19, 1774, both in Hollingsworth Correspondence, HSP; Thomas Ringgold to Samuel Galloway, September 14, 1774, Galloway Papers, LC.

[39] Hollingsworth and Rudulph to Samuel Galloway and Stephen Stewart, January 18, 1770, Hollingsworth Correspondence, HSP.

[40] *Archives of Maryland* 58:112.

tapsco, eighteen miles from the Chesapeake Bay. In the eighteenth century the Patapsco was able to accommodate ships of five hundred tons burden, but the harbor of Baltimore was shallow and ships with a draft of over eight feet could not enter. This shallowness was not detrimental because the bulk of the city's commerce was conducted at Fells Point, a narrow strip of land extending into the Patapsco at the southeastern end of town. Here hundreds of ships could anchor safely and unload their cargoes while their crews "waited not even a twilight to fly to the polluted arms of the white, the black and the yellow harlot."[41]

The year 1729 marked the founding of Baltimore, when a town was officially established for commercial purposes on the north side of the Patapsco.[42] Growth proceeded slowly, and not until 1763 was there enough trade through the town to warrant a central market.[43] Nevertheless, compared to other Maryland ports, Baltimore had become, by the 1760s, a prime shipping area. Governor Sharpe's description of the town, written to Calvert in 1764 from Annapolis, presented a scene of slow but progressive development: "With respect to the growth of Baltimore-town I must observe to you that altho there is more business transacted there than at any other of our Maryland towns it is in point of both its trade and buildings almost as much inferior to Philadelphia as Dover is to London, nor do I suppose that it contains at this time more than two hundred families, it is however increasing, and will probably very soon get the start of this city."[44]

Several considerations placed the town at a competitive disadvantage in the 1760s. Because the port lacked adequate storage facilities, the merchants there, as Lux told one correspondent, could not possibly secure outgoing cargoes as quickly as their counterparts in the more developed trading centers.[45] Nor did the town offer the purchasing market af-

---

[41] Davis, *Travels of Four Years and a Half in the United States of America* (London, 1802), p. 395; for commercial importance of Fells Point, see J. D. Schoepf, *Travels in the Confederation* [1783–1784], translated and edited by Alfred J. Morrison (Philadelphia: W. J. Campbell, 1911), p. 328; Joseph Scott, *A Geographical Description of the States of Maryland and Delaware* (Philadelphia, 1807), p. 76; duc de La Rochefoucauld-Liancourt, *Travels through the United States of North America in the Years 1795, 1796, 1797* (London, 1799), 3:256; J. F. D. Smyth, *A Tour of the United States of America* (London, 1785), p. 213.

[42] Thomas W. Griffith, *Annals of Baltimore* (Baltimore, 1824), p. 14. For a genuinely clever and perceptive essay on the port of Baltimore's growth, see C. P. Gould, "The Economic Causes of the Rise of Baltimore," in *Essays in Colonial History Presented to Charles McLean Andrews by His Students* (New Haven, Conn.: Yale University Press, 1931), pp. 225–51.

[43] Thomas Scharf, *Chronicles of Baltimore* (Baltimore, 1874), p. 56.

[44] Governor Horatio Sharpe to Secretary Cecil Calvert, August 22, 1764, *Archives of Maryland* 61:567.

[45] William Lux to Isaac and John Simon, January 15, 1767, WLLB.

forded by other advanced communities. "As our town is yet in its in-
fancy," Lux wrote Isaac Simon of Dublin in 1767, "we cannot take
cargoes off at the same terms that they do in the large cities."[46] Yet by
the middle of the following year he could proudly boast, "We have
about 350 houses in town and more adding every day—and we now have
a pretty considerable trade. I reckon there are 70 or 80 sail of vessels
loaded here yearly with tobacco, wheat, flour, flaxseed."[47]

Recognition of Baltimore's growth came in 1768 with the transfer of
the county seat from Joppa to Baltimore. Joppa's residents protested
bitterly, though correctly, that "none but persons blurred by their interest would endeavor a removal of the court house to promote the
foreign trade of Baltimoretown," but their complaints went unheeded.[48]
The interested parties in Baltimore defended the move on grounds that
since the town had become the center of commercial transactions, it
should also provide the necessary court and public services as a matter of
convenience.[49] And, in 1772, a customs commissioner, after inspecting
Baltimore, recommended that it be made a port of entry and placed
under the authority of a collector and comptroller. Such measures were
necessary, he contended, because Baltimore had become "a place of considerable and extensive trade" through its dealings with England, the
West Indies, and Europe. "Thirteen vessels" sailed each year between the
town and Lisbon alone, according to the official, and a "great number" of
other vessels plied the various colonial trades.[50]

The principal reasons for Baltimore's development seem fairly clear.
Essentially the town was a product of cooperation and competition with
Philadelphia. The focus of such cooperation and competition was wheat,
for wheat more than any other crop provided the basis for the town's
growth. Contemporary newspapers and private correspondence afford
ample evidence of the grain's importance. The wheat that passed through
Baltimore came from central and western Maryland and Pennsylvania.
An article reprinted in the *Maryland Gazette* from a Philadelphia paper
explained why Pennsylvanians shipped through the Chesapeake. The author, who sounded like a disgruntled Philadelphia merchant, complained:
"The distance is so great, the ferries so high, and the roads so bad from
Susquehanna to Philadelphia that the countrymen to the westward of

---

[46] *Ibid.*
[47] William Lux to Mrs. S. Lux, July 15, 1768, WLLB.
[48] "Petition Against Removal of County Seat of Baltimore from Joppa to Baltimoretown 1768," *Archives of Maryland* 61:567.
[49] *Ibid.*, p. 552.
[50] "Commissioners of Customs in America Respecting a Controversy between the
Collectors of Patuxent and Chester, September 28, 1772," Fisher Transcripts, MHS.

that river carry their produce to Baltimore in Maryland to the great detriment of Pennsylvania."[51] The Maryland legislature showed an early interest in Pennsylvania wheat. In 1742 it created the town of Charlestown in Cecil County specifically to help conduct the transfer of wheat from Chester and Lancaster counties in Pennsylvania. Baltimore's merchants, in a similar expression of interest, began in 1751 to request a law to erect a market so that the trade from "the back settlements of this province and Pennsylvania could be properly handled."[52]

William Lux, in his efforts to lure Europeans to trade through Baltimore, advertised the lower costs of the wheat trade as the town's most significant advantage: "The situation of our town to an extensive back country which is now well cultivated and from which we draw large quantities of wheat, flour and flaxseed renders it fair for a place of considerable trade, [and] we can always load these articles on easier terms than at Philadelphia or New York."[53] These lower costs resulted from the differing state of internal improvements in the two colonies. Maryland early built roads into its western areas as well as to the colony's border with Pennsylvania's central and western sections. Without the obstacle of major mountains to cross, the projects were not very difficult. By 1739 a road was under way between Maryland towns situated on the Chesapeake's northern shore and Pennsylvania's south central counties, the heart of the Susquehanna Valley.[54] When other roads were built to tap this rich agricultural country, the chief beneficiary was Baltimore. The town, because of its location at the base of the Susquehanna system, enjoyed a marvelous strategic position to control the valley's trade.[55] With the construction of transportation facilities into that region, Baltimore grew. In 1770 eight roads connected the town to the valley, and one major and several minor roads led west from Baltimore to the excellent wheat country of Frederick County and the Monocacy Valley.[56]

Pennsylvania, on the other hand, never constructed adequate internal improvements to secure her western resources. From the 1750s on, the inhabitants of the south central counties besieged their county courts and the legislature to build roads into Philadelphia.[57] But a suitable network

[51] *Maryland Gazette*, April 2, 1767.
[52] Griffith, *Annals of Baltimore*, p. 14.
[53] William Lux to Isaac and John Simon, January 15, 1767, WLLB.
[54] James Weston Livingood, *The Philadelphia-Baltimore Trade Rivalry 1780–1860* (Harrisburg: Pennsylvania Historical and Museum Commission, 1947), p. 5.
[55] Charles H. Lincoln, *The Revolutionary Movement in Pennsylvania, 1760–1776* (Philadelphia: The University, 1901), pp. 59–62.
[56] Livingood, *Philadelphia-Baltimore Trade Rivalry*, pp. 5–10.
[57] Walzer, "Transportation in the Philadelphia Trading Area," p. 57.

was not actually in operation until 1794.[58] The lack of interest shown by the Pennsylvania legislature in establishing such east-west links allowed Baltimore's merchants to control a major share of grain from the Susquehanna region throughout the latter half of the eighteenth century.

But wheat was not the only export down the Patapsco. Tobacco ships also put out to sea from Baltimore. In 1750 a tobacco inspection station was erected in the town and a second one followed in 1763.[59] Ships dropped anchor in the Patapsco in the 1750s and 1760s and advertised the price they were willing to give for tobacco.[60] Baltimore's merchants also became involved in tobacco exportation, though none specialized in this crop to the exclusion of wheat. Some English traders found Baltimore one of the more desirable places to take on tobacco. During the same year that William Lux sent out 500 hogsheads, William Molleson, a British merchant, told his purchasing agent, "I would not wish you to take tobacco from other rivers for him [Molleson's captain]. I would rather he lay a fortnight longer than not have been loaded from Elkridge and Baltimore."[61]

Crops alone do not build a community. Capital is also needed and Baltimore gained much of its financial support from Philadelphia. Factors from Philadelphia came to Baltimore bringing with them funds for investment. Some, after accumulating sufficient private capital, went into business for themselves.[62] Credit was extended to independent traders from Philadelphia, and partnerships, usually of a temporary nature, developed between merchants in the two ports.[63] Mark Alexander, a Baltimore merchant going into business in the 1760s, purchased flour and shipped it to the West Indies for the Philadelphia firm of Lathim and Jackson.[64] Samuel Purviance performed a similar function, shipping staves, wheat, and bread.[65] Isaac Grist worked out an arrangement with Zebulon Hollingsworth whereby he would sell goods in Baltimore that

---

[58] Gould, *Money and Transportation*, pp. 127–29.

[59] Griffith, *Annals of Baltimore*, p. 41.

[60] *Maryland Gazette*, October 23, 1760.

[61] William Molleson to Charles Ridgely, March 25, 1765, Ridgely Papers, MHS; William Lux to James Russell, July 3, 1765, WLLB.

[62] Henry Dillon to Hollingsworth and Rudulph, April 18, 1770, Hollingsworth Correspondence, HSP; La Rochefoucauld-Liancourt, *Travels through the United States*, 3:654.

[63] Samuel Purviance to Levi Hollingsworth, March 14, 1774; Jesse Hollingsworth to Thomas Hollingsworth, April 23, 1776, both in Hollingsworth Correspondence, HSP.

[64] Lathim and Jackson to Mark Alexander, October 12, 1765, Corner Collection, MHS.

[65] Andrew Cadwell and Joseph Wilson to Samuel and Robert Purviance, December 17, 1771, Baltimore Custom House Papers, MHS.

the other could not unload in Philadelphia.[66] Baltimore traders sometimes imported their goods from Philadelphia when they found it cheaper to receive them indirectly rather than directly.[67]

Yet all was not cooperation. The Eastern Shore's wheat was a prize for which Baltimore's merchants competed before the Revolution. William Lux traveled to the Eastern Shore and used all his persuasive powers to attract the wheat to Baltimore that was then going through Philadelphia.[68] But Baltimore was unable to compete effectively with Philadelphia for the Eastern Shore's grain. The town's merchants offered prices high enough to attract wheat growers in the west, but these levels were not as high as those given in Philadelphia. John Smith expressed the frustration felt by many a Baltimore merchant when he wrote a correspondent in Ireland that in order to fill his friends' wheat orders the best he could offer was 6/3 while in Philadelphia "wheat such as ours would sell for 7/."[69]

Baltimore had trouble competing commercially with Philadelphia in the years just prior to the Revolution, though the town showed signs of closing the gap. By the 1770s, some Eastern Shore wheat, possibly as much as a sixth, came under Baltimore control, but the town did not construct the facilities necessary for rivalry with Philadelphia until the war years. Baltimore, unlike Philadelphia or New York, was never closed during the war because of British occupation. Similarly, the town never suffered the widespread destruction that Norfolk experienced. Thus the Chesapeake port became a major avenue for supplies to the Continental forces. This heavy volume of trade brought merchants and concentrations of investment capital into the city. Expanding throughout the war, Baltimore cut more deeply into the trade zone previously controlled by Philadelphia, and this pattern, continuing after the war and combining with an extended western trade, contributed to the city's sustained growth. The personal history of Robert Gilmor is typical of what happened. An English immigrant, he settled during the 1760s in Dorchester County on the Eastern Shore. There he conducted a profitable wheat and lumber trade with Philadelphia. Soon after the war started he moved to

[66] Isaac Grist to Zebulon Hollingsworth, August 18, 1771, Hollingsworth Correspondence, HSP.

[67] Mark Alexander to Levi Hollingsworth, March 13, 1774, Hollingsworth Correspondence, HSP.

[68] William Lux to William Molleson, November 21, 1766, WLLB.

[69] John Smith to Warnbull and Co., December 3, 1774, Smith Letterbook, MHS; for more information concerning this competition, see George Woolsey to George Salmon, October 13, 1774, Woolsey and Salmon Letterbook, LC; and Thomas Ringgold to John Galloway, October 21, 1774, Galloway Papers, LC.

Baltimore and formed a partnership with Thomas Russell. They, in turn, established close contact with Willing and Morris of Philadelphia. During the war Russell and Gilmor made considerable profits, and after the hostilities ended, Gilmor, in partnership with Willing and Morris, established European offices for their firm. Gilmor's relationship with the Philadelphians soon ended, but on the basis of the contacts he had made, he went on to build one of Baltimore's major mercantile houses.[70]

Maryland's, and particularly Baltimore's, connections with Philadelphia were not solely economic. Political action also resulted from the relationships. Indeed, the colony's response to the Townshend Acts owed much to pressures exerted within the Philadelphia-Baltimore bond. This consideration is important because one thing was certain: Maryland's merchants did not want to adopt a nonimportation policy in 1769. Unlike the years preceding the Stamp Act, when the mercantile community suffered from an international commercial crisis, the Townshend Acts came during a period of favorable economic conditions. The economy was productive and the profit margin steady. Net returns on tobacco fluctuated from a high of £10 to a low of £6 per hogshead during the years 1766 to 1771.[71] Profitable markets returned in 1766 for both wheat and tobacco, and 1767 saw a continuation of this trend. Wheat orders poured into the colony, and in spite of the "very great prices" prevailing, the demand could not be met.[72] "We have this winter had such large orders from Europe for wheat and flour and the prices have run so high," wrote Lux, "that there was no chance of sending any to the West Indies."[73]

Tobacco went into a small decline in 1767 but the drop was by no means oppressive. Whereas in 1766 a hogshead returned from £8 to £9, the net now was £6 to £7—still a decent profit.[74] A short crop that year helped to keep the market steady and with the future outlook appearing bright, some new English firms started to solicit customers.[75] In 1768 tobacco prices rose again. Some independent merchants actually found the "extravagantly high prices" to be an obstacle in making their com-

---

[70] Robert Gilmor, "The Autobiography of Robert Gilmor," Gilmor Papers, MHS.
[71] Hill Papers, MHS. These papers contain a continuing run of prices from 1766 to 1775.
[72] William Lux to William Molleson, Baltimore to London, July 21, 1766, WLLB; for a discussion of trade revival in 1766, see chapter 2.
[73] William Lux to William Saunders, March 30, 1767; William Lux to Issac and John Simon, February 9, 1767; William Lux to William Molleson, February 14, 1767, all in WLLB.
[74] Hill Papers, MHS.
[75] Richard and John Day (London) to Clement Hill (Upper Marlboro), April 13, 1767, Hill Papers, MHS; William Molleson (London) to Basil Waring (Patuxent), November 25, 1767, Waring Papers, MHS.

missions as purchasing agents for London firms. Glasgow factors offered prices that the independent merchants could not match. William Lux told Molleson that he could not make tobacco purchases because the prices had been too high as a result of "the Glasgow stores who seem determined to have what they choose."[76] Wheat similarly maintained its high level. Thomas Ringgold informed Samuel Galloway that his profits on the sale of wheat for that year had been substantial.[77] Again, after some unsettling reports in April and May, the word of great demands in southern Europe arrived with the beginning of summer, and heavy orders continued pouring in until fall.[78] Many of the merchants, after struggling for years under adverse conditions, were at last earning a handsome profit. Good times had come and the dreams of making a "pretty fortune" seemed more readily attainable.

Tobacco held its own in 1769 and 1770. At first threats of colonial reprisals because of the Townshend Acts, including the rumor that a non-exportation policy might be adopted, boosted tobacco prices.[79] After this scare passed, a good market continued because the 1769 crop was short. During the summer of 1770, reports of excellent market conditions in Europe were heard in the colony. The factors in the prime tobacco counties, fearing that such news might raise prices to an exorbitant level, joined associations pledging to hold the line. Uniting in retaliation, the planters formed similar organizations demanding no less than a guinea per 100 weight for their tobacco. They soon won out, as the firm of Barnes and Ridgate violated the factors' agreement within one week after its formation. Brisk trading followed, and some of the large planters, believing they could secure even higher prices in England, elected to consign tobacco for the first time in several years.[80]

Through the early part of 1770 European wheat markets continued

[76] William Lux (Baltimore) to William Molleson (London), August 23, 1768; William Lux to John Norton, August 20, 1768, both in WLLB; see also Mildred and Roberts (London) to Charles Ridgely (Baltimore), March 1, 1768, Ridgely Papers, MHS; John Stewart (London) to Clement Hill (Upper Marlboro), June 1, 1768, Hill Papers, MHS.
[77] Thomas Ringgold to Samuel Galloway, June 29, 1768, Galloway Papers, LC.
[78] Jos. Williams (Head of Bohemia) to Hollingsworth and Rudulph (Philadelphia), May 9, 1768, Hollingsworth Correspondence, HSP; March and Tilebein (Barcelona) to Samuel Galloway (Annapolis), April 29, 1769; March and Tilebein (Barcelona) to Samuel Galloway (Annapolis), July 5, 1769; William Tippell (London) to Samuel Galloway and Stephen West (Annapolis), October 10, 1769, all in Galloway Papers, LC; William Brooks (Portugal) to James Brooks (Maryland), September 9, 1769, Brooks Papers, MHS; *Maryland Gazette*, July 15, 1769.
[79] Thomas Ringgold to Samuel Galloway, June 29, 1769, Galloway Papers, LC.
[80] Charles Carroll of Annapolis to Charles Carroll of Carrollton, April 25, 1770, August 12, 1770, August 27, 1770, September 15, 1770, and October 18, 1770, Charles Carroll of Annapolis Papers, MHS.

strong. For the Chesapeake traders this enormous demand for grain was a godsend. Settling accounts had been no trouble for almost four years. Merchants such as Samuel Galloway had used their grain profits to reduce measurably the balances owed their English suppliers. Soon after his ship, the *Fitzhugh*, left for Portugal in the fall of 1769, Galloway informed James Russell of the vessel's departure and expressed the hope that "before this reaches you . . . Captain Bishoprich will have remitted you £700 for her freight to that place."[81] But Galloway and others like him were making a crucial mistake in relying so heavily on the southern European market. The high demand there could not continue indefinitely, and beginning in the summer of 1770 news from that region told of good harvests for the first time since 1766. By the fall the era of "very great prices" had passed as the grain trade started to decline and level off. For the moment this drop was overshadowed by a sudden rise in prices for tobacco and lumber, but its full impact was soon to be felt.

The period from 1766 through 1770 was one of general prosperity. Credit came easy and it supported high imports which were not to prove detrimental until 1772. The exchange rate remained steady and prices were good. A secure economy produced a sense of well-being within the mercantile community. The antagonism expressed by the merchants in the early 1760s was now a faded memory. No one in Maryland appeared interested in disrupting the system, nor for that matter did the vast majority of merchants in other colonies. When politicians seeking to gain more power by asserting themselves as popular champions proposed boycotts in response to the Townshend Acts, the mercantile community strenuously fought such proposals.

Nonimportation was first proposed in the *Boston Gazette* on August 31, 1767. The suggestion was not well received, the merchants being particularly opposed to the idea. The popular leaders in Boston turned to the town meeting in hopes of gaining support for their plan. On October 28, 1767 the town meeting rejected the proposal, but it did agree to sanction a voluntary nonconsumption plan. It was not until March 4, 1768, that Boston's merchants were forced to accept a type of nonimportation agreement, and even that ban's implementation was contingent upon its adoption by neighboring colonies.

New York's merchants reacted similarly. In mid-April they too agreed to halt all importation in October of that year if Boston and

---

[81] Samuel Galloway to James Russell, December 26, 1769, Galloway Letterbook, LC; see also Jonathan Booth to Hollingsworth and Rudulph, June 22, 1770, Hollingsworth Correspondence, HSP; Lamar, Hill, and Bissell to Samuel Galloway and Stephen Stewart, March 7, 1770, Galloway Papers, LC.

Philadelphia would do the same. Philadelphia's merchants were strongly opposed to any boycott at that time and, despite a great deal of public pressure, refused to ratify the New York agreement. As a result, the New Yorkers abandoned their plan and the prospects for a general nonimportation pact diminished in the northern commercial colonies. The northern merchants had won the first round and their southern brothers remained completely indifferent to the approaching crisis.[82]

But Boston's popular agitators did not accept the Philadelphia decision as final. In July a committee chaired by John Hancock, one of the few merchants who supported nonimportation, prepared a new pact and called a public meeting on August 11 to ratify it. The proposal called for the nonimportation of all goods, with a few minor exceptions, during the year 1769. Sixty-six persons signed the agreement, but many of the merchants refused. Soon they would be coerced into implementing the ban. A similar form of action followed in New York. On August 27 the New York merchants, who were already suffering from a serious currency shortage, agreed to nonimportation. The plan they accepted was somewhat more restrictive than Boston's, since no time limit was stipulated.

In Philadelphia the advocates of nonimportation were greatly encouraged by what had occurred in Boston and New York. They mounted an arduous campaign to force the merchants into a similar boycott. By February 1769 the merchants had taken all the public abuse they could stand, and they agreed to institute nonimportation on March 10, if the Townshend measures had not yet been repealed. On that day, just a little over one year after Boston's first agreement, Philadelphia's merchants proved true to their word. Their final nonimportation measures excluded all but a few items, none of them really important commercially.

During the spring of 1769 the nonimportation movement spread into the South. In Virginia the idea of nonimportation was becoming more appealing, at least from the political standpoint. Realizing that the merchants would probably oppose such a scheme, Virginia's planter-legislators did not bother to discuss the matter with the mercantile community. On May 17, 1769, the colony's governor, Lord Botetourt, dissolved the assembly because of its open protest against Parliament's proposal that some of the more violent colonial incendiaries be taken to England for treason trials. Directly after their dismissal, the burgesses convened at a private home in Williamsburg and adopted a plan of nonimportation. The actual boycott listed a great many goods that were not to be im-

[82] In my discussion of the colonial reaction to the Townshend Acts, my debt to the work of Merrill Jensen, *The Founding of a Nation* (New York: Oxford University Press, 1968) will be apparent. See especially chapter 10.

ported after September 1, 1769. It also specified that slaves were not to be brought into the province after November 1. The plan was scheduled to remain in force until the revenue measure was revoked. In reality, however, the Virginia agreement was a meaningless nonconsumption pact among the planter-legislators. No method of enforcement was prescribed. As a result, Virginia's merchants paid the agreement no heed, and imported more goods during 1769 and 1770 than they ever had before.[83]

Throughout these years the *Maryland Gazette* accurately reported the talk of protest in other colonies, although it devoted considerably more attention to a series of hotly contested internal clerical disputes. In the fall of 1767 the paper printed a report from Boston recommending that domestic manufactures replace imports.[84] No one in the colony bothered to second this suggestion with a supporting letter. In December, John Dickinson's *Letters of a Pennsylvania Farmer* began to appear in the *Gazette*, but they too brought no response. Governor Sharpe wrote to Secretary Hamersley in February 1768 that the Townshend Act duties "have not hitherto had any great effect nor do I think they will."[85]

The sole reaction provoked within the colony during the year 1768 developed over the matter of the Massachusetts circular letter. Secretary of State Hillsborough forwarded a copy of this letter to Sharpe and the other provincial governors, directing them to order their assemblies to ignore the message. Should the assemblies disobey, they were to be prorogued or dissolved. Sharpe reluctantly went before the House in June, 1768, and communicated Hillsborough's message. As Sharpe had expected, the delegates sent an angry rejection saying they would not be intimidated from "doing what we think is right."[86] Anticipating that it would be sent home, the House immediately began to prepare a response to Massachusetts, which was sent two days after the session closed. The reply was vague and noncommittal, declaring only that Maryland agreed with the circular letter and was always more than willing to receive suggestions about the common difficulties facing the colonies.[87] Despite such assertions, this action came six months after the Townshend duties

---

[83] *Ibid.*, chapter 11.

[84] *Maryland Gazette*, November 19, 1767.

[85] Governor Horatio Sharpe to Secretary Hamersley, February 11, 1768, *Archives of Maryland*, 3:468.

[86] Charles Albro Barker, *The Background of the Revolution in Maryland* (New Haven, Conn.: Yale University Press, 1940), p. 317.

[87] *Ibid.*

went into effect, and a year would pass before Maryland signed a nonimportation agreement.

In the late summer and early fall of 1768 the *Maryland Gazette* carried the texts of the nonimportation agreements made in Boston and New York. Accompanying such reports were accounts of the arrival of troops in Boston and the ill-will that existed between the soldiers and the people. These stories elicited no local response except for a few mild statements that Boston's sufferings were common to all the colonies.[88] No one suggested that Maryland follow the example set by the commercial colonies of the north.

Nonetheless, nonimportation did become a policy for the entire colony on June 22, 1769. Ironically, the merchants themselves played a leading, albeit crafty, role in constructing and adopting the boycott. The Baltimore commercial community led the way when it agreed to nonimportation on March 30, 1769. What finally influenced the city's merchants to accept nonimportation was its adoption in Philadelphia on March 10, 1769. No sooner had the Philadelphians acted than they began applying pressure on the Baltimore merchants to do the same. The following message was sent to Baltimore from Philadelphia directly after the ratification of nonimportation: "Though the merchants and traders here have entered into this agreement without any condition, yet many will be very uneasy under it if you do not come into the like." Given Baltimore's economic ties with Philadelphia and Pennsylvania, the town agreed to institute a boycott.[89]

No copy of the Baltimore nonimportation plan remains in existence, but available evidence suggests it was lax, with few, if any, real restrictions. Essentially the Baltimore merchants acted out of respect to some pressures and in order to avoid anything more serious. Only two cases were tried under the stipulations of the Baltimore association, and in both, the examining board found the violators innocent. On November 14, 1769 William Moore imported into the town a cargo valued at £900 sterling. The local enforcement committee called Moore to explain his actions. Moore justified what he had done on the basis that when he signed the boycott it was his understanding that "he had liberty to send off for his orders for fall goods and to import the same." The board agreed with Moore. The other case involved Benjamin Howard, who went before the board seeking permission to land and vend a cargo

[88] *Maryland Gazette*, July 28, 1768.

[89] Arthur Schlesinger, *The Colonial Merchant and the American Revolution, 1763–1776* (New York: Columbia University, Faculty of Political Science, 1918), p. 138; Scharf, *Chronicles of Baltimore*, pp. 64–65.

valued at £1700 sterling. Howard's argument was that on March 30, 1769 he was not a Baltimore resident and therefore the boycott was not binding on him. He also contended that his cargo was "imported within the terms of the general association of 22'nd June." Howard received the authorization he sought.[90]

In his testimony, Benjamin Howard referred to a general nonimportation association. The call for such a ban was first made by several leading Annapolis merchants on May 11. They requested a meeting of Anne Arundel County's "merchants, traders and gentlemen" at Annapolis. On May 23 the meeting was held. By that date several other counties had already proposed nonimportation, and delegates from these areas attended the Annapolis session. At that gathering all resolved not to send orders for any goods until June 30. More importantly, the meeting called for a colony-wide convention on June 20, to consider "a general resolution of nonimportation except as to a few coarse necessary articles."[91]

The four men who proposed the May meeting were James Dick, Anthony Stewart, Nicholas Maccubin, and Charles Wallace, all of whom were wealthy and prosperous at the time. They well realized that a stringent nonimportation plan could cut their profits drastically. They further realized that pressures both external and within the community necessitated some agreement. However, they felt that if the merchants themselves took the lead in constructing the agreement a more lenient code would result. None of the four wanted a rigid boycott, and the general nonimportation association that was adopted by the colony-wide convention on June 22 was extremely weak. Moreover, James Dick and Anthony Stewart, two of the merchants who had initiated the move for a province-wide ban, committed the most notorious violation of the association. Because of flagrant violations their ship, *The Good Intent*, was refused permission to land its cargo. This was the result of a rare decision by an ad hoc enforcement committee.[92]

One characteristic marked Maryland's general boycott: the absence of many serious restrictions. Some people, especially certain ambitious politicians, may have wanted a strict association, but this is hardly what emerged on June 22. At that gathering the merchants fought hard for a weak boycott. Governor Robert Eden reported a strong current of dissension between the merchants and the politicians as they struggled to hammer out a suitable compromise: they "could hardly agree among themselves what articles should not be made use of, imported from Eng-

[90] Scharf, *Chronicles of Baltimore*, pp. 64–65.
[91] *Archives of Maryland* 62:458.
[92] "The Case of the Good Intent," *Maryland Historical Magazine* 2 (1904), 141–50.

land. I was in hopes that from the dissensions among them the meeting would come to nothing."[93]

Because of this conflict the plan was studded with exceptions. The number of goods exempted was close to the number of those included. In reality, the association read like a price-fixing agreement whose chief intent was to blackmail the British into selling their wares at a reduced level. The goods not to be imported included

oil, except salad oil . . . ribbons and millinery of all kinds, except wig-ribbon, lace, cambrick, lawn, muslin, bunting, gauze of all kinds, except boulting-clothes, silks of all kinds, except raw and sewing silk and wig-cauls, velvets, chintzes and calicoes of all sorts, of more than twenty pence per yard, East India goods of every kind, except saltpetre, black pepper and spices . . . hand-kerchiefs of all kinds, at more than ten shillings per dozen. . . . British manu-factured linens of all kinds, except sailcloth, Irish and all foreign linens, above one shilling and six pence per yard, woolen cloth above five quarters wide, of more than five shillings per yard, narrow clothes of all sorts, of more than three shillings per yard, worsted stuffs of all sorts, above thirteen pence per yard . . . rugs of all sorts, above eight shillings, blankets, above five shillings per blanket . . . hats of all kinds, of more than two shillings per hat . . . leather and skins of all kinds, except mens and womens shoes of not more than four shillings per pair . . . stone ware of all sorts, except milk pans, stone bottles, jugs, pitchers and chamber pots, marble and wrought stone of any kind, except scythe stones, millstones and grindstones, iron mongers of all sorts, except nails, hoes, steel handicraft and manufacturers tools, locks, frying pans, scythes and sickles, cutlery of all sorts, except knives and forks, not exceeding three shillings per dozen . . . and bone ware of all sorts, except combs. . . .[94]

Still the merchants were dissatisfied. After haggling and arguing over every item, many of which were placed on the "exception list," not a single trader of any importance signed the final agreement. Of the docu-ment's forty-three signers, twenty-two were members of the assembly's country party and seven others won seats at the next election in 1771.[95] Apparently the boycott found much greater acceptance with aspiring politicians who stood to gain popularity by opposing British imperial measures than it did with the colony's traders.

An even weaker code might have been constructed if the merchants, particularly those of Baltimore, had kept their alliance with Samuel Chase secure. During 1767 Chase showed a good deal of interest in strengthen-

[93] Governor Robert Eden to Earl of Hillsborough, June 23, 1769, Fisher Tran-scripts, MHS.
[94] *Maryland Historical Magazine* 2 (1904), 146.
[95] *Maryland Gazette*, June 29, 1769.

ing his ties to Baltimore. He introduced several bills aimed at improving the town's facilities.[96] Chase also tried his hand at tobacco trading and employed the services of his Baltimore ally, William Lux. The proceeds from the venture did not satisfy Chase, who believed Lux had advised him poorly.[97] An estrangement in their relationship ensued and disrupted the Baltimore-Annapolis axis that had been forged at the time of the Stamp Act. With the Baltimore merchants' power base cut substantially, the political muscle of the entire mercantile community was reduced.

As it was, the merchants were of no mind to pay much attention to the boycott.[98] Many continued to import as they had in the past, which deeply angered Philadelphia's merchants, already resentful of the numerous exceptions in the Maryland association. Samuel Coates, a prominent Philadelphia trader, complained that "Maryland was daily thriving at the expense of this province. They came after us into the agreement and made a very partial one at last allowing by far a too general importation whereby they carry'd the frontier trade to Annapolis, Baltimore, etc., by which means this province suffer'd greatly for the Marylanders were deeply in debt here and the back part of Pennsylvania also; they carry'd their ready money to purchase goods there and left us unpaid, by a shameful artifice and the most unsuspecting fraud they impos'd upon this respectable province. Their agreement among other things allowed," he observed sarcastically, "the importation of cloth not exceeding 10/ per yard by which it was understood no broadcloth should exceed that price, but shamefully prevaricating they made no scruple to order these cloths I am told of ¾ width, which made the quality superfine. What good end can be answered by our continuance after such malpractices as these and more than that our stores being stript of all goods."[99]

Coates' suspicions appear justified, though unfortunately there is no way of accurately determining the impact of the nonimportation pact. Unlike the situation in 1765, nonimportation was not now to the merchants' economic advantage. If anything, many saw the adoption of nonimportation policies in other colonies as a chance to make a quick profit. During the period of alleged enforcement more goods were shipped to Maryland and Virginia than at any time past. Indeed the trade was so

[96] *Archives of Maryland* 61:178, 195, 206–10, 355, 358, 370.
[97] William Lux to William Molleson, August 23, 1766, WLLB.
[98] Governor Robert Eden to Earl of Hillsborough, June 17, 1770, Fisher Transcripts, MHS.
[99] Samuel Coates (Philadelphia) to William Logan (London), November 26, 1770, Samuel Coates Letterbook, HSP.

heavy that Lord Hillsborough cited its enormous volume when a delegation of English merchants came before him requesting repeal of the Townshend duties because they were said to be ruining the colonial trade.[100] Maryland's agreement, unlike Virginia's, did provide for some enforcement, but a comparison of the number of ships entering Annapolis and Oxford from England for the period 1769–1770 with those of preceding and later years indicates the agreement had no substantial effect.

TABLE 4 *Ships Entering Maryland Ports*
from the British Isles, 1765–1772

Year	Annapolis	Oxford
1765	25	7
1766	33	7
1767	40	3
1768	27	12
1769	48	15
1770	48	10
1771	52	16
1772	44	13

SOURCE: Annapolis and Oxford Port Record Books, Maryland Historical Society, Baltimore, Md.

Frequently accused of chicanery, Maryland's merchants replied with similar indictments, charging their Philadelphia counterparts with openly violating all existing agreements. After hearing reports of importation into that city before the nonimportation measures were suspended, the Baltimore firm of Dillon and Carroll sent off a sharp protest to Hollingsworth and Rudulph: "We thought you were gentlemen of such great honor that you would not break through any of your resolves, at least until Parliament would break up. But now all your agreements is laughed at."[101] With so much at stake between the various mercantile communities, trust became impossible, mutual suspicion inevitable. Some feared what the Philadelphians were up to, while others such as Thomas Ringgold worried more about the New Yorkers. "The Yorkers," he told Samuel Galloway, "have really acted a most scandalous part. It plainly appears that almost all of those who pretended to oppose the importation

[100] Robert Polk Thomson, "The Merchant in Virginia, 1700–1775" (Ph.D. diss., University of Wisconsin, 1955), pp. 323–28.
[101] Dillon and Carroll (Baltimore) to Hollingsworth and Rudulph (Philadelphia), November 30, 1770, Hollingsworth Correspondence, HSP.

were secretly for it."[102] Merchants awaited the excuse to abandon the agreements once word of others' defection became known. Notice of England's repeal of duties on all items except tea reached the colonies that fall and the nonimportation movement quickly ended. Baltimore heard of Philadelphia's abandonment of nonimportation on October 10, 1770. The town's merchants quickly placed a request in the *Maryland Gazette*, urging a meeting to repeal nonimportation. They warned that should their proposition be ignored, they "would look upon the association dissolved and go into a general importation."[103] At the meeting, delegates from Queen Anne's, Talbot, and Dorchester counties as well as a majority of the assembly members attended. The association censured the Baltimore proposal and ordered the continuation of nonimportation, but the town's delegate, Jonathan Hudson, supported by the colony's merchants, sternly replied that the order would be ignored. His prediction proved correct. The merchants, as Samuel Galloway informed James Russell, were done with self-sacrifice. Referring to the recent meeting he wryly observed that "some of our merchants met and agreed to continue the non-importation agreement but it will be broke through by every person—so you have an invoice of goods which please to ship me."[104]

There was nothing particularly inconsistent about the merchants' political response to the two British taxation measures, the Stamp Act and Townshend Act. On both occasions the merchants acted on the fundamental principle of self-interest. Nowhere was this point better brought out than in a discussion between two friends, Charles Carroll of Annapolis and his English correspondent, William Graves. Carroll wrote Graves during the Townshend controversy in December 1768 to explain the colony's position. He cited and passionately supported the positions of Dulany and Dickinson but concentrated on why it was not in Britain's economic interest to tax the colonies. Manufacturers might start in America, he warned, and "many may do more and follow the Dutchman's example by taking nothing from you which by any means may be had cheaper from any other quarter. . . . Trade is of a very delicate nature; it may by imprudent measures be forced out of its old channel, but it may prove impossible to bring it back."[105]

[102] Thomas Ringgold to Samuel Galloway, July 20, 1770, Galloway Papers, LC.
[103] *Maryland Gazette*, October 11, 1770.
[104] Samuel Galloway to James Russell, November 18, 1770, Samuel Galloway Letterbook, LC; see also *Maryland Gazette*, November 1, 1770.
[105] Charles Carroll of Annapolis to William Graves, December 23, 1768, Charles Carroll of Annapolis Papers, MHS.

Graves' reply to Carroll is classic, though possibly too cynical. He dismissed the arguments of Dulany and Dickinson, commenting that "the only rule which I lay down to myself is to give implicit credit to no man in his own cause." Nevertheless, he agreed completely with Carroll that not only did England have a great deal to fear economically if she lost her colonies, but that trade considerations were a principal force affecting the current disputes. As to what the Americans might do about all this, Graves, being a student of human nature, felt certain that "what they can they will smuggle from the Dutch or French or Spanish or Danes during the present animosities." And he continued with uncanny accuracy, "What they can not obtain through those channels they will take care to leave out of the articles associated against." In his economic argument, Graves said, Carroll had clearly alluded to one of the basic determinants of political conduct—money:

A penny difference in a shilling would carry any trader from his brother to a foreigner or to the devil were he secure from violence and had no counter interest to restrain him. Profit and loss are the two objects that a merchant looks at and by which he directs himself entirely. Let laws be made unless they can be enforced, he will in spite of them deal with an enemy, a foreigner or a smuggler, if he can buy cheaper of them than of the open trader, his countryman, friend or relation. The ties of blood, religion, or patriotism will not avail against self-interest. A single person may be swayed by such motives but not the bulk of mankind; no not one out of a hundred, let the ablest orator or the most powerful preacher say what he will. Passion and resentment will not hold out against interest.[106]

As an analysis of merchant political activity during the 1760s, Graves' interpretation could not have been more correct. When times were hard the merchants were happy, even anxious, to secure their political rights by nonimportation. But when times were good, neither ideological principles nor a few additional taxes mattered a great deal.

[106] William Graves to Charles Carroll of Annapolis, January 14, 1770, Charles Carroll of Annapolis Papers, MHS.

5 : The Creation of
a Popular Movement

By 1770 the Baltimore-Annapolis coalition, created in opposition to the Stamp Act, no longer functioned. The merchants of Baltimore, as well as the colony's entire mercantile community, resented the politicians because of the nonimportation association. Where there had been unity of purpose in 1765, there was now dissension. But this division did not last long. Within three years the Baltimore-Annapolis axis had been revived and strengthened as new elements from the country and the court parties joined the alliance.

Again the coalition was forged around a conflict that had both political and economic characteristics. The basic issue was raised in the House of Delegates during the fall session of 1769, when the delegates announced their opposition to a section of the colony's tobacco inspection act. Most of the act outlined a method for regulating the quality of exported tobacco, to which no one objected. But attached to the act was a schedule of "officer fees," detailing the prices proprietary officials could charge for public services. In 1747, to secure passage of an inspection act, the proprietor had granted the delegates the power to set these fees.[1] When the legislature passed the tobacco inspection acts of 1753 and 1763, the fees were a part of the measure.

When the act came up for renewal in the fall of 1769, the members of the lower house criticized not only the high fees, but also the corruption of certain public officials who sold governmental positions. In an address to the governor, the delegates pinpointed their dislikes: "The sale of offices, now open and avowed, obliges the purchaser, by every way and

[1] *Archives of Maryland*, ed. William H. Browne *et al.* (68 vols., Baltimore, 1883——), 44:629–37.

means in his power, to enhance his fees; that is contrary to laws and leads directly to oppression."[2] The law was due to expire in November, but following this criticism a compromise measure extended the act for one more year.[3]

Eleven months later, at the start of the fall 1770 session, the lower house initiated an inquiry into the amount of revenue earned by the major proprietary officials in the conduct of their offices. Results of the study were reported on October 3. The committee's findings indicated that Daniel Dulany, as deputy secretary of the colony, made from £1,000 to £1,500 annually. His brother, Walter, reaped only a little less from his office as commissary general.[4] On the basis of this evidence the delegates drew up a lower fee schedule and sent it to the upper house for approval. To no one's surprise, the members of the upper house who held the most lucrative posts rejected the new schedule, and offered an unacceptable compromise instead. They returned their proposals on October 22, the very day the tobacco inspection law expired. No inspection measure would be enacted, they said, until the original fees were reinstated, although they might consider some alternate reduction.[5]

Because of the impasse, none of the proprietary officials could legally perform any public service after October 22, 1770. When one did, a tense encounter followed between the proprietary administration and the delegates. On October 30 the lower house's Committee of Grievances and Courts of Justice reported that William Steuart, clerk of the land office, had accepted, contrary to law, payments of excessive fees authorized by Benedict Calvert and George Steuart, land office judges. Steuart's action was clearly illegal since the law authorizing such collection had expired—a fact that Benedict Calvert and George Steuart had deliberately ignored. The house committee condemned William Steuart's behavior, and the lower house ordered him to appear before the delegates and explain his actions. When he arrived, they put him in jail. Robert Eden, the newly arrived governor who replaced Sharpe in 1769, retaliated the next day by proroguing the assembly. By this measure Eden removed Steuart from the lower house's jurisdiction and thereby released him.[6]

Eden then reconvened the assembly. The delegates immediately rebuked Eden for his high-handed tactics and brought Steuart before them once more. This time they satisfied their ire with threats of re-

[2] *Ibid.*, 62:113.
[3] *Ibid.*, pp. 59–63, 78, 82–83, 123.
[4] *Ibid.*, pp. 218–19; *Maryland Gazette*, November 15, 1770.
[5] *Archives of Maryland*, 62:272, 290, 299.
[6] *Ibid.*, pp. 304–307.

committing him. Next they passed an act for the regulation of officer fees, and added a specific prohibition against the sale of proprietary offices, aimed directly at the Dulanys. When the upper house rejected the measure, the delegates ordered the act and a series of resolves to be printed. The resolutions accused Daniel and Walter Dulany, as well as the land office judges, of conducting their offices in an "illegal and oppressive" manner. It was obvious to the public, the lower house said, that' the "Upper House, four members of which hold the Secretary, Commissary General and Land Office," rejected the bill out of "an unreasonable attachment to the emoluments of office."[7]

This assertion was significant. The wealth gleaned by the Dulanys from their offices was public knowledge, but until now the delegates had never censured that family openly. Before this session, as Charles Carroll of Annapolis said, the delegates were "in awe of Dulany." His influence was so feared that those who were interested in future public office dared not openly criticize him. What provoked the lower house members finally to defy the Dulanys? Apparently the lower house enjoyed great popularity and a new sense of dignity because of the stand it had taken on imperial issues. The supercilious condescension and arbitrary power of the proprietary officials, which had never sat well with the lower house, now seemed all the more intolerable. But it was precisely this combination of condescension and power that the governor, the Dulanys, and the upper house used in the salary dispute.[8]

The preceding year the lower house had openly and vociferously condemned the excessive salaries enjoyed by the proprietary officials. What had been the answer of these officials? To ask for higher salaries and reject as absurd the reduced fee schedule! The house had reported on October 3 that Daniel Dulany's income from fees amounted to 287,088½ pounds of tobacco and his brother Walter's, 268,149 pounds. Directly on the heels of that study the Dulanys had asked for higher fees to raise their incomes to upward of 400,000 pounds a year. The arrest of Steuart and the proroguing of the house followed, but once the assembly reconvened, the Dulanys, with aristocratic bravado, simply resubmitted their request for higher fees. Commenting on this tactic, Charles Carroll of Annapolis was furious: "The proposition you say was made by our great officers in my opinion was both foolish and insolent. Foolish in

---

[7] *Ibid.*, p. 430; see also Charles Carroll of Annapolis to Charles Carroll of Carrollton, November 30, 1774, Charles Carroll of Annapolis Papers, Maryland Historical Society, Baltimore, Md. (cited hereafter as MHS).

[8] Charles Carroll of Annapolis to Charles Carroll of Carrollton, October 18, 1770, and November 2, 1770, Charles Carroll of Annapolis Papers, MHS.

publishing what they thought the least reward adequate to their merit, vizt. £600 sterling per annum and contradicting what at least one of them is reported to have said, vizt. that the incomes of his office did not nigh amount to that sum. Insolent in presuming that the representatives of the people would demean themselves so much as to enter into any treaty with them."[9]

By November 21 Governor Eden had run out of patience. For the past several days he had received insulting letters from the lower house critical of his role in the release of Steuart. Possibly fearing the delegates might once again imprison Steuart, as they repeatedly said they would, the governor prorogued the assembly. Five days later Eden startled the colony by announcing that as governor he had decided to reestablish the fee schedule by proclamation. According to his order all officers were to charge the fees provided in the expired inspection act.[10]

The delegates were infuriated and before long they had an opportunity to show their anger. Eden, hoping for more moderate delegates, called for a new election prior to the 1771 meeting. Instead of solving his problems, the election produced further complications. The fee issue was now placed directly before the public and those elected proved to be even harder for Eden to deal with. Commenting on the character of the assembly elected, Eden wrote to Lord Dartmouth, "I sincerely wish the measures pursued by the Lower House of the Assembly had been less intemperate and offensive. In popular assemblies, particular men generally govern the rest, and the proceedings take their color from the temper and views of a few leaders. The moderate and diffident are carried with the stream; and their silence and acquiescence, by swelling the apparent majority, indicate an approbation of violence they really condemn. This was too much the case in our October session as well as in the session before it."[11]

As Eden indicated, the new delegates took up where the old ones left off. After a series of strongly worded letters between Eden and the lower house, the dispute reached its climax when the delegates approved 31 to 3 a message labeling the governor's fee proclamation as "robbery."[12] Conferences between the two houses ended in similar recriminations. At these meetings, however, the agenda was somewhat different, for while

[9] Charles Carroll of Annapolis to Charles Carroll of Carrollton, October 11, 1770, and November 2, 1770, Charles Carroll of Annapolis Papers, MHS.

[10] *Maryland Gazette*, December 13, 1770.

[11] Robert Eden to Earl of Dartmouth, Secretary of State for the Colonies, January 29, 1773, Fisher Transcripts, MHS.

[12] *Archives of Maryland*, 63:200.

the delegates condemned the high fees, their principal criticisms concerned the graft arising from the sale of offices. The lower house also passed bills to prevent the buying and selling of offices. Naturally, the upper house disapproved these measures.[13]

No agreement on any of the outstanding issues was reached until the November-December session of 1773; and then some compromise was achieved only because a depression made it imperative for the colony to bring its tobacco trade under qualitative control again. During the first year or two of the fee controversy, the colony did not suffer from the absence of tobacco regulation. No one felt any great need to regulate the outgoing hogsheads, since the prices were high. Because of the prosperity it was a time of sharp, but not desperate, politics. Unlike 1765, throughout most of 1772 no one proposed marching on the capital and no effigies went up in smoke.

William Eddis, a biased observer, saw the fee controversy as an outright grab for political power with no economic overtones. "Under pretense of supporting the sacred claims of freedom and of justice," he wrote, "factious and designing men are industriously fomenting jealousy and discontent."[14] Governor Eden, in a letter to Hillsborough in August 1772, reiterated Eddis' interpretation and further explained why, as yet, no solution had been reached: "Your lordship will observe that, on account of the old differences between the two houses concerning the officer's fees, and the clergy's salaries, there has been no revival of the inspection law, so that our staple is under little regulation, and the high price tobacco has continued to bear at home and here, ever since the law dropt, has as yet prevented the planters from being sensible of the loss of it."[15]

Unfortunately for the proprietary administration, these favorable economic conditions were swiftly nearing an end. By the fall of 1772 the first effects of a second international credit crisis within ten years began to be felt. As the depression worsened, the politics of the fee controversy became more passionate. Since the beginning of the dispute, the Atlantic tobacco market had remained sound, and the credit and debt situation continued stable. During the summer of 1771 tobacco prices rose to £10 per hogshead. With profits so high, no one thought it necessary to replace the expired tobacco inspection system. Some believed the high prices resulted from the absence of such controls. Had prices ever been better? English firms, large and small, anxiously solicited more colonial

13 *Ibid.*, 63:70, 124, 181, 330, 338.
14 William Eddis, *Letters from America* (London, 1792), October 2, 1772, 136.
15 Robert Eden to Earl of Hillsborough, August 21, 1772, Fisher Transcripts, MHS.

suppliers. Joshua Johnson, an Annapolis trader who lived in London where he represented the Maryland firm of Wallace, Davidson, and Johnson, wrote home that "it is doubtful whether or not the present crop will be more than sufficient to reduce the price."[16]

The market for lumber products was also excellent. Britain's growing mining and manufacturing industries and her expanding export trade required unprecedented quantities of wood products for packaging materials. Maryland shippers sent out cargoes of "staves" and "heading" at all-time high levels. Other colonies did the same. Still the quantities were insufficient. To augment the production of these materials in the colonies, on January 1, 1772 Parliament instituted higher bounties on staves and headings.[17]

Wheat did not do as well as tobacco or lumber in 1771. Grain prices fell everywhere, as the trade went into a sharp decline. Had it not been for a short wheat crop in southern Maryland, the market would have been much worse. John Galloway, a Western Shore trader, described the year's prospect accurately in January, 1771, when he reported, "I cannot say the markets are pleasing."[18] Eleven months later, Zebulon Hollingsworth, a dealer in Eastern Shore wheat, proved Galloway right when he wrote, "I never felt the real want of cash before. Wheat sells at 6/8 and not very good."[19]

The poor wheat trade, however, did not have a noticeable effect in Maryland. Good markets for tobacco and lumber and the high level of currency in circulation because of the emission in 1769 helped to compensate for the decline. On November 28, 1769, the House of Delegates had gone into a committee of the whole to study "the expediency and the means of issuing bills of credit for the improvement of the province and the advancement of trade."[20] On the following day the House drew up a bill to emit on loan $300,000. Despite the steadily deteriorating

[16] Charles Carroll of Annapolis to Charles Carroll of Carrollton, August 8, 1771, April 12, 1771, April 15, 1771, all in Charles Carroll of Annapolis Papers, MHS; Christopher Court (London) to Aquilla Hall (Baltimore), April 22, 1771, Harford County Historical Society Papers, MHS; Joshua Johnson (London) to Wallace, Davidson, and Johnson (Annapolis), September 15, 1771, Wallace, Davidson and Johnson Letterbook (cited hereafter as WDJLB), Maryland Hall of Records, Annapolis, Md. (cited hereafter as MHR).

[17] David Macpherson, *Annals of Commerce* (4 vols., London, 1805), 3:512.

[18] John Galloway to Samuel Galloway, January 22, 1771, Galloway Papers, Library of Congress, Washington, D.C. (cited hereafter as LC).

[19] Zebulon Hollingsworth (Head of Elk) to Hollingsworth and Rudulph (Philadelphia), November 20, 1771, Hollingsworth Correspondence, Historical Society of Pennsylvania, Philadelphia, Pa. (cited hereafter as HSP).

[20] *Archives of Maryland*, 62:53–54, 69–70, 118, 144–48, 153.

relations between the two houses, the bill met no significant opposition and became a law one month later. This law, like the one of 1766, by-passed the Currency Act of 1764 by declaring that the bills would be nonlegal tender. Still they were highly acceptable in mercantile circles because they were backed by the colony's stocks in the Bank of England. Although the new funds were quickly funneled into the economy, their first effects were not felt in a normal commercial environment until 1771.[21] Then the currency enabled traders to reimburse English merchants promptly through the purchase of bills of exchange. As a result, payment by way of the Iberian Peninsula was not as vital.

By the end of that year the colony's tobacco producers and shippers probably believed that they were living in the best of all possible worlds. The competition for tobacco among European buyers was increasingly fierce. The French had just agreed to a large purchase, and the English tobacco dealers could not get their hands on the crop fast enough. Joshua Johnson in London described the bustle that December: "I find there is a struggle amongs't the merchants who shall get their ships out first. Buchanan sends Christie out, Russell sends Person, Molleson has chartered a ship and West and Hobson is on the lookout for one. They will all sail about the first of January. I believe everyone of them carry goods for Annapolis, so that your town will be earlier supplied this year than usual and perhaps with larger quantities."[22]

The continent's demand for tobacco seemed insatiable during the first months of 1772. By February the French had already closed two major deals, which drained the English market of all available tobacco. Christopher Court, a large London trader, observed in March that "our market as well as those in Holland and Germany are not overstock'd with tobacco—tho importation was so large last year—the prices here continue without variation."[23] Other houses reported the same to their Maryland clients. In spite of the massive shipments of 1771, no decline seemed likely. With the increased buying of tobacco, Christopher Court became so anxious for the crop that he wrote his Maryland suppliers in May to charter an additional ship and send another 500 hogsheads. The costs, Court realized, would be high, but the market's strength merited the gamble. Letters similar to Court's continued to reach Maryland in the summer of 1772. Though fluctuating slightly during the most active

[21] *Ibid.*, p. 196.
[22] Joshua Johnson (London) to Wallace, Davidson and Johnson (Annapolis), December 4, 1771, WDJLB.
[23] Christopher Court and Co. (London) to Aquilla Hall (Baltimore), February 29, 1772, and March 1772, Aquilla Hall Papers, MHS.

selling season, prices remained good.[24] The exchange rate remained a consistent £155. This rate, which was a shade less than twelve points below the official exchange, indicated that English traders thought the economy sound. At this level the colony's merchants and planters could secure a good profit on their sales. The low rate indicated that no one was pressing the colonies for payment on outstanding debts. The English creditors obviously considered their massive exports to be offset by the fine tobacco markets in Europe.

All of this changed that autumn, as the effects of the European collapse began to make themselves felt in the tobacco markets. Thomas Ringgold found prices to be so unsatisfactory in September that he elected not to sell his tobacco. Charles Carroll of Annapolis told his son that tobacco prices seemed to be steadily falling at all the best landings. The merchants had suddenly stopped making tobacco purchases at reasonable rates. By year's end the full dimensions of the collapse in Europe and England were well known. Joshua Johnson in a letter to his Annapolis partners described the depressed market conditions with unmistakable clarity: "I am told that you propose sending 100 hhds tobacco home in Galloway's and Stewart's new ship and that it is the produce of the Eastern Shore. Unless you got it at a very low price you might as well have thrown your money in the river for you may be assured that you'll lose by it."[25]

Conditions in the wheat trade were similar. Excellent crops were harvested in 1772, and, according to information coming into the colony during the first half of the year, wheat prices were supposedly swinging upward. Joshua Johnson wrote in June from London to Lux and Bowly that their wheat shipments to the continent could not help but make money if they arrived at the market in time. A similar demand for wheat, he reported, existed in the West Indies.[26] Then in October Johnson, the former harbinger of good tidings, wrote again to Lux and Bowly to recant what he had said in June. He now reported European trade so deteriorated "that there is no market in Europe that will do for the wheat

[24] Osgood Hanbury and Co. to James Brooke, March 1772, Brooke Papers, MHR; Christopher Court and Co. (London) to Aquilla Hall (Baltimore), May 16, 1772, Aquilla Hall Papers, MHS; Hill Papers, MHS; Charles Carroll of Annapolis to Charles Carroll of Carrollton, June 9, 1772, Charles Carroll of Annapolis Papers, MHS.

[25] Thomas Ringgold to Samuel Galloway, September 12, 1772, Galloway Papers, LC; Charles Carroll of Annapolis to Charles Carroll of Carrollton, September 2, 1772, Charles Carroll of Annapolis Papers, MHS; Joshua Johnson (London) to Wallace, Davidson, and Johnson (Annapolis), December 8, 1772, WDJLB.

[26] Charles Carroll of Annapolis to Charles Carroll of Carrollton, September 2, 1772, Charles Carroll of Annapolis Papers, MHS; Joshua Johnson (London) to William Lux and Daniel Bowly (Baltimore), June 1772, WDJLB.

and flour, so that there must be a sure loss on the part of every adventure. The crops are said to be generally good all through Europe so that the most adventuresome speculator can have no other hopes other than from the commotions on the Continent, which may occasion a scarcity, but there is hardly a probability."[27]

The depressed conditions experienced by Maryland traders at the end of 1772 had first been felt in England during the late spring of that year. The earliest institutions hit were the banks. Johnson wrote in May that "there has been a stop in discounting bills with the bank and bankers. For some time it has thrown the continental foreign trade into confusion, and indeed every trade will soon feel it."[28] These short-term remedies applied by the bankers did not alter the trend. The refusal to stop discounting at best allowed the bankers to survive a bit longer, and in June banks began to fail, especially in Scotland. And when banks collapsed, Johnson explained, merchants soon followed: "Banks and merchants continue to stop here daily. What will be the consequence God knows, but such a conflagration there has never been in the memory of man. It's suspected all your Scotch factor bills will go back, therefore you can't use too much caution whom you buy off."[29] The enormity of the crisis also produced personal tragedies. "I mentioned pretty fully in my last the situation of affairs here since which there has been only three or four stoppages, two of whom have shot themselves," wrote Johnson.[30]

A series of economic problems now began to plague the colony. English merchants started sending out urgent calls for remittances, and currency within the colony began to go out of circulation as bills of exchange rose in price. While the price climbed, the lack of valid bills of exchange became acute because Scottish bills were worthless. English creditors categorically refused to accept Scottish bills, although these had been a primary source of international exchange. Joshua Johnson lucidly explained the bind the colonials were in: "No one is safe in taking Scotch factors' bills. It will knock down the price of tobacco and retard the remittances from your country in a very great degree."[31]

[27] Joshua Johnson (London) to William Lux and Daniel Bowly (Baltimore), October 30, 1772, WDJLB.

[28] Joshua Johnson (London) to William Hammond (Baltimore), May 17, 1772, WDJLB.

[29] Joshua Johnson (London) to Wallace, Davidson and Johnson (Annapolis), June 22, 1772, WDJLB.

[30] Joshua Johnson (London) to Wallace, Davidson, and Johnson (Annapolis), July 4, 1772, WDJLB.

[31] Joshua Johnson (London) to William Lux and Daniel Bowly (Baltimore), July 17, 1772, WDJLB. See also William Maudruit to Stephen West, July 2, 1772, Oden Papers, MHS; Joshua Johnson (London) to Wallace, Davidson, and Johnson (Annapolis), July 1, 1772, WDJLB.

By the end of 1772 the exchange rate had soared to 170. The purchase of bills from Scottish sources was no longer possible and even bills drawn on English houses were risky. Debtors in the colonies received letters demanding remittances in no uncertain terms, but also urging them to "use the utmost caution on your part that you have good indorsers to those bills you purchase."[32] Johnson described the fiscal paralysis that gripped the commercial community that fall: "What will become of your merchants the Lord only knows. Their correspondents here seem determined to ruin them or at least their credit by protesting their bills. Indeed it seems to be an invariable rule with some to note every bill that is offered to them."[33] As 1772 came to a close, the full effects of the depression staggered the colony. The massive debts accumulated during recent years of excessive importation became an unbearable hardship. Tobacco prices declined and credit restrictions were in full force. The exchange rate had risen to a point making remittances difficult, and on top of that no one could be sure a purchased bill was valid.

Throughout early 1773 trade conditions remained stagnant. "All business" wrote Joshua Johnson, was now at a total stoppage. "Was I in your situation," he told Lux and Bowly, "I would raise Indian corn and eat homina and curse the commercial business." After sizing up his own financial situation, he bluntly told his Annapolis partners that "it's probable we shall go to pot. We owe upwards of £4000 which will become due in next month and I have not a shilling to discharge it with." Complicating matters further, mercantile houses continued to fail, so that he feared there would soon be no houses upon which to draw.[34] Five hundred twenty-five bankruptcies had already occurred in England.[35]

European tobacco houses also began to suffer severely in 1773 when large firms in Amsterdam began to fail.[36] For the tobacco trade, nothing could be more catastrophic. As Johnson explained, "it has put an end to the sale of tobacco to that part of the world for some time, which you know takes much the greatest part of the Maryland." As a result, the colony's merchants continued to experience substantial losses in their sales. Wallace, Davidson, and Johnson suffered a loss of £4 per hogshead on the sale of 100 hogsheads in February. Money grew continually more

[32] Joshua Johnson (London) to Wallace, Davidson, and Johnson (Annapolis), August 20, 1772, and August 22, 1772, WDJLB.
[33] Joshua Johnson (London) to Wallace, Davidson, and Johnson (Annapolis), October 7, 1772, WDJLB.
[34] Joshua Johnson (London) to William Lux and Daniel Bowly (Baltimore), January 6, 1773, and to Wallace, Davidson, and Johnson (Annapolis), February 5, 1773, both in WDJLB.
[35] Macpherson, *Annals of Commerce* 3:524.
[36] *Ibid.*, p. 533.

scarce in all mercantile circles as prices in Britain went lower. With the advent of spring, no change appeared. Christopher Court reported in April that "the demand is still slack and the prices do not mend—the scarcity of money is very great."[37]

Slowly the painful process of restoring stable conditions began. The balance of trade had to be reversed. English merchants, Johnson said, "will ship but few goods this year." Yet trade conditions showed no sign of improving despite the cutback. In June he reported from England that "times here rather grow worse, God only can tell what will or may happen, but I much doubt whether there will be above three or four houses left in our trade if the price of tobacco keeps so low as it is at present."[38]

In Maryland domestic violence bore evidence to the desperate times. Angry mobs roamed the streets of Baltimore, and two customs officers received severe beatings for enforcing minor regulations. The two officials wisely resigned their positions and, once they had recovered, departed for Boston.[39] Not since 1765 had mob violence taken place in the colony.

Acts of violence may have offered an outlet for popular frustrations, but they could not improve the economy. Currency was badly needed, demands for remittances continued incessantly, and good bills of exchange could not be found. Conditions in Maryland deteriorated even more in June, when devastating news reached the colony that major firms dealing in Maryland tobacco had gone under. James Anderson reported from London that "I have nothing new that is good to communicate; the late stoppages in our trade of Mr. Russell, Mr. Court and Mr. John Buchanan will, it is to be apprehended, cause confusion in Maryland, as such large sums of money will be immediately demanded—I hear Mr. Russell's debts amount to upwards of £50,000 and that he has near £100,000 owing to him by his books—Mr. Court's are about £52,000 and shows about £58,000 to pay them with—Mr. Buchanan's are about £70,000 and has about £120,000 in his books. Rivalship in trade has been the

<hr />

[37] Joshua Johnson (London) to Matthew Ridley (Baltimore), January 6, 1773, and to Wallace, Davidson, and Johnson (Annapolis), February 3, 1773, both in WDJLB; Thomas Eden and Co. (London) to Aquilla Hall (Baltimore), February 14, 1773, Ridgely Papers, MHS; Christopher Court and Co. (London) to Aquilla Hall (Baltimore), April 25, 1773, Aquilla Hall Papers, MHS.

[38] Joshua Johnson (London) to Wallace, Davidson and Johnson (Annapolis), February 6, 1773, and June 17, 1773, both in WDJLB.

[39] James Gaddes to Robert Eden, May 7, 1773, Fisher Transcripts, MHS; Robert Moreton deposition, Archives of Maryland, 63:427–43.

bane of the two elder merchants—the other gentlemen pushed against the whole community."[40] The worst had come.

The depression ground on through the summer of 1773. "Such times has never been in the memory of man," wrote Joshua Johnson as he predicted, "I should not be surprised at a general revolution of the mercantile world."[41] Protested bills continued to return regularly. No one had any money and credit no longer existed. To secure payments English traders turned to the courts. One of the largest suits was filed against Charles Ridgely, a prominent Baltimore merchant, for £10,000.[42] With conditions deteriorating it was inevitable that men like Ridgely would become desperate. Angry, disillusioned, and passionately aroused, they were ready to join any struggle for some control over their lives. The people, Jonathan Boucher wrote, had been "restless and dissatisfied" before, but "it was now much worse. There was a fierceness in the opposition that was unusual."[43]

There developed during the worst months of the depression a political channel for these frustrations: the most celebrated newspaper controversy fought in Maryland before the Revolution. The argument focused on the still unresolved question of the validity of Governor Eden's fee proclamation. Out of this intense debate, which lasted from January to July of 1773, a new coalition of popular leaders emerged and gained power. From that time on, these individuals led the colony to independence and statehood.

Charles Carroll of Carrollton and Daniel Dulany were the chief protagonists in the newspaper war. Each wrote under a pseudonym, but their identities were well known. Supporters gathered around the two to give encouragement. Both men had private as well as public motives for engaging in the debate. Daniel Dulany had gone through several unsettling experiences during the previous few years, and his political security seemed once again to be threatened. The death of his father-in-law, Benjamin Tasker, in 1768 had been an unnerving experience. A member of the council since 1744, Tasker had been Dulany's strongest and most influential supporter and Dulany leaned heavily on him in his struggles

---

[40] Joshua Johnson (London) to Wallace, Davidson, and Johnson (Annapolis), May 5, 1773, WDJLB; James Anderson to James Hollyday, received June 25, 1773, Corner Collection, MHS.

[41] Joshua Johnson (London) to Wallace, Davidson, and Johnson (Annapolis), August 9, 1773, WDJLB.

[42] Harriet May to Charles Ridgely, September 25, 1773, Ridgely Papers, MHS.

[43] Jonathan Boucher, *Reminiscenses of an American Loyalist, 1738–1789* (Boston and New York: Houghton Mifflin Co., 1925), pp. 68–69.

with both Governor Sharpe and the powerful Maryland clergy, some of whom were the favorites of Lord Baltimore.[44]

Shortly after Tasker's death a new colonial governor arrived. Dulany fared no better in his relations with Robert Eden than he had with Horatio Sharpe. They resented one another and got on poorly. The uneasiness between the two was common knowledge and some speculated that Dulany's influence was on the decline. During the latter part of 1771 and through much of 1772 Dulany, possibly because of his conflict with Eden, went to England in an attempt to shore up his position within the proprietary establishment and to seek more offices for his family. At least Charles Carroll of Carrollton suspected this to be the reason for Dulany's trip when he wrote to his cousin, Charles Carroll, Barrister, several months prior to Dulany's actual departure: "The major [Daniel of St. Thomas Jenifer] tells me, Daniel Dulany still talks of going to England in the spring—whether he will or not time will show. If he goes it will be with a view, it is thought, to get his son appointed Secretary, or perhaps which I really take to be the case, to fly from the contempt and hatred of his countrymen, for altho his retainers pass him off and talk much of his past influence, it is pretty well known to be greatly in the decline—the loss of his popularity chagrins him to the quick; the improbability of ever regaining it adds to his mortification."[45]

Eden's and Dulany's relationship deteriorated even more upon his return, for the governor, like Sharpe before him, interpreted Dulany's trip to England as an attempt to weaken his authority. In October 1772, Charles Carroll of Annapolis reported with some glee to his son that Eden's "fickle behavior and mean condescension to the Dulanys justly lessens him in yours and the esteem of everyone acquainted with their pride and insolence."[46] With Tasker dead, Dulany now faced the power of Eden alone, and despite the prestige of his family the situation was uncomfortable.

But Dulany foresaw a way of improving his position. An election had to be held sometime in the late spring. Frederick, the sixth Lord Baltimore, had died in late 1771, and the province had gone to his illegitimate son, Henry Harford. As was the rule, a new election for the lower house followed a change in administration. If Dulany could convince the elec-

[44] Horatio Sharpe to Secretary Hamersley, July 25, 1768, *Archives of Maryland* 59:519; Aubrey C. Land, *The Dulanys of Maryland* (Baltimore: Maryland Historical Society, 1955), pp. 294–96.

[45] Charles Carroll of Carrollton to Charles Carroll, Barrister, August 9, 1771, Charles Carroll of Carrollton Letterbook, MHS.

[46] Charles Carroll of Annapolis to Charles Carroll of Carrollton, October 28, 1772, Charles Carroll of Annapolis Papers, MHS.

torate to return men with a more moderate stand on the governor's fee proclamation, he would undoubtedly better his position. With this in mind, he published a clever dialogue in the *Maryland Gazette* on January 7, 1773. The protagonists were called "First Citizen," an opponent of the proclamation, and "Second Citizen," who successfully defended it. After seeing his errors, "First Citizen" promised to disregard the arguments of that "designing faction of men" who wanted to destroy the government by allowing the colony to bear a mounting debt and a declining staple.

Carroll replied on February 4 under the name of "First Citizen" and the battle continued until July. The central question revolved around whether Eden's proclamation was valid. Each participant offered relevant English precedents and sophisticated historical and legal arguments. Both used the natural rights philosophy when it suited their ends, cited great literary sources to prove their points, and often employed personal invective, including some pointed insults by Dulany about Carroll's Catholicism. Dulany argued well, but by the end of the six-month debate Charles Carroll of Carrollton had become a man of considerable popularity.

During the conflict Carroll and his father were guided by one basic assumption. They believed, no doubt correctly, that Dulany designed his defense of Eden primarily to increase his popularity with the governor and, if possible, his income. They first contended privately and later proclaimed publicly that Dulany, not Eden, should be held responsible for the fee proclamation. But the Carrolls' hatred for Dulany went deeper than a dislike for opportunism. Bad blood had long existed between the families, and this attitude was complemented by the Carrolls' distaste for the proprietary structure.

Maryland did not treat her Catholics kindly and religious discrimination rankled the Carrolls. During the French and Indian War, the colony placed a double tax on Catholics. Because of this measure, Charles Carroll of Annapolis advised his son, then studying abroad, not to return to Maryland. After the war the tax was repealed, but unfair practices persisted and Catholics were barred by law from holding any of the lucrative proprietary offices.[47] This denial of public position embittered the Carrolls, and it provided one of several motives for their attack on Dulany and the system in which he flourished. Charles Carroll of Annapolis indicated his jealousy of the Dulanys in a letter to Daniel of St. Thomas Jenifer: "All that has or can be said in favor of the officers is that their

[47] David Curtis Skaggs, Jr., "Democracy in Colonial Maryland" (Ph.D. diss., Georgetown University, 1966), pp. 54–59; Kate Mason Rowland, *The Life of Charles Carroll of Carrollton, 1737–1832* (2 vols., New York, 1898), 1:47.

fees were reduced too low. Who says this? The officers. Who take upon them to decide the controversy? The officers. When the fees are reduced so low that the men next in point of *family*, fortune, understanding and merit to the present possessors shall refuse to accept the offices, then and not till then shall I think the fees too low."[48]

Since the Dulanys held the most lucrative proprietary offices, Carroll's references to "next in point of *family*," was obviously to his own. The antipathy he felt for the proprietary regulations fused with his dislike for the "insolent" Dulanys. His son, Charles Carroll of Carrollton, had shared these feelings ever since his first meeting with Daniel Dulany in 1762. While young Carroll was pursuing his studies abroad, his father urged him to look up Dulany in London. After several frustrating and unsuccessful attempts, he was finally received by Dulany. Their conversation turned to Carroll's father and Dulany spoke critically of the elder Carroll. Dulany's vain manner irritated his visitor, and this dislike eventually developed into a passionate hatred. Dulany, for his part, snubbed Carroll whenever they met thereafter.[49]

During the Stamp Act crisis, Charles Carroll of Carrollton, recently returned from England, did not take an active role in opposing the tax, yet he sympathized with his colony's position, and despite his personal feelings recommended Dulany's pamphlet to his English friends.[50] But the respect the young man had for Dulany's intelligence did not serve to improve the relationship between the two families. One sore point between them concerned the Baltimore Iron Works. The two families were partners in the company and seldom agreed on management decisions. The Carrolls actually owned more than the Dulanys, but by prior arrangement, Walter Dulany kept the books. In 1768, Charles Carroll of Annapolis began to suspect chicanery in the records. Finally, in 1771, he became convinced of misappropriations and wrote his son that he believed the evidence strong enough to warrant taking Walter Dulany to court: "In going through this matter I really am astonished that Mr. Dulany should have so little honor or even sense of that and honesty as to suffer himself to be so exposed as he must by the filing this bill. . . . Let not Cooke [Carroll's lawyer] or anyone else give Walter Dulany the least hint of it to prevent it. After his scandalous behavior we ought not

[48] Charles Carroll of Annapolis to Daniel of St. Thomas Jenifer, April 2, 1773, Charles Carroll of Annapolis Papers, MHS.

[49] Charles Carroll of Carrollton to Charles Carroll of Annapolis, January 5, 1761; Charles Carroll of Annapolis to Charles Carroll of Carrollton, April 17, 1761, both in Charles Carroll of Annapolis Papers, MHS.

[50] Charles Carroll of Carrollton to Mr. Bradshaw, November 21, 1765, Charles Carroll of Carrollton Letterbook, MHS.

to be more tender of his character than he is." The elder Carroll took particular pleasure in this discovery because the Dulanys, for the past several years, had been arguing a case through the courts claiming damages against him for illegally charging compound interest.[51]

Two other disputes inflamed the Carroll-Dulany relationship. In 1768 Daniel Dulany crossed Charles Carroll of Carrollton in a way the latter never forgot. Carroll, then preparing to marry Molly Darnall, requested the assembly to pass an enabling act giving Molly, who was still a minor, the status of an adult. He asked for the measure so that Molly might legally sign a disclaimer stating that if her husband died, she would have no right to claim the fortune. Normally such a request passed in routine fashion, but on this occasion Daniel Dulany, wanting to irritate the Carrolls, attempted unsuccessfully to block the act. The Carrolls were infuriated. Word of Dulany's malice was bantered around in upper class circles, but not till 1773 was it publicized in the newspaper. Then an anonymous muse brought up the matter while describing Carroll's attack on Dulany's first public letter:

> When your letter I read my heart
> leap'd for joy
> That I on occasion so apt
> might employ
> My rancour, and venom innate to
> let fly
> At a man I abhor—and I'll tell
> you why.
> I could not be married (you've heard
> of the fact)
> Before I got an enabling act,
> For a man you'll allow, would cut a
> poor figure
> Tho big as myself, or perhaps
> somewhat bigger,
> Who to any fair virgin his
> honor shou'd plight
> Without being enabled to do—what
> is right
> In this he opposed me.[52]

---

[51] Charles Carroll of Annapolis to Charles Carroll of Carrollton, May 30, 1771, September 15, 1771, October 20, 1769, all in Charles Carroll of Annapolis Papers, MHS.
[52] *Maryland Gazette*, June 14, 1773.

Within a year Charles Carroll of Carrollton became involved in another bitter argument with the Dulanys—this time with Lloyd, Daniel's younger brother, a cocky and impulsive man who returned in 1769 from study abroad. Hearing of his family's feud, he wrote a letter to Charles Carroll of Annapolis which the younger Carroll received first. Upon reading the contents, wherein Dulany, with calculated disrespect, characterized the senior Carroll as a crook and scoundrel, the son threatened a duel. The Carroll family's position, as wealthy Catholics in an unfriendly Protestant society, had made them extremely sensitive about matters of dignity and respect. Charles Carroll of Carrollton, being personally of a weak constitution and not much of a fighting man, did not relish the idea of a confrontation, but he had pride and courage enough to offer the challenge. He informed Dulany where he planned to ride the next morning and commented that a "brace of pistols" would be waiting.

Lloyd Dulany only sneered at this proposal. Prefacing his reply were further reflections on Carroll's father: "But as for that master of vice and profligacy your father I will still echo the universal voice of this country, that he is the deep stain of the times, and that the laws have long scandalously slept in not dragging him forth as a sacrifice to public justice." Continuing in a jeering manner he then addressed himself to the threat of a duel. "[You] desire me *to take notice* that you are not *afraid*," he said, and "I will frankly confess to you that I do discern violent struggles in your breast but they are betwixt your unparalleled and dastardly fears and your highly attenuated venom." What Carroll really wanted, Dulany maintained, was that he should make the open challenge so that the courts would hold him the aggressor punishable by law: "Tell me prithee, whither shall I fly to kiss your hands in a private place, either alone or attended by a friend? The choice of weapons shall be yours at all adventures: I waive all advantages of every punctilio. Tell me, do you wait for my making such palpable overtures as will render me the aggressor—and that you will take no legal steps—but will be punctual to an appointed meeting in a private place—why you silly little puppy," he scorned, "how can you be such a fool as to insinuate that a certain person is afraid!—afraid of whom?" Dulany then asserted that Carroll had made the threat only because he knew it impossible: "You dirty little rascal, would you propose even what you do was it not impossible from the excessive folly of it that any measure could be taken on your plan? If I do intend to chastise you I shall certainly make choice of my own time and manner." He concluded, "Either come to the point or pester me no more with your foolish impertinences."[53]

53 Lloyd Dulany to Charles Carroll of Carrollton, September 29, 1769, Charles Carroll of Annapolis Papers, MHS.

To all this Carroll replied, "Your language and character are both contemptible; I heartily despise both, your bravado doth not intimidate me in the least." The offer of a duel, as far as he was concerned, still stood. Dulany could make of it what he wished. "Tomorrow morning if the weather permits, I shall ride out at 6:00 o'clock and I shall then be prepared to give you a proper reception if you come in my way as I shall be provided with pistols," Carroll threatened.[54]

The following morning Carroll took his ride and probably breathed a long sigh of relief when Dulany failed to appear. Should they have fought, he had fully expected to lose. His honor demanded that he act with boldness, but inwardly he wanted to be restrained. Once the immediate danger had passed he confided his innermost anxieties to his father: "If such outrageous abuse should go unpunished, if the grossest insinuations are permitted to be thrown out against a gentleman's character by such scoundrels with impunity, there is an end of civil society. Every sturdy insolent fellow confiding in his strength," Carroll complained, "might insult a worthy honest man who might be weaker. But the weaker may challenge to fight with pistols and vindicate his honor—but how unequal and hard is the injured man's fate, to be under a necessity of exposing his life to imminent danger or submitting to the shame of being deemed a coward if he does not show a proper spirit. Besides," he added somewhat perversely, "the injured person may engage under great disadvantages—in the late instance had I been killed what dear connections should I have left behind me! Who would have grieved at Lloyd's death —I do not believe a single tear would have been shed on the occasion."[55]

Given the hostility between the families, it is easy to understand why the Carrolls looked upon the fee controversy as the conspiratorial product of Daniel Dulany. From the very beginning they saw him "brooding schemes of mischief and laying plans of crooked policy." As Charles Carroll of Carrollton explained, an all too obvious mixture of Dulany greed and opportunism lay at the bottom of Eden's misguided proclamation. "I cannot help saying that I am sorry to see the governor entirely swayed by the counsel of one man insolent and impolitic enough to advise such selfish measures," he wrote to Charles Carroll, Barrister. "All things here will soon be in the greatest confusion and unless a very different policy be shortly pursued the governor must bid adieu to all his happiness in his present situation. War is now declared between the government and the people, or rather between a few placemen, the real

[54] Charles Carroll of Carrollton to Lloyd Dulany, September 29, 1769, Charles Carroll of Annapolis Papers, MHS.
[55] Charles Carroll of Carrollton to Charles Carroll of Annapolis, October 2, 1769, Charles Carroll of Annapolis Papers, MHS.

enemies to government and all the inhabitants of this province."[56]

The Carroll strategy, at least in the beginning, was to attack Dulany but to avoid alienating the governor. In retrospect, the course was bound to fail. A somewhat cool relationship already prevailed between Eden and the Carrolls. The governor had in the past snubbed their offers of hospitality, and they responded by adopting a reserved manner when dealing with him.[57] But as the arguments began over the validity of Eden's proclamation, the elder Carroll grew apprehensive. Realizing the enormous influence and power exercised by the governor, he urged extreme caution upon his son. Charles Carroll of Carrollton, equally aware of the danger, took great care in his first published letter to make clear the objects of his criticism: "I impute all the blame to his ministers who if found guilty and dragged to light, I hope will be made to feel the resentment of a free people. . . . Oh unsuspicious Eden! How long wilt thou suffer thyself to be imposed on by this deceiving man!"[58]

The Carrolls made private gestures of peace to the governor through Daniel of St. Thomas Jenifer and William Paca to assure him that their quarrel lay only with Dulany. Paca was a close friend of both the Carrolls and Eden, all of whom considered him reliable. Jenifer, the proprietor's receiver-general, also had ties with both families. Unlike Paca, however, he was not trusted, although the elder Carroll tried several times to win him over. As he explained to his son, Jenifer enjoyed access to vital information and should be wooed: "I wrote to the Major [Jenifer] with a view that he might show my letter to the governor, which I doubt not he has done. It can do us no harm, it will let the governor see plainly our sentiments and if he will think these general sentiments of the people it may of course be of service to him. Besides my letter to the Major if he answers it may draw something from him and in order to that I seasoned it with some complaisance. I know him to be a courtier but I believe him to be one of the best of them. That is, he would follow his own opinion if his office did not determine him to follow the opinion of others."[59]

Always acutely sensitive to power, Charles Carroll of Annapolis persistently exhorted his son to move carefully. Not liking Eden but respecting his command, the younger Carroll preferred to maintain a re-

[56] Charles Carroll of Carrollton to Charles Carroll, Barrister, August 9, 1771, and December 3, 1771, Charles Carroll of Carrollton Letterbook, MHS.

[57] Charles Carroll of Annapolis to Charles Carroll of Carrollton, June 3, 1771, Charles Carroll of Annapolis Papers, MHS.

[58] *Maryland Gazette*, February 4, 1773.

[59] Charles Carroll of Annapolis to Charles Carroll of Carrollton, April 8, 1773, Charles Carroll of Annapolis Papers, MHS.

spectful distance. But that was not enough for the old man. Act nicely, he instructed; visit him often and suppress your personal feelings, for given these tense times "prudence directs you not to show that the governor's folly and want of spirit is mortifying to you. You may resolve to live in a desert if you will not generally associate with foolish, fickle, mean-spirited men." He emphasized: "You ought not to alter your behavior to the governor unless compelled to by some evident slight or ill treatment, which you have no reason to expect."[60]

With the "First Citizen's" letters gaining widespread popularity in the spring of 1773, Carroll's father became more insistent on this matter: "I am glad you went to see the governor last Friday and wish you had found him at home. It would," he admitted, "have been, as I think, a sort of embarrassed fête; however a conscious rectitude would have enabled you to behave with ease." Still, he wished his son would take more care in the choice of words employed in his published letters: "The word *youthful* applied to the governor I wish had been omitted. It carries too much the significance of puerility and levity and want of reflection. This is the only correction I would make in your piece." He admonished his son to remember Eden's own predicament: "The governor has a ticklish part to play. He may not see it. If Harford's guardians notwithstanding his commission should be desirous to remove him, may they not make a pretense of his unpopularity and wrong step in issuing and supporting the proclamation—he has owned it as his own act. Should he recall the proclamation and settle the fees by a law and a lower rate than by the last act will they not say he has betrayed his trust? Will they not remove him? Slight pretenses are enough to those who seek only pretenses for doing what they want to do." He advised caution along with calculation and full discussion of actions with knowledgeable friends.[61]

In late March Charles Carroll of Annapolis rejoiced to see his strategy apparently working. Eden had made no overt criticisms of the Carrolls and, more importantly, he had just invited young Charles for dinner. Certainly this seemed proof enough that he did not view Carroll's essay as personally insulting. Said the elder Carroll: "I am glad to hear the governor invited you to dine with him so soon after the publication of your answer to Antilon [Dulany's pseudonym]. Although it be no proof that your answer has not offended him, his behavior and hints which he may have dropped since will be more certain indications of his sentiment.

[60] Charles Carroll of Annapolis to Charles Carroll of Carrollton, October 28, 1772, Charles Carroll of Annapolis Papers, MHS.

[61] Charles Carroll of Annapolis to Charles Carroll of Carrollton, March 17, 1773, Charles Carroll of Annapolis Papers, MHS.

His behavior you have seen; if he has spoke you probably have heard some of the things he has said. Upon all circumstances let me know what you think he thinks." Indeed the old man insisted: "Give me every trifle that is said pro and con about the First Citizen. I may not think things trifling which you may think so."[62]

As for the younger Carroll, most of his father's hopes and instructions, while well-considered, represented sheer wishful thinking. He had written an extremely popular critique of the fee proclamation, and whatever the qualifications employed, this still amounted to direct criticism of Eden. Already he explained to his father that the dimensions of the First Citizen's success were giving "rise to the governor's resentment."[63] He felt the family had best accept this, but the elder Carroll did not. Despite his son's candid observation, he continued, not very astutely, to hope that the governor's cooling attitude might somehow be diverted. "Seem," he said, "not to perceive" the governor's hostility and "pay him the same regard you formerly showed him. From that he must infer that you think you have given him no offence." A critical period was approaching, he maintained, and caution should be scrupulously practiced: "Antilon aims much at exasperating the governor and council and making the proclamation as much their act as his—nay, making it as much as he dares entirely—the governor's act." In the next essay, he suggested, "I would have you manage the governor as much as you consistently can, with force and economy."[64]

Nonetheless, for all their well-intended tactics and thoughtful discretion, the Carrolls failed. By the end of April, Eden's hardening attitude had become evident to everyone. Actually, Charles Carroll of Carrollton was, by then, probably glad of the development. Since early April he had entertained compelling personal reasons for coming out publicly against Eden. The governor had the reputation of being a lady's man—any lady's man—and his parties were notorious. On one occasion he threw so boisterous a drunken frolic that his wife miscarried in the ballroom. The younger Carroll took a dim view of such proceedings. And at a similar sort of gathering that April, Eden apparently made some advances to Molly Carroll, Charles Carroll of Carrollton's wife. Charles Carroll of Annapolis heard of the incident from Molly's mother. He was angered

[62] Charles Carroll of Annapolis to Charles Carroll of Carrollton, March 25, 1773, Charles Carroll of Annapolis Papers, MHS.

[63] Charles Carroll of Carrollton to Charles Carroll of Annapolis, April 3, 1773, Charles Carroll of Annapolis Papers, MHS.

[64] Charles Carroll of Annapolis to Charles Carroll of Carrollton, April 8, 1773, and April 16, 1773, Charles Carroll of Annapolis Papers, MHS.

by Eden's conduct and yet proud of the way his daughter-in-law had handled the situation. To his son he wrote that the governor's "behavior to Molly as she represents it to her mother was very odd and foolish. Give my love to her and tell her I congratulate her for it; for I do not know that his smiles or intimacy redounded to the credit of any ladies on whom he has been pleased to bestow them."[65]

After this encounter Charles Carroll of Carrollton, with no trace of concern, observed that Eden "now looks very cool on me."[66] Still somewhat unhappy about the growing division, the old man agreed that the family should simply avoid the governor whenever possible. Even this tactic failed to work as relations between the Carrolls and Eden worsened. In late August the once diplomatic Charles Carroll of Annapolis reluctantly concluded that "our governor is what you say a very silly, idle, dissipated man."[67] In a sense, though, there had by then developed a difference between the old man and his son in their conceptions of politics. The caution of Charles Carroll of Annapolis reflected the traditional "outs" versus "ins" view of politics, while his son's position was more ideological, though certainly not disinterested. To the younger Carroll the greed of a Dulany and the profligacy of an Eden were becoming symbolic of a system that was unjust and not simply examples of individual wrongdoing.

Politically speaking, Eden's coolness to the Carrolls was understandable. Despite their efforts to avoid alienating him, their position inevitably offended the governor. His personal encounters with the Carrolls only gave further impetus to the deteriorating relationship. From the governor's vantage point, Charles Carroll of Carrollton's growing popularity meant trouble. The young man's stand against Dulany had attracted important supporters. Eden could see a new and extremely popular coalition forming against his administration.

As of mid-March, Carroll already enjoyed the backing of Samuel Chase, Thomas Johnson, Charles Carroll, Barrister, and Matthew Tilghman. Within this group, the barrister provided an important connecting link. He was a cousin of Charles Carroll of Carrollton and a son-in-law of Matthew Tilghman, the principal leader of the lower house's country party. Tilghman, a wealthy planter from Talbot County, had a reputa-

[65] Charles Carroll of Annapolis to Charles Carroll of Carrollton, April 8, 1773, Charles Carroll of Annapolis Papers, MHS.

[66] Charles Carroll of Carrollton to Charles Carroll of Annapolis, April 30, 1773, Charles Carroll of Annapolis Papers, MHS.

[67] Charles Carroll of Annapolis to Charles Carroll of Carrollton, June 24, 1773, and August 26, 1773, Charles Carroll of Annapolis Papers, MHS.

tion for being an aggressive organizer. Knowledgeable and capable, he consistently held executive positions throughout the revolutionary period. As a leader in the assembly, as president of all the provincial conventions, and as a delegate to the Continental Congress, he supplied critical support for the coalition forming around Carroll. Similarly, the barrister helped secure the backing of Samuel Chase, although here little encouragement was needed. Chase personally liked Charles Carroll, Barrister, for the role he had played in aiding him and his Annapolis followers in their rise to political prominence. At a meeting on March 17, 1773, three of these men met at the Carroll mansion. Charles Carroll of Annapolis wrote his son a summary of the meeting: "On Sunday about 4 o'clock p.m. I had the pleasure of Mr. Johnson's, Chase's and Tilghman's company. The evening's conversation you may naturally suppose turned chiefly on the First Citizen's paper. Their opinion of it you cannot be in doubt about. They assured me it met with a general and warm approbation."[68]

Through their connections in the lower house, both Chase and Tilghman provided the Carrolls with valuable assistance.[69] But Thomas Johnson, Jr. played an even more direct role. Possessing a keen analytical mind, marred occasionally by displays of ostentation, Johnson handled all the Carroll legal matters in a manner that invariably delighted the family. Because of his ability, he acted as their chief advisor. During the writing of the First Citizen letters, Charles Carroll of Annapolis once pointedly told his son: "Do not by any means be drawn into discussing other matters—it is Mr. Johnson's policy as well as mine."[70]

William Paca was another important Carroll supporter. He studied law with Charles Carroll of Carrollton in England and the two remained friends after their return home. Paca also got along well with Eden, and this made his presence all the more useful. A man of some ability and practical imagination, Paca enjoyed adopting a secretive manner, though in most cases he was merely bluffing. Still his peculiar sort of behavior suited the Carrolls well, for through him they could communicate with the governor. Because of his ties with Eden, Paca also encouraged young Charles to treat the governor gently, and until the Carrolls abandoned this strategy, he purveyed intelligence for both camps. A letter written

[68] Charles Carroll of Annapolis to Charles Carroll of Carrollton, March 17, 1773, Charles Carroll of Annapolis Papers, MHS.

[69] Neil Strawser, "The Early Life of Samuel Chase" (Master's thesis, George Washington University, 1958), p. 236.

[70] Charles Carroll of Annapolis to Charles Carroll of Carrollton, March 17, 1773, Charles Carroll of Annapolis Papers, MHS.

by Charles Carroll of Annapolis clearly portrayed Paca's vital position: "Paca, Chase, Johnson and Cooke dined with me last Thursday. Paca said the governor told him that he hoped, notwithstanding the present heat, all things would go on well at the next session of the assembly or something to that affect. This expression if it meant anything implied either that the governor entertained a hope of having a Lower House to his liking which I think he cannot be so weak as to expect."[71] Another early supporter of the Carrolls was William Cooke, an able Maryland lawyer often in the family's employ. Cooke was a brother of Rachel Cooke, Charles Carroll of Carrollton's first betrothed, who died before their marriage. Cooke and Charles Carroll remained good friends after her death.[72]

Chase, Johnson, Charles Carroll, Barrister, Tilghman, and Cooke provided the original nucleus of the Carroll strength. To augment their base of support, Charles Carroll of Annapolis made several attempts to attract one of the colony's most clever politicians, Daniel of St. Thomas Jenifer, the recently appointed receiver-general. Carroll knew that Jenifer, after holding only county offices, had just acquired a proprietary position and would be in close contact with the governor. Obviously Jenifer intended to do nothing that might bring official displeasure, but the elder Carroll still considered the gesture of a suggested alliance useful. As anticipated, Jenifer refused to commit himself in any way. His answer was both flattering and elusive, as befitted a consummate politician, who may well have been the shrewdest of a very shrewd lot. His language always carried a delphic double edge, and pinning him down proved impossible. His reply to Carroll was typical: "It is thought that the Whigs will not appear again; if they do not I suppose Antilon will be totally eclipsed by the shield of the man with the long name. Your son is a most flaming patriot and red-hot politician. He and I have frequent skirmishes in the field of politics, each retiring victor and of consequence always ready to renew the attack."[73]

Not to be outdone by the evasive and yet complimentary Jenifer, Carroll replied that "you and my son would not skirmish so often about politics had you not an esteem for each other." Indeed it was only for reasons of "respect and esteem" that he had written at all. The Carrolls, he wrote, simply wanted him to understand that their fight was not with the governor or the proprietary party, but rather with those "four or

[71] *Ibid.*
[72] Rowland, *Life of Charles Carroll*, 1:65.
[73] Daniel of St. Thomas Jenifer to Charles Carroll of Annapolis, March 28, 1773, Charles Carroll of Annapolis Papers, MHS.

five officers" who, to line their own pockets, were denying to the community a law "not only extremely beneficial but essential to the public
welfare." Written prior to the break with Eden, Charles Carroll of Annapolis intended this letter as much for the governor's eyes as those of
Jenifer. Feigning complete sincerity, Carroll said that he understood Jenifer's delicate position and did not expect his open support. His sole
desire was to fully apprise the man of where his son stood: "I write to
you my sentiments freely. I have ever entertained them. I never con-
cealed them; I write not to draw you into a controversy nor with hopes
that you will approve my sentiments. I know you have not leisure for the
first and I think prudence may direct you not to coincide with the
last."[74] For his part, Charles Carroll of Carrollton considered any discussion with Jenifer an utter waste of time. No commitment, he told his
father, could ever be gotten from such a person: "I must question
whether Jenifer will answer your letter and if he does it will be nothing
but flummery."[75]

Despite the Carrolls' failure to lure Jenifer, they did gain, late in the
spring, another influential ally. Their cousin, Daniel Carroll, reported to
them that Charles Ridgely, an influential Baltimore trader, supported the
First Citizen. Ridgely at that time led the Baltimore merchants, along
with Lux and Samuel Purviance. Chase had close ties with Baltimore
because of his earlier political experience. In May he began the resurrec-
tion of his former alliance, through Charles Ridgely. Chase and Lux were
still not on the best of terms, but the fact that the Carrolls and Thomas
Johnson were very friendly with Lux helped to soothe ruffled feathers.[76]
Chase wrote to Ridgely asking for support: "As I hear you stand a
candidate for Baltimore county, I take the liberty to acquaint you that
the citizens of Annapolis, the free holders of Frederick and of this
county have thought it proper to express their opinion respecting the
proclamation. They have buried it under the gallows and ordered their
representatives to return their thanks to First Citizen for his opposition
to the proclamation." But to obtain a complete repeal, he continued, the
people must be unanimous in their expression of opposition, and so "I
could wish to see Baltimore County join in sentiment with us, and if you
will exert your influence I doubt not you will be assisted." Chase con-

[74] Charles Carroll of Annapolis to Daniel of St. Thomas Jenifer, April 2, 1773,
Charles Carroll of Annapolis Papers, MHS.
[75] Charles Carroll of Carrollton to Charles Carroll of Annapolis, April 3, 1773,
Charles Carroll of Annapolis Papers, MHS.
[76] Charles Carroll of Annapolis to Charles Carroll of Carrollton, April 1, 1773,
and September 13, 1774, Charles Carroll of Annapolis Papers, MHS.

cluded, "I beg you to consult the principal gentlemen of your county—do what is right—act like a man!"[77]

Chase's appeal was successful primarily because he was able to resurrect the Baltimore-Annapolis coalition around the person of Charles Carroll of Carrollton. Carroll was both a merchant and planter, and his personal experience in these two areas provided an essential attraction for the people uniting to support him. His appeal was strong among the Baltimore merchants, the Annapolis followers of Chase, and the country party's planter legislators who saw his father's reputation as a great planter reflected in the son. Yet in his private letters to his father, Charles Carroll of Carrollton showed a greater concern for business than for agricultural affairs and his public letters criticizing Dulany contained ideas close to the hearts of many merchants. He particularly emphasized the doctrine of free trade.[78] One of Carroll's cleverest moments in his skillfully conducted debate with Dulany came in the fourth letter when, in showing why the colony could not afford higher fees, he quoted from his opponent's famous Stamp Act pamphlet. Carroll here calculated to appeal to both planters and merchants: "The attentive reader will observe that the net proceeds of a hogshead at an average are £4 and the taxes are £3, together £7—Quare—how much does the tax amount to which takes from the two wretched tobacco colonies £3 out of every £7—and how deplorable must their circumstances appear when their vast debt to the mother country and the annual burthen of their civil establishments are added to the estimate?"[79]

Carroll's education in Europe prepared him to be a merchant. The object of his higher education was law, but he could never generate any enthusiasm for the subject. To persuade him to study his father had to chide and encourage constantly.[80] What the young man did enjoy was bookkeeping—particularly the arduous Venetian accounting. This method was the most sophisticated of those employed by traders to keep their accounts, and Charles Carroll of Annapolis encouraged his son to study it.[81] Soon after he set out to master accounting, Charles Carroll of

[77] Samuel Chase to Charles Ridgely, May 26, 1773, Ridgely Papers, MHS.

[78] Charles Carroll of Annapolis to Charles Carroll of Carrollton, August 20, 1771, Charles Carroll of Annapolis Papers, MHS; Charles Albro Barker, *The Background of the Revolution in Maryland* (New Haven, Conn.: Yale University Press, 1940), p. 352; Charles Carroll of Carrollton to Edmund Jennings, May 26, 1776, and to William Graves, August 27, 1767, both in Charles Carroll of Carrollton Letterbook, MHS.

[79] *Maryland Gazette*, June 3, 1773.

[80] Charles Carroll of Annapolis to Charles Carroll of Carrollton, February 4, 1758; and December 29, 1762, Charles Carroll of Annapolis Papers, MHS.

[81] Rowland, *Life of Charles Carroll*, 1:49.

Carrollton wrote: "I have begun to learn the Italian method of bookkeeping. It is certainly useful and ought to be known by all merchants and men in business." By the start of the following year, he reported: "I think I understand the theory of Italian bookkeeping and am able to follow that method, if need be, in the transaction of my own business."[82] Practical merchant experience came later from running his father's business in Annapolis.

During the newspaper war, the coalition supporting Carroll also gained strength and popularity through another issue, about which the family rarely spoke. Here again the Carroll connection to Chase and Paca provided the essential ingredient. While seeking support for Carroll, these two were simultaneously engaged in a heated public argument with the established Anglican clergy. This debate coincided with the Carroll-Dulany letters. In defending their stands, Chase and Paca attempted to project the same popular appeal being used by Carroll. The people, they contended, were spending far too much money for the support of government officials.

Clerical appointments in the established church were a form of government patronage. Jonathan Boucher accurately explained the clergy's situation in the colony: "In Maryland the condition of the established clergy was highly respectable; and being all under the patronage of government, they naturally were on the side of government and thus, in case of competition, threw great weight into that scale."[83] Yet, despite the established clergy's position, and probably because of it, by the early 1770s the church was unpopular. Complaints filled the *Maryland Gazette* describing corruption and the lack of divine reverence among the ministers. Some of the clerics' actions were so patently vile that even the Dulanys openly denounced them.[84] Both Anglicans and non-Anglicans disliked this arm of the proprietary establishment.

An attempt to reduce the taxes levied for the clergy's support was bound to be popular in such an atmosphere. When an opportunity came to argue for reduced appropriations, Chase and Paca played the leading roles. Because of the fee schedule's expiration the argument became possible. Originally the tax levied for the clergy had been 40 pounds of tobacco per poll, but in 1747 the Tobacco Inspection Act's attached fee schedule reduced it to 30 pounds per poll. When the tobacco act termi-

82 Charles Carroll of Carrollton to Charles Carroll of Annapolis, March 17, 1762, and January 7, 1763, Charles Carroll of Annapolis Papers, MHS.

83 Boucher, *Reminiscences*, p. 68.

84 Sidney Charles Bolton, "The Anglican Church in Maryland Politics" (Master's thesis, University of Wisconsin, 1968), chapter 2.

nated in 1770, the clergy committed an error which was to cost it dearly: it asked, like the Dulanys, for higher salaries. Specifically, the clergy contended that with the tax of 30 pounds per poll expired, the former tax of 40 pounds now applied.

Several men, but most noticeably Chase and Paca, criticized the clergy's avarice. As the debate progressed and tempers rose, they claimed that the tax was based upon an unconstitutional foundation and encouraged the people not to pay it. A test case soon followed involving Joseph Harrison, a member of the lower house from Charles County. Harrison refused to pay his clerical taxes and was jailed by the county's sheriff, Richard Lee. Chase, Paca, and Johnson defended Harrison and won a popular victory. The court absolved Harrison of the charge and directed Lee to pay him £60 sterling for damages.[85] Although a higher court later reversed this ruling, Chase and Paca went on to win their fight with the clergy. After the election of 1773, the assembly passed, and Eden signed, a bill which forced the clergy to accept lower incomes.

What contributed most heavily to the clergy's undoing was an ill-advised move by its chief public spokesman, Jonathan Boucher. In the course of his newspaper arguments with Chase and Paca, Boucher accused the latter of being ungrateful to Eden because of his stand on the clergy and fee issues. According to Boucher, Paca had recently solicited and possibly been promised an office of profit from his good friend, the governor. Such a disclosure placed Eden in a highly embarrassing situation. By 1773, Paca was well-known as a supporter of the Carrolls and an opponent of the government. How could he then have been considered for a proprietary position? Paca, as a link between the Carroll forces and Eden, no doubt channelled intelligence in both directions, and his unique role allowed him to help his friend Eden. Possibly for these reasons, the governor had promised him a post in the future. But now Eden had to disclaim the promise. The public, after all, did not realize the nature of the political intrigue. Eden, in an open letter, wrote that, "Mr. Paca did not solicit from him personally or representatively any office or place of profit for himself or any other person."[86]

What prompted Boucher to make such a charge? Was it accidental or did he have a specific motive? No one knew, but Charles Carroll of Annapolis suggested that Boucher may have been purposely attempting to divide Eden and Paca. Chase, too, he believed, might have figured in the cleric's thinking: "Boucher's last address to Paca dated the 12th

[85] *Ibid.*, pp. 68–69.
[86] *Maryland Gazette*, March 18, 1773, and March 25, 1773.

instant gives me a much worse opinion of him than I formerly entertained. He cannot be ignorant of the *paper Paca has from the governor and seems in my opinion to doubt it.* Either to expose the governor or to make a difference between the governor and Paca. His aim seems to be the same in regard to Chase."[87] Whatever Boucher's motives, the embarrassment he cost Eden diminished the governor's support for the clergy. Late in 1773, when the tax bill reducing salaries of the clergy reached his desk, Eden approved the measure.[88]

The Carrolls never became publicly involved in the clerical dispute. Early in the controversy Charles Carroll of Annapolis advised his son to proceed cautiously when discussing the subject: "We may publicly disapprove their conduct but not in such harsh tones, because it may be prejudicial to us without answering any good end."[89] As Catholics they both realized that they had no business in an essentially Protestant dispute. Not wanting to give Dulany and the clergy any further propaganda material, they remained silent. But in private they encouraged Paca and Chase, since the argument helped them all to achieve wider popularity.

The testing ground for the various controversies came in the 1773 election. Dulany's primary reason for participating in the newspaper debate with Charles Carroll of Carrollton had been to persuade the electorate to send more moderate men to the lower house, altering its composition in favor of the governor. Recognizing this, Charles Carroll of Carrollton asked the public directly: "What will the delegates of the people at their next meeting say to our minister, this Antilon?"[90] To Carroll's satisfaction, Dulany suffered a crushing defeat. The voting took place on May 14, and by the day's end the Carroll camp realized, on the basis of only partial returns, that they had achieved a considerable victory. Charles Carroll of Carrollton wrote his father that evening of the election results. The letter was delivered the next day and that evening his father replied, "I am obliged to you for your accounts of yesterday's transactions. They must be mortifying indeed to the Dulanys. Their

---

[87] Charles Carroll of Annapolis to Charles Carroll of Carrollton, March 25, 1773, Charles Carroll of Annapolis Papers, MHS.

[88] *Archives of Maryland,* 64:254.

[89] Charles Carroll of Annapolis to Charles Carroll of Carrollton, November 8, 1771, Charles Carroll of Annapolis Papers, MHS.

[90] For a different interpretation of Carroll's conduct, see Thomas O'Brien Hanley, *Charles Carroll of Carrollton: The Making of a Revolutionary Gentleman* (Washington, D.C.: Catholic University Press of America, 1970). Although Father Thomas O'Brien Hanley and I view Carroll from different perspectives, I want to express my sincere gratitude for the many insights he has shared with me.

pride and insolence," he rejoiced, "is humbled, and what is still more galling they have great reason to fear an end of their powers, influence and future promotion."[91]

As a result of the election, the principal supporters of the new political faction—some were already calling it the "popular party"—gained considerable power. Soon after the new legislature met, Chase, Johnson, Paca, and Tilghman procured the most prestigious committee assignments. More significantly, all of them were appointed that fall to a new body, the Committee of Correspondence.[92] The Carrolls, being ineligible for office, continued to bide their time and proceed prudently. "Avoid public and party meetings," advised the elder Carroll to his son, and "seem not to affect popularity—I think your papers deserve and have established it." With this the son agreed. A broadly based political faction had developed around him, and for the moment he was content to consolidate and strengthen his ties to the merchants and country party.[93]

The first session of the new assembly lasted a little over two weeks. From the beginning no one really doubted the outcome. On July 2, the lower house summed up the session by resolving unanimously "that the proclamation issued in the name of his Excellency Robert Eden the governor, with the advice of his Lordship's Council of State on the 26th day of November, 1770, was illegal, arbitrary, unconstitutional and oppressive."[94] Having made their point the delegates still faced the critical problems affecting the economy. Bellicose rhetoric, while popular, was not going to bring about an upswing in tobacco prices. To alleviate the colony's failing trade the reinstitution of a tobacco inspection system and other remedies were needed. The assembly met three times in 1773 to work on the problem. Their final session produced a compromise arrangement when both houses agreed to pass a tobacco inspection measure with no fee schedule attached.

The commercial pressures present that fall forced the two houses to work together on still another economic problem. Since the depression's beginning, there had been a serious shortage of currency. The lack of a tobacco inspection system, a function of which was the channeling of a form of currency into the economy, had much to do with creating this

---

[91] *Maryland Gazette*, May 20, 1773, and May 27, 1773; Charles Carroll of Annapolis to Charles Carroll of Carrollton, May 15, 1773, Charles Carroll of Annapolis Papers, MHS.

[92] *Archives of Maryland*, 63:339; 64:16–17, 23.

[93] Charles Carroll of Annapolis to Charles Carroll of Carrollton, May 15, 1773, and October 15, 1773, Charles Carroll of Annapolis Papers, MHS.

[94] *Archives of Maryland*, 63:388.

problem. Tobacco notes were issued by the inspectors on the tobacco brought to them. These notes then served as a negotiable commercial medium. As early as 1771 there was concern that the amount of negotiable bills in circulation would not be adequate to meet commercial needs, despite the recent emission of 1769. During the November session of that year, the lower house sent up a bill to emit paper money, a measure primarily aimed at taking up the slack occasioned by the absence of tobacco notes. Bitter arguments were then raging between the two houses, and because no emergency existed, an agreement was never reached.[95]

Conditions were far different in the fall of 1773. An emergency situation prevailed and economic necessities forced a settlement between the two houses. This time neither body quibbled. A bill ordering $346,663⅔ to be emitted and put into circulation was passed. Of this sum, $266,666⅔ was made available through loans, while the rest went into the construction of public facilities.[96] The effects of the new act were not actually felt until June of 1774, but the law's passage gave everyone some breathing room. Charles Carroll of Carrollton happily reported in January 1774 to an English trader to whom he owed money that "as there will be a new emission of money in the spring, I hope I shall make a larger remittance than what I expected to be able to make before that measure was resolved on." That March Charles Grahame, a southern Maryland trader, told the same to James Russell of London: "The loan of money will enable many people to pay and I have been willing to see what that will produce before I commence suits—it is now printing and will not be in circulation till June." Alexander Hamilton, a Scottish factor, suggested similar consequences to his Glasgow employer: "The 6th day of next month the loan office will be opened for those who want to borrow money at four percent; the sum to be lent is 266,666⅔ dollars." He affirmed hopefully, "I have received many promises of payment at that time with the money."[97]

It is not perfectly clear why Eden and the upper house decided to

---

[95] *Ibid.*, pp. 330–31, 386; 64:12–13; Kathryn Behrens, *Paper Money in Maryland 1727–1789* (Baltimore, Md.: The Johns Hopkins Press, 1923), pp. 54–55.

[96] *Archives of Maryland*, 64:245.

[97] Charles Carroll of Carrollton to Joshua Johnson, January 13, 1774, Charles Carroll of Carrollton Letterbook, Arents Collection, New York Public Library; Charles Grahame to James Russell, March 21, 1774, Coutts Bank Company Papers, Letters to James Russell, microfilm in University of Virginia Library, Charlottesville, Va.; Alexander Hamilton (Port Tobacco) to James Brown and Co. (Glasgow), May 18, 1774, *Maryland Historical Magazine* 61 (1966), 156–57.

cooperate with the lower assembly and relented on their insistence that a fee schedule be enacted along with the reestablishment of a tobacco control system. Perhaps economic factors, of a very personal sort, persuaded the governor to accept the exclusion of fees from the tobacco inspection measure. Throughout 1773, as the colony's trade languished, many considered the reinstatement of regulatory controls a basic solution to the crisis. Zephaniah Turner, a trader in Port Tobacco, explained this point to James Russell shortly after the act's passage. Turner anticipated that "our tobacco will take a favorable turn in price with you, the inspection law having altered the quality greatly for the better and prevents the large quality of trash from being shipped, as was the case during the expiration of the law."[98] It was anticipated that the new measure would end the confusion which had cost so many so much. And one of those who had suffered was Governor Eden himself.

Eden had a penchant for lavish spending, and was mired in debt. Boucher wrote of Eden that "he had been in the Army, and had contracted such habits of expenses and dissipation as were fatal to his fortunes, and at length to his life . . . with an income of three or four thousand pounds a year he was always in debt."[99] Horatio Sharpe had commented that he feared his replacement would have to restrict his high living when he assumed the governorship.[100] But Eden did not, and by 1772 his personal finances had reached, as he said, so "critical" a state that he sent his wife home to see what might be done. Unfortunately for him she apparently accomplished little, for a year later Joshua Johnson wrote from London warning his partners not to lend the governor any capital: "I presume it will not be amiss to caution you against running deep with Governor Eden. He owes very large sums here."[101]

To pay off his debts and augment his income, Eden used every available means including tobacco trading. His brother, Thomas Eden, owned one of the larger firms participating in the trade, and the governor invested sizable sums in the operation. Because of his investment, he undoubtedly felt a sense of urgency when he told Dartmouth in August 1773 that he personally hoped for the reestablishment of a regulatory system because of tobacco's having fallen "into great disrepute at home

[98] Zephaniah Turner to James Russell, August 4, 1774, Coutts Bank Company Papers, Letters to James Russell.

[99] Boucher, *Reminiscences*, pp. 67–68.

[100] Horatio Sharpe to Joshua Sharpe, June 10, 1769, Ridout Papers, MHR.

[101] Joshua Johnson (London) to Wallace, Davidson, and Johnson (Annapolis), August 9, 1773, WDJLB.

since dropping the inspection law."[102] The compromise proposal that came before him that fall was not all that he wished it to be, but he took what he could get.

Thus, the growth of a popular political movement in Maryland came at a time when the colony's economy was undergoing a serious decline. Substantial dissatisfaction had resulted from the English and European credit crisis which paralyzed commercial activities through late 1772 and most of 1773. This oppressive economic situation provided the context in which the Baltimore merchant community developed the political line it later followed. The same can be said of some elements in the planter community. Economic and political causes fused dramatically as motivating forces in 1773. From a political standpoint, the traders and planters resented the Dulanys' grab for positions of profit and power. They were no longer willing to acquiesce in the established forms of corruption represented by the state and church patronage systems. From an economic standpoint they were angered by a mercantile system which seemed bent on their destruction. In the midst of this depression a strong political faction, based on widespread discontent, was forged. The party's chief goals were political power at home and control over the colony's economic destiny. Throughout the coming years these aims remained basic, though the nature and character of the party would change as a result of future conflicts.

With the passing of the year 1773 one period of political conflict ended. Until now the rhythm of contention, whether imperial or internal, had been critically influenced by economic factors. Naturally, this influence continued. Charles Carroll of Annapolis, in an angry letter written in mid-1775, specified his economic grievances. "I appeal to your reason," he asked his British correspondent, "whether we ought to be restrained from importing any goods neither produced in nor of the manufacture of Great Britain such as wines, oils, olives, fruit, etc.? Is it the intent of such a prohibition to saddle us with double freights, double voyages, etc.—for these goods under acts cannot be imported here without a clearance from Great Britain? Or is it their intent that an American shall be put to the expense of £100 that a British merchant may at least draw a commission of £2 . . 10 . . 0?"[103] But if considerations such as

---

[102] Robert Eden to Earl of Dartmouth, August 21, 1772, Fisher Transcripts, MHS; Joshua Johnson (London) to William Lux and Daniel Bowly (Annapolis), May 3, 1775, WDJLB.
[103] Charles Carroll of Annapolis to William Graves, May 20, 1775, Charles Carroll of Annapolis Papers, MHS.

these remained present they played a gradually reduced role as the imperial crisis worsened. Replacing them in the minds of Maryland leaders were concerns of a much more menacing character. Specifically, beginning in 1774 and continuing through the next several years, these men came to fear greatly the social threats posed to their class by the revolutionary movement.

6 : The Growing Revolution

Within a year after gaining power, the popular party that had emerged from the fee controversy began to face the difficult and emotional problem of the colonial conflict with England. For the faction's leaders, the basic question was how to meet the growing imperial crisis while continuing to retain political control at home. In terms of strategy two important factors had to be considered. The basic strength of the party lay in the alliance among political groups in Annapolis, Baltimore, and the lower house, and responses to the imperial controversy had to be calculated on the basis of their strain on the coalition. In the case of Baltimore's merchant community, the task of keeping the ties firm proved particularly difficult. Another problem developed with the emergence of a new political faction in 1774 under the leadership of John Hall, Matthias Hammond, and Rezin Hammond. These men hoped to win increasing political control by advocating measures more radical than the popular leaders condoned.

The division between the popular leaders and the Hall-Hammond faction first developed at a legislative meeting of the lower house in April 1774. Chase, Johnson, Paca, and their fee controversy allies were flushed with success because of their recent victory over Eden. Possibly they were worried that their victory had been too complete; the actions they took at that session indicated that having gained popularity among the people, they now hoped to reach a rapprochement with the governor. No one wanted Eden, who was preparing to leave for England, for an implacable enemy. None of the popular leaders had yet conceived of independence and it is certainly possible that men like Chase, Tilghman, and Paca still hoped to gain proprietary positions in the future.

Whatever their reasons, they made every effort that spring to have the house draw up an acceptable fee bill. When the session began a moderate table of rates was proposed, but Johnson, Paca, and Chase opposed it, and instead suggested a higher one, calculated to please proprietary circles, and not much different from the rates they had attacked the year before.[1] John Hall and Matthias Hammond criticized these recommendations, employing the same arguments previously used by the popular party. On several occasions Hall and Hammond directed successful moves to restrict the rates below what Chase and his allies considered proper. As a result, the assembly failed to enact a fee schedule. Thomas Jennings, a proprietary supporter, found the new conflict ironic and took special delight in describing the division: "Our Assembly is just broken up, after sitting a long time and doing very little as usual. There is a schism among the Patriots. Hall and young Hammond (Matthias) are as violent in their opposition to Chase, Johnson and Paca, as the latter ever were to the measures of government. Their differences have arose so high that the three last mentioned gentlemen have resolved to appear no more in the assembly...."[2]

Like their political friends in the legislature, the Carrolls did not get on well with either Hall or the Hammonds. In the past John Hall had opposed the Carrolls in an important court case which left both sides bitter.[3] Charles Carroll of Annapolis best expressed his opinion of the Hammonds when he told his son never to trust a member of that family.[4] During the fall of 1773 these feelings intensified as the Carrolls and Hammonds became locked in a bitter land dispute. Their properties bordered in Anne Arundel County and in a recent survey the Carrolls acquired 500 acres of what had formerly been Hammond land. Charles Carroll of Annapolis explained the situation to his son: "The Hammonds can not forgive my taking 500 acres by the resurvey of Chance which their father intended to take. As to what any of them say it is not to be minded. They all are noted for not observing their word. Had I gone to Rezin Hammond I must have entered into a long disagreeable contro-

---

[1] Charles Carroll of Annapolis to Charles Carroll of Carrollton, April 15, 1774, Charles Carroll of Annapolis Papers, Maryland Historical Society, Baltimore, Md. (cited hereafter as MHS).
[2] Thomas Jennings to Horatio Sharpe, April 28, 1774, in Bernard Steiner, ed., "New Light on Maryland History," *Maryland Historical Magazine* 4 (1909), 256.
[3] Charles Carroll of Carrollton to Charles Carroll of Annapolis, April 17, 1771, Charles Carroll of Annapolis Papers, MHS.
[4] Charles Carroll of Annapolis to Charles Carroll of Carrollton, October 11, 1770, Charles Carroll of Annapolis Papers, MHS.

versy with a noisy obstinate fool, not to be convinced tho quite in the wrong."[5]

The Hammonds decided to put up a legal fight. Charles Carroll of Annapolis was not particularly worried about this, feeling certain that in a court his claim would hold against the Hammond charge of partiality on the part of the commissioners assigned to delineate the boundaries. But to guarantee the outcome, Charles Carroll of Annapolis directed his son to submit an advertisement to the newspaper calculated to incriminate the Hammonds. "Pray get the inclosed advertisement inserted in next Thursday's *Gazette*," he instructed; "it will fix the odium of the fact on Hammond who can be the only person suspected and may conduce to influence the court against him."[6] His son complied. The advertisement appeared at the same time that John Hall and Matthias Hammond began their attack on the Carroll family's political allies in the lower house. No doubt the piece helped to intensify their rhetoric.

Fifty pounds reward—whereas two large stones with inscriptions cut on them in capital letters were placed last fall by virtue of a commission to perpetuate the bounds of a tract of land called Chance, contiguous to the subscriber's dwelling beyond Elk-Ridge, which stones have been lately taken up and broke to pieces and whereas he has not yet been able to fix the fact by positive proof, he hereby promises to pay fifty pounds to any person or persons who shall discover the perpetuator or perpetuators of that villainy, so that he or they be convicted thereof by a due course of law.[7]

These clashes in the assembly and the courtroom carried over into the politics of Anne Arundel County. Not only were John Hall and the Hammond brothers from this county, but also the Carrolls, Chase, and Paca. During the latter part of May a letter from Boston's Committee of Correspondence, denouncing the Boston Port Act and calling upon the colonies to adopt nonimportation and nonexportation pacts, was forwarded to Annapolis from Baltimore. On May 25 a public meeting of about 80 persons gathered to discuss the message. Charles Carroll of Carrollton, Samuel Chase, and William Paca attempted to head the gathering, but they were opposed by the Hammonds and Hall.[8] A compromise was finally arranged whereby the leaders of both factions were

[5] Charles Carroll of Annapolis to Charles Carroll of Carrollton, November 26, 1773, Charles Carroll of Annapolis Papers, MHS.

[6] Charles Carroll of Annapolis to Charles Carroll of Carrollton, March 19, 1774, Charles Carroll of Annapolis Papers, MHS.

[7] *Maryland Gazette*, March 31, 1774.

[8] *Ibid.*, May 26, 1774.

elected to the county's committee of correspondence.[9] As the meeting progressed each side attempted to outdo the other in attacking British policy. Because of the passions aroused, the meeting passed an extremely radical resolve calling on all lawyers to desist from any debt suits owed to British creditors while the Boston Port Act remained law.[10]

The proposal ignited an anxious reaction. Charles Grahame, a trader in southern Maryland, discussed the impact with his London correspondent, the prominent tobacco merchant, James Russell. "I am afraid we are going into warm resolutions on the Bostonian act of Parliament," reported Grahame, "and if the citizens of Annapolis are seconded in the country we shall have great confusion, but I am inclined to believe we shall not be so hot." Another trader, Philip Fendell, simply cried, "*God send a speedy reconciliation*, nothing else can save us from ruin on both sides of the Atlantic."[11] Daniel Dulany explained to a friend in London the actions of the meeting and the steps he had taken: "Everything passed unanimously except the fourth resolution which I confess I opposed, with about thirty more. It seems to me to carry with it so much injustice and partiality, that I am afraid it will give a handle to our enemies to hurt the general cause." Still, he maintained, with a trace of sarcasm, "I would have agreed to it if it had extended to merchants in this country as well as foreign merchants."[12] In response to the debt resolve, Dulany and 160 other persons published a letter in the *Gazette*. Among the signers were members of prominent families, proprietary officials, and some wealthy Annapolis merchants. They condemned the resolve for its illegality and for the irresponsible damage it would do to the colony's credit standing.[13]

Yet the idea had great appeal. Debts owed to England were common, and cases dealing with unpaid accounts filled the courts. Alexander Hamilton, a Scottish factor, wrote in frustration to his employers in May 1774, "I have sued a great many, few or none of which I have received any payment from yet."[14] The list of debts held by just one British merchant, William Molleson, indicates how widespread the problem was.

[9] John Thomas Scharf, *History of Maryland* (3 vols., Baltimore, 1879), 2:150.

[10] *Maryland Gazette*, May 26, 1774.

[11] Charles Grahame to James Russell, May 30, 1774, and Philip Fendell to James Russell, May 30, 1774, Coutts Bank Company Papers, Letters to James Russell (microfilm in University of Virginia Library, Charlottesville, Va.).

[12] Daniel Dulany to Arthur Lee, May 17, 1774, in Peter Force, ed., *American Archives* (4th series, 6 vols., Washington, D.C., 1837–1846), 1:355.

[13] *Maryland Gazette*, June 2, 1774.

[14] Alexander Hamilton to James Brown and Co., May 28, 1774, *Maryland Historical Magazine* 61 (1966), 159.

In all, over 1100 individuals were indebted to him, but of this number, only two owed over £1000 and fewer than ten had unpaid accounts of £100 or more. The vast majority of people owed between £15 and £50.[15] To be rid of this obligation would be a source of satisfaction for many. Stephen West received an acid letter from his chief British creditor, William Maudruit, about this. The message bitterly censured West for his conduct in backing the resolve: "The meanness of your conduct is despicable to the utmost . . . how weak must we hold you . . . who moved (to the scandal of rational beings) that the attorneys should not bring any suits. No doubt this you thought a just action; it well suits such dark minded delinquents. . . . But as you know the state of your house here, take care that you send home some effects directly, and also that Mr. Dulany is properly satisfied; and when you have paid your just debts, then you may join any, the most wretched set and you will find none more silent than Wm. Maudruit."[16]

The stand men took on the debt resolve was important politically. Anthony Stewart, a leading Annapolis merchant, firmly believed that his open stand against the resolve precipitated the public abuse he encountered in 1774 and 1775. These attacks eventually forced Stewart to flee the colony. He later wrote that those who opposed the resolve had given "great offence to the leaders of sedition" and as a result "were set down by them as marked men on whom their vengeance was to be wreacked."[17] Lloyd Dulany's widow considered this equally true in the case of her late husband. In England she told a board inquiring about loyalist activities that her husband had exercised a strong hand in organizing the protest against the debt resolve and because of this "became the marked object of the malcontents."[18]

Some disagreements arose over other sections of the Annapolis resolves, especially the part advocating the adoption of nonimportation and nonexportation. Charles Grahame reported this to James Russell in his account of a tumultuous meeting held in Charles County to discuss the Annapolis resolutions: "I found our country people on Saturday almost unanimous against that part of the Annapolis Resolves which regarded nonexportation. We chose to export at least the present crop, and to consider at some future day the expediency of entering into a nonexpor-

---

[15] William Molleson Debt Book, Maryland Hall of Records, Annapolis, Md. (cited hereafter as MHR).
[16] William Maudruit to Stephen West, July 10, 1774, Oden Papers, MHS.
[17] Anthony Stewart Papers in the British Public Records Office, London, reproductions located in Fisher Transcripts, MHS (cited hereafter as Stewart Papers).
[18] Lloyd Dulany Memorial, Audit Office, British Public Records Office, London, series 12, vol. 6 (microfilm in the Library of Congress, Washington, D.C.).

tation agreement. This point being settled, that of not paying our debts had not one advocate in the meeting which was fully as numerous as I expected." Up to this point the more responsible and wealthy growers had apparently dominated, but the situation then altered. "We had a wrangle about importation and though it was once agreed that we should have a partial one of such goods as should be thought by the general meeting of the province proper, yet towards evening the people of the inferior class growing naturally a little tumultuous the question was resumed and it was agreed we should have no importation at all."[19]

Public meetings such as this were held throughout the colony during the next several weeks to discuss the imperial crisis and select delegates for the provincial convention summoned by the Annapolis resolves, which convened on June 22, 1774. The popular leaders immediately achieved firm control. After expressing sympathetic support for Boston, the delegates turned to their major task of electing representatives for the First Continental Congress. Matthew Tilghman, Samuel Chase, William Paca, and Robert Goldsborough were chosen.[20] The faction's domination of the delegation greatly pleased its members. If anything, the imperial conflict had allowed them to increase their hold over the colony's politics.

Away from Annapolis, opinion divided sharply over these events. Alexander Cowan, a trader in southern Maryland, told ship captain Richard Jackson that the colony appeared "to be bent upon entering into resolutions neither to import or export anything to Great Britain, Ireland and the West Indies. Should that take place," he predicted, "we must all seek out some other place to get a living in for there will be no use for us here."[21] William Fitzhugh, a prominent Charles County planter, expressed similar fears to James Russell. "Everything," he complained, "seems to have a bad appearance, ten times worse than at the time of the Stamp Act and God only knows what will be the consequences; I assure you my dear sir I dread it." Another Maryland acquaintance of Russell's, James Forbes, was more positive. He disliked "the distracted situation of all the continent," but believed it was owing "to the damned unjust acts of Parliament respecting America." The proposals for reducing trade, he maintained, were justifiable: "This is a most shocking situation, but bad

---

[19] Charles Grahame to James Russell, June 6, 1774, Coutts Bank Company Papers, Letters to James Russell.

[20] *Proceedings of the Conventions of the Province of Maryland* (Annapolis, 1836), p. 5.

[21] Alexander Cowan to Captain Richard Jackson, July 2, 1774, Coutts Bank Company Papers, Letters to James Russell.

as it is it will be pressed and seems to be the only chance we have for relief."[22] Charles Carroll of Carrollton echoed these same sentiments. To one English correspondent he warned, "hear what America is doing and tremble at the consequences."[23] To another he wrote of nonimportation: "If this measure should not open the eyes of the ministry or rather of British manufacturers and through them obtain a speedy and effectual redress of our present grievances, it is the general opinion and well warranted by the color of the times—the spirit of freedom and detestation of Parliamentary tyranny so universally prevalent among us—that all exports from the old colonies to Great Britain cease in less than a twelve month from this date; in short all intercourse and connection with the mother country will be broken off."[24]

Maryland's delegates to the First Continental Congress reflected the diversity of opinion within the colony and its members managed to please both the radical and conservative factions on all the vital issues. Basically there were two problems facing the congress. The more immediate problem was deciding what form of economic pressure should be applied to bring about a repeal of the coercive acts. And, more significantly, the congress had to clarify what method of political accommodation it sought with England. On the economic question, Massachusetts' delegation wanted a policy of nonimportation, nonexportation, and nonconsumption to go into effect that fall. Maryland, along with Virginia and North Carolina, opposed implementing nonexportation until after the 1774 tobacco crop could be marketed. Virginia's instructions specifically prohibited its delegates from agreeing to nonexportation before August 10, 1775.[25]

A compromise was finally drawn up by a committee and accepted by the congress. Thomas Johnson, one of the Maryland delegates on the committee, did not want nonexportation to become effective until the fall of 1775. But he emphatically argued that a policy of nonexportation should eventually be adopted to complement the one of nonimportation.

---

[22] William Fitzhugh to James Russell, August 3, 1774, and James Forbes to James Russell, June 22, 1774, Coutts Bank Company Papers, Letters to James Russell.

[23] Charles Carroll of Carrollton to William Graves, August 5, 1774, Charles Carroll of Carrollton Letterbook, MHS.

[24] Charles Carroll of Carrollton to Wallace and Company, August 17, 1774, Charles Carroll of Carrolton Letterbook, Arents Collection, New York Public Library, New York, N.Y.

[25] Merrill Jensen, *The Founding of a Nation* (New York: Oxford University Press, 1968), p. 496.

Chase, Paca, and Tilghman agreed with Johnson's position and such a policy was exactly what the congress created.[26] Nonimportation, it decided, should begin in the fall of 1774 and nonexportation a year later.

On the subject of what terms should be offered to England for a settlement, Maryland's delegates worked hard to keep everyone happy. Chase, Johnson, and Paca frequently dined with John Adams and on such occasions they often discussed Parliament's authority in the regulation of colonial trade. What they said is not recorded, but Adams was pleased. In his diary, he wrote that he admired and respected Johnson's "extensive knowledge of trade," thought Paca a reasoned "deliberator," and enjoyed Chase who spoke so "warmly."[27]

At the same time the colony's representatives delighted the conservative James Duane of New York. Although he was disappointed that Maryland had voted against Galloway's plan of union, Duane still believed the colony to be one of New York's closest allies in Congress. He told Chase that their respective colonies were "among those that are thought most strongly attached to the parent state and probably from us will be demanded a system of union." Duane was especially encouraged about the possibility of a coalition since Maryland's views paralleled New York's on the matter of England's authority to regulate commerce. The people of his colony, Duane wrote in December of 1774, are "of your opinion that the rights of regulating our trade bona fide, as the basis of an accommodation ought to be ceded in the most express terms. The Maryland arguments in which you had so great a share on this essential point were unanswerable—they never were attempted to be answered, yet unhappily they produced no conviction."[28] Thus, Maryland's delegates left the First Continental Congress having pleased both John Adams and James Duane. In congress as in Maryland, Chase, Johnson, and Paca were liked by all and probably trusted by few.

While the congress was in session, an event of immense political importance took place in Maryland—the destruction of the *Peggy Stewart*. No other single act in Maryland played a greater role in shaping the attitudes individuals adopted toward the political conflicts both within the empire and at home.

[26] Scharf, *History of Maryland*, 2:163; Herbert James Henderson, "Political Factions in the Continental Congress, 1774–1783" (Ph.D. diss., Columbia University, 1962), p. 63.

[27] E. C. Burnett, ed., *Letters of Members of the Continental Congress* (8 vols., Washington, D.C.: The Carnegie Institution, 1921–36), 1:67.

[28] James Duane (New York) to Samuel Chase (Annapolis), December 29, 1774, *ibid.*, pp. 87–89.

On October 15, 1774, Anthony Stewart's brig, the *Peggy Stewart*, dropped anchor in Annapolis harbor. Her cargo included 2,000 pounds of tea, imported by Stewart for Thomas C. Williams and Co. Stewart, with his partner and father-in-law, James Dick, had recently experienced several financial reversals. As of April they owed between £10,000 and £12,000. To one firm alone their unpaid obligations amounted to £6,000. Making matters worse was the fact that their latest mercantile ventures had resulted in a net 33 percent loss. Throughout the first half of 1774 their firm continued to falter. They quite simply could not pay their debts.[29]

According to his contemporaries, Anthony Stewart had two motives for deciding to pay the fees on the tea. One was to recoup his financial position. Given the temper of the colonies toward tea imports, he knew that the venture would be risky. On the other hand, if a cargo could be delivered and marketed, the profits would be great. Joshua Johnson believed Stewart was importing tea on the gamble that the cargo might be gotten through. But Johnson did not think the tea had much hope of entering the colony. On August 4, about ten weeks before the ship arrived in Annapolis, he wrote prophetically, "I should not be surprised to hear that you made a bon fire of the *Peggy Stewart*."[30]

Thomas Ringgold, an Eastern Shore planter who knew Anthony Stewart, interpreted his actions in a very different light. He believed Stewart foresaw the consequences of importing tea but that he deliberately sacrificed his ship in hopes of winning British favor: "From the whole of Mr. Stewart's conduct I have no doubt but he has premeditated the exploit to endear himself to the ministry."[31]

Whatever Stewart's motives, word of the tea's arrival spread quickly. According to one account the information was purposely leaked to certain violent elements by the port's deputy collector and comptroller John Davidson. Allegedly, Davidson did this because he, along with several other officials, belonged to a rival British firm whose vessel had not yet arrived. Besides carrying tea, the *Peggy Stewart* contained a "plentiful supply of other goods from London," and with nonimportation loom-

[29] Joshua Johnson to Wallace, Davidson, and Johnson, April 25, 1775, Wallace, Davidson, and Johnson Letterbook (cited hereafter as WDJLB), MHR; James Dick and Anthony Stewart to Rogers, Cooke, Tyson, and Porticus, May 10, 1773; to Meredith and Clymen, June 11, 1773; to Archibald Boyd, August 26, 1773; to Peter Halbent, October 26, 1773; to B. Wilson, February 7, 1774; to Rogers, Cooke, Tyson, and Porticus, April 25, 1774, all in James Dick and Anthony Stewart Letterbook, Duke University, Durham, N.C.

[30] Joshua Johnson to Wallace, Davidson, and Johnson, August 4, 1774, WDJLB.

[31] Thomas Ringgold to Samuel Galloway, October 25, 1774, Hall Papers, MHR.

ing their market seemed assured. Davidson and his partners, wanting to keep the market open until their cargo arrived, plotted the ship's destruction—or so one anonymous author maintained. "Chagrined at their own disappointment," he wrote, they determined "to wreack their vengeance on Mr. Stewart. They used every means to inflame the populace, not only to prevent the landing of the tea, but also to procure its destruction."[32]

Having done poorly at the June convention, the Hall-Hammond faction had been waiting for a chance to advance its political fortunes. They seized upon this opportunity. Hearing of the tea's arrival, John Hall and Matthias Hammond promptly called a public meeting where they denounced Stewart's perfidiousness and called for a county-wide meeting to be held in four days.[33] Hand bills announcing the meeting for October 19 were distributed, and on that day a number of people gathered at Annapolis. Groups from throughout the colony, including some from the Eastern Shore, conducted heated debates for several hours. The principal controversy concerned Stewart's punishment. Some demanded that he burn his ship with the tea inside. Others contended that a public burning of the tea was punishment enough. Eventually, a vote was taken and the majority ordered that only the tea should be burned. Unfortunately for Stewart, he, along with Rezin Hammond and Charles Ridgely, a member of the popular party from Baltimore, had already left for the brig before the decision was reached and they did not know the results of the vote. The vessel's captain, Robert Jackson, described the incident: "A messenger came from the shore and told Mr. Stewart that some of the people were against burning the Brigantine but then Mr. Rezin Hammond and Mr. Charles Ridgely who were there on board told Mr. Stewart in this deponent's hearing that if he did not immediately set fire to the Brigantine that his house and family would be in danger that night and added that if he did set fire to this Brigantine they would protect him."[34]

A significant point is that the Hammonds and Ridgely, along with two unknown figures from Anne Arundel County, Drs. Charles Warfield and Ephraim Howard, were in most accounts the principal catalysts of the vessel's destruction.[35] Similarly, the two most prominent opponents mentioned were Samuel Chase, who apparently was home from the Con-

[32] "Facts Relating to a Riot at Annapolis in Maryland," in Force, *American Archives*, 2:309–10.

[33] *Stewart Papers*; Robert Caldenburg, Loyalist Transcripts, Audit Office, British Public Records Office, London, series 12, vol. 6 (cited hereafter as *Loyalist Transcripts*).

[34] Robert Jackson, *Loyalist Transcripts*.

[35] *Stewart Papers*.

tinental Congress for a few days, and Charles Carroll, Barrister. Chase was not present at the actual burning, but according to a later account, he attempted to stop a group from Annapolis who had publicized their intent to fire the brig. Chase confronted them as they marched toward the dock, hoping to persuade them to follow a more moderate course. When he finished he was rebuked by Dr. Charles Warfield, the leader of the Annapolis band. By his former patriotic speeches Chase had "inflamed the whole country and now wished to get off by his own light." Warfield called Chase a submissive coward and told his followers to head for the docks.[36] At the dockside meeting, Charles Carroll, Barrister, called for moderation, persuading the audience to vote for the burning of the tea only.[37] But he was ashore while Rezin Hammond and Charles Ridgely were on board the *Peggy Stewart*. As a result, the barrister won the audience but lost the ship.

The burning had several consequences. Obviously, the popular party's alliance was weakened. Ridgely, the man to whom Chase had written in Baltimore asking support for Charles Carroll of Carrollton, had now defected to the side advocating greater violence. Such action was to become characteristic of that town's leaders in the months that followed. Critics labeled Baltimore the colony's center of agitation where "the most violent incendiaries resided," and popular party leaders often had difficulty controlling their Baltimore allies.[38] Still it is uncertain how much the party actually suffered at this time. The Baltimore merchant community had two other powerful leaders, William Lux and Samuel Purviance, and their stand on the burning is unknown. More significantly, if the party lost some favor with the radicals, it may also have picked up support from more moderate elements because of the fire. John Galloway, a merchant present at the scene, wrote that he was shocked by what he had witnessed: "This most infamous and rascally affair which makes all men of property reflect with horror on their present situation to have their lives and properties at the disposal of a mob is shocking indeed."[39]

The anxieties expressed by Galloway were felt by many that fall. From Bladensburg a trader told his brother in Glasgow that "since the burning of the ship at Annapolis the common sort seem to think they may commit any outrage they please; some of them told the merchants yesterday, that if they would not sell their goods, they would soon find a

---

[36] Broadside located in Fisher Transcripts, MHS.
[37] *Stewart Papers*; John Galloway to Samuel Galloway, October 20, 1774, MHR.
[38] Henry Stevenson and George Chalmers, *Loyalist Transcripts*.
[39] John Galloway to Samuel Galloway, October 20, 1774, Hall Papers, MHR.

way to help themselves." Mockingly he asked, "what think you of this land of liberty, where a man's property is at the mercy of anyone that will lead the mob?"[40] Similarly shaken, Charles Grahame urged James Russell to be extremely cautious. The *Peggy Stewart*, he observed, "made an unfortunate exit." From what he could learn, the fire had been required since "nothing but the destruction of the vessel could satisfy the violent part of the people." In this incident, Grahame emphasized, "you have a specimen of what they must expect who import tea or contravene the resolution of the Congress in any shape. Let me advise you to the utmost circumspection in your conduct both as to saying, writing and doing." William Fitzhugh, in the same vein, informed Russell that it was best to behave cautiously for the time being: "I assure you at this time we are in such a situation that it might be dangerous to raise a feud amongst the people."[41]

At the end of 1774 the popular alliance remained in a strong position. Not only had it weathered the *Peggy Stewart's* destruction and in the process possibly acquired a more respectable image, but it was now gaining important support. In September the Carroll family had discovered an important division in the proprietary circle and stood ready to benefit from the split. As Charles Carroll of Carrollton told his father, Daniel of St. Thomas Jenifer had fallen out with Eden. Apparently the governor, while on his recent trip to England, had accused Jenifer of having "intimate" connections with the Carrolls and their followers. "I would not have you drop a hint of it to anyone," he advised his father, but "it seems great complaints have been made to the guardians of the major's patriotism—it has been represented that he is too intimate with the *Carrolls* and the *Pacas* and others of the popular party. That they prevailed on the major to countenance the passage of the inspection law and the law making a provision for the clergy. Did you ever meet with an instance of greater meanness? I suppose this intelligence was given to Hamersley by the governor. It is quite in his style, but does honor to the person it was meant to asperse."[42]

With Jenifer's dismissal from the court party, the correspondence of Charles Carroll of Annapolis with him in 1773 now paid unexpected

---

[40] "Extracts of a letter from a Gentleman at Bladensburg, Maryland to his Brother in Glasgow," November 11, 1774, in Force, *American Archives*, 1:953.

[41] Charles Grahame to James Russell, November 9, 1774, and William Fitzhugh to James Russell, November 24, 1774, Coutts Bank Company Papers, Letters to James Russell.

[42] Charles Carroll of Carrollton to Charles Carroll of Annapolis, September 29, 1774, Charles Carroll of Annapolis Papers, MHS.

dividends.[43] Possibly Eden had been apprised of that exchange and had misconstrued the nature of the correspondence. Whatever his reasons, Eden now alienated and lost a powerful supporter. Jenifer made the transition from courtier to rebel quite easily. Within ten months he assumed the presidency of a new and revolutionary executive body, the Council of Safety. With him on the council were the major figures of the popular party.

Eleven days after the *Peggy Stewart* incident, Maryland's delegates returned from the Continental Congress and called for the provincial convention to ratify the Continental Association. At that meeting the popular party continued to dominate the colony's politics. Because of increasing tensions within the empire, the convention decided to elect a permanent Committee of Correspondence. The men selected were Charles Carroll of Carrollton, Charles Carroll, Barrister, Samuel Chase, Thomas Johnson, Jr., Matthew Tilghman, William Paca, and John Hall.[44] Apparently the Hall-Hammond faction's engineering of the *Peggy Stewart* burning did not enable it to make any major incursions into the power of Carroll and his allies, though Hall's placement on the committee may have been a minor victory.

At the session the delegates passed one piece of popular legislation, which again focused on the debt question. A few months earlier Richard Moale, a Baltimore merchant, had written reassuringly to a London trader, "I think you may rest assured that Congress will never resolve to prevent those from paying their debts who are able and willing. It may be that lawyers will be prevented from bringing suit for a time, and as this would I think be hurtful to American credit I think they will be very cautious."[45] Moale's prediction proved partially accurate. The delegates voted that no merchant or factor who violated the Continental Congress' nonimportation directives would be allowed to collect money owed him. Theoretically this measure still permitted the collection of debts by merchants who were obedient to the congress' word, but the convention's attitude made this difficult. Those traders who had previously opposed the restrictions found themselves at a distinct disadvantage. Anthony Stewart told a friend in February 1775 that "the present situation renders the collection of debts very uncertain."[46] Even mer-

[43] See chapter 5.
[44] *Proceedings of the Conventions*, p. 10.
[45] Richard Moale to James Russell, September 20, 1774, Coutts Bank Company Papers, Letters to James Russell.
[46] James Dick and Anthony Stewart to James Russell, February 24, 1775, James Dick and Anthony Stewart Letterbook.

chants like George Woolsey, an open supporter of the convention and a member of the Baltimore Committee of Observation, reported that "the troublesome times make people very tardy in paying their debts."[47]

The December convention avoided aggravating the existing tensions. Wishing to perpetuate a sense of internal unity, the delegates adjourned, in the hope that "as our opposition to the settled plan of the British administration to enslave America, will be strengthened by our union of all ranks of men, we do most earnestly recommend, that all former differences about religion or politics and all private animosities and quarrels of every kind from henceforth cease and be forever buried in oblivion."[48] The implementation of this sentiment proved considerably more difficult than its articulation. Already a varied reaction was developing over what the congress and the conventions had done. Some strongly supported the criticisms made of England. Samuel Chew of Annapolis advised his London correspondent to "depend on it that old England has forever lost the affection of America. The Boston and Greenback bills will never be forgot." A short time later he reiterated these sentiments: "Every province is learning the life of arms—you may depend that we will die before we give up our liberties and have our property at the disposal of a damn lot of rascally ministers." Another Annapolis trader, Stephen Stewart, sincerely hoped that Parliament would respond positively "to the moderate request and resolves of the General Congress." Surely, he reasoned, Parliament "will not be mad enough to destroy themselves to distress us."[49] More forcefully, Charles Carroll of Carrollton told his English merchant that the House of Commons must make considerable amends. "A partial repeal I am satisfied will not content America; now is the time for a total redress of grievances and unless they be totally redressed," he warned, "harmony and good understanding will never be re-established between the mother country and her colonies."[50]

Others were neither sanguine nor optimistic about the future. James Forbes, a trader in Benedicktown, grew increasingly apprehensive about the extent of public participation in the confrontation: "Unless the new Parliament relieves us, the situation of this continent will be terrible and

---

[47] George Woolsey to Robert Lisle, June 24, 1775, Woolsey and Salmon Letterbook, LC.

[48] *Proceedings of the Conventions*, p. 10.

[49] Samuel Chew to James Russell, October 26, 1774, and December 6, 1774; Stephen Stewart to James Russell, December 4, 1774, all in Coutts Bank Company Papers, Letters to James Russell.

[50] Charles Carroll of Carrollton to Wallace and Company, January 8, 1775, Charles Carroll of Carrollton Letterbook, Arents Collection, New York Public Library.

must bring ruin and distress to everyone that has any property here." Surveying the scene of militia exercises, committee meetings, and court stoppages in January 1775, William Fitzhugh reached a similar conclusion and fervently wished that "the Lord grant a speedy end to this Democratical confusion!"[51] With more vigor a Baltimore trader expressed identical sentiments to a friend in New York: "In the Philadelphia papers you will perceive that some persons in this town have had the imbecility to approve of the frantic proceedings of certain men who lately styled themselves delegates to a provincial Congress (with the same truth and propriety indeed they might have called themselves electors of the Holy Roman Empire), and abandoned to every sense of decency, propriety and loyalty have also in their turn, haberdashed certain resolves extremely curious."[52] An Annapolis resident, sympathetic to this perspective, observed that "every man, in private, must think that those congressmen and their satellites, the committee-men, are the truest though absurdest tyrants that any country ever had cause to complain of." He further knew that "were it not that their leaders with horrid cunning, have rendered a retreat so difficult, I foresee thousands anxious for a defection."[53]

Governor Robert Eden did not picture things in so desperate a light. Remaining outwardly calm, he maintained close contact with the leaders of the extralegal conventions.[54] Near the end of April, with the convention then sitting in Annapolis, he reassuringly wrote home, "You must not be under any uneasiness about me. I am well supported and *not obnoxious to any*, unless it be to some of our infernal independents who are in league with the Bostonians."[55] His favorable comments were justified, considering the cautious behavior of the delegates that April.

When the convention met on April 24, its first order of business concerned a rumor that the British might be planning an invasion of Philadelphia. Although the delegates reported this to their counterparts in that city they obviously saw no immediate threat, for they next selected delegates to attend the Second Continental Congress, scheduled to convene shortly in Philadelphia. The same men who had attended the

[51] James Forbes to James Russell, December 10, 1774, and William Fitzhugh to James Russell, January 6, 1775, both in Coutts Bank Company Papers, Letters to James Russell.

[52] "Extracts of a Letter from Baltimore to a Gentleman in New York," January 27, 1775, in Force, *American Archives*, 1:1190.

[53] "Extracts of a Letter from Annapolis to a Gentleman in New York," February 17, 1775, *ibid.*, p. 1208.

[54] Daniel of St. Thomas Jenifer to Charles Carroll, Barrister, January 15, 1775, Maryland State Papers, Red Books, 13:5, MHR.

[55] Governor Eden to ———, April 28, 1775, Chalmers Papers, New York Public Library.

former congress were selected, along with one additional figure, Thomas Stone, a pronounced conservative. Having made their selection, the delegates issued a resolution of instruction: "As this convention has nothing so much at heart as a happy reconciliation of the differences between the mother country and the British colonies in North America, upon a firm basis of constitutional freedom, so has it a confidence in the wisdom and prudence of the said delegates, that they will not proceed to the last extremity, unless in their judgments they shall be convinced that such measure is indispensably necessary for the safety and preservation of our liberties and privileges."[56]

The convention then considered some of the disorders within the colony. It issued an appeal for calm, recommending to the people that they "use their utmost endeavors to preserve peace and order throughout the province." The delegates declared May 11 a day of fasting, humiliation, and prayer to "Almighty God for the preservation of the rights and liberties of America and the restoration of peace, union and happiness to the British Empire." The convention then adjourned.

When the Committee of Correspondence received news of the first fighting at Lexington and Concord, this call for prayer appeared unusually prophetic. Word of the action went first to Philadelphia and from there to Annapolis. The account written by William Ellery, a member of the Newport, Rhode Island, Committee of Correspondence, reported that the Americans had achieved a decisive victory on the 19th, suffering forty killed and wounded while British casualties amounted to nearly 300. But the real importance of the conflict, maintained Ellery, was that "the sword of civil war has been drawn by the king's troops and sheathed in the bowels of our countrymen."[57]

Despite the startling news, the committee reacted calmly and made no move to summon the convention. Had the information arrived a few days earlier, before the delegates' departures, a strongly worded resolve of support would certainly have been issued. Even Governor Eden realized this, but he still retained his sense of self-assurance. Most of the colony's leaders, he believed, were of a cautious nature. Lexington and Concord would alarm, rather than inflame, them. In May he told the Earl of Dartmouth that the proceedings within the colony "have been conducted with great temper and moderation." He assured him that Maryland's delegates to the congress were good men who sincerely hoped to "bring about a reconciliation."[58]

[56] *Proceedings of the Conventions*, p. 12.
[57] *Ibid.*, pp. 13–16.
[58] Robert Eden to Earl of Dartmouth, May 5, 1775, Fisher Transcripts, MHS.

By the end of the next convention, in July 1775, Eden was speaking in a far different manner. The Continental Congress, faced with a war in Massachusetts and suspecting that more enemy forces were coming, had recommended that the colonies organize for their protection. To do this, the provincial convention in Maryland created an official provisional government which in reality only sanctioned what already existed in fact. The convention became the colony's supreme governing authority, a role it had played since June 1774. Defensive measures had been undertaken as early as December, although these were now greatly expanded. One major departure undertaken by the July convention was the establishment of an executive branch, the Council of Safety. According to the convention, the council was to "superintend the execution of the orders and the resolutions of the convention and occasionally from time to time promote the prudent and necessary preparations for defense."[59] Initially consisting of sixteen members, eight from each shore, the membership was reduced to seven in January 1776. Daniel of St. Thomas Jenifer was selected its first president, a position he held throughout the council's existence.

Eden considered the Council of Safety a major usurpation of his authority. He told Dartmouth in August that he could no longer exercise any real power because of its creation. He also included, within the letter, some comment on the character of Jenifer:

The weakness of the civil government has so manifested itself in most of the colonies since the commotions began that your Lordship will not be surprised at the timid declining to express their sentiments—and the cautious or cunning refusing to do it. . . . It has ever, my lord, been my endeavor, by the most soothing measures I could safely use, and yielding to the storm when I could not resist it, to preserve some hold of the helm of government, that I might steer, as long as should be possible, clear of those shoals which all here must sooner or later, I fear get shipwreck'd upon. I have found great advantage in this as yet; but when the Council of Safety, as they are called, meet amongs't whom, in the convention proceedings your lordship, I am sorry to say it, must see the names of two of the Council of this Province, viz Bordley and Jenifer—(but the former has declined acting; the other is to act and . . . will I doubt not, be taken notice of) when, I said my Lord the Council of Safety meet I am under the apprehension that the authority I have hitherto supported will cease to be of any great avail.[60]

The establishment of the council helped the popular party increase and solidify its hold on the colony's power structure. From its perspec-

[59] *Proceedings of the Conventions*, p. 24.
[60] Robert Eden to Earl of Dartmouth, August 27, 1775, Fisher Transcripts, MHS.

tive the council's creation came at a most opportune time. Chase and Ridgely had recently reunited and were once more working together. Instrumental in achieving this rapprochement was Chase's promise to Ridgely to keep him informed of the congress' actions so that he might know how to guide his mercantile activities.[61] As a result, the party was again unified while its opposition, the Hall-Hammond faction, was going through a trying period. Charles Carroll of Annapolis reported that the opposing faction was fragmenting because of internal dissension among its members.[62]

At the July convention the strength of the popular faction was evident, as its members secured control of all the important positions and committee assignments. Tilghman was once again elected president. He also received a seat on the Council of Safety, as did Thomas Johnson, Jr., Samuel Chase, William Paca, Charles Carroll, Barrister, and Charles Carroll of Carrollton. Jenifer, as noted, became president of the new executive authority. These same men, with the exception of Jenifer and Charles Carroll of Carrollton, were also returned to the Continental Congress.

Yet the popular party's control, if secure in Annapolis, began to encounter some resistance in the rest of the colony, as emotions grew more taut. Recognizing the threat of unrest, the convention admonished the people to guard against taking the law into their own hands. Wanting to enhance its own image, the convention laid more restrictions on the prosecution of debt cases. From August on, a creditor desiring to sue for debt had to obtain a license from the local Committee of Observation. Presumably the convention intended that the local committees would not show any marked compassion for the creditors.

But debt alleviation alone could not quiet all the varieties of internal dissent, especially dissent centered around Governor Eden. He had left the colony for England in June 1774 to take care of personal business matters. When he returned in November, Eden encountered an extra-legal convention which had usurped the legislative powers of the assembly. The convention had ordered the counties to organize militia forces and to elect local committees to enforce the Continental Association. These acts, as well as the convention's recommendation that £10,000 be raised for defense by levy, indicated to Eden how far his authority had diminished. He quickly devised a clever plan and issued new commissions for the colony's justices of the peace at the beginning of 1775. By placing new men in power, he hoped to secure his authority at the local level.

---

[61] Samuel Chase to Charles Ridgely, May 16, 1775, Ridgely Papers, MHS.
[62] Charles Carroll of Annapolis to Charles Carroll of Carrollton, June 7, 1775, Charles Carroll of Annapolis Papers, MHS.

Robert Christie, Sheriff of Baltimore, suggested the idea to the governor. The replacement of justices, observed George Chalmers, was part of Eden's general program to create local elements of power loyal to his command: "It was part of this plan which he concerted with Mr. Christie, to bring about a change in the commissioners of the peace, as the then justices were of the utmost inflammatory part of the community."[63] The new justices were of an entirely different sort. As one of the convention supporters observed, Eden's appointees were "but too well known for their uniform opposition to every measure that has been adopted for the preservation of American freedom." They were "below contempt, having no respect or authority among the people." Eden's move thus constituted "a total revolution in the magistracy" and this convention supporter personally feared the consequences if it should be "executed throughout the province."[64] Eden did not succeed in effecting the wholesale changes planned. New justices assumed office in the counties around Annapolis, but even here the displacement was chaotic. James Christie, a relative of Robert's, complained that "we are in such terrible confusion with our politics, there is no depending on anything and that added to other things makes me wish myself out of this province."[65]

Eden next attempted to form a private paramilitary protection association. James Christie commented on the conditions influencing this decision: "We have some violent fanatical spirits among us, who do everything in their power to run things to the utmost extremity, and they are gone so far, that we moderate people are under the necessity of uniting for our own defence after being threatened with expulsion, loss of life, etc., for not acceding to what we deem treason and rebellion."[66] The defensive association which Eden organized demanded a pledge from all who joined to act as a "posse-commitatus" when one of their members was threatened. Supporters of the governor assured the men who enrolled that they would be supplied with adequate arms, but this promise was never fulfilled. How large the organization became is unknown; the only estimate surviving is one made by Hugh Kelly, a loyalist who told an English loyalist investigating commission that by the end of 1775, the entire organization including men from Virginia and Pennsylvania contained 1,900 men capable of bearing arms.[67]

[63] George Chalmers, *Loyalist Transcripts*.
[64] "Extracts of a Letter from a Gentleman in Harford County, Maryland to His Friend in Philadelphia," March 13, 1775, in Force, *American Archives*, 2:124-25.
[65] James Christie, Jr. to Gabriel Christie, February 27, 1775, Gilmor Papers, MHS.
[66] James Christie, Jr. to Lt. Col. Gabriel Christie, February 22, 1775, in Force, *American Archives*, 2:1653.
[67] Hugh Kelly, *Loyalist Transcripts*.

One of the areas in which the protective association enjoyed widespread popularity was Maryland's Eastern Shore, especially the southern counties. Already that region showed signs of developing a movement opposing the new power structure in Annapolis. In future years this pattern would intensify as the struggle there took on the characteristics of broad social protest. On November 15, 1775 the Worcester County Committee of Observation wrote the Council of Safety that "we and the rest of the friends of liberty in this county are in a bad situation; we have no ammunition and the tories exceed our number. We hope you will send us assistance as soon as you can."[68] Obviously the committee considered its prospects poor, and with good reason. A few days later Issac Hammond stood before the Worcester County Court explaining to the justices what most of them already knew—namely, that a well organized movement to overthrow the provisional government's authority had been created. Hammond told the justices that near the end of October he, along with thirty or forty others, had attended a meeting to form a loyalist association. At that time they had signed a pact which read "that all those persons who signed the same bound themselves to stand together in behalf of their king and to oppose the measures of the committee and to support each other to be in readiness in twenty-four hours warning to rescue any of their number."[69]

Appearing before the court a week later, Barclay White also discussed the organized loyalist resistance. Not only did the members intend to protect themselves, but they hoped to frustrate the provisional government's control of the region. White reported that some had engineered a kidnapping plot in conjunction with Lord Dunmore, the former royal governor of Virginia, who was then raising a slave army in hopes of retaking his colony. According to White, the conspirators intended to "take the Committee of Worcester County out of their beds in the dead of night" and transport them to Lord Dunmore. Since the authorities in Worcester had information of Dunmore's supplying their opponents with arms, White's allegations seemed entirely possible.[70]

[68] "Letter from Chairman of the Committee of Observation Worcester County to Eastern Shore Council of Safety," November 1775, in Force, *American Archives*, 3:1574.
[69] Deposition of Issac Hammond, November 20, 1775, Adjutant General Papers, located within Executive Papers, MHR.
[70] Deposition of Barclay White, November 30, 1775, *Archives of Maryland*, ed. William H. Browne et al. (68 vols., Baltimore, 1883——), 12:377; Benton Harris, Chairman Worcester County, Committee of Observation to Council of Safety, November 17, 1775, Adjutant General Papers, MHR; "Letter from Chairman of Worcester County, Committee of Observation to Eastern Shore Council of Safety," and "Deposition of Mary Robbins," both in Force, *American Archives*, 3:1574.

Similar conditions prevailed in neighboring Somerset County. There Issac Atkinson, an outspoken opponent of the provisional government, told a large gathering "that it was rebellion the way the people of Boston was going on, and that he believed the people of Boston wanted a king of their own in America." Someone in the audience shouted back that "they would back him with five hundred for he is the only man that has opened their eyes and is the man that ought to be upheld."[71] Opposition as blatant as this was naturally reported to the Council of Safety. "From what we have been able to gather," relayed a Somerset official, "an association under the most solemn oath of secrecy and entirely repugnant to the resolves of the provincial convention has been subscribed by more than one hundred of the inhabitants of these counties who are sworn enemies to the common cause of our country and are ready to receive the yoke of bondage from the hands of the British Parliament."[72] Hoping to regain some control, the Committee of Observation summoned Atkinson. He came, but refused to be cowed. Littleton Ayres, a man present that day, described what he saw. A number of men, approximately thirty, he recalled, "assembled at the court house of Somerset County where the committee sat, with short clubs in their hands, and that when said Atkinson came out of the court house, near fifty people crowded around him, and the said Atkinson said a day must be appointed and they must fight it out."[73] That day would come soon enough.

Threats to the convention's authority and to the general order of the society came from other quarters. In April, Governor Eden wrote his brother of the fears developing within the colony's leadership circle. The news of fighting at Lexington and Concord crystallized conservative apprehension on both sides of the imperial dispute. "We are at this time," Eden observed, "in a state of thorough confusion." That afternoon, he continued, "I was waited on by six gentlemen of respectable characters, requesting me, that as, in consequence of this news, they were under great apprehensions of some attempt being made by the servants or slaves for their liberty. They hoped I would commit the custody of the arms and ammunition to the freemen of the country for that otherwise they would not answer for consequences from an insurrection." Eden, thinking his visitors overstating the danger, did his best to calm them. He

[71] Depositions Concerning Issac Atkinson, November 7, 1775, Adjutant General Papers, MHR.
[72] Peter Waters to Council of Safety, November 21, 1775, Executive Papers, box 2, MHR.
[73] "Deposition of Littleton Ayres," December 1, 1775, in Force, *American Archives*, 3:1584.

pointed out that their nervous reactions "were only going to accelerate the evil they dreaded from their servants and slaves."[74] But they remained unconvinced and the governor, after consultation with his advisers, agreed to deliver "up arms and ammunition to be employed to keep the servants and negroes in order."[75]

Within a month reports coming into Annapolis seemed to confirm these fears. A grand jury investigation in Dorchester County collected evidence of insurrectionist plots. Apparently some whites were speaking openly of a desire to organize coalitions with slaves in order to implement drastic social changes. On May 22, James Mullineux told the grand jury of a conversation he had recently had with a wheelwright, John Simmons. Mullineux related that he happened to be passing Simmons "who was engaged in fishing" when Simmons "asked him what news and whether he was not going to Cambridge on Monday to muster?" Mullineux answered no and asked Simmons if he were. In anger the wheelwright replied:

. . . Yes but not to muster for he had other business, and further said to this deponent that he understood that the gentlemen were intending to make us all fight for their lands and negroes, and then said damn them (meaning the gentlemen) if I had a few more white people to join me I could get all the negroes in the county to back us, and they would do more good in the night than the white people could do in the day on which this deponent said suppose it was so, where could they get the ammunition from. He the said Simmons answered where they could find it, and further added that if all the gentlemen were killed we should have the best of the land to tend and besides could get money enough while they were about it as they have got all the money in their hands. There is Robert Goldsborough and Colonel William Ennals I'll be bound has money enough by them. I wish I had one of William Ennals bags I would put it to a better use than he does damn him would I, and from the whole tenor of the conversation that passed between them, this deponent declares that the said Simmons appeared to be in earnest and desirous that the negroes should get the better of the white people.[76]

Simmons' remarks reflected more the existence of intense social anger than any real effort at conspiratorial organization. Nonetheless during the summer fears of slave insurrection continued to be expressed. In August a minister described the tense situation to a friend in England. Not only

[74] Robert Eden to William Eden, April 28, 1775, Fisher Transcripts, MHS.
[75] Personal Record of George Chalmers, Chalmers Papers, New York Public Library.
[76] Dorchester County Court Papers, Gilmor Papers, MHS.

was the Quebec Act fraught with great danger but "to complete the horrid scene," he complained that "the governor of Virginia, the captains of the men of war, and mariners, have been tampering with our Negroes; and have held nightly meetings with them; and all for the glorious purpose of enticing them to cut their masters' throats while they are asleep. Gracious God! that men noble by birth and fortune should descend to such ignoble base servility."[77]

That fall the fear of slave insurrections continued and even grew. George Woolsey, a Baltimore merchant, reported that all eyes were riveted on the activities of Dunmore in Virginia.[78] Dunmore was then fighting Virginia's provisional government for control of the colony. To recruit the necessary manpower, he was raising a slave army as a complementary force to back his regulars. On November 15 he publicly offered freedom to all slaves and indentured servants who would repair to his banner and take up arms in support of the king. Eden recounted the impact the news made in Maryland. The "minds of the people," he told Lord George Germain, "were extremely agitated by Lord Dunmore's proclamation giving freedom to the slaves in Virginia; our proximity to which colony, and our similar circumstances with respect to Negroes augmenting the general alarm, induced them to prohibit all correspondence with Virginia by land or water."[79] What disturbed the convention even more were the activities of Marylanders who followed Dunmore's example. From Dorchester County came the following dispatch:

The insolence of the Negroes in this county is come to such a height, that we are under a necessity of disarming them which we affected on Saturday last. We took about eighty guns, some bayonets, swords, etc. The malicious and imprudent speeches of some among the lower classes of whites have induced them to believe, that their freedom depended on the success of the Kings troops. We cannot therefore be too vigilant nor too rigorous with those who promote and encourage this disposition in our slaves.[80]

Unruly debtors added to the tensions by taking advantage of the disorganized conditions. A creditor, Richard Henderson, sadly observed that "the private animosity of some men render my property insecure

[77] "Extracts of a Letter from a Clergyman in Maryland to His Friend in England," August 2, 1775, in Force, *American Archives*, 3:10.

[78] George Woolsey to George Salmon, January 26, 1776, Woolsey and Salmon Letterbook, LC.

[79] Robert Eden to Lord George Germain, January 25, 1776, Fisher Transcripts, MHS.

[80] Report of Dorchester County Committee of Inspection, Fall 1775, Gilmor Papers, MHS.

and bring my family into the utmost terror."[81] Not only were debtors refusing to pay and threatening those who might attempt to collect, but they also openly attacked the jails, freeing persons taken into custody for defaulting on their payments. To suppress these outbursts, the militia had to be called, but bands of disgruntled persons continued to roam parts of the colony, harrassing both creditors and tax collectors. During the December convention the delegates took specific notice of these disorders and resolved to suppress "the combinations in some few parts of this province against the payment of levies—such conduct evidently leading to throw this province into disorder, confusion and anarchy."[82]

But the convention failed to instill any sense of restraint in its opponents. Those against the provisional government saw little reason to curb their tongues or change their behavior, unless directly threatened. A case in point is that of Robert Davis of Anne Arundel County. Having made disrespectful remarks about the new authorities, Davis was ordered by the local committee to appear and explain his conduct. According to the committee Davis had said that he "looked on the Americans to be exceedingly wrong in their present pursuit," and "therefore he would support freedom by keeping clear." Moreover he threatened that "if the poor of the province would raise and take the Congress, he would head or back them and confine them and all our leading men." For these expressions Davis received a summons, but on the appointed day he refused to appear. After unsuccessfully requesting his attendance a second time, the committee directed a militia unit to apprehend him. When the soldiers arrived at his home, the commanding officer, Edward Norwood, went up to the house. As he approached the fence, Norwood told the committee, "Davis came out to his yard gate with a gun in his hand and said stand off you damned rebel sons of bitches—I will shoot you if you come any nearer and declared he would not attend the committee." Undeterred, Norwood persisted and persuaded Davis to go on the promise that no harm would befall him. Davis went before the committee and the convention, apologized for his excesses and was discharged without punishment.[83]

With the variety of disorders occurring throughout the colony, the need for order became increasingly apparent. Both British officials and patriots saw a crisis approaching. William Eddis wrote in September, "I

---

[81] Petition of Richard Henderson, August 4, 1775, *Archives of Maryland*, 11:50.
[82] *Proceedings of the Conventions*, pp. 114–15; Robert Christie to J. T. Chase, January 3, 1776, J. T. Chase Papers, MHS.
[83] Case of Robert Davis, Executive Papers, box 1, MHR.

am however clearly of the opinion that all power will quickly be trans-
ferred into the hands of the multitude."[84] Robert Eden reiterated these
sentiments a month later. "All power is getting fast into the hands of the
very lowest people. Those who first encouraged the opposition to government and set these on this licentious behavior will probably be
amongs't the first to repent thereof."[85]

The growing confusion also disturbed the Carroll family. Originally
they had spoken enthusiastically, almost naively, of the colony's cause.
Charles Carroll of Carrollton had written in September 1774 of his happy
anticipation that the imperial crisis would "be decided by arms." Several
weeks later his father discussed the dispute with England, concluding
with certainty that "these things considered I make no doubt the contest
will end to the entire satisfaction of America." To their friends in England they expressed similar opinions. During May 1775 the elder Carroll
rejoiced in a letter to William Graves, "our unanimity is so perfect as to
be almost incredible. No laws, human or divine, have been so implicitly
obeyed as those framed by the general congress and the provincial conventions."[86] His son told Wallace and Company of London in June, "I
have the pleasure to inform you that America is more united than ever
before." Again that September he warned that "if the British ministry
should compel us to go on fighting in defense of our just rights we shall
prove victorious, and baffle all their attempts to reduce these colonies by
force of arms to the unequal and iniquitous conditions proposed by the
ministry and Parliament."[87] But by December the Carrolls realized that
unanimity and a singleness of purpose required firm action. They were
learning that revolution was not possible without some anarchy. As
Charles Carroll of Annapolis observed to his son, the present times made
it essential to "establish a government. The convention must say what
sort of one. Rogues and enemies must be punished. Nothing essential to
the general safety can be done as things are now."[88]

[84] William Eddis, *Letters from America* (London, 1792), p. 235.
[85] Robert Eden to Earl of Dartmouth, October 1, 1775, Fisher Transcripts, MHS.
[86] Charles Carroll of Carrollton to Charles Carroll of Annapolis, September 12,
1774; Charles Carroll of Annapolis to Charles Carroll of Carrollton, September 29,
1775; Charles Carroll of Annapolis to William Graves, May 29, 1775, all in Charles
Carroll of Annapolis Papers, MHS.
[87] Charles Carroll of Carrollton to Wallace and Company, June 4, 1775, and
September 18, 1775, both in Charles Carroll of Carrollton Letterbook, Arents Collection, New York Public Library.
[88] Charles Carroll of Annapolis to Charles Carroll of Carrollton, December 1, 1775,
Charles Carroll of Annapolis Papers, MHS.

The task facing the popular party was thus growing formidable. The traditional government structure had been overthrown but a disintegrative process had set in affecting the entire society. Faced with disorder among slaves, debtors, and independent minded people—and both unable and unwilling to accept independence as a goal—the party had to proceed tactfully yet firmly to preserve a semblance of order.

7 : A Reluctant Independence

The popular party weathered the opposition and threats encountered in 1775, but the situation it faced in 1776 was no less dangerous. Disorders and rumors of insurrectionist activities among slaves, servants, and lower class whites persisted. By June the convention faced growing chaos as disaffection on the lower Eastern Shore reached the stage of an open rebellion. Angry blacks, dissatisfied whites, and passionate loyalists, including some of Dunmore's agents, had joined together in defiant resistance. Dunmore himself sailed up the bay from Virginia with his forces. Hoping to stabilize the area, the delegates sent troops there with orders to patrol the shoreline and prevent "any servants, negroes, or others," from reaching the British ships. Great efforts were necessary to discourage such flight since no issue was more sensitive to the convention than the increasing disaffection. Governor Eden's departure from the colony exemplified this. When he was leaving, several bondsmen escaped to his ship and were granted asylum. Hearing this, the Council of Safety sent up a loud, but unsuccessful, howl of protest, bitterly attacking Eden for breaking his word that he would "not receive any runaway slaves on board."[1]

Other problems were becoming more serious by the spring of 1776. Discipline among the county militias, especially those on the Eastern Shore, was rapidly deteriorating. On June 8 the Committee of Observation in Caroline County sadly reported of "information being made to

[1] Council of Safety to Robert Eden, June 23, 1776, *Archives of Maryland*, ed. William H. Browne *et al.* (68 vols., Baltimore, 1883——), 11:513; Sir Robert Eden to Charles Carroll of Carrollton, June 24, 1776, Gratz Autograph Collection, Historical Society of Pennsylvania, Philadelphia, Pa.

this committee that sundry evil disposed persons had been endeavoring to disunite the good people of this county in the common cause of America and had actually prevailed on several companies of militia to lay down their arms."[2] Officials from Somerset County relayed a similar account on June 25. "We are at this time unhappily convulsed, not only by external, but by internal enemies. A number of the people in different parts of the county particularly Merumsco and Perrehawkin, have for some days past been assembling in a disorderly and tumultuous manner, and we have reason to believe from a series of convenient circumstances that a plan has been concerted between them and the ministerial forces."[3] Three days later, on the afternoon of June 28, the Maryland convention voted unanimously for independence; but it did so only after a long and heated morning session devoted to the formulation of plans for containing the internal rebellion.

In an effort to preserve order, the convention followed several strategies. Military occupation, harsh penalties including "death without benefit of clergy," and total confiscation of property were authorized to intimidate and restrain opponents of the new order. Secondly, the convention, under the popular party's direction, drew up a constitution that placed control of Maryland in the hands of its upper class. But the implementation of such control did not come easily. To gain support and popularity for the new government, the delegates promised, and later enacted, fiscal legislation which penalized their own class dearly. None of them liked this policy, but all, with the exception of Charles Carroll of Annapolis, supported the measures as concessions necessary to retain power. The elder Carroll, considering the "popular measures" too high a price, opposed and eventually alienated all those who supported them, including his son, Charles Carroll of Carrollton.

Many of these problems were already well in evidence as the convention gathered in December 1775. Opponents of the provisional government were reportedly recruiting blacks for Dunmore and obstructing the organization of militia forces. Committees of Observation were also encountering resistance in their efforts to exercise authority. Despite the mounting tension, the popular party continued to dominate the convention as it increased its hold over all the major offices. Matthew Tilghman was again elected president. Other party men, particularly Charles Car-

---

[2] Committee of Observation, Caroline County to Council of Safety, June 8, 1776, *Archives of Maryland*, 11:481.

[3] Committee of Observation, Somerset County to Council of Safety, June 25, 1776, Maryland State Papers, Red Books, Maryland Hall of Records, Annapolis, Md., 2:101 (cited hereafter as *Red Books*).

roll of Carrollton, Thomas Johnson, and Charles Carroll, Barrister, gained the important committee assignments.[4] Daniel of St. Thomas Jenifer, while not a convention member, remained president of the Council of Safety, now reduced to seven members to make it more effective. The Maryland delegation selected to serve at the congress in Philadelphia further attested to the popular faction's control. Matthew Tilghman, Thomas Johnson, Robert Goldsborough, William Paca, and Samuel Chase were chosen. Charles Carroll of Carrollton, while not a delegation member, attended the congress as an unofficial observer. Carroll's role there was like that of a party manager. He advised the representatives and made certain that his friends back home were well informed of the congress' actions.[5]

At the December convention several defence measures were passed. The delegates authorized raising a force of 1444 troops and emitting 535,111½ dollars in paper money to finance it. Realizing the difficulties ahead, the convention recommended, as a first rule of conduct, that "all officers and soldiers . . . attend divine services when their situation will permit."[6] Having raised the troops, the delegates then showed how much they hoped never to use them by voting unanimously on January 12 against any moves toward independence: "Do not without the previous knowledge and approbation of the Convention of this province assent to any proposition to declare these colonies independent of the crown of Great Britain."[7] According to the convention, the primary task of Maryland's congressional delegation was to work for a reconciliation with England.

Soon after their assembly's adjournment the popular leaders further evidenced their desire to avoid a military conflict by undertaking a private effort to preserve peace. Daniel of St. Thomas Jenifer played the pivotal role in this sequence of events. On January 15 he wrote Charles Carroll, Barrister, of his plans: "Governor Eden is now with me and very desirous and willing to co-operate with you and Mr. Tilghman, and such other gentlemen of the convention, as are willing to disperse the cloud that has almost overshadowed and is ready to burst upon us. Let me therefore beg and beseech you to use your influence with Mr. Tilghman, Mr. Johnson, Mr. Hollyday and Mr. Stone to dine with me tomorrow if

[4] *Proceedings of the Conventions of the Province of Maryland* (Annapolis, 1836), pp. 39, 54, 55, 58, 63, 64.
[5] Charles Carroll of Carrollton to Charles Carroll of Annapolis, March 18, 1776, Charles Carroll of Annapolis Papers, Maryland Historical Society, Baltimore, Md. (cited hereafter as MHS).
[6] *Proceedings of the Conventions*, p. 98.
[7] *Ibid.*, p. 83.

the convention should break up in time, if not the next day or any other day that may suit."[8] Within a few weeks Jenifer's efforts produced concrete results. Eden, along with Tilghman, Johnson, Jenifer, and others entered into a series of discussions concerning some solutions to the imperial conflict. The governor came out of the meeting highly pleased, and soon wrote to Dartmouth of the colony's peaceful designs in the hope that a complimentary letter might lead to a settlement of the outstanding issues: "I must, my lord, do the members of the last convention as they call it, and the people of this province the justice to say, I am satisfied they are so far from desiring an independency that if the establishment of it were left to their choice, they would reject it with abhorrence, so incompatible would such a state be with their real undissembled attachment to and affection for his majesty."[9]

Clearly the colony's leaders wanted no part of independence. Their attitude on this subject remained constant, and even after July 1776 many privately yearned for a return to the empire. But by March of that year some of them were beginning to discuss openly the possibility of separation. Two letters, one by Robert Alexander the other by Charles Carroll of Carrollton, give evidence of the harsher attitude developing within the leadership circle. Both expressed strong indignation over Lord North's Prohibitory Act. Alexander, a prominent Baltimore merchant attending the Continental Congress, told the council what he thought North's actions represented. Ironically, Alexander would soon swing over to the British, for whom he served as an adviser during the war. But in early 1776 he was still a patriot. "I shall make no comments on this act," he declared, since "it is only a further step in that system of tyranny hitherto pursued by that Bastard who under the influence of a Scotch-Junto now disgraces the British throne. What measures Congress may pursue in consequence of this act I know not. With me every idea of reconciliation is precluded by the conduct of Great Britain and the only alternative absolute slavery or independency. The latter I have often reprobated both in public and private, but am now almost convinced the measure is right and can be justified by necessity."[10]

Charles Carroll of Carrollton was even more committed to independence. Carroll by this time had gained an exciting assignment from the

<hr>

[8] Daniel of St. Thomas Jenifer to Charles Carroll, Barrister, January 15, 1776, in Peter Force, ed., *American Archives* (4th series, 6 vols., Washington, D.C. 1837–1846), 4:680.

[9] Robert Eden (Annapolis) to the Earl of Dartmouth (London), January 25, 1776, Fisher Transcripts, MHS.

[10] Robert Alexander to the Council of Safety, February 27, 1776, *Archives of Maryland*, 11:189.

Continental Congress. He, along with his cousin John Carroll (a Catholic priest) and Samuel Chase, were completing the necessary preparations for an official visit to Canada. Congress had directed them to undertake the journey in hopes of securing Canadian support in the imperial conflict. Just prior to their departure Carroll evaluated for his father what he personally believed the state of things to be. "The difficulties and objections to reconciliation and dependence are every day increasing. The restraining bill or rather the bill for confiscating American property breathes such a spirit of depredation and revenge that I am satisfied peace with Great Britain is at a great distance and dependence out of the question. The colonies will never again be dependent on Great Britain," he asserted, since "we must either be totally independent or totally dependent—or in other words, entirely subdued and reduced to the condition of a conquered people to be kept under and made subordinate to Great Britain."[11] Obviously he did not favor the latter course.

After March the question of independence became an essential concern of the popular leaders. To those outside the colony, such as Carroll and Chase, the step may have seemed easy enough. No doubt their perspective from Canada or even from Philadelphia convinced them that the risks of separation could be confronted and overcome. But to those at home the decision appeared increasingly dangerous. Eventually they sanctioned the move, but they did not give their approval enthusiastically. There were too many reasons, both external and internal, for caution. Undisciplined militia forces were growing harder to control and the dependable units lacked proper arms and training. Dunmore's influence continued to grow, inspiring some and terrifying others. His agents, black and white, were said to be everywhere clandestinely inflaming the passions of servants and slaves. Spokesmen among the poorer whites were becoming bolder as their criticisms of the society's privileged classes increased. They presented a simple message. The aristocracy was leading the fight against Great Britain, so that it might enslave the poor. In early February Robert Gassaway, a modest farmer from Frederick County, spoke resentfully of this to his fellow militia men. "It was better for the poor people," he declared, "to lay down their arms and pay the duties and taxes laid upon them by the king and Parliament than to be brought into slavery and to be commanded and ordered about as they were."[12]

[11] Charles Carroll of Carrollton to Charles Carroll of Annapolis, March 18, 1776, Charles Carroll of Annapolis Papers, MHS.
[12] Proceedings of the Council of Safety, April 4, 1776, *Archives of Maryland*, 11:309; for reports of Dunmore's activities, see Benjamin Rumsey to Council of Safety, March 7, 1776, and Council of Safety to Talbot County Committee of Observation, March 12, 1776, both in Force, *American Archives*, 5:93, 185; James Murray to Council of Safety, March 15, 1776, *Archives of Maryland*, 11:249.

The council was further informed that spring of the actions of Alexander Magee, "an ordinary farmer" in Baltimore County, whose opinions were eliciting noticeably favorable responses. Magee's argument was that the common people should remain loyal because "the American opposition to Great Britain is not calculated or designed for the defence of American liberty or property, but for the purpose of enslaving the poor people thereof."[13]

All of this was reported to the popular leaders, none of whom knew what effect independence would have and all of whom wanted a guarantee of security if it came. Specifically, they hoped to prevent a divisive social and political revolution. A barrier to curb adverse currents of change had to be created. But to erect such a structure was difficult—only a man with exceptional talents could do it. Daniel of St. Thomas Jenifer possessed, in a measure more than most, the peculiar abilities necessary for the task. An incredibly devious individual, he labored through myriad channels for this purpose. The design he pursued was best illustrated by his actions during the abortive kidnapping of Governor Robert Eden. With tactics of realpolitik such as this he hoped to preserve a sense of unity between the radical and conservative elements.

The chain of events leading to the attempted abduction began on February 25, 1776. On that day, two of Maryland's congressional delegates, Robert Alexander and John Rogers, asked the Council of Safety to grant a pass to a merchant friend of theirs, Alexander Ross. Ross wanted to travel through Maryland on his way to visit Virginia's governor, Lord Dunmore. Dunmore was then battling the rebel forces in Virginia for the control of that colony, and a pass was needed to go through military lines. Both Maryland and Virginia denied the request, but Ross went anyway. He slipped safely through to Dunmore, but was arrested on his return. The apprehending officer, Captain Baron, discovered upon Ross's person documents addressed to Governor Eden from British Colonial Secretary Lord George Germain. The letters were immediately forwarded to Williamsburg, where General Charles Lee had just assumed command of the Continental army's southern department. Lee was not only concerned with military matters; he was also cooperating with such men as Richard Henry Lee in an effort to arouse greater resistance toward the British in the southern colonies. He considered Maryland's political leaders to be particularly lacking in zeal. In a letter to Richard Henry Lee, the general described Maryland's convention and Virginia's Council of Safety as "the namby pambys of the senatorial part of the

[13] Baltimore County Committee of Observation to Council of Safety, May 7, 1776, *Archives of Maryland*, 11:415–16.

continent" who were continually "growing more timid and hysterical."[14]
The intercepted letters afforded Lee an opportunity to advance his
political aims. One of the letters clearly indicated that Eden had been
transmitting confidential material to Germain concerning the feasibility
of a military landing in Maryland or Virginia. Lee decided the evidence
warranted Eden's arrest and suggested this to Samuel Purviance, chairman of the Baltimore Committee of Observation. Lee wrote Purviance
because he knew the Baltimore chairman shared his political views and
the two were good friends. In addition, William Lux, Purviance's deputy
chairman, was also a correspondent of Lee's.[15] Information received earlier by Lux lent credence to the idea that someone, possibly Eden, was
communicating military information about the possibility of a landing in
Maryland and Virginia. Joshua Johnson had written Lux from London in
September 1775 that "there is every preparation going on to enforce the
war imaginable and next spring you may expect it will be pushed with
the utmost vigor. Some say that they are contemplating a project to land
small bodies of troops at different places. If so, Virginia will very likely
be one of those places and if they are successful you may expect the next
visit."[16] This news which Lux had probably related to Purviance now
took on a new dimension. Apparently Eden had been writing to Germain
and he had to be stopped.

After receiving Lee's letter on April 14, Purviance acted quickly.
First, he forwarded Lee's letter and the intercepted message to congress,
enclosing an anonymous note characterizing the Maryland Council of
Safety and convention as "timorous and inactive" bodies that were
"afraid to execute the duties of their stations."[17] Next, he ordered Samuel Smith, a captain of the Baltimore militia, to proceed to Annapolis.
Smith's orders proposed two courses of action. If Smith found Eden
attempting to leave Annapolis, he was to arrest the governor and bring
him to Baltimore. If he did not encounter the governor, he was to ren-
dezvous with three members of the Baltimore Committee of Observation
in Annapolis, who would have additional orders.[18]

[14] "The Lee Papers Collection," *New York Historical Society Collections* (2nd
series, 80 vols., New York: New York Historical Society, 1841–1947), 1:379.
[15] *Ibid.*, p. 239.
[16] Joshua Johnson to William Lux and Daniel Bowly, September 5, 1775,
Wallace, Davidson, and Johnson Letterbook, Maryland Hall of Records.
[17] Thomas Johnson to Council of Safety, April 17, 1776, in E C. Burnett, ed.,
Letters of Members of the Continental Congress, (8 vols., Washington, D.C.: The
Carnegie Institution, 1921–36), 1:426; Richard Henry Lee to Samuel Purviance, April
22, 1776 in James Curtis Ballagh, ed., *The Letters of Richard Henry Lee* (2 vols., New
York: The Macmillan Co., 1911–1914), 1:170; see also pp. 186–87.
[18] "The Orders of Captain Samuel Smith," Purviance-Courtenay Papers, Duke
University, Durham, N.C.; *Archives of Maryland* 11:359–81.

When Smith arrived in Annapolis, he was told that Eden had not attempted to leave the capital. Because Eden was not interested in escaping, Purviance was denied the pleasure of taking him prisoner. But his letters to the congress had the desired effect. After receiving the information, congress replied with a reprimand to the Council of Safety and ordered Eden seized. The council refused to make the arrest, but did send Charles Carroll, Barrister, John Hall, and William Paca to the governor. These men extracted a promise from Eden that he would not leave the province.[19]

Once Eden had given his word, the Council of Safety angrily took up the question of Purviance's conduct. On April 24 he appeared, by order, before the council and received a rancorous tongue lashing from all the members present. Benjamin Rumsey succinctly expressed the anxiety most of them felt when he wrote "that the assumption of power intrusted to another body was a high handed and dangerous offence."[20] Obviously, the authority of the council had been challenged and chaos could have resulted. The precedent Purviance might have set was extremely dangerous. The council symbolized what law and order remained within Maryland, and Purviance's action threatened to undermine the already tenuous structure. The council members expressed this sentiment in a letter to the congressional delegation. "If," they observed, "the governor is treated with ignominy and rigor and laid under arrest and guarded we cannot tell what will be the consequence—this we are certain of—our government will be shaken to its very foundations, and in what form it would be settled again we know not."[21]

Because of the gravity of the situation the council decided that the full convention should conduct a thorough investigation. The council explained its reasoning to John Hancock when it summoned home its representatives from Philadelphia: "To dissolve the government and subvert the constitution by the seizure and imprisonment of the governor, we conceived to be a measure of too much delicacy and magnitude to be adopted without calling and consulting the convention of this province; we saw no necessity urging us to such an extreme and were therefore determined not to expose the province to immediate anarchy and convulsion."[22] In their message to the congressmen, the council referred specifically to the source of their displeasure: "Since our last nothing new has

---

[19] *Archives of Maryland* 11:359–81; Force, *American Archives*, 5:961, 963, 970, 983, 1009, 1560, 1562.

[20] Benjamin Rumsey to B. E. Hall, May 1776, Benedict Edward Hall Papers, MHS.

[21] Council of Safety to Maryland Deputies in Congress, *Archives of Maryland*, 11:355.

[22] Council of Safety to John Hancock, April 18, 1776, *ibid.*, p. 349.

occurred except the examination of Mr. Purviance before our board; he at first deny'd the anonymous letter, afterwards on recollection acknowledged it contained some of his sentiments but could not remember when he wrote them. He prevaricated most abominably. We hope the time of calling the convention will meet with your approbation, we apprehended bad consequences from delay."[23]

After the sending of these messages, the council's president, Daniel of St. Thomas Jenifer, left hastily for Philadelphia. This departure seemed odd, for on the surface he was the official most offended by Purviance's behavior. Given the tense situation in the colony and his personal stake in seeing Purviance properly punished, he had some difficulty explaining his absence. He wrote Charles Carroll of Annapolis asking him to obtain "forgiveness from my brethren for my abrupt departure from Annapolis. You must be my advocate. It was a maddened fit that came upon me; and it appeared to me from a previous question or two, that if I had asked leave in form I should not just then have obtained it." To make his leave more understandable, he further confided to Carroll that "my health required a jaunt, and I found considerable relief whilst on my journey."[24]

But, as Jenifer told Carroll, there was an additional reason for the quick trip. He had to get to Philadelphia in order "to consult upon the principal points to be discussed in the convention and the delegates to attend."[25] Jenifer had been deeply involved with Purviance in the Eden affair, and he may well have told Tilghman, Johnson, Paca, and other popular party members not to push the upcoming investigation too far. If they did, the party's ties with Baltimore would be seriously weakened. Whatever Jenifer's message, the convention passed an extremely mild censure of Purviance when it met. The Baltimore merchant was wrong in what he did, said the delegates, but only because "of his active zeal in the common cause."[26]

To the public, Jenifer and Purviance represented opposite political persuasions, but in private they worked closely and profitably together. Purviance, who kept an account of his meetings with Jenifer, recorded in March that "Mr. Jenifer received me with the warmest and most flattering expressions of behavior of our committee and the inhabitants and of myself in particular—among other things he told me had hitherto no small credit in the Council for snubbing me and finding fault with my

---

[23] *Ibid.*, p. 385.
[24] Daniel of St. Thomas Jenifer to Charles Carroll of Annapolis, April 30, 1776, in Force, *American Archives*, 5:1146.
[25] *Ibid.*
[26] *Proceedings of the Conventions*, p. 144.

conduct as an overzealous warm and hot headed man (or words to that effect). I told him I hoped he would in future derive as much credit and honor by supporting me and approving my conduct as he had hitherto done by censuring me or condemning me." Purviance further wrote that Jenifer had assured him of the propriety of forceful and independent action in a critical situation. Jenifer "gave it as his opinion," he noted, "that on extraordinary occasions Committees of Observation ought not to be limited or confined to the bare extent of their usual powers in ordinary cases, but ought to have authority to act in some measure as a Council of Safety."[27] Purviance undoubtedly remembered this sentiment at the time of the Eden affair as Jenifer led the chorus of condemnation. Using every opportunity to earn credit with the moderate and conservative members of the council and convention, Jenifer vociferously criticized the Baltimore chairman for his rash and precipitous conduct. He happily noted the acclaim which resulted not only in Maryland but in Philadelphia as well: "We are highly applauded in this city for our spirited conduct in the late conspiracy."[28] The applause was gratifying because Jenifer had probably staged the debate specifically to solidify moderate support.

Throughout the entire kidnapping affair, Jenifer knew exactly what Purviance planned. The evidence implicating him, while not complete, suggests that Jenifer not only understood but approved of all that occurred. During the official hearings, one of the most important persons to testify was Captain Samuel Smith of the Baltimore militia. He recounted how Purviance had summoned him, displayed Lee's letter and ordered a contingent of militia to Annapolis. Nothing in his public testimony implicated Jenifer, but in a private account later written by Smith, he interjected an additional paragraph which he set off by a series of dashes. Commenting on the material added, he noted that "the paragraph marked '———' I recollected since I wrote the narrative delivered to the Honorable Council." What Smith omitted seems remarkable considering the people he addressed that day. His interpolation begins just after he had arrived in Annapolis and presented his orders to the three waiting Baltimore committee men:

I went ashore and delivered a letter to Messors John Smith, Benjamin Nicholson and John Sterrett. They told me what had happened between them and the Hon. Council. I asked them whether I might not Inform the Colonel

[27] Purviance-Courtenay Papers, Duke University.
[28] Daniel of St. Thomas Jenifer to Charles Carroll of Annapolis, April 30, 1776, in Force, *American Archives*, 5:1146.

of my business. They said, that the Council had enjoined the strictest secrecy, and advised me not to mention it till I had their (the Council's) leave—next I showed them my orders, they advised me not to show them to any other person, as it was their opinion they were in some degree improper; they said they were to wait on Major Jenifer after breakfast and would let me know when they returned how I was to act. On their return to the Coffee House they told me he highly approved of the tenders being sent down, and that they were to meet the Council at ten o'clock who would give me orders.[29]

Smith never made this information public, nor was it brought out during the hearings. When questioned, Smith and Purviance scrupulously avoided any hint of Jenifer's involvement. At one session a delegate asked Purviance if Smith's instructions were "to be shown to the Council." Purviance replied, "I did not tell him to show them but presumed when he got to Annapolis he would be under their directions."[30] Purviance's response implied that such had never occurred, whereas Smith recorded that Jenifer not only received but also approved of the orders and the militia's dispatch.

Before the kidnapping affair none of Jenifer's political allies, with the exception of Charles Carroll, Barrister, knew of his involvement with Purviance. The Barrister, for his part, understood the relationship, since he often participated in the private discussions between Jenifer and Purviance. But one question still remains. Why did Purviance allow Jenifer to profit at his expense, why did he not expose him? The principal reason Purviance endured these attacks was that the council president supplied him liberally with arms. This, in turn, increased his standing within the Baltimore community. Purviance himself was under attack by men of an even more radical temper, and they were not easy to restrain. Both Jenifer and Purviance knew this and they each had reasons for wanting these elements controlled. William Lux, Purviance's principal assistant, wrote of this factor when discussing with Jenifer the conduct of Baltimore's Committee of Observation: "I have just received your favor of the 6th and am much pleased that our committee are able to justify their conduct to your satisfaction. I believe they all mean to do right; but it is quite necessary to keep them within bounds because their zeal will sometimes outstrip their prudence."[31]

To shore up his political position, Purviance carefully calculated his strategy. Whenever possible, he struck an aggressive pose, declaring his

[29] Purviance-Courtenay Papers, Duke University.
[30] *Archives of Maryland*, 11:376.
[31] William Lux to Daniel of St. Thomas Jenifer, April 10, 1776, in Force, *American Archives*, 5:836.

hatred of everything British. Bringing arms into the town greatly enhanced his image in this regard. To get these materials, all of which were in short supply, he had to work with Jenifer, since the council president directed the importation and distribution of arms. Purviance explained the nature of this relationship in his records while summarizing the events of a secret meeting he had with Jenifer in March: "In a conversation between him and me by ourselves, I observed to him how useful a parcel of long rifled guns would be for the defence of our harbor against boats and to prevent landing of forces—to which he replied do sir order whatever you think proper or necessary of that sort, and it shall be paid for."[32] This arrangement satisfied the needs of all concerned. Jenifer had his man in Baltimore, Purviance his position, and the popular cause avoided splintering. It cost the Baltimore chairman some public abuse, but to his followers this sort of critical attention seemed more a compliment than a reprimand. Indeed, Jenifer's attacks probably increased Purviance's standing with his more radical supporters.

Thus Jenifer's tactics during the Eden affair and the months preceding independence were twofold. By providing arms to Purviance and agreeing to the arrest of Eden, he solidified his ties with the more radical elements. Purviance's desires had been respected and in the end the Baltimore chairman achieved his goal. Two days after the convention's mild censure of Purviance, it voted to expel Eden from the colony. Jenifer's position is unknown, but those of the popular party who were members of the convention voted to a man for expulsion. At the same time Jenifer, by publicly denouncing Purviance and securing an apology from General Charles Lee for his interference in Maryland's internal affairs, reaffirmed his credit with the Council of Safety and the colony's conservative forces. From the end of April on he did nothing to block a move for independence. He had strong ties with men of all political persuasions, and he believed those connections would guarantee him a political future.

In May independence still seemed a dangerous step, though as one partisan of Great Britain sadly observed, the idea had been in "fashion" for some time.[33] Fearful of turmoil, the majority of the convention held fast to the position that its congressional representatives should make no moves toward separation from the empire. Richard Henry Lee depicted

---

[32] Purviance-Courtenay Papers, Duke University; see also Samuel Purviance to Daniel of St. Thomas Jenifer, February 4, 1776, *Red Books*, 14:23; Daniel of St. Thomas Jenifer to Charles Carroll of Annapolis, June 16, 1776, Charles Carroll of Annapolis Papers, MHS.

[33] —— to ——, January 22, 1776, Corner Collection, MHS.

Maryland's timidity in a letter to Charles Lee: "You asked me why we hesitate in Congress. I'll tell you my friend, because we are heavily clogged with instructions from those shamefully interested proprietary people."[34] By the end of the month this attitude had not officially changed. On May 21 the convention unanimously resolved to continue the instructions given to its delegates that December, specifically forbidding them from agreeing to independence.

Yet many of the colony's important figures were coming to the disturbing realization that independence was inescapable. Thomas Stone, a man who longed to stay in the empire, prayed for an end to the crown's intransigence. "If the commissioners do not arrive shortly," he told Jenifer, "and conduct themselves with great candor and uprightness to effect a reconciliation, a separation will most undoubtedly take place and then all governors and officers must quit their posts and new men must be placed in the saddle of power."[35] James Hollyday, an influential moderate in the convention, shared Stone's uneasiness of what independence might mean. "I think it probable," he suggested, "that men who have shown a disposition to moderation and an aversion to changes will not remain unnoticed by those who shall ascend to the top of the machine."[36] His apprehensions were justified by the existing conditions. William Eddis wrote home on June 11, characterizing the convention and those elements within the colony who were causing consternation to Hollyday and men like him: "The utmost moderation and temper, considering the complexion of the times, has indeed hitherto marked the proceedings of that body; but violent and inflammatory men, are now industriously straining every nerve to excite general confusion and plunge us fatally deep in schemes of Independence." Eddis' description of violent men referred in particular to an organization started in Baltimore that spring —the Whig Club.[37]

During the last months of the imperial crisis, Baltimore's merchants aggressively challenged England's authority. Unlike their more conservative counterparts in other trading centers, they warmly advocated separation. At the time of the Stamp Act controversy many of them had

---

[34] Richard Henry Lee to General Charles Lee, April 22, 1776, Ballagh, *Letters of Richard Henry Lee*, 1:182–83.

[35] Thomas Stone to Daniel of St. Thomas Jenifer, April 24, 1776, *Archives of Maryland*, 11:383.

[36] James Hollyday to Thomas Stone, May 26, 1776, letter in the possession of Herbert E. Klingelhofer; see Herbert E. Klingelhofer, "The Cautious Revolution: Maryland and the Movement Toward Independence: 1774–1776," *Maryland Historical Magazine* 60 (1965), 289.

[37] William Eddis, *Letters from America* (London, 1792), pp. 304, 306.

joined the Sons of Liberty, and they now formed the Whig Club. Its founding came at a crucial time. With the question of independence under serious consideration, the Whigs' swaggering presence served to create further pressures and tensions. Their aim was the expulsion of anyone opposing their conception of the American cause. Warnings signed with the code word "legion" were sent to those suspected of Tory leanings. The recipients were told to leave town immediately or face physical harm. A crown supporter living in Baltimore explained that town's attitude which was symbolized most effectively by the Whigs. In his opinion ethnic hatred was responsible. Practically all the important traders were of Scotch-Irish descent and they, naturally, despised the British: "This town is chiefly settled by Scotch-Irish (in liberality of sentiment at least three centuries behind the other British subjects in America) and it is a melancholy truth, that such are to a man violently bent on supporting the good old cause, (that is the cause of fanaticism and sedition) by taking arms against the best government (with all its imperfections) on earth."[38]

The club's harsh tone disturbed a number of the colony's leaders, including certain members of the popular faction. But in reality these people had little to fear, for most of the club's members were allied to the popular coalition. It is possible that Purviance, the Whig's principal leader, decided to form the organization as a gesture of defiance after his censure. It is also possible that a moderate such as Jenifer was delighted to have an extremist organization in Baltimore both to intimidate his opponents and to emphasize by contrast his seeming moderation. And whatever the violence of its rhetoric, the Whig Club confined its political activities geographically to the immediate vicinity of Baltimore.

On June 11 Matthew Tilghman wrote from Philadelphia that the Continental Congress was allowing the representatives of the middle colonies to return home for consultations on independence. "This postpone was made to give an opportunity to the delegates from those colonies which had not as yet given authority to adopt this decisive measure to consult their constituents." He advised, "it would be well if the delegates to the convention were desired to endeavor to collect the opinion of the people at large in some manner or other previous to the meeting of the convention." He knew such discussion would promote considerable tur-

---

[38] "Extract of a Letter from Baltimore to a Gentleman in New York," January 27, 1775, Force, in *American Archives*, 1:1190. For an interesting study of the ethnic composition of Baltimore's merchant community, see James Leroy Votto, "Social Dynamics in Boom-Town: The Scotch-Irish in Baltimore, 1760–1790" (Master's thesis, University of Virginia, 1969).

moil, but unfortunately there was no alternative: "We see with the deepest concern the attempts from various quarters to throw the province into a state of confusion, division and disorder, but trust, the exertions of those who are the true friends of virtue and the American cause will be adequate to the surrounding difficulties and dangers. From every account and appearance the king and his ministers seem determined to hazard everything upon the success of the sword."[39] Five days later, Daniel of St. Thomas Jenifer gave the same message to Charles Carroll of Annapolis. Congress, he said, had directed the middle colonies' representatives to return home in the hope that those provinces would "take off their restrictions and let their delegates unite in the measure."[40]

Tilghman, Jenifer, Johnson, Charles Carroll, Barrister, and all the popular party members were ready for the move. With their coalition solidly organized and, thanks to Jenifer's labors, their standing good in both conservative and radical ranks, they could anticipate their continued control of the convention. If further encouragement were needed to persuade those still cautious, it soon arrived in the persons of Samuel Chase and Charles Carroll of Carrollton, who returned to Philadelphia from their Canadian mission on June 11. Four days later they were in Maryland, campaigning vigorously for separation. Chase concentrated his efforts among the county delegates. On the 21st he wrote John Adams "that a general dissatisfaction prevails here with our convention. Read the papers and be assured Frederick speaks the sense of many counties. I have not been idle. I have appealed in writing to the people. County after county is instructing."[41] Besides Frederick, other counties including Anne Arundel, Charles, and Talbot soon issued resolutions for independence, though some complained bitterly that the meetings were "engineered."[42]

Charles Carroll of Carrollton worked equally hard but in a different and ultimately unsuccessful direction. Happy that independence was at last here, he quickly recognized the importance of his friends' continued domination of all the major institutions. With dissent growing on the shore, as rumors of slave and tenant insurrections spread, with the breakdown of discipline among some militia units, and with the increasingly passionate and demagogic extolment of democracy by certain politically

[39] *Archives of Maryland* 11:478.
[40] Daniel of St. Thomas Jenifer to Charles Carroll of Annapolis, June 16, 1776, Purviance Papers, MHS.
[41] Adams Papers, MHS.
[42] Force, *American Archives*, 6:1017–19; Oswald Tilghman, *History of Talbot County, Maryland, 1661–1861* (Baltimore, Md.: Williams & Wilkins Co., 1915), 2:92.

ambitious elements hoping to ride the crest of upheaval to power—with all of this, the need for secure authority was obvious. In this situation a correctly guided military force could play the decisive role, and such a body had recently been created.

A request from the Continental Congress for military personnel had been on the convention's agenda since June 3. On June 25 the delegates agreed to contribute 3405 men for service until December 1, 1776. To command the force, the convention selected, to the delight of people such as Carroll, Thomas Johnson and awarded him the rank of Brigadier General. Johnson's election assured the popular faction of further institutional power, but there remained one disquieting fact. The convention had also adopted a resolution making militia officers ineligible for service in future conventions. Carroll was both elated and concerned because he considered Johnson's presence in the convention of great importance. "We cannot do without him in the convention and yet," he complained, "if the vote above mentioned is not repealed he cannot be a delegate to the convention."[43] Several confusing changes rapidly followed. At the convention's first full session in July, the delegates rescinded the resolve barring officers from political participation. Johnson, at that time, enjoyed a Brigadiership, held a seat in the Continental Congress, and another in the convention. But three days later the delegates reconsidered the question of multiple office holding, and on July 4 revoked Johnson's military commission, he having apparently indicated his preference for remaining in the convention.

It cannot be determined at exactly what time the convention decided for independence. Most likely the decision came before its actual vote on June 28. Charles Carroll of Carrollton, in a letter to his father written on the morning of that day, gave the impression that the matter had already been decided and most of the delegates were now preoccupied with the desire to return home. "The instructions to our deputies in Congress will certainly be rescinded," he observed, for "the impatience of the members to get home in time enough for the harvest will conspire with the instructions to render this a short session."[44] On the 28th, Samuel Chase provided further inducement by reading a message he had received from John Adams. The letter reported that New Jersey, Delaware, and Pennsylvania had instructed their delegates to vote for independence. With this information in hand the delegates realized that all the colonies with the possible exception of New York favored independence. Adams con-

[43] Charles Carroll of Carrollton to Charles Carroll of Annapolis, June 28, 1776, Charles Carroll of Annapolis Papers, MHS.
[44] *Ibid.*

cluded his letter saying, "I hope that before Monday morning we shall receive from Maryland instructions to do right."[45] The convention granted Adams his wish by a unanimous vote that afternoon.

With the coming of independence, the popular party remained firmly in control. The Carrolls, Chase, Tilghman, Johnson, Paca, and Jenifer continued to act collectively. Their ties to Baltimore were still strong and their credit with all political persuasions was generally secure. Now, as Chase told Richard Henry Lee, a "new government" had to be established.[46] Chase and his fellow party members wanted one that they could dominate. In the creation of a constitution, the party would show its basic conservative and aristocratic characteristics, but because the men of the party were political realists, they simultaneously continued to promote popular measures. Such was the price of power. Such too was the price of any hope of revolutionary success.

[45] Charles Francis Adams, ed., *The Works of John Adams* (10 vols., Boston, 1850–1856), 9:413–14.
[46] Samuel Chase to Richard Henry Lee, June 29, 1776, Chase Papers, MHS.

8 : The Search for
a Vanishing Authority

Once independence was accepted, Samuel Chase and Charles Carroll of Carrollton immediately turned their attention to the process of forming a new government.[1] In some respects, the very ideology of self-determination that they had employed to justify their opposition to Great Britain now worked against them. The idea that the people should govern had been widely expressed. Orators at public meetings and writers in the colony's newspapers asserted this theme again and again.[2] Chase, Carroll, Johnson, Paca, and the party's other leaders had not meant for the message to be taken literally. What they actually wanted was an orderly society whose direction would remain in the hands of the rich and well born. Those popular leaders who had guided the colony haltingly toward independence now worked to establish a highly conservative constitution. During the Constitutional Convention, the aristocratic characteristics of the popular party came to the surface. The party leaders were determined to shape the institutions of the new government in a fashion that would insure their future control.

From the very beginning these men encountered strong opposition. On July 3 the provincial convention called for an election on the first day of August for delegates to a convention that would draw up a constitution.[3] The election order stipulated that the property qualifica-

---

[1] Samuel Chase to Richard Henry Lee, July 29, 1776, Chase Papers, Maryland Historical Society, Baltimore, Md. (cited hereafter as MHS).

[2] For a timely example of such arguments see *Maryland Journal*, July 3, 1776.

[3] *Proceedings of the Conventions of the Province of Maryland* (Annapolis, 1836), July 3, 1776, p. 184.

tions for voting of the proprietary era were to remain in effect, but on election day five counties flagrantly ignored the prescribed voting regulations. Election judges in Kent, Prince George, Frederick, Queen Anne's, and Worcester counties were forcibly thrown out and those who took over allowed all taxpayers who bore arms to vote.

The men elected to the convention were not to the popular party's liking. When they convened in August, Samuel Chase immediately moved to disqualify the delegates from these counties on the grounds that people not qualified to vote had participated at the polls.[4] The convention approved Chase's motion and new elections were conducted in the five counties. This time the property qualifications were enforced, but the effect of their application was minimal. Eighteen of the twenty men originally elected were returned; Chase's attempt to alter the composition of these delegations proved completely unsuccessful.

These election results suggest that discontented political forces were at work. Forty-three of the seventy-six delegates elected had never before served in a convention. More significantly, the very leaders of the popular party came under strong attack. In Anne Arundel County, they ran into strong and well-organized opposition. The earliest election reports indicated a trend against them. The Council of Safety wrote Charles Carroll of Carrollton and the other deputies attending the Continental Congress in Philadelphia, "Yesterday our election for this county began and it is not yet ended. We are sorry to inform you that Messrs. Johnson and Paca and Carroll of Carrollton from present appearances will not be elected. Worthington, Carroll, Barrister, Chase and R. Hammond are greatly beyond others on the poll."[5] These early reports proved correct as the popular party's adversary, the Hall-Hammond faction, achieved an important victory in placing Rezin Hammond on the county's delegation. By continuing to emphasize their democratic sympathies, particularly on election day, the Hall-Hammond faction appeared to be cutting into the popular party's political base.

A post election investigation into possible voting irregularities in

[4] *Proceedings of the Convention*, pp. 213–18; *Calendar of Maryland State Papers*, in Maryland State Papers, Red Books, no. 4, 1:46 (8 vols.; Annapolis: Maryland Historical Records Commission, 1943–58). These calendars, prepared under the general direction of Dr. Morris L. Radoff, Mr. Gust Skordas, and Mr. Roger Thomas, constitute an excellent guide to the materials contained in the Maryland State Papers, which are located at the Maryland Hall of Records, Annapolis, Maryland (cited hereafter as MHR). For this study I have used the unpublished Maryland State Papers, which are bound into a series of volumes designated by the titles, Red Books (cited hereafter as *Red Books*), Black Books, Blue Books, and Brown Books.

[5] Council of Safety to Maryland Deputies, August 2, 1776, *Archives of Maryland*, ed. William H. Browne et al. (68 vols., Baltimore, 1883———), 12:163.

Anne Arundel County graphically revealed the rhetoric and tactics employed by the Hall-Hammond people. According to one witness, Samuel Godman, the polls had just opened when "Mr. R. Hammond told the people present that every man that bore arms in defense of his country had a right to vote, and if they were allowed no vote they had no right to bear arms."[6] Another witness, Thomas Henry Howard, testified that he heard Rezin Hammond "address the people from the hustings, and in his address he advised the people to lay down their arms if they were denied the privilege of voting, for it was their right and they ought not to be deprived of it."[7]

Because of Hammond's fiery rhetoric, which played on the genuine dissatisfaction of those people excluded from voting, an election disturbance of some sort occurred at the Anne Arundel polls. Although the investigating panel eventually decided that the wrongs committed did not warrant a new election, the events in Anne Arundel County reflect the nature and form of the disorders that occurred throughout the province on election day. James Disney, Jr., one of the clerks at the poll in Anne Arundel, told the examiners that soon after the officiating judges had ordered the voting to begin, they "were interrupted by a number of people present which insisted on every man's having a vote that bore arms." The judges, Disney continued, promptly refused and began reading the order of the convention requiring each voter to have at least 50 acres of land or property worth 40 pounds sterling. Disney himself was then told to read the order once more, but just after he began, several of the bystanders cried, "Pull him down, he shall not read, we will not hear it, and if you do not stop and let every free man vote that carries arms we will pull the house down from under the judges."

The presiding officials judiciously adjourned the proceedings briefly, but when they reopened the polls, several people again presented themselves to vote who were not qualified. Prominent among those, Disney reported, were soldiers of a military unit, the "Flying Camp," which was proceeding northward to join the Continental forces. One of their officers, upon seeing his men's actions, interposed and told them bluntly that they were not qualified. Angry over the rebuff a group of the enlisted men then "drew up on Gallows Hill, and there was recommended to lay down their arms and go home, and if any of their officers interrupted them to knock them down—and if they do not support Mr. Hammond's election, they would all be slaves and if they did, they would all be

[6] Deposition of Samuel Godman, August 27, 1776, *Red Books*, 11:8.
[7] Deposition of Thomas Henry Howard, August 27, 1776, *ibid*.

free."[8] The committee found out that the men encouraging this action were Thomas Harwood and Matthias Hammond, Rezin's brother. Samuel Godman overheard Matthias Hammond tell the soldiers the evening of the dispute, "Gentlemen, Mr. Rezin Hammond has stood as a candidate for this county and as many of you think him worthy of your trust, we hope will come and vote for him." But the soldiers were by then discouraged. One of them plainly told Hammond "that they could not vote unless they were worth 40 sterling at least," and another observed sarcastically that "the whole company was not worth 40 sterling."[9]

As the election turned out, Hammond did not need the soldiers' support. His victory, along with that of B. T. B. Worthington, came at the expense of several leading popular party members, including Charles Carroll of Carrollton, William Paca, and Thomas Johnson. Chase and Charles Carroll, Barrister, were elected along with Hammond and Worthington but the Anne Arundel results indicated the party was in trouble. The election in Annapolis, which was authorized to send two delegates to the convention, gave seats to Paca and Carroll of Carrollton, but the Carrolls were still worried because Thomas Johnson would not be a member.[10] For a time they hoped that the election investigation would invalidate their county's results so that Johnson might get another opportunity to run, but a turn of events in Caroline County made this unnecessary. William Richardson, a delegate from Caroline, received a colonelcy in the "Flying Camp" and promptly resigned his convention seat. Johnson held enough property in the county to gain a place on the ballot, and with the help of his party's organization, he won the vacated seat.[11]

The Carrolls and other popular party members were not the only ones dissatisfied with the August election. Their rivals in Anne Arundel, John Hall, Matthias Hammond, and Rezin Hammond, who had wanted to secure at least one more seat, were equally displeased. As the Anne Arundel delegation stood after the August election, the popular party still held sway. Charles Carroll, Barrister, and Chase were really opposed only by Rezin Hammond, because B. T. B. Worthington was not a member of either political organization.

The Hall-Hammond faction still hoped to make John Hall a member of the convention by reviving a strategy they had originally employed to gain popularity in the county before the August election. Their preelec-

[8] Deposition of James Disney, Jr., August 27, 1776, *ibid.*
[9] Deposition of Samuel Godman, August 27, 1776, *ibid.*
[10] *Proceedings of the Conventions*, pp. 209–12.
[11] Charles Carroll of Carrollton to Charles Carroll of Annapolis, August 20, 1776, Charles Carroll of Annapolis Papers, MHS.

tion plans had centered on using the county's militia as a vehicle for political activity. At a meeting dominated by Hall and the Hammonds on June 26, the Anne Arundel County militia proposed a radical form of government, which was made public in the middle of July. Essentially, the militia program outlined a governmental system very democratic and decentralized in structure consisting of three branches, with the legislative the most powerful. The legislature was to be made up of two houses elected annually by the people and was to have the power to choose a governor without a veto and to make all the major judicial appointments. All transactions of the legislature were to be recorded and published annually. At the county level, the people and not the central government were to choose all officials. The militia additionally called for two very popular measures. It proposed a permanent restriction on all suits of law to stop debt proceedings until the end of "this time of public calamity." And it urged that all taxes be raised by "a fair and equal assessment in proportion to every person's estate and that the unjust mode of taxation heretofore used be abolished."[12]

Once the Hall-Hammond faction obtained the militia's endorsement of this program, it published the scheme in the colony's newspapers during the middle of July. Then the leaders of the organization began circulating the proposals throughout the county. Within a month they had gained enough signatures to make their next move. They realized the complexion of the Anne Arundel delegation and could accurately gauge the response that would be forthcoming. On August 22, the *Maryland Gazette* printed a series of instructions to the delegates of Anne Arundel County, signed by 885 freemen. These instructions largely duplicated the plan formulated by the militia. The only feature added was that all freemen who paid taxes should be allowed to vote. No doubt Hall and Hammond had developed this proposal in response to the turmoil that had occurred over this very issue on election day. Prior to the instructions' publication, the county's delegates had been sent advance copies, so that the *Gazette* also included the delegation's response. Naturally, Rezin Hammond heartily endorsed the proposals while Chase, Charles Carroll, Barrister, and B. T. B. Worthington disagreed. Essentially, they objected that the instructions would not provide a "proper security for liberty or property." These three delegates announced that they would hold a public meeting on the 26th in Annapolis to discuss these issues.[13]

Charles Carroll of Carrollton's conduct during this confrontation is

[12] *Maryland Gazette and Baltimore Advertiser*, July 23, 1776; *Maryland Gazette*, July 18, 1776.
[13] *Maryland Gazette*, August 22, 1776.

instructive. For the first time, he began fully to appreciate the very serious social and political problems created by the Revolution. His loss of innocence proved a painful experience. After the decision for independence in June, he continued optimistic about the future and steadfast in his allegiance to the American cause. He went to the Continental Congress at Philadelphia in July, and shortly after his arrival informed his father of the Howe brothers' proposals of peace and pardon "to those who will lay down their arms and return to their duty." But since these proposals constituted only "a preliminary condition" they were, he continued, "treated with contempt and indignation by every good and honest American." Carroll happily observed that at last "every man's eyes must now be opened: the blindest and most infatuated must see and I think, detest the perfidy and tyranny of the British Constitution, Parliament, and Nation."[14] Strong words these, but Carroll's attitude was to change dramatically within a short time.

Indeed, within nine days he began to express some mild uneasiness. "The Hammonds," he wrote, "are making interest against me because I voted against instructions which I deemed to be dishonest and which I was convinced were not agreeable to the sense of the majority of my constituents unless I could suppose the majority dishonest." Specifically, Carroll was referring to his vote in an earlier convention against a measure "for stopping public interest" because "it would have subverted public credit and struck at our paper money."[15] In other words, he knew that such a measure would undermine the value of the province's currency and thereby make the paying off of old debts an easy matter. Carroll, a creditor, didn't like that and he, along with 40 other members of the convention, had voted against that resolve, while only five had voted "aye." Though Carroll himself managed to win reelection in August, it was significant that of the 41 who voted against the resolve only 18 were reelected.

This sort of criticism did not deeply bother Carroll; if anything he considered it an unavoidable consequence of public life. But the Hall-Hammond instructions were a different matter. Neither the reforms advocated nor the threat posed to his party's control could be dismissed lightly. He noted disapprovingly that the people were already contending too much about "forms of government and liberty." Once he and Chase had time to digest the proposals, they decided to respond through

---

[14] Charles Carroll of Carrollton to Charles Carroll of Annapolis, July 20, 1776, Charles Carroll of Annapolis Papers, MHS.

[15] Charles Carroll of Carrollton to Charles Carroll of Annapolis, July 29, 1776, Charles Carroll of Annapolis Papers, MHS.

the tactic of an open debate. Carroll hoped to stage the public confrontation so that Chase and Charles Carroll, Barrister, would emerge the vic-
tors. To insure a triumph, he requested his father's assistance: "Hammond has been persuading the people not to meet at Annapolis. Do use
the Howards and prevail on them to get the people to attend at Annapolis on the day mentioned in the printed letter. If two or three hundred of
the substantial free holders were to meet a check might be given in time
to the desperate designs of the Hammonds, and such fellows who are
endeavoring to involve their country in the utmost confusion in this time
of danger and distress."[16]

Unfortunate results were sure to ensue, Carroll continued, if Hall and
the Hammonds were not firmly checked. The convention must establish a
form of government that would preserve order, authority and stability.
Such a design as that envisioned by the published instructions was abomi-
nable. "Should their schemes take place," he wrote, "and it is probable
they will unless vigorously counteracted by all honest men, anarchy will
follow as a certain consequence; injustice, rapine and corruption in the
seats of justice will prevail, and this province in a short time will be
involved in all the horrors of an ungovernable and revengeful Democracy and will be dyed with the blood of its best citizens." Now was the
time for the right thinking to take a bold and resolute stand. The moment was at hand when something truly positive could be achieved: "If
gentlemen who really mean well to their country and sincerely wish it
prosperity will oppose the designs of selfish men, who are busy everywhere striving to throw all power into the hands of the very lowest of
people, in order that *they* may be their masters from the abused confidence which the people have placed in them, I say if the honest part of
the community will now behave themselves as their duty requires them
we shall be able to establish a very good government in this state."[17]

Despite Charles Carroll of Carrollton's efforts, Chase and Charles Carroll, Barrister, lost their public bid to have the instructions rescinded.
These two men, along with B. T. B. Worthington, then resigned their
seats. A new election was held on September 4. Chase and Worthington
were returned to the convention, but Charles Carroll, Barrister, lost his
seat to John Hall.[18] For the popular party and for Charles Carroll of
Carrollton particularly, the Barrister's loss graphically confirmed a sense

[16] Charles Carroll of Carrollton to Charles Carroll of Annapolis, August 17, 1776
and August 20, 1776, Charles Carroll of Annapolis Papers, MHS.
[17] Charles Carroll of Carrollton to Charles Carroll of Annapolis, August 20, 1776,
Charles Carroll of Annapolis Papers, MHS.
[18] *Maryland Gazette*, September 12, 1776; *Proceedings of the Conventions*, p. 248.

of danger. Carroll now began to perceive sinister conspiracies in all who disagreed with him. His private letters reveal this deepening anxiety. On August 23, he characterized his opponents as "men of desperate fortunes, or of desperate and wicked designs," who, he maintained, "are endeavoring under the cloak of procuring great privileges for the people to introduce a levelling scheme by which they, these evil men, are sure to profit."[19]

Specifically, Carroll referred to an opposition party he observed forming in the convention, where two distinct political factions had developed. One, composed primarily of those men who had united together at the time of the fee controversy, included himself, Samuel Chase, William Paca, Matthew Tilghman, Thomas Johnson, Robert Goldsborough, and George Plater. These men formed the conservative leadership. Throughout the session, they recommended high property qualifications for voting and holding office, long terms for all legislative officials, and a strong centralized form of government. Authority, they said, should be dictated from above, not from below. From the very beginning, another group appeared in opposition to the conservatives. Late in August, even before any serious discussion had started, Carroll forewarned his father of certain delegates: "Col. Fitzhugh is most outrageous and acts a very weak, and I think a very wicked part; he is united with Hammond, Cockey Deye, and such men and seems desirous of impeding business and throwing everything into confusion."[20]

Fitzhugh deserves special examination. He was one of the wealthier men in the colony, and up to the very last minute hobnobbed with Governor Eden and the top proprietary officials. In late 1774, after Walter Dulany's death, Fitzhugh had secured the lucrative post of commissary general but, as he told his English merchant friend, James Russell, the office brought him nothing but grief: "I am truly sensible of the sincerity of your friendly wishes that I may live long to enjoy the office of Commissary General. It has been a good office when the fees were regularly paid and I hope will be again, whenever these troublesome times cease." Unfortunately, he went on to say, not everyone shared his ambitions, especially "our patriots," who were pushing a plan "to destroy the office." Such attempts as these, he continued, "do not proceed from any grievance or complaint of the people, but from the spirit of opposition to the government and the common passion of the *outs* to destroy

---

[19] Charles Carroll of Carrollton to Charles Carroll of Annapolis, August 23, 1776, Charles Carroll of Annapolis Papers, MHS.

[20] Charles Carroll of Carrollton to Charles Carroll of Annapolis, n.d., Charles Carroll of Annapolis Papers, MHS.

the *ins.*" The confusion the popular party created had lessened his fees so that his holding of the position actually cost him money. "Too many people," he complained, are "under the influence of our patriots" and as a result have refused to pay anything.[21]

In his next letter to Russell, Fitzhugh named his enemies and gave his opinion of the popular party and its principles. "Charles Carroll of Carrollton (a Papist) and Samuel Chase, a fractious and desperate lawyer, are the ring leaders of mischief in this province. Nor has their address," Fitzhugh observed critically, "been less than their iniquity: to throw this country into general confusion. They have lately at their county meeting at Annapolis resolved that every person who will not contribute money toward carrying on their diabolical machinations, shall be advertised as an enemy to the country and be treated accordingly. Some talk of the *moderate* punishment of tarring and feathering, but those two mild patriots humanely prescribe jibbings, house burnings, etc." For his friend's edification, Fitzhugh was sending along some "hand bills, which are specimens of those gentlemen's politics and will show their views." He deplored that "a country" could be "led by such notorious and barefaced incendiaries."[22]

By the time of the Constitutional Convention in August 1776 all of this was past history, and from Fitzhugh's perspective, Carroll was now in and he was out. For him this may have been reason enough to play the part of the democratic incendiary. His metamorphosis was certainly exceptional and, whatever his motives, Fitzhugh advocated in the coming month some democratic reforms that appeared shocking to all the popular party members. Other men who voted with him in the radical minority included Rezin Hammond from Anne Arundel, Cockey Deye from Baltimore, Charles Ridgely and John Stevenson from Baltimore County, John Mackall of Calvert, and the delegates from Montgomery and Harford counties. Ridgely and the Baltimore area delegates had once more quit the camp of their original party allies to join with those who had been primarily responsible for the *Peggy Stewart's* destruction. In the future Ridgely and the Baltimore community would continue to vacillate between the various political forces in the state. Their defection at this time, however, was offset by a very surprising move. John Hall, the man who had worked so closely with the Hammonds to restrict the popular

---

[21] Wm. Fitzhugh (Charles County) to James Russell (London), November 24, 1774, Coutts Bank Papers, microfilm in the University of Virginia Library, Charlottesville, Va.

[22] Wm. Fitzhugh (Charles County) to James Russell (London), January 25, 1775, Coutts Bank Papers.

party's dominance on the Anne Arundel delegation, altered his stand perceptibly during the convention proceedings. Instead of voting consistently with the Hammonds, Hall, for unknown reasons, adopted an independent attitude and did not align himself with any specific faction.[23]

Charles Carroll of Carrollton's fear of the men opposing his party grew intense. His correspondence during the convention shows clearly that he seriously believed the conservative forces were losing control. Actually, the very opposite occurred. During the convention, the popular party's conservative leaders clearly dominated. The influx of new members to the convention may have been unsettling, but the old political leaders asserted leadership without too much difficulty and drew up an extremely conservative constitution. Charles Carroll of Carrollton's consternation notwithstanding, the radicals never gained enough strength to endanger the program he advocated. Only on one occasion, during the debate over property qualifications for voting, were his opponents able to mount a serious, albeit unsuccessful, attack.

The military situation and the degree of unity within the general community largely dictated Carroll's state of mind. When these two elements were favorable he was reasonable, if anxious and uneasy. On September 6, after reviewing for his father a satisfactory military situation, he commented that "our internal affairs, I mean of this province, seem to be but in an indifferent way. I am afraid that there are some men in our convention not so honest as they should be. It is certain we go on slowly."[24] Carroll remained rational at this time despite the Hall-Hammond controversy and the opposition elements in the convention. But during the month of October, as the internal disorders grew worse in Maryland and the military situation deteriorated, his anxieties rose to a feverish pitch.

His most irrational fears focused on the Constitutional Convention. When the convention first convened in August, it selected a committee to prepare a plan of government. Its members were the same men who had dominated in politics since the time of the fee controversy. Matthew Tilghman, who was also president of the convention, Charles Carroll of Carrollton, William Paca, Samuel Chase, Robert Goldsborough, and George Plater were designated to serve.[25] Charles Carroll, Barrister, was also appointed to this post before he lost his convention seat.

Charles Carroll of Carrollton thought the proposed structure pre-

[23] *Proceedings of the Conventions*, pp. 268–69.

[24] Charles Carroll of Carrollton to Charles Carroll of Annapolis, September 6, 1776, Charles Carroll of Annapolis Papers, MHS.

[25] *Proceedings of the Conventions*, p. 222.

pared by the committee excellent, but had some misgivings about its eventual fate. To his father he wrote of the plan: "I believe you will approve of it but I am sure the House will not, at least they appear to dislike it very much at present."[26] The committee reported the proposed constitution to the convention on September 11. The convention voted to postpone consideration until September 30 so that the deputies of the Continental Congress could be present. This adjournment was important to the conservatives, for it insured them of having all their major leaders present for the crucial debate. Chase, Paca, and Johnson were members of the congressional delegation which had just recently departed for Philadelphia, but they would be home by the 30th to enter the convention lists.[27]

The document prepared by Carroll and his associates was clear in intent. Their constitution made the possession of extensive property the fundamental basis of government. No one could participate in public life without large amounts of material wealth. To qualify for membership in the lower house a man had to own a minimum of £500 real or personal property. Seats in the upper house were to be held by individuals possessing a minimum of £1,000. The governor's position was to go only to a man holding an estate valued at or above £5,000. Eligibility for the governor's executive council, the position of congressional delegate, and the local office of county sheriff required estates of £1,000.[28] Table 5, based on a thorough examination of Maryland's tax lists, presents figures that indicate the number of free, white, male voters eligible for office in both the lower and upper houses because of these property qualifications which were included in the final constitution.

The committee's proposal similarly outlined an election method designed to insure the selection of an aristocratically oriented government. This process, combined with the property requirements, made it a certainty that the rich and well born would rule. Voters could directly elect individuals to only two positions: the lower house and county sheriff. As proposed by the committee, lower house elections were to be held every three years. The election of a sheriff constituted something of a reform since, prior to this time, he had been appointed. Yet with a property qualification of £1,000 attached to the office, the concession to popular rule seems hardly dramatic.[29] Senate members were to be selected by an

---

[26] Charles Carroll of Carrollton to Charles Carroll of Annapolis, September 13, 1776, Charles Carroll of Annapolis Papers, MHS.
[27] *Proceedings of the Conventions*, pp. 252–53.
[28] *Ibid.*, pp. 316–26.
[29] *Ibid.*, pp. 324–25.

TABLE 5 *People Eligible for Holding Office in Maryland*

County	Number of Free White Males	Eligible for Lower House		Eligible for Upper House	
		Percent	Number	Percent	Number
Worcester	1,733	8.2	143	3.8	65
Somerset	1,638	12.7	208	7.4	122
Talbot	1,478	10.0	147	6.9	102
Kent	1,495	13.7	205	9.2	138
Dorchester	1,828	9.1	167	6.2	113
Caroline	1,293	7.2	93	3.2	42
Cecil	1,200	11.2	135	6.2	74
Charles	1,725	14.3	247	9.7	167
Montgomery	2,160	10.9	236	5.6	120
Baltimore	3,165	9.5	302	7.6	239
Harford	2,243	7.8	173	5.4	121
Anne Arundel	2,229	15.3	342	13.3	297
Calvert	894	11.3	101	11.1	99
State average		10.9		7.4	

NOTE: Satisfactory population and tax statistics for four Maryland counties—St. Mary's, Frederick, Prince Georges and Queen Anne's—were not available for this analysis.

electoral college. The voters could choose only electors who had estates valued at a minimum of £500. These electors, in turn, selected the Senate. Nine members of that body were to come from the Western Shore and six from the Eastern Shore.[30] An election to the Senate was to be held every seven years. Lastly, the governor of the state was to be selected annually by the legislature.[31] He could continue in that office no longer than three successive years.

Obviously the form of government proposed in the Anne Arundel County instructions had not won much favor in the committee. Only one county office in the new plan, that of sheriff, had been made elective. Instead of annual elections to the assembly, delegates to the lower house were to be selected at intervals of three years, and senators at seven. One specific modification concerning suffrage was made in the proposed plan of government. Under the proprietor the right to vote had been based on the possession of a 50-acre freehold or property worth a minimum of £40 sterling. The committee recommended a lower requirement of a 50-acre freehold or property at the value of £30 current money. Thirty pounds

[30] *Ibid.*, pp. 319–21.
[31] *Ibid.*, pp. 322–25.

current money was equal to about £20 sterling. In essence, the new property value qualification reduced the old one by 50 percent.[32]

This plan of government came before the convention at the beginning of October. Almost as soon as discussions started, Carroll began to lose his nerve. At first angered, he quickly became horrified at the attack mounted against the committee's report. "I execrate the detestable villainy of designing men," he told his father, "who under the specious and sacred name of popularity are endeavoring to work themselves into power and profit and to accomplish this, their end, want to establish a most ruinous system of government." To him it all seemed part of an insidiously widening pattern of internal decay, and he was of the opinion that all further proceedings should be "postponed till there is a greater certainty than we have at present of possessing a country and people to govern. In my opinion our affairs are desperate and nothing but peace with Great Britain on tolerably rational terms can save us from destruction. Our Army is badly provided, exposed to the inclemency of the weather, inferior in numbers to the enemy, etc. etc. etc.—but these," he lamented, "are not the greatest difficulties we have to contend with."

We are miserably divided, not only colony against colony, but in each colony there begins to appear such a spirit of disunion and discord that I am apprehensive, should we succeed against Great Britain (which I think very improbable under our circumstances) we shall be rent to pieces by civil wars and factions and that no free government can be established during such contention is self-evident.

Even that archpatriot, General Charles Lee, Carroll informed his father, now favored starting negotiations. Lee had traveled through Annapolis the other night and supped with Carroll. "What do you think," he asked, "even Lee admires peace?" Lee believed that safe and honorable terms might be secured. While Carroll doubted this, he contended that if "safe and honorable terms can be had we had better return to our old connections and forms of government under which we were once happy and flourished than hazard civil wars amongst ourselves and the erection of a despotism as a sure consequence."[33]

Six days later Carroll remained of the same mind as the struggle over the constitution became more bitter, or so he believed. He reasoned that a "considerable majority of the House" were favorably disposed toward

---

[32] *Ibid.*, pp. 349–50.
[33] Charles Carroll of Carrollton to Charles Carroll of Annapolis, October 4, 1776, Charles Carroll of Annapolis Papers, MHS.

the committee's report, but felt that the irrational tactics of the minority could "plunge us into worse difficulties than those from which we are endeavoring to extract ourselves." The wisest solution to these "insurmountable difficulties" lay in immediate negotiations with England and a reunion of some sort. His dreams of American independence were all gone because "the seeds of disunion are sown, and I am much mistaken if the soil will not be exceedingly productive."[34]

Carroll's worst moments came during the next few weeks. On October 18, he wrote his father a long and elaborate letter characterized by pessimism and despair: "If we remain independent of Great Britain our distractions will increase and civil wars among ourselves will surely follow." To illustrate this point he described what had recently taken place at the convention: "We began yesterday on our plan of government. From the alterations that were made in it yesterday and this morning I am satisfied we shall have a very bad government in this state." Because of this, he was "in hopes this winter some negotiations will be set forth which will lead to peace on safe terms to the colonies." He was optimistic that a settlement might be arrived at with the English authorities. Spain's declaration of war against Portugal might soon bring peace to the Empire. The outbreak of fighting on the continent, he reasoned, would "be an inducement to the ministry to accelerate a peace with the colonies and to grant them full security for the enjoyment of their rights and liberties provided they will return to their former state of allegiance and dependence." If such a reconciliation did not take place soon, he felt certain that the colonies "will be ruined not so much by the calamities of war as by intestine divisions and the bad governments which I foresee will take place in most of these united states: they will be simple Democracies, of all governments the worst and will end as all other Democracies have, in despotism."[35]

From what Carroll wrote at this time he obviously believed that his kind of people, his style of leadership, and his ideas were threatened with extinction. He thought the convention was turning against him in a tide of disorder that was sweeping forward with the Revolution. But nothing of the sort happened. Only two material alterations were made in his committee's plan and these, while significant, were hardly crucial. "We have made some little progress in our government," he wrote a few days later. "We are to have but two branches, a Lower House and Senate; the only material alteration respecting the Senate from the draft of the Committee is its continuance being reduced from seven to five years—instead of triennial elections for the Lower House they will have annual which in my opinion they err exceedingly and will have cause to repent of that alteration. God knows what sort of government we shall get."[36]

The unsuccessful attacks by the radical minority on the suggested governmental structure were largely a symbolic exercise. Besides the alteration of legislative terms, there was only one instance when a move to amend the conservative's scheme almost succeeded. This came over the issue of suffrage. Two resolutions aimed at lowering the suffrage requirements were submitted to the convention. One proposal recommended reducing the property qualifications for voting from £30 to £5 current money. The measure lost by a close vote of 23 to 20. A second motion suggested the elimination of all property qualifications. According to this measure, all taxpayers should be allowed to vote. This measure was also defeated, but again the margin was narrow—29 to 24.[37]

Other motions submitted in an effort to alter the conservatives' plan never came near passing. Significantly, none of the measures introduced attempted to modify the basic structure of the proposed government. Such fundamental features as the electoral college for the Senate, and the high property qualifications for office holding were never challenged by the radical minority.[38] This minority, it is true, did persuade the convention to limit the tenure of seats in the legislature. To Carroll this may have seemed a serious setback, but the fact that this was the only change made suggests clearly that he and his supporters firmly held the reins of power in the new state.

The questions about the Maryland constitution are many. Why was it so conservative? Why did the leaders of the popular party continue to dominate a convention that contained 43 new members? And what were those elements of internal decay in Maryland that caused Charles Carroll of Carrollton to see catastrophe in the moderate changes suggested? A complete answer to these questions is not possible, but the broad outlines of the situation can be reconstructed. The members convened at a time of growing division, when disorder and chaos were rapidly replacing the traditional forms of authority. A radical few hoped to ride the crest of this upheaval to power, but the majority of men attending were with

[36] Charles Carroll of Carrollton to Charles Carroll of Annapolis, October 20, 1776, Charles Carroll of Annapolis Papers, MHS.
[37] *Proceedings of the Conventions*, pp. 330, 331.
[38] *Ibid.*, pp. 267, 274, 302–303, 308, 310, 330–31, 336–37, 345–48.

good reason deeply concerned. Carroll may have underestimated the conservatism of the convention, but his fears and those of the other delegates are understandable. If there was dissension in the halls of Annapolis, there was turmoil in the society outside. A full-scale insurrection was underway on the Eastern Shore. Loyalist organizations existed throughout the state and were rumored to have arms. Other groups, while not active loyalists, refused to pledge fealty to the new government. At the other extreme, the Whig Club of Baltimore employed violent measures to enforce its aim of banishing all those elements not fully sympathetic to the American cause. These internal conflicts made the need for stability obvious. The new constitution with its conservative characteristics promised order, but to achieve it was another matter.

Various forms of loyalism confronted the convention, each representing a different threat to orderly rule. One was the protection society originally founded by Governor Robert Eden. Despite his departure, the organization he built continued. Late in 1776 some of the society's members, after being harassed by the Whig Club, took up arms. Several pitched battles occurred in the Baltimore area. The loyalists, outnumbered at first, were beaten, but they received support from the town's free Negroes who offered protection in their quarters. The loyalists remained there for a short period until they were able to depart safely and in secret to New York.[39]

The black community joined with the loyalists in other parts of the state and together they posed a serious threat to the conservative leaders, particularly on the Eastern Shore, where Lord Dunmore had sent several agents to establish a resistance movement. By the time of the August convention the organization was well developed. To counter this threat the June convention had authorized "several independent militia companies" to suppress the "insurrection." At the same time the Continental Congress sent advice. John Hancock wrote the Maryland Council of Safety on June 25 that he was forwarding resolves containing explicit instructions which "are calculated to prevent insurrections and to introduce good order and obedience to the laws."[40] But organized military force, rather than paper directives, was needed to suppress Dunmore's white and black followers, who were said to be "very smart fellows."[41] As the disorders grew, it became more difficult to raise militiamen from

---

[39] Henry Stevenson Testimony, Audit Office, British Public Record Office, series 12, vol. 6 (cited hereafter as *Audit Office*).

[40] John Hancock to the Council of Safety, June 25, 1776, *Red Books*, 6:62.

[41] Examination of Thomas Sawyer and James Johnson, a prisoner and deserter from Dunmore's fleet, Executive Papers, box 2, folder 54, MHR.

the Eastern Shore territory, where many were indifferent and others sympathetic to the insurrectionists. Nearly all were afraid to leave their families. On July 22, Thomas Johnson wrote the Council of Safety from the Eastern Shore that men "reluctantly leave their own neighborhoods unhappily full of Negroes who might, it is likely, on any misfortune to our militia become very dangerous."[42]

Throughout the summer, slaves attempted to escape to Dunmore as word of his activities spread. In one particularly brutal and well-publicized incident during August three slaves in Dorchester County killed a white man in their unsuccessful bid for freedom. An example had to be made of them, the County Court decided: "They were to be taken to the place of execution and there each of them to have their right hands cut off and to be hanged by the neck until they were dead; their heads to be severed from their bodies and their bodies to be divided each of them in four quarters and their heads and quarters to be set up in the most public places of the county."[43] The message was obvious.

The following month another trial, the first of its kind, convened for one of Dunmore's sympathizers, Isaac Costin. The charges specified that he had organized approximately 200 people in the middle of June to oppose any moves toward independence. He had openly, in the company of his armed followers, "damned the Whigs and rebels." For this offense, Costin was found guilty of showing himself "inimical to the cause of American freedom," and sentenced to jail.[44] But popular pressure soon forced his release. His discharge emphasized the real problem which the provincial authorities faced. Support for Dunmore within Maryland was symptomatic of a much wider feeling of discontent present in large sections of the society. To suppress Dunmore's movement and other insurrectionist elements required the cooperation and support of the community, but these were lacking. Great numbers of the people, to use the term current at the time, were "disaffected"—they had no sympathy for the revolutionary government and frequently resented the new authorities.

By the summer of 1776, the Council of Safety was becoming well acquainted with the dimensions of the problem. The British were brazenly landing supplies in Somerset County to aid the insurgents. Local militia commanders ordered their men out, but the effort to protect the

[42] Thomas Johnson to the Council of Safety, July 22, 1776, *Archives of Maryland*, 12:92.
[43] Dorchester County Court Proceedings, August 2, 1776, Maryland State Papers, Black Books, 8:101–103, MHR.
[44] *Proceedings of the Conventions*, pp. 236, 258.

coast was futile. Thomas Ennals, a prominent Eastern Shore official, reported that militia officers had informed him that people in the area were almost impossible to work with. "I am further informed by them," he advised the council, "that they found many of the people in that part of the country very lukewarm in the opposition, difficult to be got together, and when collected, in such bad discipline they are not (in their opinion) to be relied on, paying but little regard to the instructions of their officers."[45] The situation in Dorchester County was similar. At the time of Ennals' report, another government official observed to the Dorchester County Committee of Observation, "we are sorry to inform you that we have lately discovered such an unfriendly disposition in many of the inhabitants about the islands in this county, that we are convinced it will be productive of very ill consequences unless some steps are immediately taken to keep them in proper order."[46]

The Shore's situation continued to worsen. During late September and October, the months when Charles Carroll of Carrollton's fears were rampant, word came to Annapolis of widespread disorder in Caroline and Dorchester counties. From the original areas of discontent in Worcester and Somerset, the trouble now appeared to be spreading northward. As it expanded, the military units commissioned to control the turmoil proved less and less competent. Instead of solving the problem they were becoming part of it. From previously quiet Queen Anne's County, a militia colonel, Thomas Wright, wrote the council that the people had decided they should elect all their officers by popular ballot: "The people have been induced to believe they ought not to submit to any appointments but those made by themselves." He, of course, opposed the demand. Consequently the militia of his county had become completely inoperative. "I most heartily wish," he concluded, "that some mode could be adopted to restore harmony to this distracted county but which way it can be effected I know not."[47]

Colonel Wright's problems were minor compared to those of militia units stationed on the southern part of the Shore. In Worcester County desertion had become so frequent and the lines of communication so disorganized, that the officers there bypassed the executive authority of the province, the Council of Safety, and went directly to the Maryland

---

[45] Thomas Ennals to the Council of Safety, July 2, 1776, *Archives of Maryland*, 11:542.

[46] James Murray to Dorchester County Committee of Observation, July 12, 1776, *ibid.*, 12:37.

[47] Colonel Thomas Wright to Council of Safety, September 20, 1776, *ibid.*, pp. 288–89.

delegates at Philadelphia for help. The congressional representatives, in turn, informed the council of what they had done: The officer who had come to see them, Lieutenant Long, was on his way back "to Worcester to endeavor to get the deserters to return to their duty, under an assurance which we have presumed to give that on their immediate return the past shall be forgiven." The congressmen further told the council that they had decided to remove certain unpopular officers and to put men into positions of command who were more acceptable to the troops. They reported, for example, that Captain Watkins was on very "ill terms" with his men. "The Captain has beat some of them. He says he had great cause. They say he had none. Some of the men have said nothing shall induce them to continue in the company under Captain Watkins. We shall endeavor to keep the remnant of the company together under the care of the third Lieutenant until your orders can interpose."[48]

As the fall set in and a shortage in vital supplies became apparent, conditions deteriorated further. In Dorchester County a militia Captain led a salt riot, confiscating 14½ bushels from James Murray, a member of the Dorchester County delegation to the provincial convention. An investigation into this matter brought sharply into focus the dilemma affecting the Eastern Shore. The Dorchester County Committee of Observation ordered the rioters to appear before it for an explanation of their conduct. At the first session, when only a few came, they "appeared agreeable to the summons and behaved orderly." The officials present ordered the hearing postponed until all the rioters appeared. At the second session they may well have regretted that decision. The rioters showed up in numbers equaling "upwards of 100 armed men headed by Captain Andrew" and "the company behaved so riotously and disorderly," the committee told the Council of Safety, "that it was out of our power to proceed in the business."[49]

That was not the worst of it. "Many of the men swear," reported the committee, that "they will support what they have done at the hazard of their lives as it seems they have associated to do, and by their declarations against the present measures of the country, and in favor of the king, show themselves entirely disaffected to our cause. If these men were all we have to contend with," the report went on, they might be brought under control, "but from the very best information we can obtain, we

[48] Maryland Deputies (Philadelphia) to the Council of Safety (Baltimore), September 20, 1776, *ibid.*, pp. 291–92.
[49] Dorchester County Committee of Observation to the Council of Safety, November 15, 1776, *ibid.*, pp. 449–51.

are of the opinion they have a very formidable number to protect them from Caroline, Worcester and Sussex in Delaware." In addition the action of Captain Andrew's men had established a precedent, "as (since their outrages) several companies in this county have taken salt nearly in the same way which will of course stop them from opposing them if they do not join them." There was only one conclusion to be drawn, according to the committee—the rioters could not be stopped: "We are unanimously of the opinion that it is very improbable there can be in General Hooper's brigade a sufficient number of militia raised who would on the present occasion take up arms to suppress and stop the progress of these rioters and their adherents, and bring the offenders to justice; and we therefore think it most prudent to decline making the attempt as a failure would be very deterimental to our cause, and give strength and spirits to their party and friends."⁵⁰ Upon receiving this account, the Council of Safety immediately wrote John Hancock that "it gives us concern to find from information just now received from Dorchester and Caroline counties of the Eastern Shore that there are likely to be disturbances in those counties (for want of salt, it is said) of a serious nature."⁵¹ Of that prediction the council could be sure.

The disorders, insurrections, and instances of militia resistance were not confined to the Eastern Shore. The Western Shore and the patriot stronghold of Baltimore, home of the Whig Club, also experienced increasing difficulties. In the beginning the central focus of concern was Dunmore and his slave rebellion. John Dent, a district military commander, confidently reported in July from St. Mary's County that the chief threat there consisted of "not more than 50 regulars of the 14th Regiment, about 150 Tories and 100 Negroes that bear arms." His strength, he told the council, was at present "about 400 militia exclusive of the *Independent* [a Maryland naval vessel] and Captain Forrest's company." He considered the situation to be well in hand.⁵² No doubt the council wanted to believe him, but there were other unsettling signs coming to their attention. Slaves from as far away as the western county of Frederick had been reported escaping to serve under "the command of Lord Dunmore."⁵³ As word of his activities spread, the council fully realized the threat posed by the blacks, and it urged an increased surveil-

---

⁵⁰ *Ibid.*
⁵¹ Council of Safety to John Hancock, November 2, 1776, *ibid.*, p. 465.
⁵² John Dent (Charles River Headquarters) to the Council of Safety (Annapolis), July 19, 1776, *ibid.*, pp. 83–84.
⁵³ Deposition of Capt. George Cook, Frederick County, July 1776, Maryland State Papers, Blue Books, 5:2.

lance of all slaves. Fearful of that community's mounting rebelliousness, the council suspected that Dunmore had infiltrated black agents into the province. "The Negro you mentioned that escaped from the guard," it told Major Thomas Price, an officer stationed in southern Maryland, "may have been sent on purpose to seduce the slaves in this neighborhood."[54]

By August the same problems associated with the Eastern Shore military units were also apparent in St. Mary's County. The troops sent there from outside the area quickly proved to be a serious disciplinary problem. Dissatisfied because of local hostility, poor equipment, meager facilities, and the unhealthy conditions of the swampy regions in which they were stationed, the troops became resentful. Soon after their arrival, they began to create disturbances so great that the St. Mary's Committee of Observation, which had originally asked for help, begged their removal. The soldiers, the committee said in its appeal, had engaged in "licentious behavior since they had been at this place, in killing and destroying people's property and threatening to disband and return should any of their company fall sick. And being as we perceive," the committee wrote, "under no control or command of their officers, we fear they will rather prove a disadvantage than service to the people of this county. Under these circumstances and for these reasons," concluded the appeal, "we have taken the liberty to remonstrate to you and entreat their removal from hence, hoping that this act (which we conceive to be for the good of the whole) can not meet with your censure or disapprobation."[55]

Military personnel outside of the sensitive areas were similarly dissatisfied. With growing frequency, they complained of the elite notions of their officers. In Anne Arundel County one militia company petitioned the Council of Safety for a new election of officers for two reasons. They believed the original ballot had been improperly conducted, but, more importantly, they were making the request because "we do complain of our Captain and Ensign speaking in public company against the poor people in general." To support their petition, the soldiers forwarded the following deposition of one of their members: "I, Gilbert Hamilton Smith, of the county above mentioned [Anne Arundel] heard Captain Richard Chew of the said county say that no poor man was entitled to a vote, and those that would insist upon voting, if he had his way, should

[54] Council of Safety to Major Thomas Price, July 25, 1776, *Archives of Maryland*, 12:114.

[55] St. Mary Committee of Observation to Council of Safety, August 7, 1776, *ibid.*, pp. 184–85.

be put to death and I do affirm also that I heard his brother, Samuel Chew, say that a poor man was not born to freedom but to be a drudge on earth."[56] Thirty-nine signatures accompanied this petition, sixteen of them with a mark.

Two days later reports of a similar nature reached the council from Charles County, after an entire battalion refused to obey the order given them to muster. Instead they "broke their ranks and collected together in a crowd," where they told the officers they disapproved of the manner in which the battalion was run. "I said everything I could," wrote the reporting officer, "(and so did many other officers) to show them the absurdity of such conduct but to no purpose. I then ordered them to be dismissed until I should hear from the Convention and hope it will not be long before some step is taken to reduce them to order."[57]

Conditions were no better in the patriot stronghold of Baltimoretown and Baltimore County. Samuel Purviance, the most popular political figure in the area, told the council in November that morale was low and disrespect for law and authority widespread. Here, there were two additional unsettling elements, the Whig Club and an active nonassociator community. The membership of the Whig Club, a secret and frequently violent patriotic organization, included merchants, tavern keepers, and, as one report said, "one Poe, a wheelwright (who seemed at the head of the lower class)."[58] Since July, this organization had worked hard to harass and eliminate all elements not totally committed to support of the Revolution. People whom the club members suspected of being disloyal in any way were ordered to leave the province upon threat of serious physical harm or death. One such message was sent to Robert Christie, a former proprietary official: "Your conduct has been such in the state during our struggle for liberty that we are at this moment determined that unless you leave this town instantly and the state within six days, your life will be sacrificed by an injured people."[59] Afraid for his life, Christie left for New York, but others were less easily frightened. These were assaulted in the streets by members of the club.[60]

For such actions, the Baltimore Committee of Observation, as well as the Provincial Council of Safety, reprimanded the club on several occasions.[61] Above all else the governing authorities wanted some measure of stability. In straightforward language, the council told the Baltimore

---

[56] Petition of Chew's Company, October 5, 1776, *ibid.*, p. 323.

[57] Jesias Hawkins to Matthew Tilghman, October 7, 1776, *ibid.*, p. 325.

[58] Robert Christie to Daniel of St. Thomas Jenifer, December 10, 1776, *ibid.*, p. 517.

[59] *Ibid.*

[60] Henry Stevenson, *Audit Office.*

[61] Thomas W. Griffith, *Annals of Baltimore* (Baltimore, 1824), p. 69.

Committee that the Whig Club threatened "the peace of the state." They wanted the club members arrested and brought to "trial." At this delicate time the council urged "we must press upon you to an exertion of your authority to prevent all irregularities and disorders tending in their consequences to prejudice the common cause; for on steadiness and unanimity amongst ourselves depend our success; whereas the conduct of the Whig Club, if truly represented to us, will manifestly introduce anarchy and a total end of all regular government."[62]

The Whig Club particularly despised the nonassociators—people who, while not actively participating in organized resistance, openly refused to adhere to the new government. In July 1775 the convention had drawn up a document entitled the *Association of the Freemen of Maryland*. All those loyal to the American cause were asked at that time to sign the association. Each county's Committee of Observation was ordered to undertake the task of securing signatures. Those who refused to sign were listed as nonassociators.[63]

The July convention had not prescribed any penalty for those refusing to sign, but by January, 1776, the colony's internal situation had substantially deteriorated, and nonassociators were regarded more suspiciously. They were required to give parole for their good conduct, higher taxes were placed on them, their arms were confiscated, and the convention instructed the local committees to watch them carefully.[64] No one could be sure what they would do in response to the prevalent disorders. If their neutrality developed into open hostility, a serious civil conflict would result. The exact number and social character of the nonassociators is unknown, as few quantitative records concerning this group remain. In 1780, the commandant of the Maryland Loyalists, John Chambers, claimed that "there certainly are 12,000 non-jurors [nonassociators] in Maryland" but this probably exaggerated figure cannot be verified.[65]

Court records about the nonassociators have survived, however, which indicate some of the attitudes that fed the discontent. Alexander Magee, a nonassociator brought before the examining committee, expressed the frustration of many who participated in the disorders. He stated his belief "that the American opposition to Great Britain is not calculated or designed for the defense of American liberty or property, but for the purpose of enslaving the poor people thereof." He added,

[62] Council of Safety to Baltimore Committee of Observation, December 13, 1776, *Archives of Maryland*, 12:526.
[63] *Proceedings of the Conventions*, p. 18.
[64] Robert Buchanan Testimony, *Audit Office*.
[65] John Chambers to ———, "Aspinwell Papers," *Massachusetts Historical Society Collections*, 4th series, 10:797–801.

"signing a paper did not alter the heart and he knew there was thousands among us who had enrolled that was still of his way of thinking."[66]

Nonassociators often resisted forcibly. The case of Vincent Trapnell and James Bosley is distinctive. Bosley, a collector of fines for the Baltimore Committee of Observation, left his home on November 14, 1776 to begin what was for him a very bad day. When he came to the home of Trapnell, the latter "swore he would blow my brains out," and went to get his gun. Trapnell's wife urged him not to use this weapon, so, he "picked up a large stick, swearing and cursing, and with both hands struck my head," screaming that he would not pay the fine. Considering a retreat in order, Bosley began running, but Trapnell continued hot on his heels, "swearing he would kill me." Finally making his way off Trapnell's farm, Bosley turned and intrepidly screamed that he intended to acquaint the committee of this reception. Trapnell responded that "the committee and I might kiss his arse and be damned, pulling his coat apart behind." In his opinion they were all "a parcel of roguish, damned, sons-of-bitches and if they came here, he would use them in the same manner as I have done you."[67]

The unruly conduct of men such as Trapnell made the job of keeping order difficult. "We are sorry to inform you," wrote Samuel Purviance to the council, "that the spirit of violence and opposition to the measures which have been adopted for our common safety, grows extremely daring and outrageous in this county, so that the officers appointed to carry into execution the resolves of the Convention dare not proceed without further assistance." Worse still, he advised that "the militia threaten to lay down their arms unless the fines of non-enrollers who daily insult them are strictly collected." It was his opinion that "some speedy and vigorous measures are necessary to preserve union among the people and effectually to destroy the rising hopes of internal enemies."[68]

In early 1777, the problems continued unchanged. On January 27, the Council of Safety reviewed another case involving James Bosley and his brother, Charles. According to the account, the two brothers were going to a distraint sale for one Richard Rhodes, who had not enrolled. Prior to reaching their destination, they encountered a group of armed men carrying clubs and guns, all of whom seemed "devilish inclined." Finding their path blocked, the Bosleys threatened to come back with more men. At that instant one of the nonassociators jumped up, "knocking his heels

[66] Examination of Alexander Magee, Non-Associator, August 29, 1776, *Red Books*, 13:54.
[67] Testimony of James Bosley before Committee of Observation, November 14, 1776, *Archives of Maryland*, 16:87–88.
[68] Samuel Purviance to the Council of Safety, November 18, 1776, *ibid.*, p. 87.

together, swearing by God that he was bottom for them, and turned round to his company crying, 'Huzza Boys, we can get any day 500 men to our assistance.' " Another man warned James Bosley that he "had better quit collecting fines and if he did not he would be as surely killed, as he was born—and that there were men there who came on purpose to kill him."[69] Given such resistance, the Council of Safety's recent directive to the Baltimore Committee of Observation must have seemed a product of wishful thinking. It read, "we hope effectual measures will be taken to keep those who are disaffected or too much inclined to riotous and extra-judicial proceedings within proper bounds."[70] Orders were also sent to all the local military commanders to "be ready at all times to aid and obey the Committee of Observation in Baltimore County in preserving the peace of the state and putting a speedy end to all riots and tumults within the said county or Baltimoretown."[71]

Despite all of these adverse conditions, there was one thing the Western Shore authorities had to be thankful for—the Chesapeake Bay, which separated them from the Eastern Shore, where social violence verged on permanency. Because of the growing shortages of salt and the high prices that prevailed, salt riots continued to erupt and invariably the primary targets were the leading families. In Caroline, the rioters raided the storehouse of James Murray, a convention delegate; in Talbot, the same happened to another member, James Lloyd Chamberlain. The rioters not only vandalized the storehouses, but they also expressed anger over the engrossing and exploitative tactics of the upper class. One of them, John Gibson, put the matter bluntly when he said that he was not really against the Revolution and, in fact, was committed to his country's cause to a greater degree than any of the "engrossers of salt here." He wished only that "our leading gentlemen on this side of the bay was as little inclined to party designs and self interest," as the raid's organizer, Jeremiah Colston.[72]

James Lloyd Chamberlain considered the conduct of Colston and his followers as anything but justified. Indeed Chamberlain became so disgusted with the disorder surrounding him that he decided to quit all public life, including his post as brigadier general of the militia. He returned his commission with the explanation that existing conditions precluded the carrying out of his duties. "Many of us," he believed,

[69] Deposition of Aquila Wilmot, January 27, 1777, *ibid.*, pp. 91–92; deposition of Charles Bosley, January 27, 1777, *ibid*, pp. 99–100.
[70] Council of Safety to Baltimore Committee of Observation, January 18, 1777, *ibid.*, pp. 59–60.
[71] Executive Papers, box 2, folder 132, MHR.
[72] John Gibson to the Council of Safety, January 4, 1777, *Archives of Maryland*, 16:16–18.

"[are] rather disposed to quarrel with his neighbor than face the enemy." And he concluded, "a general discontent prevails," which produces an "unwillingness in the people to do any duty" or to obey "any sort of order."[73]

Chamberlain's somber analysis was correct enough. Doing one's duty was often not only futile but also hazardous, as Thomas Sparrow, a recruiter, told the convention. Sparrow had received a commission to raise a force of Eastern Shore men for artillery duty in Annapolis. He first stopped at the town of Cambridge in Dorchester County, where he spoke at a picturesque county chapel. Just after he had risen and begun to read the recruitment order, one of the men present shouted that "it was false and if any man should enlist, he would be sent to Philadelphia and not to Annapolis and that they were damn fools that would go to either, to fight against their king." Sparrow recounted that he then told the man that "he was a Tory," and "another told me I should not come there to find anything else." Sparrow retorted that he "hoped to find it otherwise." A young man then came up to Sparrow to hear more of the proposal, and the recruiter began again to read, "but one of the company struck the paper and many of them made such a noise that prevented me from informing those who wanted to enlist." A few minutes later, another man approached Sparrow and told him to flee or be murdered. "I took his advice," he continued, but "it being dark I knew not the road perfectly. In a few minutes I heard some horses in full speed coming up after me, on which I took to the woods and made my escape for that time. It would take up too much time to relate what I suffered in that night which almost cost me my life." Angered by his experience, Sparrow "complained to many of the committee and in particular to Captain Daffen and Mr. Ennals, who told me the night I came away they were sorry I was so ill used, but it was out of their power to help it."[74] They were right.

The lawlessness on Maryland's Eastern Shore, particularly the lower counties, was by now drawing a good deal of attention from Philadelphia. Samuel Chase wrote the Council of Safety from that city on January 8 that he "believed many reasons will occur to convene the General Assembly as soon as possible. Many reports from Somerset County cause uneasiness here, and if true, demand speedy and vigorous measures." A little less than a month later Chase informed the council "that the Tories in Sussex, Somerset and Worcester Counties have been assembling" and

[73] James Lloyd Chamberlain to Daniel of St. Thomas Jenifer, December 26, 1776, *ibid.*, 12:552–53.
[74] Memorial of Thomas Sparrow, January 5, 1777, *ibid.*, 16:19–21.

were well armed. Their weapons included artillery pieces as well as rifles, and they were intending to "seize the magazine and destroy the property of the Whigs." The next day he promised that the congress would provide "every assistance in their power to prevent any communications between the insurgents and the men of war" that were operating in the bay.[75]

None of this was new to the leaders of the state government as they convened for their first legislative session in February. Still the conspicuous absence of the Somerset delegation forcefully conveyed the dimensions of the problem. A report later presented to the delegates explained some of the difficulties the Somerset election officials had experienced. Shortly after the polls opened, "a number of men, armed with firearms to the amount of thirty and a number with sticks and spears fixed in the end of them, came from several parts of the county to the place of election."[76] Their demonstration worked, no elections were held, and no seats were won that day. The course of action to be adopted was painfully clear to the General Assembly. As its first order of business, the legislature authorized 2,000 troops for duty on the Eastern Shore to suppress what it officially proclaimed to be "that dangerous insurrection." Within a few days the shape of that conflict became all the more threatening. A report containing some very unpleasant news arrived from the congress. Reliable intelligence sources had reported that "the enemy meditate an expedition to the bay of the Chesapeake in the ensuing campaign and that the Eastern Shore is the first object or place of landing."[77] There the British fully realized they would meet some who were the king's friends, and others who were the patriot's enemies. For the untried state government, a difficult year lay ahead.

[75] Samuel Chase to the Council of Safety, January 8, 1777, February 6, 1777, and February 8, 1777, *Archives of Maryland*, 16:27, 122–24.
[76] *Votes and Proceedings of the General Assembly of the State of Maryland*, House of Delegates, February Session 1777, March 5, 1777.
[77] Resolution of Congress, February 17, 1777, *Red Books*, 13:21.

9 : The Wisdom
of Sacrifice

O n January 29, 1776, Colonel Richard T. Earle sat in his study, a puzzled man. Just a short time before, the convention in Annapolis had appointed him colonel of a battalion of Eastern Shore militiamen. Grateful for this honor, he realized that his newly acquired position presented several difficulties. Earle, a comfortable planter who knew little about the arts and organization of the military, required information immediately. Where could he turn? To ask the authorities in Annapolis for advice would be embarrassing. Instead, he looked to his merchant friend in Philadelphia, William Barrell, for some elementary information. He desired a manual "with some instructions, particularly with respect to dress. How," asked Earle, "are the colonels, majors and captains when in regiments to distinguish themselves? Some wear shoulder knots on the right, and some on the left. Some wear small swords and some cutteaus. Some carry fuses and cartridge boxes. Do any above the rank of captain do this?"[1] Colonel Earle obviously had much to learn and his predicament symbolized the confusion and ineptness of the government's military forces as they struggled to control the divisiveness that gripped the province.

No doubt by the end of 1776 Colonel Earle and others like him knew what sword to wear, but they had shown little ability to utilize their weapons. The Continental Congress, viewing the situation in Maryland with increasing alarm, urgently recommended to the state's Council of Safety that it take measures to bring about some semblance of order.[2]

[1] Richard T. Earle to William Barrell, January 29, 1776, Stephen Collins Papers, Library of Congress, Washington, D.C.
[2] Council of Safety to Brigadier General Hooper, February 3, 1777, *Archives of Maryland*, ed. William H. Browne *et al.* (68 vols., Baltimore, 1883——), 16:110.

The council wanted to do just that, but on February 6, 1777 it wrote President John Hancock that, considering the scope of that "alarming and dangerous insurrection in Somerset County," the size and effectiveness of "the force of this state which can be immediately collected together" was "insufficient to quell it." Maryland required not directions from the congress but the military assistance of Continental forces.[3]

The Maryland leadership knew that its request for aid could not be met. Nonetheless it was apparent that some steps had to be taken. With the legislature then gathering in Annapolis, an assertion of authority seemed necessary. As a first step the council directed the Eastern Shore's Brigadier General Henry Hooper to move into the areas of Somerset and Worcester counties and apprehend "as many of the leaders of those banditti as you possibly can."[4] But Hooper's untrained militia could not do the job, as no one knew better than the general himself. He needed and fortunately received outside help. A sizeable force of Virginia troops under Maryland's highest ranking general, William Smallwood, and certain regular army units commanded by Colonel Mordecai Gist entered the disaffected area in the latter part of February to suppress the insurrection. Smallwood was given authorization to call in more Continental troops should they be needed. To further assist him, political commissioners accompanied his men with orders to enforce the decrees of the provincial government and Continental Congress.[5]

At first Smallwood minimized the difficulties of his assignment. Believing that too many men were being allocated, he discharged Hooper's militia. The people, he first reported on March 3, were "generally quiet and peaceable."[6] They seemed well inclined to accept the General Assembly's proclamation calling for a halt to all disorders. The entire operation, he confidently assured Annapolis, would be quickly executed. But what Smallwood actually perceived was not submission but a deceptive calm. The insurgents were waiting to measure his strength, and once they discovered their superiority the general found his authority openly flouted. By March 14, he was no longer optimistic. "The proclamation will not have the desired effect," Smallwood reported. Each day he was encountering more difficulties in bringing a return to order. "What have you to expect from those who have cut down liberty poles, and in direct opposition thereto, have erected the King's standard and in an avowed

<hr>

[3] Council of Safety to John Hancock, February 6, 1777, *ibid.*, p. 122.
[4] Council of Safety to Brigadier General Hooper, February 7, 1777, *ibid.*, p. 124.
[5] Council of Safety to Brigadier General Hooper, February 13, 1777, *ibid.*, p. 134; Oswald Tilghman, *History of Talbot County, Maryland, 1661–1861* (Baltimore, Md.: Williams and Wilkins Co., 1915), 2:106–7.
[6] William Smallwood to Daniel of St. Thomas Jenifer, March 3, 1777, *Archives of Maryland*, 16:157–58.

manner drank his health and success and destruction to Congress and conventions." Smallwood asked rhetorically, "What can be expected from the inhabitants of a place which becomes the reception of deserters, escaping prisoners, and most of the disaffected who have been expelled from the neighboring states?" He told the council, "you may rely on it, there are few circles of the like extent in New York or the Jersey states which abound more in disaffected people."[7] To secure that part of the peninsula would take time, patience, and men.

None of these ingredients was available. Soon after writing this account, General Smallwood left for duty elsewhere. The remaining officials, realizing the strength of the resistance, knew they could not handle the situation. From Worcester, Joseph Dashiell, the county lieutenant and son of a leading family, told the council that few people were bothering to take advantage of the state's proclamation promising them immunity from punishment if they stopped their unlawful activities. Those so refusing "may be arranged under three classes." Some were sick and unable to make the journey, others simply wanted to remain home and cared not to openly enroll on either side, and finally there were "those who held out, from a blind and obstinate attachment to the old form of government, and whose wish and inclination was still to fall down and worship the golden image of royalty."[8] But who were these worshipers of royalty—the rich, the refined, the well born? Dashiell, himself of a wealthy family, reported they were rather the dregs of society. "Humanity can scarce forbear to drop a tear on reflecting on the circumstances of many of them," he told Governor Johnson. "With a poor wretched hut crowded with children, naked, hungry and miserable without bread or a penny of money to buy any; in short they appear as objects almost too contemptible to excite the public resentment: yet these are the wretches," he complained, "who set up to be the arbiters of government; to knock down independence and restore the authority of the British King in Parliament which by testimony taken by us was the avowed design of some of the principles, although they have sworn directly the reverse. Yet, despicable as those creatures really are they have their influence within their own peculiar sphere."[9]

In the government's opinion, these individuals had to be brought

[7] William Smallwood to Daniel of St. Thomas Jenifer, March 14, 1777, *ibid.*, p. 175.

[8] Joseph Dashiell to Governor and Council, April 2, 1777, Executive Papers, box 7, Maryland Hall of Records, Annapolis, Md. (cited hereafter as MHR); to Gov. Thomas Johnson, April 12, 1777, Maryland State Papers, Red Books (cited hereafter as *Red Books*), MHR, 14:21.

[9] Joseph Dashiell to Gov. Thomas Johnson, April 12, 1777, *Red Books*, 14:71.

under control. Local authorities did what they could and the council sent in what forces might be mustered, but more general guidelines were needed. The General Assembly set about providing these in its first session. The basic enforcement measure passed was "An Act to Punish Certain Crimes and Misdemeanors and to Prevent the Growth of Toryism." In the early discussions the Senate and House versions differed somewhat and notes flew back and forth between the two chambers in support of the various proposals. The essential point of difference concerned the manner in which those who spoke pessimistically or spread false rumors should be punished. Zealous delegates of the lower house maintained that "a liar is one of the most detestable of characters" and should be punished severely by either banishment or death. To the Senate a liar was equally distasteful, but it maintained that the House version went too far in that it would "have the effect of suppressing all communications."[10] By its very language, the House bill could authorize the punishment of those who even spoke of reconciliation short of complete independence. Since most Senators thought in these terms, they saw no reason to enact a law which might eventually be turned against them by ambitious political opponents.

The Senate stood firm and secured the qualifications it desired. The bill prescribed the death penalty for any person who committed treason by levying war against the state. Any person who had information about such activities but did not report it could have his entire estate confiscated. For activities short of treason, that is for attempts to persuade others to resist the government, to obstruct recruitment activities, or to oppose "with force, the execution of any of the laws of the state," the General Assembly instituted a series of fines and prison sentences. To strengthen enforcement procedures the assembly increased the governor's powers. During an invasion he was authorized to suspend habeas corpus and to limit to a specified area any persons he believed dangerous. Finally the assembly published a list naming fourteen leaders of the Eastern Shore rebellion who were not to be pardoned under any circumstances.[11]

Legislation alone could not stop the Eastern Shore's insurrection. What the situation demanded was a permanent force of Continental troops serving in an occupational capacity. Benjamin Rumsey, a Maryland congressional delegate, agreed with Governor Johnson that the sta-

[10] *Votes and Proceedings of the General Assembly of the State of Maryland,* House of Delegates, February 1777, pp. 80, 91.
[11] William Kilty, *Laws of Maryland* (Annapolis, 1799), chap. 20, February 1777, p. 1; *Votes and Proceedings,* House, February 1777, p. 7.

tioning of a battalion of Continentals in Somerset County "would keep the three counties inclined to Toryism in order."[12] Not everyone in government considered this necessary. Robert Morris, head of the congress' powerful secret committee, was strongly opposed to keeping any significant concentration of forces in the area when, if General Washington were reinforced, a "capital stroke" might be delivered. "I wish you would think of this," he told Governor Johnson in May, just after the state had managed to procure a few units for Eastern Shore duty. "Order them to move on," he urged, "other means may be found to keep the forces in order there." The troops Morris referred to in his letter were some 300 men recently authorized by congress to secure the area.[13]

Although Morris did not know it, what he asked of Johnson was impossible. The men existed on paper only. True, congress had authorized that Maryland raise a battalion for duty within the Continental command structure to serve as occupational units, but the state could not recruit the men. Congress' orders directed Colonel William Richardson, a Continental officer from Caroline County, to secure the disaffected area with a battalion of troops supplied by the state. To raise the men the Council of State, successor to the Council of Safety, wrote to the colonels heading the county militias on May 5. It hoped to obtain from them enough volunteers to make up the 300 men slated for the battalion.[14] No sooner had the request gone out than it began to encounter resistance. From Caroline County came word that "such a backwardness prevails generally amongst us that I am almost certain the number (though so very small) can not be got voluntarily; nothing but a draft will accomplish the design." Unfortunately, Colonel William Whitely continued, the men here do not even turn out for normal musters: "Two thirds of the people remain at home abusing and ridiculing the honest few who think it their duty to attend constantly." Most of his officers and men, he sadly admitted, "deliver sentiments very prejudicial to our cause." Similar reports came from other counties.[15] By the end of June only fourteen volunteers had been raised. These sad statistics caused Joseph Dashiell to observe sarcastically that "it is indeed a melancholy truth that the greatest part of our men appear to have just courage enough to disobey orders but not enough to face an enemy. They are so totally lost

[12] Benjamin Rumsey to Gov. Thomas, April 17, 1777, *Archives of Maryland*, 16: 217; Gov. Thomas Johnson to John Hancock, April 21, 1777, *ibid.*, pp. 222–23.
[13] Robert Morris to Gov. Thomas Johnson, May 1, 1777, *ibid.*, pp. 236–38; Gov. Johnson to Gov. Henry, *ibid.*, p. 227.
[14] Council of State to Col. John Dickinson, June 11, 1777, *ibid.*, 284.
[15] William Whitely to Gov. Thomas Johnson, May 19, 1777, *Red Books*, 18:66; Christopher Birckhead to Gov. Thomas Johnson, June 3, 1777, *ibid.*, 22:156.

to every sense of virtue and regard for the interest and happiness of their country, that no measure but that of a compulsory nature will have the least effect with them."[16]

Frustrated, Colonel Richardson tried other expedients, including the enlisting of servants. But this proved counterproductive, as he explained to Governor Johnson. "So general a desertion prevails amongst the servants enlisted into our Army," wrote the colonel, "that I have ordered my officers to forbear enlisting any more of them, seeing that it was only recruiting men for the enemy not for us."[17]

Complicating matters further, those units that could be scraped together by Richardson and others were of an extremely inferior quality. The officers could not trust the men; the men resented their superiors.[18] One of the primary duties of the forces on the Eastern Shore was to protect the coast against British raiding parties and also to cut off the extensive intercourse between the British and the shore people which served to embolden the resistance. But the untrained, poorly disciplined, and undermanned militia units were no match for the British, who triumphed decisively in the few encounters that occurred. Normally they captured upwards of one-third of the militia's arms. Even had the Maryland troops been better, their leaders more resourceful, and the men more dedicated, they would still have experienced difficulty in interdicting the British supply lines. William Paca came to this conclusion after touring the area in September 1777. Whatever military forces existed, he said, were needed to control both the "Negroes" who were continually "flocking down" from the interior and the rising disaffected. The interior must be guarded, he felt, even if that meant ignoring the British.[19]

These conditions produced two general consequences. By the fall some of the wealthy residents on the Eastern Shore began to relocate their "distressed families" in safer areas across the bay.[20] But if the shore no longer appealed to them, it did to the British general, Sir William Howe. His decision to go to Philadelphia in 1777 by way of the Chesapeake was based partly on the sympathy and support he expected to receive from the inhabitants of that region. Howe considered the Delmarva peninsula to have military potential and believed the area was

---

[16] Joseph Dashiell to Gov. Thomas Johnson, June 28, 1777, *ibid.*, 22:59.

[17] William Richardson to Gov. Thomas Johnson, June 13, 1777, *ibid.*, 16:106.

[18] John Done to Col. Joseph Dashiell, June 9, 1777, *ibid.*, 16:33; Col. Joseph Dashiell to Col. William Richardson, June 9, 1777, *ibid.*, 16:34.

[19] William Paca to Gov. Thomas Johnson, September 26, 1777, *ibid.*, 4:96.

[20] Edward Lloyd to Thomas Johnson, August 31, 1777, Executive Papers, box 8, MHR.

well able to serve as a supply base for the British army.[21] While Howe never occupied the Eastern Shore, his thoughts certainly encouraged the Tory forces there.

After entering the Chesapeake in his 1777 campaign, Howe issued a proclamation on August 27 addressed to "The Province of Pennsylvania, the Lower Counties on the Delaware, and Counties on the Eastern Shore of the Chesapeake Bay," promising protection, security and a pardon to all men who disavowed the rebellion and supported George III.[22] Captain Walter Griffith on board H.M.S. *Nonsuch* issued another proclamation directed specifically to the Western Shore's residents, concerning the special status the British were according the Eastern Shore. He warned "the inhabitants of the several towns, and of the sea coast on the western side of the Chesapeake that if they, in any manner, molest (either in their persons or property) the inhabitants of the Eastern Shore, who may be disposed to return to duty and allegiance, they may expect to feel the full force and weight of retribution and resentment from his Majesty's forces."[23] Obviously the British were well aware of the sentiment for them on the peninsula and the difficulties of the Maryland authorities there.

Howe emphasized to his men that in dealing with the local residents they should remain on excellent behavior. Some who disobeyed were reportedly lashed "1,000 times." A young British officer similarly encouraged his men to act like gentlemen, since he knew the people there disliked the patriot forces for being too often "in their cups." He humorously absolved the rebel officers for allowing their men to drink, since he understood that only by giving them an "extraordinary quantity of strong liquor" could they be persuaded to fight.[24]

From the perspective of Annapolis, the Eastern Shore seemed ready to secede. Governor Johnson believed rightly that the British intended "to cut off the Eastern Shore from the Western Shore."[25] In September a plot was discovered which aimed at the takeover of the Eastern Shore's southern counties. The plan, attributed by some to Lord Dunmore, envi-

[21] For this information I am indebted to Edward Papenfuse, Assistant Archivist of the State of Maryland; see also G. Harlan Wells, "The British Campaign of 1777 in Maryland Prior to the Battle of Brandywine," *Maryland Historical Magazine* 33 (March 1938), 318.

[22] *Ibid.*

[23] "Proclamation by Walter Griffith on Board H.M.S. *Nonsuch* to the Inhabitants of the Western Side of the Chesapeake," *Red Books*, 18:5.

[24] Wells, "British Campaign of 1777," pp. 11–13.

[25] Gov. Thomas Johnson to the House of Delegates, November 6, 1777, *Archives of Maryland* 16:410.

sioned the seizure of all public arms, starting with the magazine located at Snow Hill, the county seat of Worcester. How the men intended to proceed is not clear, but one of the participants said that the whole venture was devised because they wanted "liberty and to be free." Just prior to the attack, word came from Somerset to abandon the project because "the matter would soon be settled for them" in another manner, presumably by the British.[26]

When the General Assembly convened that fall, one of its first considerations was the passage of a law providing the death penalty for any person who would "willfully and maliciously burn or destroy or attempt to conspire to burn or destroy any magazine of provisions or naval stores."[27] This act and the Worcester County conspiracy emphasized the seriousness of the situation. Everyone was alarmed, including General Washington, who directed one of his best Maryland officers, Colonel Mordecai Gist, to take command of the area.[28] Previously Washington, needing reinforcements, had contemplated asking for some militia forces from the shore. Possibly he thought they were doing no real good and could be put to more effective use. Whatever his reasons, he now changed his mind. As the Council of State told Joseph Dashiell, "General Washington we hope and expect, will not want the assistance of your county militia. We are sorry there is so much occasion for them at home and therefore countermand the former order for their marching."[29]

At Annapolis conditions on the Eastern Shore were not the only worry. With British forces controlling the bay, the state's leaders faced the possibility of a military collapse on the Western Shore as well. Discipline, always poor, deteriorated even further. Enlisted men frequently refused to muster, threatened their officers openly and grew increasingly surly. Whenever a unit was activated, desertions began almost immediately. In one battalion of approximately 300 men, fifty desertions occurred on a march of some sixty to seventy miles.[30] "Desertions," as General Smallwood told the governor in September, "are still frequent

---

[26] See depositions of Samuel Dreadon, John Hasher, Thomas Tyler, Ephraim Henderson, Selby Newton, and Hezekiah Cary in Executive Papers, box 8, MHR.

[27] Kilty, *Laws of Maryland*, vol. 1, chap. 1, October 1777.

[28] Mordecai Gist to Gov. Thomas Johnson, September 1, 1777, Maryland State Papers, Brown Books, MHR (cited hereafter as *Brown Books*), 3:51.

[29] Council of State to Joseph Dashiell, September 22, 1777, *Archives of Maryland*, 16:383.

[30] John H. Stone to Gov. Thomas Johnson, July 24, 1777, *ibid.*, p. 318; Zadok Magruder to Gov. Thomas Johnson, June 20, 1777, *Red Books*, 14:21; General William Smallwood to Col. James Rhodes, September 24, 1777, Executive Papers, box 8, MHR.

and I am apprehensive will become more so."[31] Concerning a regiment of over one hundred men from Anne Arundel County, Smallwood reported in October that only twenty-eight remained. "The men from Elkridge and some other parts of Anne Arundel," he commented bitterly, "will shine more at an election than in the field—their disorder and licentiousness under our present regulations will ever render them contemptible in the field."[32] Still these men were needed to meet the threats of disaffected elements, both white and black, particularly with the expanded British presence. In Harford County a militia officer placed his company near the neck of a river "to prevent the Negroes, servants, and disaffected peoples from going to the enemy." Already, he reluctantly admitted, "several Negroes are gone from our parts on board, and some white people and without a good lookout, a number more will go." Another official from Cecil reported that he did not possess the troops necessary to give his county "security and take up a number of the Negroes that, at present, have nobody to stop them from going to the enemy."[33] Similar conditions were found throughout the Western Shore. Colonel Richard Barnes reported from St. Mary's that his county was exposed, poorly defended, and weakened by internal dissension. "No part of the state, I am satisfied," he said, "is worse armed than this county, added to our internal weakness, the Negroes who, I am informed, in the lower part of the county are beginning to be very insolent."[34]

All of these difficulties were further compounded in the first week of October, when large-scale rioting broke out in Baltimore County. Some accounts estimated the number of rioters at 700 men.[35] There the tensions produced by an unruly militia as well as restive servants and slaves were aggravated by the bravado of the nonassociators. The case of Henry Guyton is illustrative of how open was the defiance. Guyton, a nonassociator, refused to have any dealings with the new government, including the payment of a fine required of people in his category. A

[31] General William Smallwood to Gov. Thomas Johnson, September 8, 1777, *Archives of Maryland*, 16:366.
[32] General William Smallwood to Gov. Thomas Johnson, October 14, 1777, *ibid.*, p. 398.
[33] Charles Rumsey to Gov. Thomas Johnson, October 8, 1777, Executive Papers, box 8, MHR; Aquilla Hall to Gov. Thomas Johnson, August 28, 1777, *Red Books*, 18:91.
[34] Col. Richard Barnes to Gov. Thomas Johnson, September 15, 1777, *Red Books*, 17:177; see also Thomas Stone to Gov. Thomas Johnson, December 9, 1777, *ibid.*, 4:31; Executive Papers, box 8, MHR.
[35] Andrew Buchanan to Gov. Thomas Johnson, October 2, 1777, *Red Books*, 17:180.

distraint sale was then scheduled to make good his fine and an unsuspecting individual by the name of George Brown bought Guyton's heifer and steer. But when Brown went to pick up his cows he encountered Guyton who "came up to him in a great rage and singing a hymn (he being one of the people called Methodists)" asked him if he wanted to fight. Next Guyton sent for "eight white men and one Negro to prevent" Brown from claiming his merchandise. Wisely, George Brown decided that "he would not contend with them but would take the law of them and said Henry answered him that he would wipe his ass with his law." Guyton then directed Brown "to go about his business and seek his recompense, and then turned up his ass and said a fart for them that will give it to you."[36]

The October rioting was sparked by a similar incident. Many of the county inhabitants, rather than serve in the military, requested that substitutes be raised. Some replacements were found, but when the sheriff attempted to levy the executions needed to pay for the soldiers acquired, somewhere between 200 and 700 men rose in resistance.[37] Immediately the Council of State acted. It requested military assistance from other counties, asked the lieutenant of Baltimore County's militia to contain the riots, and ordered a large matrosse company stationed in Annapolis into the area "to suppress an insurrection in the upper part of that county." These well-armed troops, along with a strongly worded proclamation promising severe punishment, brought the disorders under control.[38] But this precedent did not curb the dissension that continued to plague the province. A very worried and disgusted colonel in St. Mary's County summed up the situation best when he informed the governor that the militiamen under his command were openly threatening "that they will shoot several of their field officers: it really begins to be high time," he pressed "to put our government in full force and some examples made or nothing but anarchy and destruction must ensue."[39]

Several decades ago, one historian concluded in an influential study of Maryland that there "the masses of inarticulate citizenry remained, on the whole, inarticulate. When they did raise their voices to demand a

[36] Charge against Henry Guyton, *Archives of Maryland*, 16:76–77.
[37] Andrew Buchanan to Gov. Thomas Johnson, October 2, 1777, *Red Books*, 17: 180.
[38] Council of State to Aquilla Hall, October 3, 1777, *Archives of Maryland*, 16: 388–89; Council of State to Andrew Buchanan, October 3, 1777, *ibid.*, 388–90; Resolution passed in Council, October 3, 1777, Executive Papers, box 8, MHR.
[39] Col. Richard Barnes to Gov. Thomas Johnson, December 20, 1777, *Red Books*, 17:192.

share in state making, they were either squelched or disregarded."[40] This evaluation would amuse the state's early leadership. True, the aristocratic members of the popular party fashioned a conservative constitution and gained firm control of the government. When the first legislature convened in February 1777, all of them were present. Charles Carroll of Carrollton, Daniel of St. Thomas Jenifer, Matthew Tilghman, Charles Carroll, Barrister, Robert Goldsborough, and Thomas Johnson won seats in the Senate.[41] Samuel Chase directed the popular coalition's forces in the lower house. On February 13, 1777, the legislature elected Thomas Johnson the state's first governor. The complete vote in the election reflected the party's strength. All five of the individuals nominated were members of the popular faction. The balloting gave Thomas Johnson forty votes, Samuel Chase nine, Matthew Tilghman one, George Plater one, and William Paca one.

Theoretically, the members of the popular party were in a strong position. They commanded the established institutions. But to examine these institutions alone is to miss the far more significant actions occurring in the general society. Men like Chase, Carroll, Johnson, and Jenifer knew full well that their authority was tenuous and insecure. Their domination of the government was comforting, but the constitution had been structured to insure this control. Most of the popular leaders were senators who in accordance with the constitution owed their seats to wealthy electors and only indirectly to the people. They governed with no popular mandate. Whatever their popular base had once been, it was now rapidly disappearing under a spreading wave of discontent.

When the Senate first met that February, several members were not present, among them Daniel of St. Thomas Jenifer. Carroll wrote urging him to attend so the Senate might act quickly to deal with the deteriorating conditions. Jenifer, always a sensitive observer, replied that he believed the new government weak, unpopular, and unable to act effectively. Because of the constitution's "many gradations and exclusions" he anticipated "that there will not be men enough found of sufficient abilities to turn the machine with the velocity which the present exigencies of our affairs require. Besides," he continued, "the Senate does not appear to me to be the child of the people at large and therefore will not be supported by them longer than there subsists the most perfect union between the different legislative branches. How long that may be, you, who know mankind full well as I do, may easily determine." Once the

[40] Philip A. Crowl, *Maryland During and After the Revolution: A Political and Economic Study* (Baltimore, Md.: The Johns Hopkins Press, 1943), p. 19.
[41] *Votes and Proceedings*, February session, 1777.

assembly undertook to provide for the war, he fully expected a violent confrontation to engulf and ultimately bring down the government. To meet the financial requirements of the military effort "taxes must be laid and the money made a legal tender." These measures "may not alike suit every man, hence will arise diversity of sentiment, warmth will ensue and your government immediately be dissolved."[42]

Jenifer was not the only man holding these opinions. With the prospects of growing insurrections, spreading riots, and continuing military disobedience, all the state's leaders feared the future. They and their close supporters constituted society's wealthy elite, and they had the most to gain or lose on the outcome of the next few years. The immediate problem was to popularize themselves and the revolutionary cause in order to gain support. With this in mind, the legislature enacted two radical measures during its first session. One altered and reformed the taxation system, and the other almost eliminated the burden of debt owed within the state.

The new taxation structure created in 1777 differed dramatically from its colonial predecessor. Prior to 1776, two separate tax bases were employed in Maryland. Land was the basis for proprietary dues, while provincial and county taxes were raised by a poll tax. The Calvert family, concerned more with its own profits than with development of the colony, managed an extremely productive quit-rent system. From 1738 to the time of the Revolution, the quit rent set by the proprietors was four shillings per hundred acres of land. Zealous local officials were instructed that this was a minimum rate and that they could opt for a higher assessment. The governor, secretary, or judges of the land office could increase the quit-rent rate whenever they deemed the planters could bear it. The rent was collected in two ways: the governor could either appoint private persons (known as farmers of the rent), or he could designate receivers, usually sheriffs. To facilitate the collection of revenues, the governor also appointed two general rent roll keepers, one for each shore. Their tasks were mainly of a supervisory and coordinating nature. They received the duties collected, kept the rolls for each county of their shore, and from these rolls calculated the quit rent owed by each county. To perform their jobs the keepers received a constant stream of information from the judges of the land offices concerning all the changes in land ownership, and all new grants or surveys made. The proprietary instructions outlining this system created an organized body

[42] Daniel of St. Thomas Jenifer to Charles Carroll of Carrollton, February 2, 1777, *Archives of Maryland* 16:108–09.

of minor officials apart from the government and independent of any legislative control. It paid off handsomely. For example, in the period from 1768 to 1774, an average income of £10,267 was collected for the proprietor.[43]

Once the Revolution began, the proprietary system was abolished and the entire taxation process came under legislative control. Taxation was not a new responsibility for the legislature. During the colonial period, the lower house levied a poll tax to secure funds for the provincial government. All freemen of the province sixteen or older, with the exception of clergymen, plus male servants over ten and all slaves, male or female, were defined as taxable. Sheriffs and constables of each county were required to make annual written reports to their county courts of the number of tithables living within their districts. In turn, the justices forwarded this information to the legislature in Annapolis. After the assembly calculated the government's expense for the coming year, a tax was set on the basis of the county court's reports. The sheriff and his subordinates collected the tax under the watchful eye of the county justices.[44]

From the founding of the colony up to the Revolution, the head tax formed the basis of the tax structure.[45] Since the poor as well as the rich paid the same rate, the system was regressive. With the heightened political tensions in the years immediately preceding the Revolution the tax structure came under serious criticism. Responding to this, the Constitutional Convention categorically abolished the poll tax, and the first legislature restructured the entire system.[46] A graduated property tax became the basis for the calculation of the rate. According to the law passed on February 5, 1777, each inhabitant of the state was to pay a tax of 10 shillings for every £100 worth of property he owned. Property was then defined solely in terms of land. If a man's holdings were not equal to £100, a ratio was to be calculated. Specie value formed the basis of the assessment, but the tax was payable in depreciated currency.

The definition of property was soon expanded. During the years 1777

---

[43] Clarence P. Gould, *The Land System in Maryland, 1720–1765* (Baltimore, Md.: The Johns Hopkins Press, 1913), pp. 28–59; Charles Albro Barker, *The Background of the Revolution in Maryland* (New Haven, Conn.: Yale University Press, 1940), p. 141.

[44] James Allen Kinnaman, "The Internal Revenues of Colonial Maryland" (Ph.D. diss., University of Minnesota, 1952), p. 250.

[45] *Ibid.*, p. 59.

[46] *Proceedings of the Conventions of the Province of Maryland* (Annapolis, 1836), p. 312.

to 1781, the legislature passed ten tax measures.[47] In October 1777, the lower house enlarged the term property to include all improvements the owners had made on their land. Besides these, the assessors were to consider all the mines and raw ore that might be located on the property. The term raw ore specifically included pig and bar iron, for which the legislature established special rates per ton. Similarly, if the property holder owned any silver plate, it was to be taxed at a definite rate per ounce. Slaves were also graded. A healthy male Negro in 1777 was, for tax purposes, worth £75, a Negro tradesman, £125. Later, in 1780, the tax on slaves was extended to include males and females from the age of fourteen. Town lots and buildings were similarly taxed on a scale reflecting their commercial value. To facilitate the assessor's computation, the assemblymen designed a rating scale as a guide for the assessors to employ in computing a tax rate. An acre of choice land was worth £4 and the lowest rate for poor land was pegged at 7s. 6d. All other assessments were to fall between these two limits.[48] Merchants were taxed on the basis of each £100 worth of property they held, including all ships and stocks in their possession.[49]

To encourage the payment of taxes, the legislature gave preferential treatment to certain lower classes, especially tenants and debtors. People living on rented land were permitted to pay the value of the assessment and deduct the tax from the rent tendered the owner.[50] Debtors received a similar inducement. All persons indebted at the time of assessment by judgment, mortgage, bond, bill, or other means upon which yearly interest accrued, were allowed to deduct the sum they paid in taxes each year from the annual interest rate owed to their creditors. The legislature directed all creditors to respect this reduction. If a creditor did not, and notice of such disobedience was brought to the attention of the county court, the creditor was to forfeit all interest due on the debt. To mitigate these provisions, the assembly declared that it would not calculate mortgages, bonds, and promissory notes in determining the property tax of a

---

[47] Session Laws of Maryland, February 5, 1777, "An Act to Assess and Impose an Equal Tax on all Property within this State"; the General Assembly passed tax laws during the following sessions: February 1777, October 1777, March 1778, October 1778, March 1779, October 1779, March 1780, November 1781.

[48] Session Laws of Maryland, October 31, 1777, "An Additional Supplement to the Act for the Assessment of Property."

[49] Session Laws of Maryland, November 1779, "An Act for the Assessment of Property within this State"; November 1781, "An Act for the Raising of Supplies for the Year Seventeen Hundred and Eighty-Two."

[50] Session Laws of Maryland, 1777–1781. This provision was contained in all Maryland taxation acts passed during the Revolution.

creditor.[51] In other words, the taxable estate of a creditor would not include monies owed him. Since, for some wealthy families, the credit held constituted as much as 25 percent of their total estate, this provision considerably lessened their tax burden.[52] Still, the deduction formula was clearly in the debtors' interest. In effect, the assembly, to gain the debtors' favor and encourage them to pay, was penalizing the creditors.

Surprisingly, this measure was the less radical of the two offered to achieve popularity that session. The other, concerning paper money, far exceeded the tax law in its efforts to rally large-scale support. The law proposed to make paper money a legal tender for all debts including those contracted in sterling before the separation from England. Since the value of paper money was already beginning to depreciate and it was likely this trend would continue, the proposal would reduce considerably the value of debts owed to creditors. No other state yet had written such an explosive piece of legislation.

Some of the leading proponents of the 1777 tender law were further motivated by personal considerations. Two of its chief supporters, Samuel Chase and Charles Ridgely, owed sizable debts.[53] Still, what is significant here is the broader social role the measure was designed to play. Practically the entire upper class, including both houses of the assembly, endorsed the legislation. Naturally, they were not very enthusiastic, since the provisions placed a disproportionate burden on the rich. But all of them realized they must make sacrifices to retain their leadership position. The more astute, including Charles Carroll of Carrollton, aptly defined the measure as the "price of Revolution." Real insight can be gained into the aristocracy's attitude on this question by a close examination of Carroll, who by now had regained his self-composure. Immediately after the act's passage, he and his father entered into a bitter dispute lasting over three years. Charles Carroll of Annapolis, after working hard all his life to build one of the greatest fortunes in North America, now saw much of it disappearing under a flood of worthless paper. His son disliked the financial loss as well, but strove unsuccessfully to convince

[51] *Ibid.*

[52] In 1764, Charles Carroll of Annapolis estimated that the monies he had out on loan constituted approximately 25 percent of his estate's worth. Charles Carroll of Annapolis to Charles Carroll of Carrollton, January 9, 1764, Charles Carroll of Annapolis Papers, Maryland Historical Society, Baltimore, Md. (cited hereafter as MHS).

[53] Charles Carroll of Annapolis to Charles Carroll of Carrollton, March 22, 1777; Charles Carroll of Carrollton to Charles Carroll of Annapolis, March 28, 1777; Charles Carroll of Annapolis to Charles Carroll of Carrollton, November 7, 1777; Charles Carroll of Annapolis to Daniel of St. Thomas Jenifer, June 20, 1778, all in Charles Carroll of Annapolis Papers, MHS.

his father that it was one of the social requirements demanded by a popular revolution. On occasion, the dispute came close to driving them apart. One thing, however, was certain—both men knew they were fighting for survival in a Revolution that had both external and internal dimensions. Knowing this, they were much wiser than many who have since written of them.

From the moment the law was suggested, Charles Carroll of Annapolis opposed it violently. The tone of sharpness and desperation present in his earliest words on the subject indicated how great he considered the challenge. "Should a law pass to make the Continental and our currencies a legal tender in all cases it will surpass in iniquity all the acts of the British Parliament against America. The Parliament only declares it has a right to take away our property, the duties they have imposed are trifling. But the act which you say will pass, takes away a real and universal medium of commerce by substituting a medium which eventually may be of no value." He did not want to be unreasonable, he said, for "if creditors are rigorous it is necessary a law should pass to give all reasonable indulgence to debtors, but it can not be consistent with justice to bestow the property of creditors on debtors and I shall look on every man who assents to such a law as infamous and would as soon associate with highway men and pickpockets as with them. I shall detest them as I do the British Parliament, because like that they act unreasonably, unjustly, iniquitously and tyrannically." He therefore advised his son "to draw up a strong and nervous protest against the law, setting forth your reasons at length. Many obvious and unanswerable ones must occur to you. Lose no time in preparing your protest, and if the law passes, give it and quit a station which you can not keep with honor."[54]

Charles Carroll of Carrollton agreed completely with his father's criticisms, but he was more politically aware and therefore subscribed to a different set of priorities. He felt it especially important to remain in political office to keep the leverage he had in the popular coalition. "I entirely agree with you as to the injustice of the law," he replied, "but I can not follow your advice to withdraw: where shall I withdraw?" Because of his intimate association with the day-to-day politics of the state he fully appreciated the seriousness of the current disorders. The government was struggling to attract support and the act was therefore necessary. He cautioned his father to gird himself for even greater attacks

[54] Charles Carroll of Annapolis to Charles Carroll of Carrollton, March 13, 1777, Charles Carroll of Annapolis Papers, MHS; for an interesting analysis as to the extent of debt holdings in Maryland, see Aubrey C. Land, "Economic Behavior in the Chesapeake Area," *Journal of Southern History* 33 (November 1967), pp. 469–85.

against the rich. "It can not be expected," wrote the younger Carroll, "that such great revolutions should happen without much partial injustice and suffering. I have long foreseen the consequences of this unhappy civil war and therefore have so tempered my mind that I can bear adversity with firmness, and have gradually prepared myself against the worst event."[55]

The old man would have none of this. Ignoring his son's warning, he explained the necessity for withdrawal from politics should the tender law pass. His reasoning was simple. Never give in—never allow the creation of such a precedent. Once it was established, the wealthy would soon be destitute. Should the tender act pass, he told his son, "you may naturally expect many more levelling laws. *Principis obsta*, ought to be the inflexible rule of every man of honor and honesty . . . why upon the principles of the law in question may not a law pass that no man shall hold above 500 acres of land—that he shall sell all above that quantity at the rate of £100 current per thousand? Why should not the landholder be obliged to part with his land as well as the sterling money holder be obliged to part with his sterling?"[56]

Within the next few days, Charles Carroll of Annapolis received more dismaying news; one of his closest associates, Samuel Chase, was a major backer of the bill. Up to that point he had been advising his son to work with Chase in blocking the measure. Now that this was no longer possible, he completely astounded the younger Carroll by suggesting another course of action. He directed his son to form a working alliance with Daniel Dulany! Naturally, he advised discretion: "You can not concert an opposition directly with Dulany, but you may do it indirectly." He realized how objectionable such a partnership was, but to persuade the Senate to use its veto, "the influence of all who are likely to suffer should be exerted. *Vis unita fortier*." Lastly, to drum up some support, the old man suggested that his letters be shown to the more influential members of the assembly.[57]

Charles Carroll of Carrollton considered nothing of the kind. Out of respect for his father's wishes, he was speaking against the measure even though he believed it necessary. But these latest suggestions were both preposterous and politically disastrous. Such letters could hardly be shown to anyone. "Your advice is very imprudent," he explained. The

[55] Charles Carroll of Carrollton to Charles Carroll of Annapolis, March 15, 1777, Charles Carroll of Annapolis Papers, MHS.
[56] Charles Carroll of Annapolis to Charles Carroll of Carrollton, March 18, 1777, Charles Carroll of Annapolis Papers, MHS.
[57] Charles Carroll of Annapolis to Charles Carroll of Carrollton, March 19, 1777, Charles Carroll of Annapolis Papers, MHS.

letters could not be distributed because "they discovered too much warmth, and it might be supposed that my opposition to the bill proceeded from interested motives and your entreaties. A man, if he wants to succeed in any public measure, must be cool and dispassionate or his opposition will surely be imputed to interest and consequently his arguments have less force on others." Similarly, any talk of withdrawal was not productive. "If I withdraw, I shall become obnoxious and be heavily assessed." Remembering his father's early fire for the revolutionary cause, he observed that "although injustice be done to individuals, my country on the whole is in the right; I mean that our public cause is just." Unfair sacrifices were demanded by the people but they were at least being made for a worthy cause. "These are the times in which men do not stick at trifles; they mean to cancel debts under a pretense of keeping up the value of the currency." That they were going to do so was "predetermined" and the best one could do was to be patient.[58]

Charles Carroll of Annapolis did not consider patience a virtue, as he told his son a few days later. "Your withdrawing will prove your detestation of rogues, your conduct may evince your patriotism. You had better be obnoxious to the multitude than associated with villains." America was correct, he agreed, but "the right is not to be asserted by unrighteous means." Because of the principles of "honor and honesty," he persisted, "you can not, I think, with honor continue to sit with men whose actions show them to be villains. Not one of them shall ever hereafter darken my door."[59]

By this time Charles Carroll of Carrollton was becoming annoyed with the obstinacy of his father, who refused to accept his son's definition of the correct way to proceed. Again, he promised to make a strong protest against the bill, but he respectfully reminded his father that it would pass since he alone would be in opposition. It was only sensible for him to acquiesce and make himself "easy on this score." The Revolution was going to cost them dearly. "I have long considered," young Carroll wrote, "our personal estate, I mean the money part of it, to be in jeopardy. If we can save a third of that and all our land and negroes, I shall think ourselves well off." When the legal tender proposal reached the Senate a few days later, Charles Carroll of Carrollton did as he said he would. He denounced it vigorously, but his oratory swayed no one. At the time of the vote, his was the only hand raised in opposition. By so

[58] Charles Carroll of Carrollton to Charles Carroll of Annapolis, March 22, 1777, and March 28, 1777, Charles Carroll of Annapolis Papers, MHS.
[59] Charles Carroll of Annapolis to Charles Carroll of Carrollton, April 1, 1777, Charles Carroll of Annapolis Papers, MHS.

acting, he considered that he had done all he could. Indeed he worried
that his vote might produce considerable ill will. One observer, the
former proprietary official William Eddis, shared his opinion. As he
wrote the former governor Robert Eden: "The bills passed for payment
of sterling debts with Congress and convention money will be attended
with the most distressing consequences to many persons, especially to the
friends of government who have large sums upon loan. Several of the
Senate, whether from *principle* or *interest*, I know not, expressed without doors, their highest disapprobation of this act, but only Carroll of
Carrollton had resolution to oppose it in the proper place. He animad-
verted on the injustice thereof, and protested against the same being
passed into a law; but his objections procured him no great reputation as
it was generally believed that he was not altogether actuated by sentiment alone."[60]

Charles Carroll of Carrollton wished that his father would consider
factors similar to those expressed by Eddis. But the old man had other
ideas. After receiving word of the bill's approval, he immediately wrote
asking, "who were present in the Senate when the bill past? Invite none
of them here for I shall turn them out of doors."[61] Within the next few
days the General Assembly adjourned, and the younger Carroll gratefully
left for Philadelphia to take his seat in congress. From there he patiently
continued to instruct his father that moderation was the only sensible
course. Try to reason with your debtors, he said near the end of May:
"When the debtors tender no more than the interest, I would not write
to them about the injustice of tendering the interest money at par." Give
in on this point but "when they tender more than interest, it would be
proper to expostulate with them on the injustice of the profferred payment." Above all, he implored, do "not bring yourself into trouble about
this law, although it is unjust it hath passed and we must submit to it or
take the consequences of a refusal."[62]

But Charles Carroll of Annapolis could not brook injustice and soon
tired of his son's caution. By June he refused to submit any longer.
Rather than deal with his son, he now decided to write the bill's primary
sponsor, Samuel Chase. From the beginning their exchange took on harsh
overtones. The elder Carroll, a direct man, bluntly accused Chase of
promoting an unjust law solely to win popularity. "The laws in all well
governed states," he began, "favor creditors—this law ruins them." It

[60] William Eddis to Gov. Robert Eden, July 23, 1777, Fisher Transcripts, MHS.

[61] Charles Carroll of Annapolis to Charles Carroll of Carrollton, April 13, 1777,
Charles Carroll of Annapolis Papers, MHS.

[62] Charles Carroll of Carrollton to Charles Carroll of Annapolis, May 27, 1777,
Charles Carroll of Annapolis Papers, MHS.

encourages debtors to "cheat as far as they are able." At the beginning of the dispute with Great Britain, recounted Carroll, Parliament "declared they have a right to take away our property—you have carried such a right into execution; where you will stop who can tell; why not take away our lands as well as our money; our right to both is equal." With ill temper, Carroll charged that such consideration "could not escape a man of your sagacity and abilities; if they did not I can not continue to entertain a favorable opinion of you, unless you show them to have no force by refuting them. I have heard you should say the law was a bitter pill to their honors, but that they must swallow it. If this be true," he concluded, "it adds to the unfavorable opinion I entertain of your behavior as your words imply a consciousness that you was promoting a law which you knew to be unjust."[63]

Chase, a proud and hot-tempered man who did not take criticism gracefully, replied the next day. "I have a right to respect notwithstanding our disparity of fortune," he announced. Carroll's letter lacked any measure of decency and employed an "asperity of language and a coarseness of expression applicable only to the coarsest and vilest of mankind." Carroll's personal opinion of him mattered nothing. "I am totally indifferent whether you *continue* to entertain a favorable opinion of me, or whether anything you have heard *adds* to that unfavorable opinion of my behavior or not."[64]

Upon receiving Chase's reply, Carroll vigorously denied that his previous letter contained coarse language. "I can not see any coarseness, indelicacy or asperity," he observed; "I believe every injured creditor will deem the questions they contain very proper and the language very mild." He should expect such treatment, maintained Carroll, for "when you voted for the law, you merit the coarsest and most opprobrious epithets which can be put upon paper. You have promoted, you have voted for a law by which creditors are robbed," and "you say you *are wholly indifferent and etc.*—why do you make use of that common evasion and pretense of infamous persons taxed with crimes they can not deny?" The old man then compensated for any lack of coarseness in his first letter:

E.G. A public strumpet taxed with her vices may say she is wholly indifferent what people say and whether they entertain a favorable or unfavorable opinion of her; yet notwithstanding her pretended indifference tho she

[63] Charles Carroll of Annapolis to Samuel Chase, June 5, 1777, Charles Carroll of Annapolis Papers, MHS.
[64] Samuel Chase to Charles Carroll of Annapolis, June 6, 1777, Charles Carroll of Annapolis Papers, MHS.

may be of a punk of quality, no one will scruple to call her a whore. In my last, I am not sensible that I fail'd in the respect due to your private or public station.[65]

During these heated exchanges, Charles Carroll of Carrollton remained in Philadelphia, complaining wearily of the tedium "of public business" and attempting to console his father. Despite the law's patent injustice, he cautioned it must be accepted in order not to "incur the odium of a whole people."[66] Besides the question of popularity, other considerations lay behind his advice. The power he now enjoyed was a product of his membership in the popular coalition. His father's repeated attacks served no meaningful purpose and endangered this connection. With the law receiving enthusiastic acceptance and Chase's popularity growing, the younger Carroll believed it both expedient and necessary to maintain his alliance with Chase. Even if such an arrangement might now be personally distasteful, he and his father must for the moment swallow their pride. Hearing of his father's angry exchange, he bluntly told the old man that if necessary he should "submit to be plundered," but more importantly he must stop his arguing with Chase. "If you love me, you will pursue this conduct," he implored.[67]

Another advisor to Charles Carroll of Annapolis and member of the popular party, Daniel of St. Thomas Jenifer, also told the rich patriarch to be more cautious. He fully agreed the law was corrupt and evil, but realized the people loved it. Jenifer had heard that Carroll was refusing "continental money" for debts owed: "I think you had better bend to the times than suffer yourself to be prosecuted which is talked of. There can be no doubt but that the tender bill will be hard upon monied men, but what is provoking the people will not allow them even to complain of the injury. For my own part I have always taken it without hesitation and have now a very considerable sum by me that I do not know what to do with it." He wished his old friend would do the same.[68]

Like Charles Carroll of Carrollton, Jenifer's correspondence reflected accurately the apprehensive attitude of many in the upper class. Shortly after the Senate had adjourned its first session, Jenifer wrote a young

[65] Charles Carroll of Annapolis to Samuel Chase, June 9, 1777, Charles Carroll of Annapolis Papers, MHS.
[66] Charles Carroll of Carrollton to Charles Carroll of Annapolis, May 24, 1777, and June 10, 1777, Charles Carroll of Annapolis Papers, MHS.
[67] Charles Carroll of Carrollton to Charles Carroll of Annapolis, June 16, 1777, Charles Carroll of Annapolis Papers, MHS.
[68] Daniel of St. Thomas Jenifer to Charles Carroll of Annapolis, June 18, 1777, Charles Carroll of Annapolis Papers, MHS.

lady of whom he was fond, warning her not to be so outspoken in her criticism of the new government. Be "cautious and well guarded in your expressions," he advised, since there are "many envious and malicious people in the world who are always waiting an opportunity to take advantage of their neighbors." Remarks such as ones she had recently made were dangerous because of those "whose violent patriotism would not allow them the smallest time for reflection." He completely concurred that if the patriots possessed a measure of intelligence "our affairs would be conducted with more propriety; but on the contrary many of them are thrown into confusion." Still these men currently enjoyed great power, and he suggested that her views be "softened and converted into those of a *mild* Whig." Being a cautious man, he naturally requested her "to be kind enough to burn" his letter "without showing it" to anyone.[69]

Charles Carroll of Annapolis reluctantly listened to the advice of his son and Jenifer, accepting, as they put it, the judgment of "yielding to the times."[70] With his father at last acting reasonably, Carroll now turned his attention to the General Assembly meeting that June. During that session, his assumptions about the viability and worth of his alliance with Chase proved correct. Soon after the legislature convened, rumors began circulating that Chase planned to move for a general confiscation of all British property. William Eddis commented on this to Eden, saying he expected a speedy "confiscation of estates and property belonging to absentees, and others attached to the British Constitution."[71] Carroll vigorously opposed any such scheme as dangerous and ill-advised. He judged the seizure of private property a much greater threat than the tender act. He further worried that any confiscation in Maryland might jeopardize the extensive holdings still retained by the Carroll family in England.[72] Working within the popular coalition, Carroll seemed assured by the end of the month that Chase would not back the measure.[73] For Charles Carroll the politician this looked to be proof enough that his former friend Samuel Chase remained a reasonable, albeit ambitious, man.

Throughout the summer and into early fall, Charles Carroll of Annapolis obliged his son. But his dispute with Chase had not ended. At the beginning of November, the cantankerous old man finally gave in to his frustrations. Once again he resurrected all the old charges in a long letter

[69] Daniel of St. Thomas Jenifer to Polly Riche, May 25, 1777, Society Collections, Historical Society of Pennsylvania, Philadelphia, Pa.

[70] See n. 68.

[71] William Eddis to Gov. Robert Eden, July 23, 1777, Fisher Transcripts, MHS.

[72] See chapter 10.

[73] Charles Carroll of Carrollton to Charles Carroll of Annapolis, June 26, 1777, Charles Carroll of Annapolis Papers, MHS.

to Chase laced with sarcastic remarks. Up until now, he said, the friendship Chase enjoyed with his son had served to curb his passions. Yet after careful reflection, he now fully realized the necessity of speaking his mind, since the very concept of friendship could mean little to a man of Chase's caliber. "As you promoted and voted for so iniquitous a law," charged Carroll, "you may be as little influenced by a sense of friendship as by a regard for honesty and justice." After explaining his temporary silence, he suggested that if Chase wanted to regain the Carroll family's affection, he should have the law repealed: "I have also heard you declared you esteemed me and valued my friendship. Is the promotion and voting for a law which flagitiously robs me of a great part of my property a proof of the veracity and sincerity of that declaration? I have also heard that you expressed your wonder that in preference to others I chose to address you. I answer I looked upon many to be ignorant, upon you as a man of abilities, as a leader, as a man knowing the law you patronized to be unjust or as you expressed yourself, a bitter pill. . . . If I was not mistaken, if you did not sin with your eyes open, if you desire to be esteemed an honest man it is incumbent on you to labor the repeal of the law with as much sincerity, warmth and application as you promoted it. Should you miscarry, you may in some measure find your conscience eased by your endeavors to make restitution to the injured." But, he warned, "your pride, the contrariety of your conduct and many more such obstacles will present themselves to you and make the step painful. It is with you to determine whether reason, justice and honor ought to prevail."[74]

Chase never read these words. Charles Carroll of Carrollton saw to that. The letter reached him before Chase, and upon reading the message he stopped its delivery. He had thought the dispute over; he was angry to find his father once again causing trouble. Now fully aware of his father's intransigence, he wrote questioning his wisdom and defending Chase. Considering the social disorder that threatened them all, Chase's conduct was not nearly so bad as that of those men who had secretly opposed the act, but "sacrificed the convictions of their own consciences to popularity founded in injustice." Chase had at least been completely open in his support of the bill and Carroll appreciated such honesty. In addition, he could not help but suspect his father's motives. How much of the old man's arguments were grounded in personality and how much in principle? "Does your sentiment proceed," he asked, "from any reflec-

---

[74] Charles Carroll of Annapolis to Samuel Chase, November 1, 1777, Charles Carroll of Annapolis Papers, MHS.

tion thrown on your character by Chase?" Was it really a sense of conviction that gave rise to such bitter censures or was it more a matter of wounded pride? "I entreat you to forbear and no longer fret yourself with the empty impertinence of a man, who whatever he might have said in the gust of passion, I am sure esteems, nay more, I am sure has still an affection, at least a great regard for you."[75]

But like a wall of granite the old man refused to be swayed. "I wrote to Chase," he replied, "with reflections, and cool deliberation" and "I do and must continue to look upon him as a rogue unworthy the society of honest men." Chase was the one, contended the elder Carroll, who debased the argument into a contest of vindictive prose: "He wrote to me he was wholly indifferent whether I continued to entertain a favorable opinion of him—is not that the language of all hardened and incorrigible villains? The iniquity of the law is evident and he says he is unconcerned at his promoting it. I strongly suspect his enmity to Dulany prompted him. His pretended friendship for us, a regard to justice were motives too weak to combat his malice." Considering both the fiduciary and moral principles at stake, he had to speak out. All those afflicted should protest until the assembly reversed the measure. And to his way of thinking the mildness, indeed meekness, of his son was not flattering. "Who is more injured than myself," he asked, "and consequently who more forceably called upon to expose the villainy? Believe me your meekness of temper, you may think it prudence, is out of season." He considered all who supported the act, either overtly or covertly, to be despicable, and he firmly requested his son to see the letter delivered. "Cover it again and order Skerrett to direct and deliver it. It would give me pain to deny you anything, but the suppression of this letter. I advised you to quit the company of the rogues who voted for the bill, but left you at liberty. I hope I may meet with the same indulgence from you."[76]

Carroll ignored his father's abrasiveness. Instead he continued to emphasize the enthusiastic acceptance of the law, the nature of popular revolutions, and the inappropriateness of concentrating on Chase as a target of abuse. "I beg you to consider well and suffer not your passion or your interest to get the better of your understanding," for Chase, he pleaded, was of all the tender measure's advocates "the most improper to be singled out." Besides, Chase could not alone bring about a repeal, and

[75] Charles Carroll of Carrollton to Charles Carroll of Annapolis, November 2, 1777, Charles Carroll of Annapolis Papers, MHS.
[76] Charles Carroll of Annapolis to Charles Carroll of Carrollton, November 7, 1777, Charles Carroll of Annapolis Papers, MHS.

the law, now in effect for several months, enjoyed enormous popularity. "Reflect on this," he implored, "that the number of offenders lessens the ignominy of the crime; a common reproach is no reproach; perhaps there are not in this state more than 500 men who disapprove of the law although thousands would acknowledge the injustice of it. The reason is obvious, *virtus laudatum, et alget*; the bulk of mankind admires that virtue, that justice, that rectitude in others which they themselves find it inconvenient to practice." Carroll then brilliantly conceptualized what he believed to be the demands forced upon the rich:

The law suits the multitudes, individuals must submit to partial losses; no great revolutions can happen in a state without revolutions or mutations of private property. Were the injury more personal and fewer interested in the doing of it, or applauding it when done, you might be right in stigmatizing the authors.[77]

Surely after intelligently weighing all the relevant factors, his father would not want the letter delivered. Not so, came the immediate reply. All of his son's arguments the elder Carroll dismissed as inappropriate, and he demanded his wishes be respected. "I judge you have not ordered it may be delivered. It is needless to reason any further on the matter. If I was certain," he maintained, that "imprisonment and even death were to be the consequences of my letter I would not countermand it."[78]

At last the son agreed. He went personally to deliver the message hoping to mitigate its caustic manner. But when told of its contents, Chase refused to accept it. He politely told his friend he would not read the letter because, "I wish to avoid an altercation with your father." Carroll reported all this to the old man, commenting that he personally considered Chase's attitude sound and eminently mature: "I really think to speak my mind freely he has acted with more wisdom than you have done and I hope you will not trouble yourself any more with letters to him or anyone else on the subject." Not only did such conduct damage the family's political standing, but it also placed all of them in danger. The circulation of "imprudent, virulent publications, which would be quite out of season, might injure all connected with you," he warned. There is no knowing what the consequences might be if a letter, such as the one sent to Chase, were published. And again, with obvious impa-

---

[77] Charles Carroll of Carrollton to Charles Carroll of Annapolis, November 8, 1777, Charles Carroll of Annapolis Papers, MHS.

[78] Charles Carroll of Annapolis to Charles Carroll of Carrollton, November 10, 1777, Charles Carroll of Annapolis Papers, MHS.

tience, he offered some remarkable guidelines on the ways of revolutionary politics:

If no consequence should happen to your person very many, I am sure, would
happen to our property. There is a time when it is wisdom to yield to injustice and to popular heresies and delusions. Many wise and good men have
acted so—when public bodies commit injustice, and are espoused to the public
and can not vindicate themselves by reasoning, they commonly have recourse
to violence and greater injustice towards all such as have the temerity to
oppose them, particularly when their unjust proceedings are popular.[79]

Despite these strong words, Charles Carroll of Annapolis predictably
dismissed his son's "fears and prudence as idle and out of season." Indeed,
he found the young man's political character distasteful. "Are you not
too fond of popularity," he questioned, "and has not that fondness biased
your judgment?"[80] To this rebuff, Charles Carroll of Carrollton replied
that a wise man should know when to give up a lost contest. "I assure
you I am not fond of popularity," he told his father, "because I am
convinced it is often gained by the unworthy. I would wish to deserve
the good opinion of the good and discerning," he continued; "now I am
sure the bulk of mankind are neither good, nor discerning and 'tis for this
very reason I wish to avoid publications relative to the tender bill. They
will answer no good purpose, and may subject us both to very disagreeable consequences, particularly if written in the same intemperate style
of your letter to Chase." Because of the indisputable correctness of these
observations, he maintained, "your reasoning however just will not be
understood or listened to by the people—it is too much against their
interests to believe what you say. And if they should believe they will
pretend not to believe and impute your invectives against the injustice of
the act to your particular interest. I am never for showing my teeth till I
can bite."[81]

For a time these abrupt words convinced Charles Carroll of Annapolis
that his son's opposition was final. As he had done in the past, he again
turned to the Senate President, Daniel of St. Thomas Jenifer, for support.
But Jenifer felt every bit as strongly as the younger Carroll that both the
legal tender measure and the man, Samuel Chase, were too formidable to

[79] Charles Carroll of Carrollton to Charles Carroll of Annapolis, November 13,
1777, Charles Carroll of Annapolis Papers, MHS.
[80] Charles Carroll of Annapolis to Charles Carroll of Carrollton, November 14,
1777, Charles Carroll of Annapolis Papers, MHS.
[81] Charles Carroll of Carrollton to Charles Carroll of Annapolis, November 15,
1777, Charles Carroll of Annapolis Papers, MHS.

oppose. "I would most cheerfully communicate your letter to Chase, to others, would it produce any good consequences," he told Carroll, "but our patriots seem determined that all property shall bend to their frenzy."[82] For Jenifer that constituted the unfortunate reality and the only intelligent alternative required bending "with the times."

But Charles Carroll of Annapolis was not a man given to expedient solutions, particularly ones that cost him money. Encountering persistent and determined resistance from his son and all of his social contacts, he nevertheless continued unsuccessfully to rail against the tender measure. He never accepted what his son, Jenifer, and others in the Senate and lower house believed to be essential. They knew that the legal tender act, like the reformed taxation scheme, was demanded by the turbulent conditions if their class were to survive as a leadership force. They knew that the estranged, the aggrieved, the disgruntled must be detached from the committed Tory element. All of them agreed on this. Each time the measure came up for renewal it went through without dissent. Not until late in 1780, with an eased social situation, could the act be repealed. But in those early revolutionary years the strong support given by the entire Senate and House indicated clearly that all these gentlemen concurred with Charles Carroll of Carrollton's interpretation of the forces unleashed by the popular revolution. "No great revolution can happen in a state without revolutions or mutations of private property," he had told his father, and none except the old man showed any sign of daring to think differently.

In a very real sense the revolutionary leaders struck a clever bargain with the people. Amidst great confusion the political and wealthy elite prepared and implemented a highly conservative constitution specifically designed to preserve a structured class society. But unable to ram such an arrangement through in the high-handed and indifferent manner they undoubtedly preferred, these men intelligently pursued a course designed to achieve acceptability. When Charles Carroll of Annapolis accused his son and Chase of courting popularity, he struck at the heart of the matter. If the maintenance of public control and proper ruling institutions required such measures, both men gladly sacrificed principle for power.

There was, in addition, a third and quieter way in which the new government sought institutionalization. Support was needed at the local level. To establish a loyal force for the new authority, the revolutionary leaders created a host of positions. The purpose for this was simple. It

---

[82] Daniel of St. Thomas Jenifer to Charles Carroll of Annapolis, November 27, 1777, Charles Carroll of Annapolis Papers, MHS.

was to tie large numbers of people in a very personal and profitable way to the new order. Since the majority of individuals coming into the positions had never before held office, their loyalty could be counted upon. William Eddis commented on this tactic to Eden: "You know, sir, it has long been popular in this country to exclaim against the [former proprietary] administration on account of the number of officers, and the salaries, fees, and etc. granted for their support, but most true it is, that exclusive of army and navy appointments the persons now employed, greatly, very greatly, exceed every former establishment, and if their paper can be supposed of any real value, the present rulers most amply reward the laborers in their vineyard."[83] Figures available for office holding during the Revolution bear out Eddis' observation. Between 1776 and 1778 some 913 new positions were established at the county level to enforce the various administrative programs adopted by the legislature. Tax commissioners, purchasing agents, loan subscription committees, and other such agencies came into existence. In all, the General Assembly selected 414 people to serve, and of that number 335 entered a position of authority for the first time. Their presence at the county level represented a reliable force aiding the state's authorities in the efforts to establish control.[84]

Throughout 1777 and into 1778 Maryland's political leadership fought hard and skillfully on two fronts for survival. Internally the waves of discontent seemed perilously close to engulfing them. Externally, British ships sailed at will in the bay. Destruction from without and within looked all too possible as the reports from militia authorities continued to pour in, emphasizing the extent of desertion and disobedience, which rendered their commands ineffective.

The more immediate factors precipitating this unrest can be easily isolated and described. Certainly some opponents to the new government were persuaded by a sense of loyalty to Britain as well as by the British agents sent in to encourage opposition. Enemies of the revolutionary government frequently expressed their support of the crown. But an equal number maintained vigorously that they opposed the British. Some of them claimed the mantle of true revolutionaries more committed to the rebellion than the lordly gentlemen whose homes they sacked. Simi-

[83] William Eddis to Gov. Robert Eden, July 23, 1777, Fisher Transcripts, MHS.
[84] The names of all county officials appointed during the Revolution are located in the Journals of the Senate and the House. Each time a position was created, such as tax collector, loan subscriber, purchaser, etc., the individuals appointed to implement the measures were listed by county. For county positions held before the Revolution, see Oliver Goldsmith's unpublished Civil Lists of Maryland, MHS.

larly, the traditional categories of patriots and loyalists are no help in explaining the intense division present in the militia units and the wider society as underlined by the nonassociators' open defiance. An analysis of the currents motivating the varieties of resistance must ask a more fundamental question than simply where a man pledged his loyalty. Specifically, some answer must be given to explain why so many people in the lower and middle ranges of the society rose up in opposition to the new authority. What was it about the revolutionary government and the context in which it operated that made it an object of resentment for large numbers of people? Why did the Whig ideology fail to arouse these people for the confrontation? Or more correctly, why were the exponents of that ideology unsuccessful in marshaling sufficient support to maintain stability?

Situations of social dislocation present individuals with difficult choices because men are creatures driven by an array of frequently contradictory sentiments. A man is a father, husband, and provider, so he must be cautious. Yet he may also be confronted by difficult economic conditions that threaten his ability to carry out his responsibilities. Resentful because of the hardship he endures, his anger becomes directed against all those who hold positions of dominance in his immediate environment. Normally his feelings of insecurity may tell him to go slow, wait, and be sure to support the more powerful side. But when having to make dangerous decisions in a tense social situation, his frustrations may reach a point where he flails out against all those forces beyond his control causing him such intense anxiety.

Within Maryland one point can be seen clearly amidst the confusion. All the differing forms of disorder were characterized primarily by a strong resentment of authority. As the established standards of conduct began to erode under the social disarray and emotionalism created by the Revolution, the traditional leadership came under attack. People in the lower orders, possibly a majority in some Eastern Shore communities, having lived with the economic and psychological disadvantages of being a subordinate class, now lashed out in anger at those figures dominating their immediate lives. The actions expressing this hatred varied. Some actively aided the British by taking up arms. Others pillaged locally with no particular direction. The majority openly, indeed defiantly, refused to be disciplined and showed contempt when their betters demanded respect and deference. Because of such a diverse pattern the resistance movement had the appearance of an undirected social eruption so intensely passionate and yet so chaotic that it was not susceptible to any one form of explanation or to any clear political channeling.

Some partial understanding of the people who participated in these disorders is possible. During the years 1778–1781 the general court tried many of them for treason, insurrection, and riotous behavior. Joseph Dashiell, the county lieutenant of Worcester, had called them wretches of the earth. They were not quite that, though his supercilious remark explains much about why he personally was unable to command authority. By examining tax records remaining from the late revolutionary years, an economic profile of the men indicted can be reconstructed. Out of a total of 194 individuals so charged, 100, or approximately 52 percent, were located.

TABLE 6   *Acreage Holdings of Men Indicted by the General Court*

Acreage	NL*	0–50	50–100	100–150	150–200	200–300	300–400	400–500	500+
Percent Indicted	34	6	5	17	10	14	5	5	4

* NL = nonlandowner.

As table 6 indicates, 34 percent of the men held no land. Presumably most of these were either tenants, renters, or part of a roving labor supply hired by others. Some may also have been related to and living with parents or siblings who owned property. Of the land holders, the greatest proportion lived on farms ranging from 100 to 300 acres. A more complete picture of this group emerges from an examination of their total taxable worth, which comprised the value of their lands, slaves, and important possessions (see table 7).

TABLE 7   *Value of Estates Held by Men Indicted by the General Court*

Value (£)	0–50	50–100	100–150	150–200	200–250	250–300	300–400	400–500	500–750	750–1,000	1,000+
Percent Indicted	21	16	13	11	8	13	5	5	5	2	1

These statistics show a marked concentration of estate values in the lower categories. Eighty-two percent possessed estates of £300 or less, with 50 percent ranging from £150 down. Such estates again give clear evidence that these men were typical of the ubiquitous small farmer, be he tenant, renter, or owner, who scratched out a crude but bearable living. While a few well-to-do people participated in the disorders, the typical individual put on trial came from the lower propertied element.

Too much importance should not be attached to these statistics. The economic profile of the men indicted differs little from that of the colony in general. Still the lot of most of them was not a pleasant one. Even the most cursory examination of their estates indicates that they possessed little, and because of this condition, their frustrations were sharp. Feelings of dissatisfaction inhere in any class of subordinate people, but except in times of marked social disorder, these attitudes rarely find overt expression. The Revolution created such an abnormal situation. Generally these people directed their anger at the local leaders rather than the Annapolis government. For them the Revolution held out no real prospect of improvement. They saw the break from England being led by the traditionally powerful families who had always been well off. This apparent immunity from hardship was reason enough for the disaffected to hate their betters. Now with latent animosities surfacing in a mixture of compelling envy and resentment, large numbers of them became conscious that a social and political opportunity was present to express and act upon emotions long suppressed. Most felt secure in their actions. With the uncertainty of authority evident and with the broader community sharing their hostility, they believed themselves protected from any real punishment. Their assumption proved correct. When the courts, by the middle and latter part of 1778, mustered enough courage to begin trying these men, the sentence of guilty was invariably accompanied by only a minor fine. The judges dared do no more. On the few occasions when the court ordered harsher punishments, it soon had to back down.

A variety of economic pressures fueled these emotions. On the southern part of the Eastern Shore, the people experienced a difficult and increasingly unstable existence in the years immediately preceding the Revolution. During the 1760s and 1770s farmers there found market conditions unstable and future planning difficult. Because of the poor soil, the inferior tobacco that was raised could only be sold profitably under good conditions. With wheat they did better and the shift to that was pronounced. Similarly, that area developed a profitable trade in lumber products to England. All of these markets began to collapse in 1771, and the subsequent depression hit this region particularly hard. The farmers lost any sense of commercial orientation; they were totally confused as to which crops to grow. On the Western Shore conditions never deteriorated that far. Everyone agreed that tobacco was the commodity to raise. Whether the market were good or bad producers here continued to raise a high quality tobacco and never wondered what to plant. They lived in a more secure environment than their counterparts across the bay.[85]

[85] See chapters 1 and 5.

After the institution of nonexportation in the fall of 1775, the producers on the Eastern Shore faced even greater difficulties. The courts in the area had been clogged with debt cases before the war.[86] With access to most markets closed because of the fighting, the situation became increasingly desperate. For some, especially those who faced the prospect of losing their land, the Revolution truly took on the appearance of an elitist plot. Many of them had endured intense anxiety because of market conditions since 1771. They had not settled upon a satisfactory means of commerce, they were insecure, often in debt, fearful of the changes occurring, resentful of their social superiors, who were almost always their creditors, and not given to concerns about individual liberties and natural rights. What they wanted was economic stability and freedom from debt. The Revolution in the beginning promised nothing of the kind.

Another intriguing dimension to the riots and insurrections involves the role played by Methodist clergymen. William Paca, in a report from the Eastern Shore in September 1777, pointed to the Methodists as a primary cause of the widespread dissension: "I am sorry to inform you of an insurrection of Tories on the borders of Queen Anne's and Caroline Counties headed by some scoundrel Methodist preachers. A body of eighty, assembled in arms, were dispersed—three have since been apprehended. The Captain and Chief Methodist Preachers are among the captives."[87] Paca's critical remarks may be partially attributed to his strong Anglicanism, but during the war the Methodists were often identified as sympathetic to the British cause. Nathaniel Potter, a military man stationed on the Eastern Shore, wrote to the governor in disgust that "the spirit of Methodism reigns so much amongst us that few or no men will be raised for the war. . . . It is a general practise amongst us," he continued, "when there is any call for raising men for their preachers to be continually attending their different posts day and night which I am fully persuaded is the greatest stroke the British Ministry ever struck amongst us."[88]

Some ministers promoted the British cause in a more active manner. A militia officer in Queen Anne's County charged Martin Roddy, a prominent minister, with having "read General Howe's declaration to a company of people who had declared their disapprobation to the Consti-

[86] Somerset County Court Judicial Record, 1775–1784; Provincial Court Records, 1770–1775, MHR.
[87] William Paca to Gov. Thomas Johnson, *Archives of Maryland*, 16:364.
[88] Nathaniel Potter to Gov. Thomas Sim Lee, August 23, 1780, *ibid.*, 45:23.

tution of Maryland and the proceedings of the colony in general."[89] At a much higher public level John Wesley, the founder of Methodism, wrote in opposition to the colonial cause. His writings caused Francis Asbury, the leader of American Methodism, much anxiety and embarrassment. "I am truly sorry that the venerable man," he once said, "ever dipped into the politics of America."[90]

In Maryland the concern over Methodism was particularly intense because of the denomination's outspoken opposition to slavery. The growing hostility of the black community during the early war years resulted in many anxious moments for the Annapolis leadership. Some believed that the Methodists were largely responsible for the unrest. Francis Asbury, who spent most of the war years in neighboring Delaware, spoke out forcefully for the "freedom doctrine." In 1780, a conference of Methodist leaders meeting in Baltimore passed a declaration sponsored by Asbury calling on all members of the faith, and especially the preachers, both to educate the blacks and exert pressure for their emancipation.[91]

Long before this conference, Methodist preachers at the local level vocally criticized the institution of slavery. Thomas Rankin, a minister active in Maryland and Virginia, began making abolitionist speeches in 1775. A close friend of his, William Watters, spent some time with Rankin before taking up preaching on the Eastern Shore during the early war years. An insight into Watters' commitment can be seen in his memoirs. In 1775 he recounted going to see his dying brother in Harford County after a round of preaching on the Shore. What bothered him most, he remembered, was that his brother passed away "before there was much talk if any amongst us about the impropriety of holding our fellow creatures in slavery."[92] Nelson Reed, an itinerant Methodist preacher on the Western Shore, kept a record of his activities in a private journal. After speaking one Sunday he wrote that "several black people came in desiring I would advise how to serve God and save their souls, telling me that their masters never suffered them to go hear preaching; I gave them some advice for which they seemed grateful. The blacks in these parts seem much reformed, and if allowed to tend preaching would become good Christians." But the planters rarely gave such permission.

[89] Deposition of Martin Roddy and George Green, Red Books, 14:57, MHR.

[90] W. W. Sweet, Religion in the Development of American Culture, 1765–1840 (New York, Scribner, 1952), p. 30.

[91] Donald G. Matthews, Slavery and Methodism (Princeton, N.J.: Princeton University Press, 1965), pp. 7, 8.

[92] William Watters, A Short Account of the Christian Experience and Ministerial Labor of William Watters (Alexandria, Va., 1806), p. 40.

TABLE 8 *Methodist Church Membership for Maryland's Eastern Shore*

County	Date	White	Black
Talbot	1770s (late)	632	332
Talbot	1785	1,077	544
Caroline	1785	657	243
Dorchester	1787	594	135
Cecil	1789	257	252

SOURCE: A. Z. Hartman, "History of the Methodist-Episcopal Church in Maryland," Manuscript in Maryland Hall of Records, Baltimore, Md.

"O," he hoped, "that God may give masters and servants the knowledge of the salvation." Still on occasion Reed managed to speak with blacks for an extended period. For him these were rare and beautiful moments. On one Sunday in September he recorded that at Brother Wilson's, "we had a love feast. The Lord was present with us and a number of blacks who feared God being present; it was wonderful to hear how sensible and feeling they spake of the work of grace on their hearts."[93]

The most outspoken Methodist minister in Maryland was Freeborn Garrettson. Francis Asbury knew him well and especially appreciated his dedication to the "doctrine of freedom." During the war years, Garrettson preached on the Eastern Shore whenever possible. Frequently arrested, harassed and beaten, he persisted in his calling and found popularity among many, both white and black. When released from jail on one occasion in 1780, he told of how angry the people of Dorchester County were, but that the love of the Lord prevailed: "O! how wonderfully did the people of Dorset rage; but the word of the Lord spread all throughout that county, and hundreds both black and white have experienced the love of Jesus."[94]

Not only did the Methodists preach to the slaves but whenever possible they also established mixed churches, drawing largely from the free black population. Church membership figures for some Eastern Shore counties survive for the years during and after the Revolutionary War, testifying to the high degree of black participation (see table 8).

To stop the Methodists from preaching, the General Assembly passed an "Act for the Better Security of the Government" in October 1777. A

[93] Journal of Nelson Reed, June 19, 1781, and September 26, 1781, at Lovely Lane Methodist Church, Baltimore, Maryland.

[94] Matthews, *Slavery and Methodism*, p. 7; Nathan Bangs, *The Life of the Rev. Freeborn Garrettson* (New York, 1829), pp. 65, 114.

major provision of the measure required any man desiring to preach to take an oath of fidelity to the state. The assembly designed this statute specifically for the Methodists, since their religion, like that of the Quakers and other pietistic sects, prohibited oath taking. That this legislation was passed with the Methodists in mind can be seen from the act repealing it, adopted in 1782, which stated "that no person of the sect, society or profession of the people called Methodism shall be fined for preaching the gospel without taking the oath of affirmation proscribed by the 'Act for the Better Security of the Government.' "[95] While the measure was in effect, serious efforts at enforcement were made. Some preachers went to jail, generally without the opportunity of either bail or appeal. More vocal ones were summarily ordered to leave the Eastern Shore by courts at both the county and provincial level. Even on the Western Shore, the general court tried twenty-eight ministers within a single year for violation of security provisions. The fines meted out ranged from £30 to £300. Local citizens who enjoyed mobbing and tarring complemented the government's actions and in one bizarre case even attempted to assassinate a preacher.[96] Despite these tactics, or possibly because of them, the Methodists' appeal continued to grow during the war years. Because the ministers enjoyed substantial popularity, the government could not effectively control them. It is not possible to measure quantitatively their actual contribution to the disorders. No doubt their religious convictions spurred on many a black in his desire for freedom. Similarly, the Methodists' message of evangelical egalitarianism may have caused considerable numbers of yeomen to resent their patriot superiors. That the ideas of Methodism contributed to the insurrection and turmoil of that period seems unquestionable.

As the year 1778 began, reports continued to arrive in Annapolis from officials on the Eastern Shore detailing the chaotic nature of the area. No one, not even the lowest mechanic, complained Joseph Dashiell, paid the state authorities any mind: "I should have got a much larger quantity of shoes if the disaffected shoemakers would have made them up. But as soon as they heard the shoes was wanted for the army they

[95] Kilty, *Laws of Maryland*, vol. 1, chap. 20, October 1777; Tilghman, *History of Talbot County*, 2:14.

[96] A. Z. Hartman, "History of the Methodist-Episcopal Church in Maryland," manuscript in MHR, p. 32; Rev. John Patterson and Thomas Wright to Governor and Council, December 3, 1777, *Red Books*, 16:159; Appeal of Rev. John Bowie, March 29, 1777, Executive Papers, box 7; Western Shore General Court Records, 1778–1780 and Eastern Shore General Court Records, 1778–1780, MHR. For much of this information, I am indebted to Reverend Edward Scheel of the Lovely Lane Methodist Church, Baltimore, Md.

raised the price from five to fifteen shillings."[97] Not only do the people refuse to supply the Americans, said another government official, but they also come and go on British ships "without being called on to answer for their offense." But he feared attempting to apprehend or even restrain such behavior because of the reaction that might follow: "I am informed of a number of deserters from the army being among us and as the endeavors of their officers to apprehend these people brought on the late insurrection in the county, I make no doubt but that something similar to it will happen should it now be attempted."[98]

Nathaniel Potter, a militia officer in Caroline County, offered another explanation for the difficulties. The state of Delaware, he maintained, was responsible for much of the current disorder: "I am fully satisfied if something is not done with that petty, insignificant state of Delaware they will poison the minds of the greatest part of our people." This was so because there the "infernal Tory party . . . carries everything before them and I believe deters many of the inhabitants of our country from doing their duty." Should nothing be done, he warned, "I will move to the Western Shore."[99]

Potter told the truth. The Tory party of Delaware roamed freely and enjoyed a well-entrenched position, as did the disaffected elements in Maryland. But if Tories persuaded some to side with the British out of fear, the misconduct of the government's troops convinced others. Admittedly these soldiers faced a difficult task because of the local population's hostility or open defiance. For all practical purposes the government forces occupied a minority position, and they had good reason to feel a sense of isolation. On occasion this insecurity manifested itself in some unpleasant ways calculated only to worsen feelings. Regular soldiers were sometimes reported to be robbing and abusing the local population, and instances of harassment normally occurred when the government forces attempted to assert a measure of control. They were known to wake up suspects during the middle of the night and march them to headquarters for questioning. Thomas Holloway, a victim of this treatment, complained that the soldiers even refused him the "liberty" of putting on his breeches and shoes.[100] Similar tactics were employed for purposes of recruitment. The raising of troops in these communities was

[97] Joseph Dashiell to Gov. Thomas Johnson, January 24, 1778, Red Books, 16:39.
[98] George Dashiell to Gov. Thomas Johnson, February 2, 1778, ibid., p. 38.
[99] Nathaniel Potter to Gov. Thomas Johnson, March 9, 1778, Maryland State Papers, Blue Books, MHR, 4:912; see also John Dennos to Gov. Thomas Johnson, March 18, 1778, Executive Papers, box 10, MHR.
[100] Deposition of Thomas Holloway, February 2, 1778, Executive Papers, box 10, MHR.

always a problem, and the frustrations felt by the recruiters were evident in the methods they employed. Eli Showell, a young man of military age, testified about this treatment to the Worcester County Court. After refusing to enlist, he was taken prisoner and put into detention. The next morning an officer "went into the prison with his sword drawn and said to him, 'Eli, now God damn your soul but that your life is your own, if you do not enlist I will run you through.'" Other abusive measures continued, and then he was put back in his cell. The following morning two sergeants took him out and wrapped "a pair of bridle reins round his neck and choked him for some time," threatening to kill him. Still he held out until one of them disgustedly said to put the "son of a bitch" back. On the third day of his ordeal, Showell told the court he finally enlisted, no longer strong enough to resist. Such stories circulated constantly in the disaffected areas.[101]

To make matters worse, a regular Continental Army officer from Caroline County, Colonel William Richardson, told the Council of State in June 1778 that high ranking militia officers often employed "cruelty, oppression and corruption," simply to line their own pockets: "I hear that a combination was entered into by a militia colonel, a constable and a subaltern of the Maryland troops for the purpose of seizing and selling the inhabitants in which they have succeeded so well as to make upwards of a thousand pounds by the business." Richardson elaborated on the scheme explaining that the constable would arrest a man and carry him before the colonel who would declare him a vagrant and hand the victim over to the subaltern for transportation to the camp. The man would then be forced to enlist and sold to the highest local bidder as a substitute. Worse yet, said Richardson, "in some instances they have been sold to inhabitants of different counties. Consequently they will be twice numbered which will occasion a deficiency in the general quota although each county will appear to have furnished its proportion."[102]

The effect of all this unrest was that neither side controlled the Eastern Shore in the first half of 1778. Local military personnel in the region favored the British as much as the Annapolis government. An occasional zealous officer might attempt to assert some authority, but normally this display only worsened the situation. When convenient, the people signed the loyalty oath, but as one of them said it meant nothing "more than a blank piece of paper."[103] Men like George Dashiell, leader of the Somer-

[101] Deposition of Eli Showell before the Worcester County Court, March 8, 1778, Executive Papers, box 10, MHR.

[102] Col. William Richardson to Gov. Thomas Johnson, June 14, 1778, *Red Books*, 20:122.

[103] Deposition of John Taining, Daniel Bryan, Levin Langroff, William Bishop, and Daniel Spring, Executive Papers, box 11, MHR.

set County militia, realized how complete the disaffection was. He could not possibly order out the men of his command because of "there being more than three to one disaffected." Governor Johnson had to face the hard reality, wrote Dashiell, that "it is a fact not to be controverted that three-fourths of the Somerset militia are unfriendly to our cause." Because of this he dared not even issue arms since "we are well assured that it is their desire to act against us."[104] Johnson dispatched Luther Martin on an inspection tour of the Eastern Shore in the spring of 1778. He traveled much and saw nothing he liked. The disaffected inhabitants "have arrived to so daring heights of insolence and villainy," he observed, "that there appears but very little security for the lives or property of any person who from political or other reasons are obnoxious to them. Bodies of armed men pass unhampered through the country and disaffected leaders openly recruit followers." Anyone who opposes them, Martin continued, puts his own life in danger. Just the other night a militia captain had been shot "though it is hoped not mortally" for attempting to carry out his orders. For loyal government officials the situation had reached the point, he concluded, where their lives were in constant danger. To survive they must be always on the alert, moving only in certain areas and avoiding large sections nominally under their jurisdiction.[105]

Such were the conditions when the General Assembly met in March 1778. Governor Johnson and the legislators realized that additional action had to be taken. The assembly quickly passed another control measure aptly entitled "An Act to Prevent and Suppress Insurrection." In the act's preface the legislators said that "whereas there have been frequent insurrections and outrages committed in Somerset County and in some other counties by the disaffected inhabitants," the governor's and council's powers had to be expanded. They were to be given total authority to use all necessary military force to contain the troublesome activities. More important, the assembly authorized the permanent stationing of a company on the southern part of the Eastern Shore for a three-year period. Similarly, it directed the placing of several armed galleys to patrol the waters off Somerset continually. As a temporary measure, until the authorized forces were ready, the legislators ordered the matrosse companies serving in Anne Arundel and Baltimore to proceed to the region.[106]

---

[104] Col. George Dashiell to Gov. Thomas Johnson, March 12, 1778, Executive Papers, portfolio 4, folder 60Y, MHR.
[105] Luther Martin to Gov. Thomas Johnson, March 18, 1778, Executive Papers, portfolio 4, folder 60Z, MHR.
[106] Kilty, *Laws of Maryland*, vol. 1, chap. 8, March 1778.

The immediate reaction to this legislation was not very encouraging. Less than a month after its passage, another insurrection, reportedly involving between 600 and 700 men, erupted in Queen Anne's County.[107] A romantic figure by the name of China Clow (also a Methodist) led the uprising. His followers all wore a queue as a symbol of identification. Clow organized his partisans in the spring of 1778 and for a time caused considerable consternation both within the state and at the Continental Congress. That April Charles Carroll of Carrollton wrote to Governor Johnson from congress that "we are informed of an insurrection of the forces at a place called Jordan's Island ten miles from Dover—Smallwood apprehends this insurrection may become very serious unless speedily suppressed." Carroll lamented how weary he was of the never-ending disorder. "Is it not strange," he asked, "that the lust of domination should force the British nation to greater exertions than the desire of liberty can produce among us? . . . Try, for God's sake," he pleaded, "and the sake of human nature to rouse our countrymen from their lethargy."[108] Unfortunately, all he and congress could offer was moral support and direction, including a resolution requesting Maryland to detect and defeat "all disaffection, conspiracies and insurrections in the neck of land comprehended betwixt the Delaware and Chesapeake Bays."[109] But when a Maryland delegate requested more concrete aid in the way of troop assistance, congress turned him down.[110]

Within the state the authorities grappled with the threat as best they could. Clow's insurrection appeared particularly dangerous, since it was occurring not far from a vast concentration of war stores located at the head of the bay, a vital supply center for the Continental forces. Fearing that region might be lost, Johnson had recently ordered a report detailing the consequences should the area fall under British control. Henry Hollingsworth, the man in charge of the staging area, completed an inventory entitled "An Account of Stores and Provisions now laying in the States of Maryland and Delaware which from their present Situation appears to be in danger of falling into the Enemy's Hands unless speedily removed" (see table 9).

Immediate action was required to protect these stores. Troops and

[107] Samuel Patterson, April 15, 1778, *Red Books*, 7:115; William Henry to Col. William Bordley, April 13, 1778, portfolio 4, folder 61BB; William Bordley to Gov. Thomas Johnson, portfolio 4, folder 61hh; Bangs, *Life of Freeborn Garrettson*, p. 64.
[108] Charles Carroll of Carrollton to Gov. Thomas Johnson, April 21, 1778, *Archives of Maryland*, 21:49–50.
[109] Congressional Resolutions, April 23, 1778, *Red Books*, 7:118.
[110] Benjamin Rumsey and William Smith to Gov. Thomas Johnson, April 28, 1778, *Red Books*, 4:170.

TABLE 9 "An Account of Stores . . . in the States of Maryland and Delaware"

Where Laying	Bushels Wheat	Barrels Flour	Barrels Bread	Barrels Beef	Pork			Bundles Salt Fish
					Hhds.	Tierces	Barrels	
Appoquinimink, Delaware State	7,000	760						
Durhams Mill on the road from Middletown to Red Lyon		100						
Charles Town, North East		650	358	52	10	28	523	250
Elke and the mills in that neighborhood	10,000	3,000						
Harford		600*						
Total	17,000	5,110	358	52	10	28	523	250

Where Laying	Barrels Tallow	Barrels Lard	Barrels Beans	Salt		Hhds. Rum	Hhds. Molasses	Bushels Corn	Bushels Oats
				Bushels	Barrels				
Appoquinimink, Delaware State									
Durhams Mill on the road from Middletown to Red Lyon									
Charles Town, North East	1	6	1	2,041	100				
Elke and the mills in that neighborhood			75		40	7	6	2,500	1,000
Harford									
Total	1	6	76	2,041	140	7	6	2,500	1,000

SOURCE: "An Account of Stores and Provisions now laying in the States of Maryland and Delaware which from their present Situation appears to be in danger of falling into the Enemy's Hands unless speedily removed," manuscript located in Executive Papers, Maryland Hall of Records, Annapolis, Md.

* Plus a large quantity of wheat ordered there from the Eastern Shore to be manufactured.

artillery companies from both shores were dispatched to the area.[111] For once the state's actions produced favorable results. The two military men in charge of the operation, General William Smallwood and Colonel William Bordley, wrote to the governor on April 20 that the situation had been brought under control. Smallwood further reported that he thought the strength of Clow's forces was exaggerated: "Some say there were seven or eight hundred being joined by British officers and soldiers but there is generally more smoke than fire. I believe these latter reports were groundless."[112] Colonel Bordley concurred with Smallwood's analysis, but he cautioned that while the partisans had retired to the swamp for security, they were still dangerous. To completely eliminate the threat Clow posed, Bordley recommended the permanent placement of a large contingent "to keep him in the swamps until he could be turned out."[113] His suggestion was sound, but never acted upon. Clow's men continued to roam the area for the next several years.[114] But Clow, while a definite nuisance, never raised a sufficient force to threaten the supply base at the bay's head. Once the British shifted the concentration of their military campaigns to the South, men like Clow no longer constituted the grave threat they had posed in the early war years. Still, it was not until 1782 that the colorful career of China Clow ended with his capture at a swamp hideaway, used for many years by his followers.

Beginning with the warmer weather in the spring of 1778, the long ordeal faced by the Maryland government began to pass. A combination of factors accounts for the reprieve. Unless Charles Carroll of Carrollton is judged a totally inaccurate observer, the revolutionary government can be said to have won by then some measure of popularity. Its leaders had shown the ability to endure adversity, and in this process they convinced some of their tenacity. In this regard, their record seemed better than that of the British, who were now pulling out of Philadelphia for New York under a new commander, Henry Clinton. For the next several years, his army would sit in that city while other troops, under Cornwallis, raided throughout the South. There were to be no more elaborate Chesapeake campaigns—the "lobster backs" were leaving for good. With the British shift to other military theaters, the indigenous elements loyal

---

[111] Instructions to Lt. Gule, April 17, 1778, Executive Papers, box 1; William Bordley to Gov. Thomas Johnson, April 16, 1778, portfolio 4, MHR.

[112] General William Smallwood to Gov. Thomas Johnson, April 20, 1778, *Brown Books*, 2:33.

[113] Col. William Bordley to Gov. Thomas Johnson, April 20, 1778, *Red Books*, 19:51.

[114] Broadside, located in Lloyd Papers, Legal Cases, box 2, MHS; Harold Bell Hancock, *The Delaware Loyalists* (Wilmington, Del.: Historical Society of Delaware, 1940), p. 63.

to the crown no longer enjoyed the prestige and security that had been theirs. Now the Annapolis government constituted the only visible and immediate authority.

Nonetheless caution was still in order. Disaffection within the state continued strong, and the Eastern Shore remained turbulent. Slowly the government began to assert its authority. Since September 1775 no major courts had dared meet on the Eastern Shore. A few minor county courts, still symbolically styling themselves "his Lordship judges," did manage to gather in 1776 and 1777 for abbreviated and ineffectual sessions.[115] Then in April 1778 the state's second highest judicial body, the general court, convened in Easton. In May the same court met in Annapolis. Since cases for treason, insurrection, and riot fell within its jurisdiction, the general court's primary purpose was to bring about a return to order and stability.

At first the court proceeded carefully. The three presiding judges, William Paca, Nicholas Thomas, and Alexander C. Hanson, understood perfectly well their tenuous position, and accordingly decided to hear only one case involving a charge of riot. They found the man guilty and fined him £30. Having made the point that their court, while a gracious and kindly institution, was one that could try men and presumably would do so in the future, the three judiciously concluded their session and retired to the more congenial atmosphere of Annapolis.[116] Their conduct was admirably tailored to the existing conditions. They proved that a court could meet and exercise a degree of control. Had they attempted anything more, their authority might well have been openly flouted and disobeyed. By conducting themselves prudently, the judges had instead achieved some respect.

During the general court's recess, a few lower county courts started functioning more effectively. In Worcester a man appeared before the local justices "for speaking words tending to discourage the good people of this state from supporting the independence thereof by swearing the Whigs were all damned rebels." The court rebuked the man mildly and released him on a promise of good behavior. Another individual, Daniel Johnson, came before the authorities "for opposing the constable of the hundred and preventing him from doing his duty in suppressing the strolling and tumultuous meeting of Negroes." He received the same punishment—being released on a bond of good behavior.[117]

---

[115] Somerset County Judicial Record, August 1776; November 1776; March 1777, MHR.

[116] Eastern Shore General Court, Criminal Prosecutions, April 1778, MHR.

[117] Worcester County Court, The State vs. John Brittingham, August court, 1778; and The State vs. Daniel Johnson, both August court, 1778, MHR.

In September 1778 the general court met for a second time and took a slightly more aggressive stance. The judges heard five treason and nine riot cases as well as two for murder and one for larceny and rape. Benjamin Shockley, an insurgent leader, was charged with treason and indicted for "being a wicked and seditious man of unquiet and turbulent disposition," who, according to the court, "did falsely, wickedly and seditiously conspire, consult and agree to make an insurrection within the said state." Finding him guilty the judges ordered Shockley to pay a fine of £30 and his followers, £10. In another case one Beauchamp Andrew and others had been charged with "riotously" assembling with "force and arms, that is to say with sticks and staves and other offensive weapons." The men then marched to the "mansion house" of a leading resident of Caroline County where they broke in and did "take and carry away" some valuable possessions. For this crime the judges required Andrew and his men to pay a fine of £5 each.[118]

The punishments prescribed in the two cases were typical of those handed down at the September session. For treason the court outlawed only those persons who had already gone over permanently to the British. For those who remained the fines imposed ranged from £10 to £30. Persons found guilty of riot or insurrection normally received fines of £5 to £20. The reasoning behind the light penalties, which were payable in the state's badly depreciated currency, was simple. The judges, wishing to assert their authority, realized they could do so only by taking those actions acceptable to a hostile population. Thus they acted with restraint. Only once they miscalculated. The case involved John Tims, who on April 20, 1778, led an attack on the Queen Anne's County Court House to free the men held prisoners there. The judges sought to make an example of Tims and ordered him "to be drawn to the place of execution and be there hanged by the neck and cut down alive and that his entrails be taken out and burnt before his face and his head be cut off and his body divided into four quarters and his head and quarters disposed of at the pleasure of the state."[119] The people were to know that the law could be harsh. Such a tactic appeared deliberately planned, since the court had been lenient with all the accused except Tims. But the theory behind the tactic proved wrong. Tims could not be executed because the local community refused to allow it. William Wright, the county sheriff

---

[118] Eastern Shore General Court, Criminal Prosecutions, The State vs. Benjamin Shockley, September 1778; and The State vs. Beauchamp Andrew, September 1778, MHR.

[119] Eastern Shore General Court, Criminal Prosecutions, The State vs. John Tims, September 1778, MHR.

charged with carrying out the sentence, understood the situation and appealed on his prisoner's behalf to the governor's council. Tims, he said, was a good family man with "two small children." More important, the judgment could not possibly be carried out in his county because "near two-thirds of the people were Tories ingrained."[120] The council agreed with Wright's assessment, reversed the general court's decision, and issued Tims a pardon in March 1779.[121]

Despite this setback, the general court could reflect on a good year's work by the end of 1778. Altogether the Eastern and Western Shore branches of the court used the Tory Act in 150 prosecutions, forty-seven of which produced indictments for riot and insurrection. In twenty-three of these cases the men confessed and received small fines. Three others required jury trials and in one of these—that of Tims—the court ordered the death sentence. The other two defendants given trials received minor fines. Another eighty cases under the Tory Act involved charges of trading and assisting the enemy. Of this number only fifty-four produced indictments, from which seven confessions and three trials resulted. All the guilty received insignificant fines. Most of the others indicted under any of these charges could not be found, presumably because they had gone over to the British.[122]

During the April and September terms of 1779 the Eastern Shore's general court increased its prosecutions. Table 10 demonstrates how the court operated in persistently bringing people to trial although, as before, only small fines accompanied the guilty sentence.

The general court's moderate conduct helped greatly to stabilize conditions by the end of 1779. The disaffected and the government seemed to arrive at a tacit acceptance of one another. For the moment, both sides were content to live in a state of mutual animosity and tolerance. Disruptions still occurred but at a reduced level. In early 1781, when the British appeared ready to renew military activity in the Maryland-Virginia region, some of the government's former enemies took heart and renewed the old fight. But this time the over-all tone of the disorders and the reaction of state authorities differed considerably from the earlier years. No cries of hysteria now emanated from those in official positions. There was no talk of serious social disruption. Sometimes they acted in a jaunty,

[120] William Wright to Gov. Thomas Johnson, September 29, 1778, *Red Books*, 20:13.
[121] *Archives of Maryland*, March 20, 1779, p. 325.
[122] Eastern Shore General Court, Criminal Prosecutions, 1778–1782, MHR. For a thorough study of loyalism in Maryland see Richard Arthur Overfield, "The Loyalists of Maryland During the American Revolution (Ph.D. diss., University of Maryland, 1968).

TABLE 10 *Proceedings of the Eastern Shore's General Court, 1779–1781*

Charge	April 1779	September 1779	April 1780	September 1780	April 1781
Riot	51	21	16	2	1
Treason	5	15	17		
Breach of duty	12		4		
Assault and battery	1	2	1		3
Contempt	1		1	2	5
Felony		1			

SOURCE: Eastern Shore General Court, Criminal Prosecutions, MHR.

almost nonchalant manner about the problem of exercising control. This attitude is reflected in a report from Joseph Dashiell in March 1781. At an earlier time he had despaired of ever achieving order, but he now could write the Council of State with a touch of humor that "there was taken up and brought to me yesterday that old offender, Leven Deshroon, who has been in every insurrection. . . . He was insolent enough the other night, in the house of a certain George Parsons, Jr., to sing sundry disaffected songs." With the British so close these days, men such as this were reinvigorated, but Dashiell expected that they could be handled.[123]

When a special state court sitting that summer uncovered a sizable conspiracy in Frederick County, none of the state's officials was appreciably unnerved. Over one hundred men were reportedly involved in a plan to promote riots and assist the British. The courts decided to try only the leaders. Seven men were indicted, found guilty of high treason, and sentenced to die by hanging. Unlike former times, no one questioned whether the state had sufficient local support to carry out the punishment. After a series of appeals, four received pardons and three were executed.[124] Possibly an even better (though admittedly questionable) indicator of the declining social tensions and return to normal pursuits is the 1779 criminal docket for Queen Anne's County. Twenty-four people were fined for assault and battery, one for Sabbath breaking, one for neglect of highways, one for indecent behavior, and sixty for fornication![125]

Order and stability thus returned to Maryland because of several

[123] Joseph Dashiell to Gov. Thomas Sim Lee, March 13, 1781, *Archives of Maryland*, 47:120–21.
[124] Frederick County Treason Papers, MHS.
[125] Queen Anne's County Criminal Docket, MHR.

factors. The political leadership, by adopting policies designed to court popularity, gained acceptance—or so men such as Carroll, Chase, and Jenifer believed. Complementing this program, the state, by using the courts in a moderate manner to cautiously extend its new authority, slowly acquired a sense of permanence and legitimacy. Lastly, after the spring of 1778, the government was able to carry out its responsibilities without the nearby presence of major British troop concentrations, which until then had eroded the state's ability to command respect. A proposal, discussed by Charles Carroll of Carrollton with his father in 1781, illustrates the confidence of the political elite in its ability to maintain social control. The legislature was about to pass a law raising a regiment of black troops. Giving the blacks arms no longer concerned Carroll, but he complained rather of the expense involved: "We shall pass a law tomorrow for raising a Negro regiment of 750—every person having six Negroes between fourteen and forty-five years of age may have a Negro taken from him if the Negro should be willing to enlist for the war." He did not fear that the blacks might rise in insurrection or flee to the British lines. What annoyed him was that "this law appears to me to be unequal and consequently oppressive to a particular set of men—I hope none of our Negroes will enlist. The price, if paid in ready and solid coin, is not equal to the value of healthy, strong young Negro men."[126]

For Carroll the early revolutionary years, where wealth had gladly been sacrificed for power, formed part of a past happily forgotten.

[126] Charles Carroll of Carrollton to Charles Carroll of Annapolis, June 4, 1781, Charles Carroll of Annapolis Papers, MHS.

10 : The End of
the Popular Party

The popular party under Carroll in the Senate and Chase in the House survived the years 1776 and 1777. As long as a working coalition existed between these two men the party remained viable. Some stresses had developed within the alliance, particularly in the Baltimore sector, but these tensions were not fatal. Only with the final break between Charles Carroll of Carrollton and Samuel Chase in 1780 did the popular coalition cease to be an effective vehicle of political and social control.

Chase and Carroll, working together since 1773, had shaped much of Maryland's politics. Despite their personal differences, they had always sought accommodation and adjustment when matters of substance separated them. But in late 1778 a different situation began to develop. The controversies between them became too fundamental, the passions too heated. By the end of 1780 neither was agreeable to a union based on compromise. Now that the internal stability of their society seemed assured, neither felt compelled to subordinate his self-interest in order to retain unity. As a result they became increasingly antagonistic on the vital political questions.

Prior to the Carroll-Chase split, divisions had already taken place in other areas of the party. The Baltimore wing was rapidly disintegrating under a variety of internal and external pressures. Charles Ridgely, James Calhoun, William Lux, and Samuel Purviance, the four principal leaders of that community, had fallen out badly. James Calhoun, chairman of the Baltimore Committee of Observation, precipitated a major break when at a public meeting on March 4, 1777 he vigorously denounced Charles

Ridgely.[1] On the basis of information supplied him by William Lux, he accused Ridgely of uttering statements aimed at dividing the people in their opposition to Great Britain.[2] Naturally Ridgely denied ever expressing such sentiments.

Complementing this division was another involving Samuel Purviance. Throughout the war years, he commanded considerable influence in Baltimore, serving as secretary on all the important committees.[3] But his leadership there was not accompanied by a similar success within the popular party, with whose leaders he now was at odds. The issue that set Purviance apart centered around the matter of western lands. Men such as Chase, Thomas Johnson, and Charles Carroll of Carrollton were investors in the Illinois-Wabash, Indiana, and Vandalia companies.[4] These companies were locked in a dispute with Virginia over western claims. Purviance, unlike the others, invested in western lands through Virginia, whose claims he naturally hoped would be vindicated.[5] Such hopes, of course, alienated his former political allies, and Purviance, throughout the Revolution, did not play an important role outside of Baltimore.

Because of these differences, the Baltimore wing of the popular party no longer functioned as a unified body. Up to 1776, valuable support had come from this seaport town. The Baltimore community had rendered vital assistance to the party's leaders in their quest for political control, but after 1776 such support evaporated. In fact, by 1779 the political role of the commercial community within the party had become so unessential that Charles Carroll of Carrollton did not consider it a liability to sponsor a resolve making all merchants ineligible to represent the state in congress.[6]

Strains existed between other leaders of the party by 1779. Samuel Chase had grown to dislike and to disdain Thomas Johnson. When some members of the upper house introduced a resolution thanking Johnson for his services as governor, Chase prevented the resolve's passage in the

---

[1] *Votes and Proceedings of the General Assembly of the State of Maryland,* House of Delegates, March session, March 4, 1777.

[2] Daniel Bowly Statement Concerning a Conversation between Charles Ridgely and William Lux, n.d., Ridgely Papers, Maryland Historical Society, Baltimore, Md. (cited hereafter as MHS).

[3] Samuel Purviance to Governor Thomas Johnson, February 15, 1779, Executive Papers, box 8, Maryland Hall of Records, Annapolis, Md. (cited hereafter as MHR).

[4] Merrill Jensen, "The Cession of the Old Northwest," *Mississippi Valley Historical Review* 23 (1936), 27–48.

[5] George Mason to Samuel Purviance, May 20, 1782, Purviance-Courtenay Correspondence, Duke University, Durham, N.C.

[6] Philip A. Crowl, *Maryland During and After the Revolution: A Political and Economic Study* (Baltimore, Md.: The Johns Hopkins Press, 1943), p. 99.

lower house.[7] At the same time, Charles Carroll of Carrollton was writing harsh words to his father about the duplicity of Daniel of St. Thomas Jenifer. Carroll believed that Jenifer had given clandestine support to the legal tender law when it was first adopted and had been lying since in saying that his advocacy of the measure was solely based on considerations of political expediency: "In my opinion it ill becomes *that man* to talk of our want of virtue who was *instrumental* in promoting a law contrary to every principle of justice, thereby setting an example to the common people to disregard both private and public faith—I say instrumental for altho' he did not openly vote for it—I am persuaded as a popular measure, it had his secret approbation."[8] To those sentiments the old man replied in kind three days later: "We do not differ in our opinion about the major. He shall only have from me what I think proper."[9]

But in reality all these disputes were incidental to the alliance's functioning. As long as Chase and Carroll operated together and each maintained sway in his respective house—a task more difficult for Chase, who faced constant opposition—the coalition could accomplish its purpose.[10] Not until late in 1778 did the structure visibly begin to crack. Within a short time, little remained of the original edifice.

Chase's speculation caused the first break. In the fall of 1778, rumors circulated of a massive flour scandal. That September, Governor Johnson received a report from Philadelphia of "various complaints" having "been lately made to Congress purporting that some traders at Baltimore are engrossing the flour and other provisions and shipping off the same in direct violation of the embargo."[11] Less than a month later, Alexander Hamilton publicly accused Samuel Chase of organizing such an operation. Hamilton detailed the scheme in a caustic letter printed in the *New York Journal and the General Advertiser*. Writing from Poughkeepsie, New York, he charged that Chase, on the basis of secret congressional information, had formed partnerships to corner the flour market:

When you resolved to avail yourself of the extraordinary demand for flour which the wants of the French fleet must produce, and which your official

---

[7] Samuel Smith to Otho Holland Williams, November 22, 1779, Otho Holland Williams Papers, MHS.

[8] Charles Carroll of Carrollton to Charles Carroll of Annapolis, May 15, 1779, Charles Carroll of Annapolis Papers, MHS.

[9] Charles Carroll of Annapolis to Charles Carroll of Carrollton, May 21, 1779, Charles Carroll of Annapolis Papers, MHS.

[10] Daniel of St. Thomas Jenifer to Charles Carroll of Annapolis, November 27, 1777, Charles Carroll of Annapolis Papers, MHS.

[11] Francis Lewis to Governor Thomas Johnson, September 15, 1778, Maryland State Papers, Red Books, 7:17, MHR.

situation early impressed on your attention, to form connexions for monopo-
lizing that article and raising the price upon the public more than one hundred
per cent—when by your intrigues and studied delays you protracted the
determination of the committees of Congress, on the proposals made by M.
Wadsworth, commissary-general for procuring the necessary supplies for the
public use—to give your agents time to complete their purchases,—I say, when
you were doing all this and engaging in a traffic infamous in itself, repugnant
to your station and ruinous to your country, did you pause and allow yourself
a moment's reflection on the consequences? Were you infatuated enough to
imagine you would be able to conceal the part you were acting. Or had you
conceived a thorough contempt of reputation and a total indifference to the
opinion of the world.[12]

Chase's actions in this affair are not completely known, but a general
outline can be reconstructed. Colonel Jeremiah Wadsworth, the commissary general of the Continental Army, had sent a letter to his deputy,
Ephraim Blaine, describing the French need for provisions. This letter
was subsequently read to congress on July 31, 1778 and referred to a
committee for examination. Chase was not a member of that committee,
but Robert Morris, a man with whom he had had dealings before, was.[13]
The other members of the committee were Gouverneur Morris and
Samuel Holten.[14] On August 24, congress began its consideration of the
committee's report, which recommended "that the Commissary General
be directed to purchase 20,000 barrels of flour in the states of Pennsylvania, Delaware, Maryland and Virginia."[15] Chase, possibly through
Robert Morris, got word of the committee's report before it was presented to congress. He sent for his partner, John Dorsey, and instructed
him to begin purchasing as much grain as possible. Dorsey returned to
Baltimore and began buying frantically. By the day congress received the
committee's report, he had secured considerable quantities of grain.[16]

Hamilton's virulent attack on Chase produced serious repercussions in
Maryland politics. Immediately after the scandal's exposure, the legisla-

---

[12] *The New York Journal and the General Advertiser*, October 26, 1778; see also
Harold C. Syrett, ed., *The Papers of Alexander Hamilton* (13 vols., New York:
Columbia University Press, 1961-), 1:570.

[13] W. C. Ford, ed., *Journals of the Continental Congress, 1774-1789* (34 vols.,
Washington, D.C.: U.S. Government Printing Office, 1904-1937), 11:734; Kathryn
Sullivan, *Maryland and France 1774-1789* (Philadelphia: University of Pennsylvania
Press, 1936), pp. 75-80.

[14] Ford, *Journals of the Continental Congress*, 11:734.

[15] *Ibid.*, p. 831. The resolve passed by Congress read: "That the commisary general of purchases do procure in Pennsylvania, Delaware, Maryland, and Virginia, on
the most reasonable terms, twenty thousand barrels of flour."

[16] The best account of the flour scandal was written by John Cadwalader and published in the *Maryland Gazette and Baltimore Advertiser*, September 24, 1782.

ture was called upon to take a stand. Tempers and feelings were bound to be hurt, but the situation could not be ignored. Nor did some Senators want to let Chase's malfeasance go unnoticed. Indeed, they jumped at the opportunity to crucify the common people's champion. In righteous indignation, the Senate drew up a set of instructions which contained an explicit reprimand of Chase. Charles Carroll of Carrollton was one of the men involved in composing these instructions. Whether he advocated a severe or mild censure is not known, but for years Chase held Carroll responsible for the Senate's attack. The Senate declared that "reports have circulated, much to the disadvantage of some of the delegates; they have been accused of combining with the monopolizers and engrossers of the necessaries of life, and sharing in iniquitous gain. The resolves of Congress, recommending proper measures and laws to check these pernicious practices, will lose much of their efficacy and force, while members of their own body under the suspicion of the same guilt, are suffered to retain their seats in that assembly."[17] The General Assembly then proceeded to dismiss Chase from its congressional delegation.

Chase's rebuttal took a curious and unexpected form. He did not confront his detractors in open debate, but contented himself by professing his innocence to the assembly members. He realized that the evidence implicating him in the flour scandal was of substantial proportions. His best tactic was to let the matter lie for a few months and then open a vicious attack on the integrity of the Senate. As a result the scene was quiet and no political harangues shattered the fall and winter air. Then suddenly, in March 1779, Chase replied with the accusation that there were "traitors in the Senate!" He labeled Matthew Tilghman, Charles Carroll, Barrister, and Samuel Wilson as men especially tainted by treasonous activities.

On March 17, 1779, the Senate summoned Chase to give testimony concerning his charges. Chase came before the Senate and quickly demonstrated that he would not be cowed. "He had obeyed the summons of the Senate," he said, "though by no means admitted the power there of." With that assertion, Chase proceeded to detail his charges. The indictments concerning the conduct of Matthew Tilghman and Charles Carroll, Barrister, he said, came from an irreproachable source, Samuel Adams! According to Chase, Adams had told him that in December, 1776, when General Howe was approaching Philadelphia, Tilghman and Carroll had urged sending "propositions of reconciliation or accommoda-

17 *Ibid.*

tion." Samuel Wilson, Chase continued, had "expressed sentiments adverse to the independence of America" to William Paca.[18]

After making these charges, Chase offered some remarks concerning two other members of the Senate. From reports he had received, Chase said, "he could give the Senate some information of Mr. Jennings" which he thought would justify the "expulsion of him." Next, when asked if he had anything further to declare, Chase said "it might look like partiality if he passed by the president," Daniel of St. Thomas Jenifer. The president's conduct was very suspicious, or so it seemed to Chase. Jenifer had recently held meetings with a Doctor Craik in New York in which he had, Chase contended, given it as his opinion that negotiations should begin at once with the British. Jenifer arose and instantly replied "that the intimation relative to the conversation between himself and Doctor Craik was groundless as he had not been more than once in Doctor Craik's company for eighteen months or two years."[19] With that abrupt denial, the Senate adjourned.

On the next day, the Senate formally dismissed all of Chase's accusations as groundless. Nevertheless, it agreed to conduct an investigation into the charges, if only to remove any suspicion of doubt from its accused members. For the next several months the Senate, in a rather haphazard manner, conducted its probe and concluded, not surprisingly, that all its members were innocent. Samuel Wilson, the Senate recorded, had indeed made some pessimistic and apprehensive statements about the immediate future. Given the military situation at the time, there was some reason to be concerned. But Wilson's remarks, so the Senate found, in no way conceded defeat or the need for accommodation.[20]

As to the report of perfidy concerning Charles Carroll, Barrister, and Matthew Tilghman, Chase had simply lied. Daniel of St. Thomas Jenifer went to see Samuel Adams, the man who was Chase's "impeccable" source. The visit confirmed what the Senate suspected. From Philadelphia, Jenifer wrote in May that "Sam Adams declared to me in the presence of McHenry [a Maryland congressional delegate] that he never said or heard that Mr. Tilghman or Mr. Carroll proposed sending to General Howe to know what terms he had to offer and that Chase must have been mad."[21] A few days later, Jenifer elaborated more fully on Chase's conduct in a letter to Charles Carroll of Annapolis: "Mr. Chase

[18] *Votes and Proceedings*, Senate, March session, March 17, 1779.
[19] *Ibid*.
[20] *Ibid*, March 18, 1779; July 29, 1779; July 30, 1779; August 2, 1779.
[21] Daniel of St Thomas Jenifer (Philadelphia) to ———, (Baltimore), May 26, 1779, Gilmor Papers, MHS.

has been much censured for his attack upon the Senate as well as for his speculations. I have been informed by Major Mercer that Chase denied to him that he speculated in flour and Sam Adams informed me before McHenry that he never said, or heard that Mr. Tilghman and Mr. Carroll or either of them had proposed to send to General Howe when in Jersey to know what terms he had to offer."[22]

The Senate called Chase to appear before it on August 2, 1779. There he heard his charges categorically denied. Chase was enraged, and in the words of Jenifer, he made a "poor figure." The Senate's president, who by this time had come to loathe Chase, concluded that the entire affair had been a sham and was pleased that Chase had suffered another public defeat. Chase, whom Jenifer described as "the most wretched has lost much ground, indeed in the opinion of all thinking men sunk, even below contempt."[23]

The Senate was still not through with Chase. Samuel Wilson, the man whom Chase had labeled as a traitor, had been very active in the latter part of July with moves designed to bring further disgrace upon his accuser. Wilson's strategy was to resurrect and once more illuminate Chase's role in the flour scandal. For this reason, he sponsored "An Act to Restrict Delegates of this State from Engaging in any Trade either Foreign or Domestic."[24] The act eventually passed both houses. Since the vote is not recorded, it is impossible to determine how close the count was in the lower house. Apparently the matter was so open and controversial that Chase's forces had to agree to the restriction and the censure it implied.

Throughout this period, Jenifer continued privately to discredit Chase with the Carrolls. Since Charles Carroll of Carrollton still appeared willing to work with Chase, he concentrated his efforts on the elder Carroll, who was more than receptive. In August Jenifer obtained a letter written by Chase to his commercial partner in Baltimore, John Dorsey, and promised a copy to the Carrolls. Charles Carroll of Annapolis explained to his son, "I hear a letter of Chase's to John Dorsey has been intercepted, opened and that it gives great offence in Baltimoretown. It is said to avow the principle of making a fortune at any rate. I am promised a copy of it."[25] Two days later, Jenifer forwarded the letter, expressing

[22] Daniel of St. Thomas Jenifer to Charles Carroll of Annapolis, May 24, 1779, Charles Carroll of Annapolis Papers, MHS.
[23] Daniel of St. Thomas Jenifer to Charles Carroll of Annapolis, August 2, 1779, Charles Carroll of Annapolis Papers, MHS.
[24] *Votes and Proceedings*, Senate, July session, July 24, 1779.
[25] Charles Carroll of Annapolis to Charles Carroll of Carrollton, August 10, 1779, Charles Carroll of Annapolis Papers, MHS.

the hope that because of it Chase might be "banished." Essentially, the letter outlined a scheme designed to make a handsome profit off the sale of tobacco. A congressional embargo was then in effect but Chase, although not in congress, had secured information of its being lifted in the near future. Naturally the price would climb rapidly, and he urged Dorsey to buy as much as possible. He specifically asked "will old Carroll take £15 per hundred?" Chase hoped so, since he estimated the future market price to be "60 to 65 dollars per hundred" or more.[26]

Nothing could have made the Carrolls angrier. If Jenifer aimed at further disgracing Chase he had certainly calculated correctly. Chase apparently intended to build his personal and political fortunes at their expense. Charles Carroll of Carrollton now agreed completely with his father as to the character of Chase and took an increasingly hard line on his former friend's conduct. In April 1780 he remarked to his father that "Chase I am informed said something in the house reflecting on me but the reflections of such a man I esteem honorable to me."[27]

During the assembly's first session in 1781, the matter of whether the prohibition against engaging in trade should be extended for another year was on the agenda. While the subject was being argued, Chase published a defense of his conduct and a profession of innocence concerning the flour scandal. After reading the article, Charles Carroll of Annapolis queried rhetorically, "should a man talk of virtue, liberty and patriotism . . . who betrayed the secrets of Congress?"[28] His son thought not and decided that Chase's article demanded a reply. He believed Chase guilty and felt there should be no question about his chicanery. While not naming Chase directly, but referring instead to merchants in general, Carroll's signed letter was clear in its accusations:

Merchants are useful members of the community, and as such ought to be countenanced and encouraged by the legislature; but the spirit of the times and circumstances, may justify a temporary exclusion of that order of men from the public councils. If all merchants were men of known propriety, and tried integrity, the exclusion would be improper; however as past occurrences have discovered that all are not to be trusted, it is prudent to exclude the latter which cannot be done, but by a general law; for certainly in times, when an insatiable thirst of accumulating wealth and of rising into opulence instantane-

[26] Daniel of St. Thomas Jenifer to Charles Carroll of Annapolis, August 12, 1780, Charles Carroll of Annapolis Papers, MHS.
[27] Charles Carroll of Carrollton to Charles Carroll of Annapolis, April 8, 1780, Charles Carroll of Annapolis Papers, MHS.
[28] Charles Carroll of Annapolis to Charles Carroll of Carrollton, June 14, 1781, Charles Carroll of Annapolis Papers, MHS.

ously, and not by the gradual progress of unremitting industry has taken the place of a sober and well regulated spirit of trade, when occasions present themselves of making thousands by one bold though publicly injurious stroke of speculation, mercantile men can more readily turn such occasions to their own emolument, than others not engaged in trade.[29]

Chase's commercial speculations and his attacks on the Senate's integrity provided the ground work for the conclusive break with Carroll. But at the heart of their division lay the persistent question of legal tender currency, which became increasingly tied up with the matter of confiscating British property. Within the Senate circle the old man never for a moment let up in his criticism of the tender measure. During the assembly's spring session of 1778 he busily wrote his son and Jenifer, urging them to labor for repeal. He proposed a petition campaign to have the law removed, and if that failed he sardonically suggested reenacting the measure under the title "an act to take away the money of all creditors and give it to all their debtors."[30]

As president of the Senate, Jenifer reluctantly acceded to Charles Carroll of Annapolis' wishes and raised the matter of repeal but, as anticipated, his colleagues voted him down. The members present felt they could do nothing else. All those present "reprobated the act making paper money a legal tender and wished it had never passed," wrote Jenifer, "but conceived any attempts towards a repeal would be fruitless." Continuing, he recalled the elder Carroll's early fire for the revolutionary cause and appealed to his sense of history: "Are you not opprobrious in your epithets bestowed on those who were for the bill? I still think that all our money must go to support the war and if our liberty be established (which I doubt) and we can keep our lands and Negroes we shall be well off—no people ever yet procured their liberty so as to be benefitted themselves—to do it for posterity to reap the advantage is what has ever been aimed at."[31]

To Charles Carroll of Annapolis such animadversions on his sense of patriotism no longer meant anything. Nor did the negative reports he received from his son and Jenifer.[32] With characteristic tenaciousness he continued to demand repeal. Near the end of May Jenifer had to repeat

---

[29] *Maryland Gazette*, August 23, 1781.
[30] Charles Carroll of Annapolis to Daniel of St. Thomas Jenifer, March 13, 1778, Charles Carroll of Annapolis Papers, MHS.
[31] Daniel of St. Thomas Jenifer to Charles Carroll of Annapolis, April 16, 1778, Charles Carroll of Annapolis Papers, MHS.
[32] Charles Carroll of Carrollton to Charles Carroll of Annapolis, May 24, 1778, Charles Carroll of Annapolis Papers, MHS.

that the chances for the measure's suspension were very remote. "The same reasons that spurr'd on *some men* to promote passage of the law will actuate them to oppose repeal. I therefore think that it will not be worth your while to trouble yourself any further about this business." A little over a week later he reiterated the same advice, this time placing it explicitly within the context of the society's agitated conditions: "Altho the Senate may reprobate the tender law which the violence of the times might induce it to pass; yet as the same threat of temper has not abated it would at this time be dangerous to attempt at repeal of the law."[33]

Charles Carroll of Annapolis predictably rejected Jenifer's cautious hint that he face reality. Instead he sharply rebuked what he saw as Jenifer's lethargic, compromising, and even demagogic attitude: "If the law is iniquitous and productive of manifest injustice, it is the duty of every honest man to endeavor a repeal of it; men of a different character such and such only who prefer popularity to justice will oppose them."[34] Now Jenifer became annoyed. Like the elder Carroll, he did not tolerate insults lightly. Not wanting to alienate the old man completely he decided to parry Carroll's remarks with ones designed to irritate obliquely. If the revolutionary forces should prove victorious, he said, "you ought to pay your share towards the doing of it. And I believe the debt is and will be so great, that your share of it, will take much the greatest part, if not the whole of your monied estate to pay it off. And if it would," he asked, "where will be the great loss to you for surely you would not desire to go scot free in this business." Jenifer moralistically taunted "money is not necessary to procure happiness. I am convinced it is the cause of great inquietude of mind, and has been the destruction of the bodies and souls of millions. That it is the 'root of all evil,' you cannot deny. Why then should we be so fond of it?"[35]

The elder Carroll, having worked hard his entire life to expand his family's fortune, hardly appreciated this cavalier attitude. "Seneca before you has moralized and philosophised on the contempt of money and riches," he reminded Jenifer. "His reasons have not had and yours will not have any influence on the world, and are not as I think pertinent to the present subject as they do not tend to show that it is just to rob creditors to bestow the stolen goods on their debtors." Then in specific answers to Jenifer's question he said, "I expect to pay my share of the

---

[33] Daniel of St. Thomas Jenifer to Charles Carroll of Annapolis, May 30, 1778, and June 10, 1778, Charles Carroll of Annapolis Papers, MHS.

[34] Charles Carroll of Annapolis to Daniel of St. Thomas Jenifer, June 14, 1778, Charles Carroll of Annapolis Papers, MHS.

[35] Daniel of St. Thomas Jenifer to Charles Carroll of Annapolis, June 18, 1778, Charles Carroll of Annapolis Papers, MHS.

charge of the war but I do not think it just to pay more than my share."
Isn't "honesty," he wondered, still "the best policy?"[36]

That fall Charles Carroll of Carrollton cautiously raised with some
Senate members the possibilities of repeal. "I have spoken to all the
members of the Senate respecting the tender bill," he informed Charles
Carroll of Annapolis, and "they all admit its injustice but I am convinced
I should not be seconded were I to move for a committee to be appointed
to bring in a bill to repeal it."[37] Taking matters into his own hands, the
elder Carroll submitted a petition to the lower house requesting that the
measure be struck down. The delegates dismissed the appeal, terming it
"highly indecent and justly exceptionable." Undeterred, Carroll resubmitted his petition at the spring and summer sessions of 1779. Both times
he failed miserably. Jenifer pleaded with him to "let the tender law
sleep." To this Carroll replied, "No I will not let the tender law sleep,
not the rogues who have taken advantage of it, not the men who ought to
repeal it!"[38]

With the convening of the next General Assembly Charles Carroll of
Annapolis took heart. For the past several years, he had railed alone, but
the political climate that autumn showed some slight improvement, some
glimpses of change. Chase continued to dominate the lower house, but
opposing factions were growing. William Fitzhugh, the former aristocratic companion of proprietary circles who had turned vengeful demo-
crat once independence became a reality, was now speaker of the house
and could stack the committees in his favor. Originally a furious foe of
the popular party's leaders, his attitude toward the Carrolls seemed to be
mellowing. Similarly, John Hall, the old radical enemy of the Carrolls,
had recently defeated Chase in a close house vote and appeared interested
in putting out some tentative feelers toward them. With their political
positions secured, the two no longer considered popular demagoguery a
constant necessity.

Fitzhugh made the first hesitant move. It was he who originally had
intercepted Chase's letter about the lifting of the tobacco embargo. Immediately after receiving it he had several copies drawn up, one of which
he gave to Daniel of St. Thomas Jenifer.[39] During that same month,

[36] Charles Carroll of Annapolis to Daniel of St. Thomas Jenifer, June 29, 1778,
Charles Carroll of Annapolis Papers, MHS.

[37] Charles Carroll of Carrollton to Charles Carroll of Annapolis, November 1, 1778,
Charles Carroll of Annapolis Papers, MHS.

[38] Daniel of St. Thomas Jenifer to Charles Carroll of Annapolis, July 25, 1779;
Charles Carroll of Annapolis to Daniel of St. Thomas Jenifer, July 20, 1779, Charles
Carroll of Annapolis Papers, MHS.

[39] Daniel of St. Thomas Jenifer to Charles Carroll of Annapolis, August 12, 1779,
Charles Carroll of Annapolis Papers, MHS.

August 1779, Fitzhugh agreed to present Charles Carroll of Annapolis' petition to the house. With some obvious satisfaction, the elder Carroll described to his son Fitzhugh's courteous conduct: "You know I sent my petition under cover to the speaker. He presented it, Chase objected and insisted it ought to be presented by a member on the floor. The house were of Chase's opinion. The speaker returned my petition with a polite letter and I sent it under cover to Mr. John Hanson, desiring him to present it on the floor."[40]

All of these developments had an influence on Charles Carroll of Carrollton. With his alliance to Chase seriously ruptured, the tender law's retention could no longer be justified on the grounds of political expediency. At the same time his father remained indefatigable. In public, the elder Carroll kept trumpeting repeal. He requested permission from the *Maryland Gazette* to publish an open letter of protest but the editor, Anne Greene, refused, fearing the issue too inflammatory. No doubt she remembered the experience of William Goddard, editor of Baltimore's *Maryland Journal*, who had been severely beaten and his shop wrecked for printing unpopular opinions. Privately, Carroll persistently pointed out to his son and Jenifer their collective lack of courage. When the younger Carroll once complained of high taxes, the old man shot back, "You ought not to claim of being robbed nor do you deserve any property."[41]

Convinced finally that the tender law was no longer serving any useful purpose, Charles Carroll of Carrollton began planning to move for repeal: "If I find an opening, a proper disposition and unanimity in the Senate for the bill on a plan that will please *all* or *nearly all* the Senate I will urge the matter though I am sure the House of Delegates will reject it; neither will they care for being stigmatized as rogues; I think you must or ought to be convinced of this."[42] Having fought alone for almost three years, Charles Carroll of Annapolis hardly appreciated this advice. He did not care a whit for the sensibilities of the House: "I see no necessity of calling the delegates rogues but it is certainly necessary to couch the reasons for the repeal of the law in such plain and strong words as to prove them to the world to be rogues unless they repeal the law." He further desired that his son be more determined, "I wish you had a great deal more warmth and earnestness in your temper. You say you will urge the matter though I am sure the House of Delegates will

---

[40] Charles Carroll of Annapolis to Charles Carroll of Carrollton, August 10, 1779, Charles Carroll of Annapolis Papers, MHS.
[41] Charles Carroll of Annapolis to Charles Carroll of Carrollton, November 4, 1779, Charles Carroll of Annapolis Papers, MHS.
[42] Charles Carroll of Carrollton to Charles Carroll of Annapolis, November 7, 1779, Charles Carroll of Annapolis Papers, MHS.

reject it—men seldom, if ever act with spirit who despair of success."[43]

But the younger Carroll proved correct. He persuaded the Senate to come out openly against the tender bill, but the law was still extremely popular and the House, as expected, voted the matter of suspension down 41 to 5.[44] As he told his father, the repeal process would be long and difficult: "A repeal of the tender law I fear cannot be expected—you know how much private interest is against the repeal of that law." Of course, he agreed that "it is certainly vexatious to see oneself openly robbed by a set of rascals with impunity and without any public advantage; however, if the war should continue longer we may be robbed of our own lands as well as money." For the present he could see no real alternative: "You say such a bill should be enforced by such arguments as to secure the passage or convince the public that the patrons of the tender law are determined villains: what man of any reflection is not already convinced of this? In short so those patrons can benefit themselves they value very little their reputations. The law is so palpably unjust, and of this the feelings of every man must be the strongest evidence that it is impossible by words to put its injustice in a stronger light than what the common sense of every man does at first instant discover—would you set above to prove that at noonday it is night?"[45]

Pleased at last with his son's behavior, Charles Carroll of Annapolis now reversed his position and urged young Carroll not to work so hard. "The oppression of honest men and the dominion of rogues is certainly vexatious," he agreed. Still the tender law was not everything. "I fear you take too much of the public business on yourself—drudge not; let others draw, you may correct, nothing is dearer to me than your health, therefore I beg you will follow my advice."[46]

Despite the repeal measure's defeat that fall, rumors were rife of its possible success when the assembly convened in the spring of 1780. James Dick, an Annapolis merchant, told a Philadelphia correspondent that the law might be rescinded since most loans had already been paid off. "I wrote you that near all our outstanding debts sterling and currency were discharged according to the iniquitous tender act, the money now lying in the loan office certificates, and it's thought the tender act will be repealed but in what manner is not yet certainly known, with or without

[43] Charles Carroll of Annapolis to Charles Carroll of Carrollton, November 9, 1779, Charles Carroll of Annapolis Papers, MHS.

[44] *Votes and Proceedings*, Senate, November session, November 20, 1779.

[45] Charles Carroll of Carrollton to Charles Carroll of Annapolis, December 4, 1779, Charles Carroll of Annapolis Papers, MHS.

[46] Charles Carroll of Annapolis to Charles Carroll of Carrollton, December 8, 1779, Charles Carroll of Annapolis Papers, MHS.

retrospect."[47] Dick's letter was wrong on both counts. A great many outstanding loans had not yet been paid off and never would be. As a result the homes of creditors such as Edward Lloyd were raided after the tender law's repeal, with his bonds the specific object of his attackers. Dick's prediction was also overly optimistic. The Senate voted repeal and again the lower house rejected it 42 to 9.[48] Angry over this setback, Charles Carroll of Carrollton complained of the carnival atmosphere that prevailed in Annapolis. "I believe the assembly will rise by the end of next week," he told his father late in April. "It has been a most expensive session and no good done—in short the billiard table has been more attended by the leading members of the House of Delegates than public business."[49]

But progress was clearly being made. With the beginning of the next session political negotiations became intense. By July a partial compromise had been hammered out and a limited repeal enacted. Essentially Chase and his followers agreed to a repeal for reasons of self-interest. The critical part of the rescinding act concerned the requirements regarding future loan procedures. The measure prescribed that all currency emitted by congress, the assembly, and the conventions would not be a legal tender for debts contracted from the date the act went into effect. Since men like Chase were now wealthy enough to make loans, they did not want to be paid in paper trash. To insure their future as creditors, they agreed to the act's passage. Charles Carroll of Carrollton lucidly described this to William Carmichael, a friend of his then in Madrid on a diplomatic mission.

Thus you perceive there are two rules laid down for the payment of old and new debts. A man who lent on the 4th day of last July gold and silver, must be content to receive paper in payment tho not equal perhaps to a fiftieth part of the debt; but he who lent gold and silver since the 5th day of that month may in virtue of an act passed on that day recover gold and silver— Do you want to know the reason of this different treatment of two creditors equally entitled to justice? Let those who to their disgrace suffer two currencies, the one supposed to be no times better than the other, to be a tender for sterling debt at one and the same rate of exchange, vizt. at 66⅔ per cent assign the reason for this difference. The solution of all this inconsistency must

[47] James Dick (Annapolis) to Henry Hill (Philadelphia), April 6, 1780, James Dick and Anthony Stewart Letterbook, Duke University, Durham, N.C.
[48] *Votes and Proceedings*, House, April session, April 10, 1780; Lloyd Papers, legal cases, box 12, MHS.
[49] Charles Carroll of Carrollton to Charles Carroll of Annapolis, April 29, 1780, Charles Carroll of Annapolis Papers, MHS.

be sought for in the iniquity of those who have plundered this state, and individuals to benefit themselves, and are determined at the expense of their representation to preserve the gains they have made by such scandalous frauds.[50]

Carroll's point was clear. Men had made fortunes by fraud and they now intended to increase their earnings by adopting more fiscally responsible measures. Naturally he and his father were not happy with the halfway repeal. The question of how debts contracted before June 1780 should rightfully be paid remained a major grievance with them. But even a limited requirement would help the Carrolls and other creditors in terms of future loans. Still, the new law was another "bitter pill" for the Carrolls. They realized full well that by agreeing to it they were helping Chase create a field of lucrative speculation. As Charles Carroll of Carrollton explained, "I think the conduct of the House of Delegates must open the eyes of the people—Chase rules there, without control—I believe a majority do not see into his schemes and views—the acts of that branch of the legislature respecting money matters seem calculated to answer his particular contracts and interests."[51]

With this measure on the books, hopes for a broader one were increased and that fall a more inclusive repeal was enacted.[52] John Ridout, a friend of Horatio Sharpe, jubilantly wrote the former governor explaining the new law. "It is also with pleasure I inform you that an act hath been pass't this session repealing in a great measure the iniquitous tender law: Debts contracted before September 1, 1776 and not already paid off, are to be satisfied with only solid coin or with bills of credit equivalent not nominally but really, regard being had to the depreciation at the time of payment."[53] Charles Carroll of Annapolis echoed the same sentiments. He disliked the form of repeal but was pleased to see the last of the tender bill: "I must doubt the assembly ever doing justice to the public and creditors, however it is a comfort that we are not now exposed to be robbed."[54]

The rescinding act also contained a highly unusual provision making

[50] Charles Carroll of Carrollton to William Carmichael, August 9, 1780, Charles Carroll of Annapolis Papers, MHS.

[51] Charles Carroll of Carrollton to Charles Carroll of Annapolis, May 6, 1780, Charles Carroll of Annapolis Papers, MHS.

[52] "An Act for Calling Out of Circulation the Quota of this State of Bills of Credit Issued by Congress, and the Bills of Credit Emitted by Acts of Assembly Under the Old Government and by the Resolve of the Convention," Session Laws of Maryland, November 1780.

[53] John Ridout to Horatio Sharpe, December 27, 1780, Ridout Papers, MHR.

[54] Charles Carroll of Annapolis to Charles Carroll of Carrollton, December 17, 1780, Charles Carroll of Annapolis Papers, MHS.

it very attractive to those owing debts abroad. In December 1779, the lower house had passed a law allowing individuals to discharge debts owed to nonresidents by payment of depreciated currency into the state treasury. At that time the Senate rejected the proposal. But in October 1780 the same provision was incorporated into the bill repealing the legal tender act.[55] Obviously the revolutionary government had taken good care of its debtors. First this group's internal and now its external obligations were made easily dischargeable through the tender of depreciated currency.

The state similarly provided well for its speculators. Samuel Chase saw to that. Charles Carroll of Carrollton loathed the conduct of Chase, who seemed devoid of any shred of morality. A man of principle, he was fully repulsed by Chase's opportunism. Originally the Revolution had contained for him some real hope of virtue. But Chase had debased it completely by his demagoguery and surreption. To save the Revolution and to preserve his class's position of social control, Carroll understood the need for economic radicalism. He could even play the role of the democratic politician but he could not tolerate Chase's naked acts of self-aggrandizement.

During the first half of 1780 the fashioning of fraudulent schemes reached a fever pitch. One plan of Chase and his supporters was to agree to the tender law's repeal in order to establish a safe loan market for themselves. Another of Chase's projects was first discussed by Charles Carroll of Carrollton in May of that year. The tax bill just then suggested by the house, he said, had been specifically designed to aid those men now speculating heavily in the state's currency. One of the provisions of the proposed legislation was to pledge "the faith of this state for the redemption of our state certificates and convention money at 66⅔ per cent." Carroll objected to this clause because "I have been informed that certain persons have been busily engaged in buying up our state certificates—they are becoming a great object of speculation."[56] In his mind one man, Samuel Chase, was responsible for this scheme. Chase ruled the lower house "without control," observed Carroll, and shaped all money matters to enhance his "particular contracts and interests."[57] Over a year later, he publicly accused Chase of attempting to establish, by legislation, a lucrative market for currency speculation. Referring to the proposed tax law of 1780, Carroll told his readers: "Had a distinction been made

[55] *Votes and Proceedings*, House, November session, January 4, 1780; "An Act for Calling Out of Circulation . . . ," Session Laws of Maryland, November 1780.

[56] Charles Carroll of Carrollton to Charles Carroll of Annapolis, May 8, 1780, Charles Carroll of Annapolis Papers, MHS.

[57] Charles Carroll of Carrollton to Charles Carroll of Annapolis, May 6, 1780, Charles Carroll of Annapolis Papers, MHS.

between the continental and convention money it would have opened a new field for speculation."[58]

The division separating Chase and Carroll on matters of finance paralleled their differences over the question of property confiscation. Here, too, the question of legal tender was involved. As early as November, 1777, congress had recommended to the states that they confiscate and sell British property and invest the proceeds in Continental loan office certificates.[59] The matter of confiscation had been raised within Maryland, but the earlier efforts had been blocked by the united opposition of Chase and Carroll.[60]

That was the situation until December 1779, when Chase changed his mind. At that session of the assembly, the lower house unanimously passed a bill authorizing the confiscation of British property.[61] A mixture of public pressure and the anticipation of private profits motivated the delegates. It was common knowledge by that time that speculators were getting rich, or at least many people assumed such was happening. A letter written by Otho Holland Williams, one of the state's military leaders, reflected this opinion: "Tis all in vain my dear Benedict, tis all in vain to oppose the prevailing vices, which like a torrent rapidly involve in inextricable difficulty every virtuous political scheme, however wisely conceived. When I reflect upon the present situation of our affairs I curse the speculatory cause of all the evils attending it and find no better way to banish my disagreeable apprehensions than by keeping myself as ignorant as possible of the danger in which my bastard brethren the engrossing patriots and weak legislators have involved my country."[62] Another military commander, Mordecai Gist, expressed identical sentiments to a merchant acquaintance and promised vengeance on the speculator element.

The practice of speculation which however strong it may operate on your mind as an incentive to interest, permit me to tell you it implies a want of public virtue, depreciates our currency and unnerves the sinews of war. It consequently (if you are guilty) must render you contemptible in the eyes of a virtuous army now exposed to innumerable hardships, who are determined when they have sufficiently humbled the pride and arrogance of Britain to

[58] *Maryland Gazette*, August 30, 1781.
[59] Ford, *Journal of the Continental Congress*, 9:971.
[60] Daniel of St. Thomas Jenifer to Charles Carroll of Annapolis, December 12, 1777, Charles Carroll of Annapolis Papers, MHS.
[61] *Votes and Proceedings*, House, November session, December 15, 1779.
[62] Otho Holland Williams to Benedict Edward Hall, May 27, 1779, Benedict Edward Hall Papers, MHS.

take signal vengeance on such men as their next greatest enemy and do justice to themselves by a general seizure and equal distribution of their property.[63]

By passing a confiscation measure which, in theory at least, offered land to everyone, the delegates hoped to dampen such feelings.

Whatever the House's reasons, the Senate did not see the matter in the same light. Its rejection of the measure was written by Charles Carroll of Carrollton. He strongly opposed confiscation because he considered the violation of private property exceedingly dangerous to the state's political and social structure.[64] Moreover, he suspected the proposal was being pushed by men who wanted to realize gains on their speculation in inflated currency. Carroll made his feelings on the subject very plain to Benjamin Franklin in December of that year: "I think the measure impolite, contrary to the present practice of civilized nations, and because it may involve us in difficulties about making peace, and will be productive of a certain loss, but of uncertain profit to this state, for as this business will be managed, it will be made a job of, and an opportunity given to engrossers and speculators to realize their ill gotten money."[65]

Carroll publicly aired these same opinions on the front pages of several consecutive issues of the *Maryland Gazette*. His essays left scars, and in future years Chase frequently referred to these particular pieces and the harshness of the charges made. One of the most important accusations involved the curious time schedule proposed by the lower house. "One great objection," Carroll wrote, "to the proposed hasty sale of part of this British property, at so inclement a season of the year, was, that few would probably attend the sales and that engrossers and speculators becoming the purchasers would turn into a private job what might have been intended for public benefit. That the purchasers would have consisted chiefly, if not altogether, of engrossers and speculators, I am induced to think from these two circumstances—they have the *most money* and could not speculate to so great an advantage in anything else, as in buying up confiscated property at a quarter perhaps of the real value." To emphasize his point Carroll noted that the house had first held up the bill till December. Then it had proposed to confiscate and sell enough loyalist property to raise 5,220,000 dollars, all "in the space of one month (January), generally the most inclement in the year; a few

---

[63] Mordecai Gist to William Hammond, December 29, 1779, Gist Papers, MHR.
[64] *Votes and Proceedings*, House, November session, December 23, 1779.
[65] Kate Mason Rowland, *The Life of Charles Carroll of Carrollton, 1737–1832* (2 vols., New York, 1898), 2:25.

only would have had notice of the sales and few consequently (however great the number of persons inclined to purchase might have been) could have attended then and become purchasers. It is probable, that twenty or thirty persons, at the outside, would have been bidders; might they not," asked Carroll, "have previously agreed upon their respective portions of the property put up to sale to avoid a competition of purchase and over bidding each other." If this scheme had worked, he suggested, the property "which under more favorable circumstances would have commanded 20,880,000 dollars for instance would not have sold for more than 5,220,000 dollars."[66]

But Carroll's essay did not explain all of the reasons for his opposition. No doubt much of it was grounded on principle and political animosity, but much of it was also based on economic self-interest. Carroll particularly feared the personal financial costs involved should the British retaliate by confiscating the investments held by families such as his in England. To prevent this loss, Carroll sent orders to his agent in France. He wrote in November of 1779, prior to the Senate's rejection of the confiscation bill and his sharp public attacks: "Our general assembly is now sitting and I believe will confiscate all British property in the state. How far the laws of nations will warrant such a confiscation I am not sufficiently read in them to determine. The manner in which the enemy has carried on the war has given us sufficient cause and provocation for to go all lengths; but I am inclined to think a confiscation at this time an impolite measure and I really cannot help feeling for the distress that will be brought on many innocent persons—No doubt the British Parliament by way of retaliation," observed Carroll, "will confiscate our money in their funds and all private property belonging to the people in this state to indemnify the sufferers in G.B.—altho you wrote to me formerly that you had taken steps to secure my money in your hands on your leaving London I cannot help giving you this timely caution to put that and all other property belonging to the inhabitants of Maryland and to yourself beyond the possibility of seizure."[67]

Again the following May Carroll wrote his agent urging him to be sure that all the property had been removed: "My letter of the 27th November informed you of a scheme proposed and warmly urged at that time and lately by the house of delegates for the confiscation of British property—the Senate hath hitherto successfully opposed that measure and the people seem averse to it—however the weight of taxes and resentment against the British may at last overcome the dictates of justice

[66] *Maryland Gazette*, February 18, 1780.
[67] Charles Carroll of Carrollton to Joshua Johnson, November 27, 1779, Charles Carroll of Carrollton Letterbook, Arents Collection, NYPL.

and sound policy, and that period may be at no great distance. I therefore again advise you to secure all your own and your correspondent's property which may be in England in such a manner that it may be out of the reach of the British government in case it should make use of reprisals."[68]

As Carroll indicated, the two houses were hotly debating the matter of confiscation that spring. And in the process this issue was being linked to the still pending issue of legal tender. Carroll made this connection clear to his father. "The Senate," he reported, "passed a bill for the suspending the tender law—this was rejected by the delegates. This day we rejected the confiscation bill. The delegates have done nothing in pursuance of the resolution of Congress for revising the tender laws. I wish to God this session may end well but Chase's violence I fear will throw all into confusion." The causes for the impasse were obvious. Chase and his supporters sought to realize a handsome profit by purchasing confiscated land with depreciated currency. "In short," said Carroll, "some men want to lay out their continental in the purchase of British property and nothing less than the confiscation and speedy sale of that property will serve them."[69]

Carroll determined they should not realize these profits. In early May he drew up another strong protest, repeating many of his earlier criticisms. Concerning this message, he told his father that although it "will be addressed to the delegates it is as much intended for the people to let them into the views of their representatives. Such a shameful waste of time, and shameful schemes to enrich individuals at the expense of the public, I believe no age ever produced—if the people will not open their eyes and trust their affairs to honest men they must be undone. There are many gentlemen among the delegates who wish to promote their country's good, perhaps a majority, but their leaders, or rather leader, is all for himself; all his measures have a tendency to promote his own interest which is incompatible with that of the public." He could only hope that some of the more responsible delegates "will be a curb on the most prostitute scoundrel who ever existed!"[70]

Despite his feelings, Carroll soon agreed to confiscation. In June, he reluctantly concluded that the measure was indeed necessary. The force behind his decision did not come, as might be expected, from a deal with

---

[68] Charles Carroll of Carrollton to Joshua Johnson, May 1, 1780, Charles Carroll of Carrollton Letterbook, Arents Collection, NYPL.

[69] Charles Carroll of Carrollton to Charles Carroll of Annapolis, April 18, 1780, and April 21, 1780, Charles Carroll of Annapolis Papers, MHS.

[70] Charles Carroll of Carrollton to Charles Carroll of Annapolis, May 11, 1780, Charles Carroll of Annapolis Papers, MHS.

Chase. Rather, the pressures that influenced him came as a result of decisions made in England.

Fifteen years before, in 1764, the Maryland legislature had invested provincial funds in stock issued by the Bank of England. Two years later, these stocks, the value of which then equaled £26,800 sterling, were pledged for the redemption of a provincial currency emission. In 1779, these bills became due and the state treasurer attempted to draw on the bank stock fund, but the trustees refused to honor the commitment. Following this, the assembly in June of 1780 passed an act authorizing an emission of £30,000 in new state currency. This act further directed the Western Shore treasurer to draw bills of exchange to the amount of £35,000 sterling on the trustees. These bills were to be used for the redemption of the £30,000 emission. If the trustees protested these bills of exchange, and if the bank stock could not be obtained, the assembly ordered that the new bills of credit should be redeemed by selling an equivalent value of British property.[71]

Carroll did not like the conflict that developed over the province's bank stock. Still he could hardly vote against the confiscation of British property when people in England were seizing what was, in effect, Maryland property. He reluctantly explained this conclusion to his father: "As to ways and means I fear we shall be pushed to agree upon that point; the delegates will propose probably the sale of some part of British property. We think of a new emission on the credit of our bank stock vizt. £27,000 sterling subject to our disposal; and in case at the end of the war Great Britain should refuse to pay it to make British property to that amount in this state liable."[72]

During the October session the assembly received word that the trustees had protested the bills of exchange drawn on the bank stock. With the news confirmed, the Senate agreed to the confiscation of all British property for the use of the state. Only one form of property was exempted. At the Senate's request, an amendment to the confiscation act exempted debts owed to loyalists or British subjects from seizure.[73] Such a concession was not particularly important since a debtor could easily pay off whatever he might owe by turning in his worthless continental currency to the state treasury.

[71] "An Act to Enable the Treasurer of the Western Shore to Draw and Sell Bills of Exchange and for an Emission of Bills of Credit if Necessary," Session Laws of Maryland, June 1780.

[72] Charles Carroll of Carrollton to Charles Carroll of Annapolis, June 23, 1780, Charles Carroll of Annapolis Papers, MHS.

[73] "An Act to Seize, Confiscate and Appropriate all British Property within this State," Session Laws of Maryland, November 1780.

Both Carroll and Chase had something to cheer about when the legislature adjourned from its 1780 fall session. Carroll had his repeal of the legal tender provision and Chase his confiscation measure. But the two remained deeply divided throughout the rest of 1780 and 1781. The bitterness of their division was reflected in an exchange published in the *Maryland Gazette* during August 1781. Earlier that summer, Chase had written an essay in which he professed complete innocence to all the charges previously directed against him. He had not speculated in flour in 1778; he had not attempted to corner the market. His dismissal from the Maryland congressional delegation had been grossly unjust. More recently because he "was a warm advocate for the confiscation of British property," his enemies, "to induce the unwary and unthinking part of the people to reject the proposal," had "assiduously circulated that it was a deep scheme of his to realize large sums of continental money. The assertion was false and ridiculous," said Chase. So too was the claim that he "opposed the repeal of the tender law because he had benefited himself by paying debts in depreciated paper. This allegation [was] without any foundation," as was the rumor that he "opposed the calling in the convention money by giving one new dollar for forty of that emission, because he had, in person, or by emissaries, bought up large sums of convention money."[74]

Charles Carroll of Carrollton wrote his father the day after Chase's article appeared. He considered Chase's defense absurd. As soon as the legislature rose he promised to compose an answer proving conclusively Chase's guilt: "You will see in reading over the last Annapolis paper that I am under a necessity of answering Chase's publication under the signature of censor. I shall write a letter to him and publish it in the same gazette and sign it with my name—I shall state facts, draw conclusions from them and conclude that in my opinion that he was guilty of a breach of trust in revealing the secrets of Congress—I shall not write this letter until the session is over and I have collected facts."[75]

Carroll did not complete his reply until August. The *Gazette*, making the most of the controversy, divided the message into two parts, publishing one half on August 23 and the other on August 30. Within the letter, Carroll not only condemned Chase's speculations, but he also traced their personal relationship and resurrected many of the old charges. He began by freely admitting that he had helped draft the congressional instructions of 1778 which had severely criticized Chase. Nevertheless, he de-

[74] *Maryland Gazette*, June 21, 1781.
[75] Charles Carroll of Carrollton to Charles Carroll of Annapolis, June 22, 1781, Charles Carroll of Annapolis Papers, MHS.

nied Chase's charge of being "guilty of the *'ungenerous and perfidious conduct of a false friend.'* " Rather he had executed his proper duty because of the concrete evidence. Chase's conduct, by that time, he recounted, was already suspect.

A similarity of sentiments on public questions first gave rise to our acquaintance, which gradually grew into familiarity and friendship. I am free to own your public character and conduct appeared to me decided and for a long time disinterested. You had great merit in helping to form our constitution; you opposed popular prejudices, at the hazard, nay with the loss of your popularity for a time, though your talents peculiarly fitted you to take the lead in a democracy. You had the wisdom to despise the precarious ascendancy, which the vices of that form of government would have given you, and courage enough to encounter and defeat the opposition of those who wished our constitution to be more democratical. Your first deviation from the line of true policy (perhaps of rectitude, if you acted from view of interest) was your advising and supporting the resolve of congress recommending to the several states to make continental bills of credit a legal tender in all cases. But to speak with candor, I ascribed your conduct at the time to an error in judgment, and to an impetuosity of temper, which often prevents you from examining subjects with that patience of thought, so requisite to form a true judgment in all cases of moment. I impute not to you so much sagacity, as to have foreseen the numberless frauds since committed under the tender laws, nor the intention, to profit by them. But the temptation was too strong to be resisted in the sequel. When the injustice of suffering the tender law to remain in force became evident, when the pretext for its passage no longer existed, you still opposed its repeal. Have you not taken unjustifiable advantages of that law? Have you not paid away more monies than you have received under it?[76]

Carroll then raised all of his traditional objections, concluding that everything Chase designed was for his personal aggrandizement.

To enliven the debate, the *Gazette* ran a companion piece to Carroll's article, written, of course, by Samuel Chase. Naturally, his views differed considerably. He explained with much passion, if little light, that he had severed all ties when Carroll became the "advocate of disaffected tories and refugees; because he opposed the confiscation of British property, and insolently and falsely imputed my maintaining the propriety of the measure to base and interested motives; because he changed his political conduct, and published principles destructive of freedom and Independence of America; because in and out of Congress he betrayed an unmanly fear of success in the war; because he possessed an inherent heredi-

[76] *Maryland Gazette*, August 23, 1781.

tary meanness and avarice of soul incapable of friendship or love to the public."[77]

From such an exchange, any moves toward reconciliation seemed impossible. But in January 1782 Chase and Carroll began a partial effort toward settling their differences. At the time, the lower house was reviewing Chase's conduct as a congressional delegate. On January 24, the house declared him innocent of all charges, with only two dissenting votes. A mutual acquaintance, encouraged by this development, urged Carroll to write Chase privately specifying all of his complaints. He agreed, and in more restrained language reiterated all the charges that had been aired publicly. Three days later, Chase replied in a lengthy well-argued letter. For most of the seventeen pages, he contended that all of the evidence purported to show his involvement in flour speculation was based on hearsay. Somewhat wistfully, he remembered that until that fall, Carroll had been one of his closest companions. He could not understand why he had not first raised the matter privately: "I really thought, and still think, that the part you took in the draft of the instructions was ungenerous and unfriendly." Carroll's conduct in the controversies over currency and confiscation had been similarly unjustified, but Chase held out some slight hope for the future: "Peace may immediately take place if you incline to cease hostilities, but time, and a return of good offices, and confidence can alone restore our former amity. I do not feel my mind so embittered against you as I think I discover yours to be against me."[78]

Carroll replied that Chase was mistaken in several instances. Concerning the flour market scandal, the evidence had been considerable: "These reports were confidently and publicly spoken of; the Commissary General, Mr. Wadsworth, complained loudly of your conduct, many minute circumstances respecting these reports were mentioned at the time, but now forgotten, that impressed me with the belief of their being true." Still, he would grant one point. Chase maintained that once the scandal broke he had vigorously protested his innocence. Carroll could not recall any declarations of this sort, but admitted their possibility: "The several declarations which you say you made respecting the falsity of the reports circulated against you, have all, I assure you, upon my honor, escaped my memory; I do not mean to insinuate that you did not make these declarations at the several respective times mentioned in your letter, but you

[77] *Ibid.*
[78] Samuel Chase to Charles Carroll of Carrollton, January 28, 1782, Charles Carroll of Annapolis Papers, MHS.

must excuse me for saying that an appeal to the public, in my opinion, in answer to Publius [Hamilton's pseudonym] would have been much more satisfactory, and a stronger evidence of the falsity of the reports, and of your innocence, than all those declarations."[79]

Carroll also showed some willingness to bend on another issue. He agreed that the evidence implicating Chase in the speculation of convention money was not conclusive: "I was informed that affidavits were produced and read in the House of Delegates to prove Mr. Dorsey's speculating in convention money. I really concluded as a partnership subsisted between you, that you were to keep the benefit of that trade also. . . . If my conclusion was wrong and you will say you was not concerned in these purchases I shall not have the least objection to acknowledge, that the insinuation was not warranted by the fact."[80] But on the matters of legal tender and confiscation, Carroll held to his original charges.

Chase waited eight days before replying. He began aggressively telling Carroll that "I desire no explanation of or apology for your conduct, and the many insinuations and charges you made against my character, on general reports, because I do not think your *opinion* sufficient to maintain the truth of the allegations, or necessary to evince my innocence." Having made clear his feelings, Chase accepted Carroll's general explanation in a more conciliatory vein. As to the establishment of some sort of compromise, Chase gave Carroll permission to "show his letter to any one or to publish it if you think proper."[81]

Carroll answered four days later, saying he would publish certain extracts from the letter. He specifically intended to print the following two extracts, which appeared in the *Maryland Gazette* on February 28, 1782.

In your address to me, as a corroborating circumstance, that the reports circulated (in the fall of 1778) injurious to my character, were true, you asserted *"that I remained silent three years under the imputation of a breach of trust."* In my answer I said that this assertion was contrary to the truth, and your knowledge of the fact. I have fully proved, and can maintain, that your allegation, that I remained silent three years, under the imputation of a breach of trust was contrary to truth. I admit that the latter part of my answer was improper and that I cannot maintain that your assertion *was contrary to your*

[79] Charles Carroll of Carrollton to Samuel Chase, February 3, 1782, Charles Carroll of Annapolis Papers, MHS.

[80] *Ibid.*

[81] Samuel Chase to Charles Carroll of Carrollton, February 11, 1782, Charles Carroll of Annapolis Papers, MHS.

own knowledge of the fact; and that I *now* believe from the evidence lately disclosed, it was not warranted by the fact.

The second matter in my answer to your address which *gives* you offence is my assertion *that I did not believe that you gave credit to the reports circulated against me in 1778, which occasioned the instructions.* I am now satisfied that in this assertion also, I was mistaken and *now* admit that you did give credit to the reports at the time you drew the instructions. When I made this assertion I had no doubt of the truth of it, this circumstance which induced me to make it, was related to me by several persons of unquestionable veracity; but the testimony lately given and your declaration that you was misunderstood influence me to this admission.[82]

This matter settled, Carroll reminded Chase of an outstanding debt of £95/5/11 owed his father since 1770. Chase tersely responded that he would take care of the loan immediately. As to their differences, "I have no inclination to continue our controversy. Neither the public nor either of us can be benefited by it, and my time, like yours, can be more usefully employed."[83]

With that agreement, Chase and Carroll tolerated each other amicably for the next several years. Not everyone was pleased with this. One of Carroll's admirers wrote that he had previously viewed Carroll's behavior "in a favorable light," but was altering his opinion because of "a report now circulating of a compromise being on foot." He reported that many considered Carroll's conduct "guided by fear or apprehension of the consequences or inconvenience that may result from a dispute with so popular a figure as Chase." Stop all discussion now, he suggested, for it was the "opinion of the world in this matter," that "a compromise immediately after Chase's acquittal is a kind of acquiescence therein."[84]

Carroll's adviser did not have to worry. The truce with Chase lasted but a few years, though the feud did not flare up again until the latter half of the 1780s. In the spring of 1783 some difference of opinion developed as Chase's forces in the lower house began pressing for legislation to restrict the court's role in aiding British creditors to collect their unpaid balances. Although Carroll and his friends in the Senate did not approve

[82] Charles Carroll of Carrollton to Samuel Chase, February 15, 1782, Charles Carroll of Annapolis Papers, MHS; *Maryland Gazette*, February 28, 1782.
[83] Charles Carroll of Carrollton to Samuel Chase, February 15, 1782; Samuel Chase to Charles Carroll of Carrollton, February 23, 1782, both in Charles Carroll of Annapolis Papers, MHS.
[84] ———— to Charles Carroll of Carrollton, February 20, 1782, Charles Carroll of Annapolis Papers, MHS.

of the measure, they wisely decided to accept it.[85] From 1783 until late in 1785, with Chase in England much of the time attempting to recover Maryland's bank stock, the state's politics remained relatively tranquil. Even after he returned to Maryland, the bank stock issue consumed most of his interest. But when the legislature convened in December 1785, Chase began pushing for an act which he knew would anger Carroll. He proposed a new emission of paper money, ostensibly to ease the burdens of the state's inhabitants suffering from deflationary pressures.[86] While this was true, Carroll and Chase both understood that the paper emission was also designed to serve the interests of a select group of land speculators.

After the confiscation measures of 1780 had passed, the speculators, as Carroll predicted, rushed to buy enormous tracts of land. Chase, naturally, was a big investor, but so were several of Carroll's former political allies, particularly Jenifer and Paca. By late 1785, the burdens these men had assumed were weighing heavily and they looked to cheap money for relief. The lower house passed a bill that December to emit paper money, but Carroll persuaded the Senate to reject it. After suffering this defeat, Chase organized his lower house supporters and his new allies into a cohesive political unit, which worked to have Carroll and his fellow conservatives unseated in the Senate election of 1786. Their effort failed when Carroll and nine other conservative members of the old Senate were reelected.[87] Having met defeat at the polls, Chase, in frustration, turned to the press, where he berated Carroll bitterly because of his opposition to paper money. Carroll, as expected, replied in kind.[88] Indeed, the two now came to distrust one another so deeply that both refused to attend the Constitutional Convention in Philadelphia for fear of what the other might do at home.[89]

[85] For a well-executed study of the period, see William Arthur O'Brien, "Speculative Interests and Maryland Politics, 1780–1788" (Master's thesis, University of Wisconsin, 1967), pp. 18, 32.

[86] *Ibid.*, p. 39.

[87] *Ibid.*, pp. 49–50, 69.

[88] *Maryland Journal*, February 2, 1787, March 2, 1787; *Maryland Gazette*, March 15, 1787.

[89] O'Brien, "Speculative Interests," pp. 65–67.

Coda : Economics, Politics, and the Revolution in Maryland

The revolutionary era in Maryland was marked by extremes. Of all the state constitutions written during the period, Maryland's was by far the most conservative in character. The document was designed specifically to insure the continuance of elitist rule. In every respect the new charter successfully fulfilled that purpose. The government's legislative, executive, and judicial branches were firmly controlled by a small ruling class of wealthy men. And yet, these men designed and enacted the most radical fiscal legislation of the revolutionary years. No state came near duplicating these financial measures, which alleviated the burden of debt at an enormous expense to the creditor class. The Revolution in Maryland cost the aristocracy dearly, both in terms of capital and prestige. Why did such contradictions occur? The principal aim of this study has been to answer that question.

The story began in the early 1760s, when economic and political dislocation helped lay the foundations of a coalition determined to gain power within the colony. In its early stages, during the Stamp Act crisis, the coalition encompassed two specific factions. Samuel Chase led one of the wings. By 1765, he had built a strong political following in Annapolis and Anne Arundel county. His power came as a result of bitter political infighting with certain members of the proprietary or court party. The Baltimore merchant community, the coalition's other division, was also well organized. Merchants in that town joined to seek answers to their common economic problems. They were all suffering from the recessions and depressions that afflicted the trading community in the 1750s and 1760s. These two elements united at the time of the Stamp Act to form the Sons of Liberty in Maryland.

The Baltimore-Annapolis axis was a shifting alliance which went through several stages of formation and disintegration in the late 1760s. Because merchants formed a major component of the coalition, the strength of the organization was dependent on trade problems within the empire. During the Townshend Act controversy, credit and commerce were good, and, as a result, the merchants opposed the economic boycotts proposed by politicians. Only after these traders were subjected to extreme pressure did they agree to the politicians' nonimportation program, and even then they flagrantly violated the bans whenever possible. As a result, the political and merchant communities in Maryland were seriously divided as the 1770s began.

A permanent and widely based political organization was not established until 1773. At that time, the effects of a severe depression played havoc with the colony's economy. Within Maryland this depression was linked to a fight over the regulation of "officer fees." Out of this conflict there came a new or "popular party." Its principal base was once again the Baltimore-Annapolis axis, and Samuel Chase was one of those responsible for resurrecting it. His job was made easy this time because he had a popular figure to build a political faction around—Charles Carroll of Carrollton. The colony's tobacco or fee controversy had made Carroll the people's champion against the proprietor's chief advocate, Daniel Dulany. Both men argued their positions in the colony's newspaper and, as the debate progressed and Carroll's popularity grew, various elements within the province came to his support. It was a simple matter for Chase and Carroll's father, Charles Carroll of Annapolis, to shape these supporters into a political party.

The goals of the party that emerged from the fee controversy were not new. Basically its leaders were conservative men. They desired the traditional advantages of power—money, prestige, and influence—but they wanted to enjoy these benefits within the existing society. To accomplish this aim, they had launched vicious attacks against the proprietor and his agents on matters of provincial concern. Imperial issues had not played a significant part in their campaign. But once in power they were forced to contend with the Anglo-American conflict. The structure of politics required them to take a stand. Other power-seeking elements, particularly the Hall-Hammond faction, also sought to exploit the imperial dispute. Thus the very shape of the imperial conflict and the prodding of the radicals forced the popular party to make decisions and take actions which most of its members regretted.

When the popular party first came to power in 1774 it reflected a variety of attitudes over the imperial question. Chase had the reputation of an incendiary, Tilghman of a reasonable man, and the Carroll family's attitudes were not widely known. These differing opinions were still present two years later. The Carrolls and Chase were by then strongly opposed to Britain's policies and enthusiastically embraced the idea of independence. For Chase independence held out the possibility of increased political and economic power, for Carroll the opportunity of significant reform. Other leaders more intimately aware of the internal dangers involved, particularly Jenifer and Tilghman, were apprehensive, though they recognized the inevitability of separation. For all of the party's leaders, however, the decision took considerable courage and conviction since independence meant that even greater demands would be made on the people than the comparatively mild tyranny being overthrown.

The practical problems of holding popular support were formidable. By the summer of 1776 Maryland was in an uproar. Bitter internal conflicts were raging throughout the colony. On the Eastern Shore a particularly serious insurrection against the provisional government was in progress. Marauding loyalist bands were roaming the countryside. Extremist groups had been formed on both sides of the imperial question, and fighting among these civilian organizations had taken place. The political and social control exercised by the popular party leaders through the mechanism of the provisional government appeared to be rapidly disintegrating. Independence, the very thought of it, terrified many members of the upper classes. Chaos seemed everywhere and the possibility that a dangerous new social order might be established looked all too real.

Once independence was declared, the party's heads moved to establish strong controls. To accomplish this, the June convention ordered an election for a new convention to draw up a constitution. At that meeting, the popular leaders hammered out the most conservative of all the new state constitutions. The document was structured to insure the wealthy a controlling voice in the government. But the establishment of a conservative government was not by itself enough to insure stability and order. At least this was the assumption made by the party's leaders. They were frightened, though sensible men, who concluded that their authority would have no effectiveness unless their rule was acceptable to the people. To gain popular support and to prevent what they foresaw as civil if not class warfare, they agreed to enact radical fiscal legislation on an unprecedented scale. These measures, Charles Carroll of Carrollton was convinced, were "the price of Revolution." If the wealthy refused to acquiesce, the Revolution would have no hope of success and their class no hope of survival. The vast majority of them agreed and willingly submitted. They feared "a revengeful democracy." If this democracy were not pacified, they believed the province might well be "dyed with the blood of its best citizens."

After passing this legislation in 1777, the party's leaders, particularly Carroll and Chase, anxiously waited to see if the policies would win support for the government. As the years of 1778 and 1779 went by and the social convulsions diminished, their sense of urgency and anxiety gave way to a feeling of security and stability. With the lessening of fear and with the government's gradual assertion of authority, the party began to develop internal divisions; Chase and Carroll divided sharply. The return of a stable social order allowed Carroll to act upon his basic convictions. He considered Chase's profiteering reprehensible and made his position publicly known. Chase returned this abuse with equally sharp language. He believed Carroll's sense of morality to be a luxury enjoyed by only the rich. As the arguments became more unrestrained, the party broke into cantankerous factions. Chase controlled his followers in the lower house; Carroll directed his in the upper. By the end of 1780 the party that had directed Maryland for the past seven years lay in ruins. Its demise signaled the completion of the party's primary task and the end of a chaotic era. With the processes of disintegration checked and the demands for radical change held in bounds, the establishment of independence and stability was insured.

Index

This book was composed in Janson text and Caslon display type
by Maryland Linotype Composition Company from a design by Victoria Dudley.
It was printed on Warren's 60-lb. Sebago paper, and bound
in Holliston Roxite cloth by The Maple Press Company.

Library of Congress Cataloging in Publication Data

Hoffman, Ronald, 1941-
    A spirit of dissension.

    (Maryland bicentennial studies)
    Includes bibliographical references.
    1. Maryland—Economic conditions. 2. Maryland—
Politics and government—Colonial period. 3. Maryland
—Politics and government—Revolution. I. Title.
II. Series.
HC107.M3H63   975.2'03   73-8127
ISBN 0-8018-1521-5

DATE DUE
